Justice and the Social Contract

Justice and the Social Contract

Essays on Rawlsian Political Philosophy

SAMUEL FREEMAN

UNIVERSITY PRESS

2007

OXFORD
UNIVERSITY PRESS

Oxford University Press, Inc., publishes works that further
Oxford University's objective of excellence
in research, scholarship, and education.

Oxford   New York
Auckland   Cape Town   Dar es Salaam   Hong Kong   Karachi
Kuala Lumpur   Madrid   Melbourne   Mexico City   Nairobi
New Delhi   Shanghai   Taipei   Toronto

With offices in
Argentina   Austria   Brazil   Chile   Czech Republic   France   Greece
Guatemala   Hungary   Italy   Japan   Poland   Portugal   Singapore
South Korea   Switzerland   Thailand   Turkey   Ukraine   Vietnam

Published by Oxford University Press, Inc.
198 Madison Avenue, New York, New York 10016

www.oup.com

Library of Congress Cataloging-in-Publication Data
Freeman, Samuel Richard.
Justice and the social contract : essays on Rawlsian political philosophy /
Samuel Freeman.
    p. cm.
Includes index.
ISBN 978-0-19-530141-0

1. Justice. 2. Social contract. 3. Rawls, John, 1921– Theory of justice.
I. Title.
JC578. F697 2006
320.01'1—dc22   2005058991

9 8 7 6 5 4 3

Printed in the United States of America
on acid-free paper

To my mother, Clara Smith Freeman,
who taught me to persevere,
and in memory of my father,
Frank Freeman,
who, in a small Southern town,
first taught me about Justice

Acknowledgments

Chapter One: Originally published in *Philosophy and Public Affairs* 19, no. 2 (Spring 1990): 122–57. Copyright 1990 by Blackwell Publishing; reprinted by permission of the publisher.

Chapter Two: Originally published in *Philosophy and Public Affairs* 23, no. 4 (Fall 1994): 313–49. Copyright 1994 by Blackwell Publishing; reprinted by permission of the publisher.

Chapter Five: Originally published in *The Cambridge Companion to Rawls*, ed. Samuel Freeman (Cambridge: Cambridge University Press, 2003), 277–315. Copyright 2003 by Cambridge University Press; reprinted by permission of the publisher.

Chapter Six: Originally published in *Chicago-Kent Law Review* 69, no. 3 (1994): 301–50. Copyright 1994 by Chicago Kent Law Review; reprinted by permission of the publisher.

Chapter Seven: Originally published in *Fordham Law Review* 68 (April 2004): 101–48. Copyright 2004 by Fordham Law Review; reprinted by permission of the publisher.

Chapter Eight: Originally published in *Social Philosophy and Policy* 23, no. 1 (January 2006): 29–68. Copyright 2006 by Cambridge University Press; reprinted by permission of the publisher.

Chapter Nine: Forthcoming in *Rawls's Law of Peoples: A Realistic Utopia?* ed. Rex Martin and David Reidy (Oxford: Blackwell, 2006). Copyright 2006 by Blackwell Publishers; reprinted by permission of the publisher.

Contents

Abbreviations

CE	Amaryta Sen, "Consequential Evaluation and Practical Reason," *Journal of Philosophy* 97 (September 2000)
CP	John Rawls, *Collected Papers*, ed. Samuel Freeman (Cambridge, MA: Harvard University Press, 1999)
CPP	Will Kymlicka, *Contemporary Political Philosophy* (Oxford: Oxford University Press, 1990)
DP	Joseph Raz, "Disagreement in Politics," *American Journal of Jurisprudence* 43 (1998)
JLK	Susan Hurley, *Justice, Luck, and Knowledge* (Cambridge MA: Harvard University Press, 2003)
KC	John Rawls, "Kantian Constructivism in Moral Theory: The Dewey Lectures," *Journal of Philosophy* 77 (1980)
LCC	Will Kymlicka, *Liberalism, Community, and Culture* (Oxford: Oxford University Press, 1989)
Lectures	John Rawls, *Lectures in the History of Moral Philosophy*, ed. Barbara Herman (Cambridge, MA: Harvard University Press, 2000)
MA	David Gauthier, *Morals by Agreement* (Oxford: Oxford University Press, 1986)
Methods	Henry Sidgwick, *The Methods of Ethics*, 7th ed. (Indianapolis: Hackett, 1981)
OC	John Rawls, "The Idea of Overlapping Consensus," *Oxford Journal of Legal Studies* 7 (1987)
PL	John Rawls, *Political Liberalism* (New York: Columbia University Press, 1993; paperback ed., 1996, 2004)
Restatement	John Rawls, *Justice as Fairness: A Restatement*, ed. Erin Kelly (Cambridge, MA: Belknap Press, 2001)
RC	Kent Greenawalt, *Religious Convictions and Political Choice* (New York: Oxford University Press, 1988)

SS   Brian Barry, "John Rawls and the Search for Stability," *Ethics* 105 (July 1995)

SV   Ronald Dworkin, *Sovereign Virtue* (Cambridge, MA: Harvard University Press, 2000)

TJ or *Theory*   John Rawls, A *Theory of Justice* (Cambridge, MA: Harvard University Press, 1971; revised ed., 1999)

Justice and the Social Contract

Introduction

John Rawls is widely recognized as the most significant and influential political philosopher of the twentieth century. His main influence lies in two separate works, A *Theory of Justice* (1971) and *Political Liberalism* (1993).[1] Rawls revised his account of justice considerably in the twenty-two years intervening between these books, but there is a good deal of disagreement and confusion about how his views about justice changed. Some suggest that Rawls became more conservative, that he abandoned the difference principle, or that he altogether gave up on the idea of the original position and his social contractarianism. Others contend that in *Political Liberalism*, Rawls changed his thinking as a response to communitarian criticisms, or that he was primarily motivated to accommodate religion. In this book, I argue that all these claims are mistaken. There are powerful interconnections between A *Theory of Justice* and *Political Liberalism* that have not been sufficiently acknowledged in the literature. If one understands these connections, then one can better understand Rawls's project not only in *Political Liberalism* but also in A *Theory of Justice*. In this brief introduction, I provide the intellectual context for the chapters that follow, first by discussing the background to Rawls's transition to the doctrine of political liberalism and its basis in his social contractarianism, and then by foreshadowing the arguments of each chapter.

I. Rawls's Contractarianism and the Stability of a Well-Ordered Society

Rawls's aim in A *Theory of Justice* is to develop a theory of justice from the idea of a social contract found in Locke, Rousseau, and Kant.[2] He seeks to present

1. John Rawls, A *Theory of Justice* (Cambridge, MA: Harvard University Press, 1971; rev. ed., 1999) (cited in text as *TJ*; sometimes referred to as *Theory*); *Political Liberalism* (New York: Columbia University Press, 1993; paperback edition, 1996, 2004) (cited in the text as *PL*; references are to the paperback edition).
2. Rawls, *Collected Papers*, ed. Samuel Freeman (Cambridge, MA: Harvard University Press, 1999), 614 (cited in text as *CP*).

a contract theory that is not subject to objections often thought fatal to contract views and that is superior to the long-dominant tradition of utilitarianism in
moral and political philosophy. Utilitarianism, Rawls believed, for all its strengths
and sophistication is nonetheless incompatible with freedom and equality, the
fundamental values of justice in a democratic society. By appealing to the social
contract tradition Rawls hoped to derive a conception of justice more compatible with the values and ideals of a democratic society and with our considered
convictions of justice.

Many contend that the idea of a social contract does no genuine work in
Rawls, since (among other reasons) the parties' ignorance of facts in the original
position prevents their bargaining and renders them all, in effect, the same person. I explain in chapter 1 how the original position involves an agreement that
is not a bargain, but rather a joint precommitment to principles of justice. But in
many respects, whether there is an agreement in the original position is beside
the point. For, the way in which Rawls's justice as fairness is a social contract position has far more to do with his idea of a well-ordered society than does the original position. Rawls describes a well-ordered society as one in which all reasonable
persons accept the same public principles of justice, their agreement on these
principles is public knowledge, and these principles are realized in society's laws
and basic social institutions. It is this general agreement among the members of a
well-ordered society that mainly drives the contractarian element in Rawls's view,
not simply the original position. The parties in the original position seek to discover and agree upon principles that reasonable persons with a sense of justice in
a well-ordered society can generally accept and endorse as a public basis for justification. A well-ordered society is then one in which everyone can justify their
social, political, and economic institutions to one another on reasonable terms
that all accept in their capacity as free and equal, reasonable and rational citizens.
It is (to use T. M. Scanlon's term) this "contractualist" idea of *reasonable agreement* among free and equal persons that is predominant in Rawls's social contract
view, not the Hobbesian idea of rational agreement among persons motivated by
their own interests that takes place in the original position.[3]

The overriding concern in Rawls's account of justice, early and late, is to
describe how, if at all, a well-ordered society in which all agree on a public conception of justice is realistically possible. This accounts for Rawls's concern for
the stability of justice as fairness. All along, Rawls aims to describe the conditions under which a "social contract"—general agreement upon principles of
justice among free and equal persons with a sense of justice—can be achieved as
a real possibility in the world. This continuing quest for the conditions of a stable
social contract accounts for many controversial moves in Rawls for which he has
been widely criticized—for example, it explains why he thinks that tendencies
of human psychology, and general facts about social cooperation and economic
relations, are relevant to the justification of fundamental principles of justice;

3. Rawls remarks that he considers the works of Locke, Rousseau, and Kant to be definitive of
the contract tradition: "For all its greatness, Hobbes's *Leviathan* raises special problems" (*TJ*, 11n/10n
rev.).

it also clarifies why he thinks the publicity of principles of justice is a condition upon their justification (see chap. 3). As I argue in this book, the reason that Rawls devotes so much attention to the question of the feasibility and stability of a well-ordered society of justice as fairness is, first, in order to show that justice is within the reach of our capacities and compatible with human nature and, second, to show that doing and willing what justice requires for its own sake is not just compatible with but also is an intrinsic aspect of the human good.

Rawls's "Kantian Constructivism in Moral Theory" (The Dewey Lectures, 1980)[4] was an attempt to perfect the project Rawls began in the early 1950s and culminated in A *Theory of Justice*. Rawls sought to develop the Kantian interpretation of justice as fairness (*TJ*, sec. 40) and show how it informed the setup of the original position and the "construction" of principles of justice. Rawls's Kantianism was then at its most intense. With Kantian constructivism, he brought to fruition the primary problem that justice as fairness was designed to address. What conception of justice (if any) would be both generally acceptable and stably enduring among reasonable and rational people who regard themselves as free and equal and who are members of a well-ordered society where this conception is fully public, would be regulative of their social relations, and would provide citizens the public basis for political justification and criticism? Rawls hypothesized that modern moral awareness, our "sense of justice," had implicit within it democratic ideals of persons as free and equal, and of social cooperation on grounds of mutual respect. He did not think these ideals were a priori, as Kant might have; most likely Rawls believed that they were socially instilled.[5]

Noticeably, the problem Rawls set for himself in Kantian constructivism resembled Kant's contractarian formulation of the categorical imperative, often called "the formula of the Kingdom of Ends." (Because of his democratic sentiments, Rawls always preferred "Realm of Ends.") Kant's contractarian formula says (in effect) that in deciding what moral principles to act upon, we are to imagine ourselves as members of an ideal society, the members of which are all morally motivated to do what is right and just for its own sake; then we are to determine and will only those principles which these ideal moral agents would willingly accept and legislate as equal members of this Realm of Ends. The resemblances to Rawls's idea of a well-ordered society should be readily apparent. Rawls assumed there was a solution to the social contract problem he poses. To discover it, he sought to provide content to Kant's enigmatic notion of "autonomy," conceived as practical reason giving principles to itself out of its own resources. Already, in A *Theory of Justice*, Rawls had referred to the Kantian ideal of moral personality as "the decisive determining element" of principles of justice, and to the original position as "a procedural interpretation of Kant's conception of autonomy and the categorical imperative" (*TJ*, 256/222 rev.). Kantian constructivism is Rawls's attempt to develop this suggestion, in order to provide visible content to the Kantian idea of moral autonomy within a contractarian framework. Rawls did so by

4. See CP.
5. See Rawls's rejection of Kant's "dualisms" at the beginning to the Dewey Lectures, CP, chap. 16.

"modeling" the ideal conception of the person and of society that he thought implicit in our considered convictions of justice into a "procedure of construction," the original position. This deliberative procedure is designed to incorporate "all the relevant requirements of practical reason" (*PL*, 90) — "relevant," that is, to justice and to justifying principles of justice. If it can be shown that the same principles of justice can be derived from this deliberative procedure by all who "enter" or apply it, and we are confident that it incorporates all relevant aspects of rationality and reasonableness, then it might be said that the principles of justice that result are not only reasonable and objective; they have been "given to us" by our practical reason. And insofar as we act according to these principles' demands, and desire to do justice for its own sake, we can be said to be morally autonomous.

It is because of the failure of the argument for stability of a well-ordered society as defined in A *Theory of Justice* and within Kantian constructivism that Rawls is driven to make the revisions in the justification of justice as fairness that result in *Political Liberalism*. Kantian constructivism was an ambitious project. It was masterful in that it provided content to some of Kant's most influential but also enigmatic ideas; among these are the idea of autonomy conceived as reason giving principles to itself out of its own resources, and the idea of practical reason itself constituting the domain of morality. Rawls sought to do this without presupposing Kant's dualisms between analytic/synthetic, a priori vs. a posteriori concepts, or necessary vs. empirical truth, and in a way that he thought was compatible with (though clearly not derivative from) twentieth-century scientific naturalism. But during the 1980s, Rawls gradually came to see that the Kantian project so conceived could not succeed. While many credit communitarians for this transition, Rawls himself avers that communitarian ideas and criticisms had nothing to do with his discovery of the problems that eventually led to political liberalism.[6] Rather than communitarianism, the reason Rawls saw Kantian constructivism as flawed and overly ambitious is that its idea of a well-ordered society did not describe a feasible and enduring social world. This became evident to him once he clarified the "full publicity" condition of a conception of justice, to require that a conception must be capable of serving as a generally accepted basis for public justification in a feasible and enduring social world. (See chap. 6 of this volume.) For, what the full publicity of the Kantian interpretation and Kantian constructivism required for the stability of a well-ordered society was that citizens generally acknowledge the Kantian conception of agency and the person underlying their social relations, and that they endorse the public view that justice has its origins in practical reason and that moral autonomy is an intrinsic part of each citizen's good. But because of certain empirical limitations Rawls

---

6. See *PL*, xixn. Rawls had very little to say in response to his communitarian critics, other than to say that they misunderstood his position. See also *PL*, 27n. Rawls was puzzled by communitarianism, for it seemed to him to be a term used to signify several philosophical and political positions: Thomism, Hegelianism, cultural relativism, anti-liberalism, social democracy, and so on. He regarded it at its best as a kind of perfectionism that regarded the human good as the pursuit of certain shared ends.

calls "the burdens of judgment" (*PL*, 54–58), reasonable people will always have different and conflicting moral, philosophical, and religious beliefs. It is then highly unlikely in any feasible social world that free and equal citizens will all come to agree on the Kantian foundations of justice or in any other "comprehensive moral doctrine" (*PL*, 59). Given the stability and publicity conditions that he imposed upon the justification of a conception of justice, Rawls came to see that no conception of justice, including justice as fairness, could meet the conditions for general agreement among members of a well-ordered society set forth in *A Theory of Justice* and in "Kantian Constructivism in Moral Theory."

It is these problems internal to the justification of justice as fairness that led to the revisions found in *Political Liberalism*. There, Rawls altered not his commitment to the difference principle or the argument from the original position, but the conditions needed for the stability of justice as fairness, conceived as a fully public conception of justice for a well-ordered society of free and equal citizens. This means that Rawls remained true to his contractarianism, and to justice as fairness and the liberal egalitarian requirements that it imposes, to the end. For, all along he is guided by the confidence that a well-ordered society, where free and equal, reasonable and rational citizens can all agree upon a public conception of justice, is a realistically possible aspiration for us, one that is compatible with the human good.

The underlying unity of Rawls's work, I argue, is further manifest in *The Law of Peoples*,[7] where Rawls extends his contractarian theory to international relations. Rawls's cosmopolitan critics argue that the absence of a global distribution principle is evidence of disunity in Rawls's account, due to his failure to understand the implications of his own position.[8] But Rawls is a social contractarian, not a global contractarian; the social/domestic grounding of distributive justice and the absence of a global distribution principle are integral to Rawls's social contract position. I contend that they are required by his ideas of the social and political bases of economic relations, the reciprocity of democratic social cooperation, and the conditions of political autonomy within a well-ordered society.

I discuss Rawls's idea of the stability of a well-ordered society in several chapters of this book (chaps. 3, 5, and 6). As suggested, my view is that it is difficult to understand what Rawls is doing in both *Political Liberalism* and *A Theory of Justice* (and also in *The Law of Peoples*) without understanding the central role of the stability argument in justifying justice as fairness. The extraordinary fact is that, though thousands of articles have been written upon *A Theory of Justice*, there are very few written on the role of the stability argument in *A Theory of Justice* and virtually none on Rawls's primary argument for stability based in the congruence of the right and the good. (An exception is chap. 5 of this volume, originally published in 2003.) But it is mainly this argument and the subsequent problems

7. Rawls, *The Law of Peoples* (Cambridge, MA: Harvard University Press, 1999) (cited in text as *LP*).

8. See Thomas Pogge, "Incoherence between Rawls's Theories of Justice," *Fordham Law Review* 72 (2004): 1739.

Rawls finds with it that lead him to political liberalism and his reformulation of the argument for justice as fairness.

II. Outline of Chapters

In many of the papers in this volume, I focus on issues and aspects of A *Theory of Justice* and its aftermath that have not been discussed much (if at all) in the literature on Rawls heretofore. As already indicated, a good deal of attention is given here to part III of A *Theory of Justice*, the argument for the stability of justice as fairness. This is not to say that parts I and II of that book have been neglected. The first four chapters of this book deal mainly with topics connected with them and with Rawls's original motivations. In particular, in this volume I devote attention to Rawls's conception of the social contract (chaps. 1 and 6); his difference principle and account of distributive justice (see chaps. 3, 4, 8, 9); his criticisms of utilitarianism and consequentialism (chaps. 2 and 3); and the Kantian background and structure of his view (chaps. 2, 5, and 6). Other recurring topics in these papers are Rawls's idea of public reason (chaps. 1, 6, and 7), and his account of international justice in *The Law of Peoples* (chaps. 8 and 9).

A good deal of the discussion in these chapters is not directly interpretation or defense of Rawls, but rather involves extensions or applications of Rawls's positions. (Thus, rather than subtitling the book "Essays on Rawls," I have used "Essays on Rawlsian Political Philosophy.") This is particularly true of the discussions of public reason and contractarian agreement in chapter 1, consequentialism in chapter 3, luck egalitarianism in chapter 4, distributive justice in chapters 3, 4, 8 and 9, and judicial review in chapters 6 and 7. I do not pretend that Rawls would have addressed these subjects exactly in the same way I do, however, much of my approach is informed by his framework. I do feel they share the spirit of his position.

Six of the seven previously published papers in this volume are presented with minor changes from the originals. Most changes were introduced to reduce repetition within overlapping discussions and to remedy infelicitous expressions. Four of the papers (chaps. 1, 2, 5, and 6) were written and (except for chap. 5) published over 10 years ago. Chapters 3, 4, 7, 8, and 9 were written over the past two years. I have incorporated a good deal of new material into chapter 9 since its original publication. Chapters 3 and 4 are heretofore unpublished.

In the following remarks, I foreshadow the main ideas in each chapter.

A *Theory of Justice*

Rawls says in the preface to A *Theory of Justice* that his aim in the book is to revive the social contract tradition by drawing on the natural rights theories of Locke, Rousseau, and Kant, in order to offer the most appropriate moral conception of justice for a democratic society. Before Rawls, social contract doctrine had laid dormant since the eighteenth century—largely due to Hume's and Bentham's still-influential criticisms. Partly as a result, it is often difficult to see how Rawls's work ties in with social contractarian doctrine. In chapter 1, "Reason and Agreement in Social Contract Views" (1990), I seek to fit justice as fairness within the liberal and democratic social contract tradition of Locke, Rousseau, and Kant, and show how its conception of practical reason and general agreement differ significantly from the alternative Hobbesian contract tradition. I mainly contrast Rawls's contractarianism with the Hobbesian position set forth by David Gauthier. I discuss the two different kinds of reasons Rawls recognizes, stemming from his distinction between reasonable and rational. I defend Rawls against Gauthier's and others' objection that Rawls does not have a genuine contractarian position since there is no role for bargaining between the parties in the original position due to the veil of ignorance. The general aim of the paper is to show that there is a distinctive idea of agreement underlying Rawls's contractarian position, which stems from the idea of reasonableness that is so integral to Rawls's account of practical reason. My suggestion is that the parties to Rawls's original position rationally agree to principles of justice in so far as they jointly precommit themselves to upholding cooperative institutions that mutually benefit everyone. This rational agreement among the parties in the original position is designed to reflect the reasonable agreement among free and equal citizens in a well-ordered society who are motivated by their sense of justice, and want to cooperate on grounds of reciprocity and mutual respect.

I discuss here an idea of "public reason," distinguishing it, as Rousseau does, from an idea of "private reason," which I construe as the particular reasons that enable a person to decide what is rational to do. It is the idea of practical rationality as a person's private or particular reasons that exclusively informs the Hobbesian tradition. At the time that Rawls initially revived Rousseau's and Kant's idea of public reason (implicitly in "Kantian Constructivism" [1980] then explicitly in "Political not Metaphysical"[9] [1985]), he seems to have conceived of it as roughly synonymous with the idea of "the Reasonable" (or so I believed at the time), which he contrasts with "the Rational" or the idea of a person's good. This is how I treat the concept in the first chapter. As the idea of public reason subsequently developed in Rawls's thought within the context of political liberalism, it took on a different meaning than Rousseau's or Kant's uses of it, coming to be defined in terms of the considerations that reasonable and rational persons can accept in their capacity as free and equal democratic citizens. (Rawls's developed sense of public reason is discussed in chaps. 6 and 7.)

Rawls says in the preface to A *Theory of Justice* that he seeks to revive social contract theory in order to offer an alternative conception of justice to utilitarianism, which he regards as the dominant tradition in moral and political philosophy. In chapters 2 and 3, I take up Rawls's relation to, and major differences with, utilitarianism and consequentialism and topics related to them. In chapter 2, "Utilitarianism, Deontology, and the Priority of Right" (1994), I discuss utilitarianism in order to clarify Rawls's distinction between teleological and deontological moral conceptions and his idea of the priority of right over the good. Ronald Dworkin and Will Kymlicka have argued that utilitarianism is not

---

9. Rawls, "Justice as Fairness: Political not Metaphysical," *Philosophy & Public Affairs* 14, no. 3 (Summer 1985) (cited in text as JF).

teleological as Rawls asserts but is as deontological as any other position, for it is grounded in a conception of equality that requires giving equal consideration to everyone's interests. I discuss why this is a mistaken understanding of Rawls's distinction between teleology and deontology, which addresses the substantive content and requirements of moral principles and not the reasons used to justify or apply those principles. Simply because utilitarians invoke justificatory principles requiring equal consideration does not render the substantive content of the principle of utility itself an egalitarian or deontological principle. The principle of utility is teleological since it says we are to maximize the aggregate good of individuals' happiness without regard to how it gets distributed. I then discuss and clarify Rawls's idea of the priority of right, which is often confused with deontology (by Sandel, Kymlicka, and many others as a result). Rather than being a claim about the justification of a moral conception (such as Sandel's mistaken claim that Rawls relies only on principles of right and no conception of the good in arguing for his principles), the priority of right over the good addresses the structure of the practical reason of reasonable moral agents. Instead of aiming to maximize individual or social good (such as individual or aggregate utility), a reasonable moral agent is one who regulates his/her deliberations about the good according to requirements of moral principles of right and constrains the pursuit of ends accordingly. This basically is what is meant by Rawls's idea of the priority of right—it is a claim about the composition of the practical reasoning of conscientious moral agents and their commitment to regulate their ends and pursuits by moral requirements of justice.

Chapter 3, "Consequentialism, Publicity, Stability, and Property-Owning Democracy," is heretofore unpublished. The paper begins with a discussion of consequentialism and why I believe Rawls did not devote attention to many alternatives to utilitarianism proposed by contemporary consequentialists. Only utilitarianism, Rawls believed, could provide anything near the degree of systematicity and ordering of moral judgments that is required by a practical moral conception of political justice. (Here it is interesting to reflect whether Rawls would have been more amenable to a form of non-utilitarian pluralist consequentialism, given his apparent change of view later regarding the degree to which a political conception of justice can provide anything resembling a decision procedure or ordering method for resolving problems of justice.) This leads into a discussion of a distinct problem with pluralist consequentialist views that seek to incorporate rights and other moral principles into the state of affairs to be maximized or otherwise instrumentally promoted. Positions of this kind have been suggested by Amaryta Sen and others, and they are popular among consequentialists who seek to avoid the gross distributive inequalities allowed by utilitarianism. I contend that these positions are confused, and that in the end they are forms of non-consequentialist intuitionism.

In sections III and IV of chapter 3 (along with chap. 6), I discuss the ideas of publicity and the stability of a moral conception of justice, which Rawls heavily relies upon to argue that the principles of justice would be chosen over the principle of utility in the original position. The main question I consider is why Rawls regards the publicity and stability of a moral conception of justice as conditions of its justification (as opposed to its application), especially given the fact that publicity and stability both depend upon facts about human nature and social cooperation. This question is of particular significance in light of criticisms (by G. A. Cohen, Juergen Habermas, and many consequentialists) that the publicity and stability of a moral conception are not relevant to its justification but rather are important factors to take into account in applying a moral conception to regulate human conduct.

Finally, chapter 3 ends with a discussion of alternative economic frameworks supported by utilitarianism and justice as fairness. It takes up Rawls's rejection of the capitalist welfare state, which he regarded as having primarily a utilitarian justification. Rawls argues instead, on the basis of justice as fairness, for a property-owning democracy, in part because it results in less inequality of primary goods than the welfare state and provides for widespread ownership and control of the means of production, mitigating the control of production by a capitalist class and the resulting wage-relationship that workers must tolerate. In this regard Rawls's account of distributive justice is guided not by welfarist concerns as is often assumed but by concerns similar to those that Mill and Marx had for the dignity and self-respect of working people and their control of their productive capacities. Related to these discussions are my later discussions of economic justice and the difference principle in chapters 4, 8, and 9. There I discuss why Rawls regards distributive justice and the difference principle as based in democratic social and political cooperation. This explains in large part why Rawls later rejects the idea of global distributive justice.

Chapter 4, "Rawls and Luck Egalitarianism," is also a new paper, prepared for the 2005 APA Meetings, Pacific Division, for a session on Susan Hurley's book *Justice, Luck, and Knowledge*. While I largely agree with Hurley's criticisms of so-called "luck egalitarianism" in her book, I take issue with her and others' claims (e.g., Richard Arneson and Will Kymlicka) that Rawls himself starts from or is committed to a position that seeks to equalize the consequences of fortune (especially the "natural lottery" [*TJ*, 74/64 rev.]) in deciding distributive justice. I show why this is a misunderstanding of Rawls's supposed remarks that people do not deserve their natural talents and that natural talents should be regarded as a "common asset" (e.g., *TJ*, sec.12). To begin with, Rawls never said these things. Instead, he said that "differences" in natural talents are undeserved and are to be regarded as a common asset, which, I explain, is a very different claim than those attributed to him. In any case, whatever Rawls said, it does not commit him to the position that distributive justice requires that the consequences of the "natural lottery," or any other effect of (mis)fortune, be equalized or that misfortune be compensated. Rawls does think the effects of luck should be "mitigated" and not allowed to "improperly influence" distributions, but he intends this to mean something which is very different than luck egalitarians think and which is entirely compatible with the aims of the difference principle. I also discuss in this paper the differences between Rawls's and Ronald Dworkin's positions that markets are to be used to hold people responsible for their choices. Unlike Rawls, Dworkin assigns a greater role to markets in determining just distributions since they reflect people's choices. I question the wisdom of allowing people's "value to others" to serve as any kind of benchmark for just distributions. I end this chapter with a brief defense (in response to G. A. Cohen's criticism) of Rawls's appeal to incentives in justifying inequalities of income and wealth under the difference principle. The primary reason Rawls builds incentives into the difference principle is not to encourage capitalist self-seeking but to accommodate the plurality of goods and citizens' freedom to determine and pursue their conception of the good.

In chapter 5, "Congruence and the Good of Justice" (2003), I take up Rawls's discussion in part III of A *Theory of Justice*, his argument for the stability of justice as fairness. I discuss here (continuing the discussion begun in chap. 3) the importance of the stability requirement to the argument for justice as fairness. There are two reasons Rawls focuses on the stability of a conception of justice: First, he seeks to show that regularly doing what justice as fairness requires of us is within human capacities and moral sentiments. Second, the purpose of the stability argument is to show how justice and having a sense of justice are not self-destructive and do not undermine our pursuit of important goods but rather are compatible with our good. Rawls makes more than one argument in *Theory* for stability (among these is his argument from social union). I discuss what I take to be the central argument Rawls provides for the stability of a well-ordered society: Rawls's Kantian argument for the "congruence of the Right and the Good" (*TJ*, sec. 86). The purpose of the argument is to show how in a well-ordered society it can be in everyone's rational interest to act not just according to but also for the sake of principles of right and justice. I show how this argument relies upon the Kantian interpretation of justice as fairness, particularly the idea of moral personality and realization of the moral powers as the condition for free moral and rational agency. The implication of the congruence argument is that we fully realize our moral and rational capacities by acting for the sake of justice, and to do so is to achieve moral autonomy, an intrinsic good for each person in a well-ordered society. I discuss some potential problems with this argument, problems which I contend, here and in chapter 6, lead Rawls to think that this argument for the stability of a well-ordered society is unrealistic. These problems lay the background for Rawls's project in *Political Liberalism*.

Political Liberalism

Chapter 6, "*Political Liberalism* and the Possibility of a Just Democratic Constitution" (1994), begins with a discussion of why Rawls made the changes to the justification of justice as fairness that led him to *Political Liberalism*. As suggested earlier, the main reasons are problems he found with the Kantian philosophical commitments implicit in the congruence argument.[10] I then discuss the main changes and new basic ideas in *Political Liberalism*—including the domain of the political and a freestanding political conception of justice, the overlapping consensus of reasonable comprehensive doctrines, and public reason as a basis for public justification—and provide an account of why each of these ideas is necessary once Rawls gives up the Kantian congruence argument.

---

10. See *PL*, 388n, where Rawls confirms this interpretation as one of his reasons for the transition to political liberalism.

Chapter 6 (and also, to a degree, chap. 7) ends with a discussion of Rawls's position regarding the role of the institution of judicial review in a democracy. It is a common criticism that judicial review is incompatible with democracy. Here it is relevant that Rawls does not regard democracy simply as a form of government but rather as a kind of constitution and more generally as a particular kind of society. His aim from the outset was to discover the most appropriate principles of justice for the basic structure of a *democratic society* (*TJ*, viii/xviii rev.), including its democratic constitution and economic and legal systems. It is within this framework that he argues that there is nothing intrinsically undemocratic about the practice of judicial review — it is not incompatible with a democratic society so long as it is needed to maintain the social and political institutions constituting the basic structure. In the context of the conditions necessary for a democratic society, the frequent criticism that judicial review is nonetheless incompatible with a democratic government appears rather limp, for if democracy is simply defined as nothing more than a voting procedure incorporating equal voting rights and majority rule, then of course the objection is a truism. But why should we artificially truncate a conception of democracy in this way? Rawls has a far more robust conception of democracy as a society of free and equal citizens who possess constitutive political power and design social and political institutions that maintain their status as equals cooperating on a basis of mutual respect. This conception of democracy puts democratic voting procedures in their proper context, enabling us to understand their intended purpose as well as their limits.

Chapter 7, "Public Reason and Political Justifications" (2004), is a discussion of Rawls's idea of public reason as it develops and emerges from his work in its final form, of its centrality to political liberalism, and its role in his account of political justice. Here I distinguish Rawls's idea of public reason from accounts and misunderstandings by others. I explain how public reason, rather than being simply reasons that are shared by people of different persuasions, is an idea patterned upon Rawls's conception of democracy. Public reason has to do with the reasons and political values that free and equal citizens can reasonably accept in their capacity *as* citizens, and on the basis of their fundamental interests as citizens. Here I also discuss how the complex idea of reasonableness is to be understood in Rawls's later works. It differs from others' accounts of reasonableness and even from Rawls's own earlier account insofar as that was influenced by a Kantian account of practical reason. I defend the idea of public political justification and public reason against objections by Joseph Raz and Ronald Dworkin. I also show how one can apply the idea of public reason to address the political debate over abortion and therewith justify a limited political right to abortion. I conclude this paper with further thoughts on the proper role of judicial review, discussing its relationship to Rawls's idea of public reason.

The Law of Peoples

Chapters 8 and 9 begin with general discussions of what Rawls is trying to achieve in this much-misunderstood final work of his. I defend Rawls against numerous frequent objections by cosmopolitans and others. I discuss the role of the idea of human rights in *The Law of Peoples* and their relation to the duty of assistance owed to burdened peoples; why Rawls sees human rights as distinct from liberal rights; and why he did not see it to be the role of liberal peoples to impose liberalism upon "decent" societies. I mainly focus, in both papers, on why Rawls does not extend the difference principle globally as many have suggested, or indeed why he does not endorse any global principle of distributive justice. Here I emphasize the centrality of social and political cooperation to Rawls's account of distributive justice. In chapter 8, "The Law of Peoples, Social Cooperation, Human Rights, and Distributive Justice" (2006), I argue that Rawls regards distributive justice as domestic rather than global, largely because he sees it not as an allocative problem but as a question of how to design basic social institutions within a democratic society. This is a question for democratic political cooperation, which does not exist at the global level. The absence of a global basic structure, particularly a democratic world-state and global legal system, underlies the domestic rather than global reach of principles of distributive justice. In chapter 9, "Distributive Justice and the Law of Peoples" (2006), I discuss why distributive justice for Rawls ultimately involves the political design and social maintenance of basic social institutions (particularly property and economic relations) that make social cooperation possible. Part of the explanation is that, for Rawls, decisions regarding appropriate principles of distributive justice involve the task of deciding on reasonable terms of social cooperation *among free and equal persons*, on a basis of *reciprocity* and mutual respect. Free and equal persons are conceived as socially productive and politically cooperative citizens, each of whom does his fair part in contributing to economic and political life. I argue that it is not reasonable, and there is no reciprocity involved in structuring social and political relations among democratic citizens so as meet the requirements of a global distribution principle. It is this idea of social cooperation among free and equal citizens on a basis of reciprocity and mutual respect that supplies the argument for the difference principle; outside of that democratic context the argument for the difference principle cannot succeed.

III. Acknowledgments

I am indebted to a good number of people over the years for providing helpful discussions and critical comments on these papers and their subject matter. Primary among them are R. Jay Wallace, Joshua Cohen, Samuel Scheffler, Rahul Kumar, K. C. Tan, Thomas Ricketts, T. M. Scanlon, and John Rawls. I am grateful to Mardy Rawls for her suggestions in writing the biographical material that appears in the appendix. I also appreciate the editorial work that Kathleen Moran has done in preparing this volume. I am indebted to my sister, Betsy Freeman Fox, for proofreading the entire manuscript. Finally, I am grateful to my wife, Annette Lareau, for her editorial suggestions and constant support in helping me bring this work to completion.

Part I

A Theory of Justice

1

Reason and Agreement in Social Contract Views

Social contract views work from the intuitive idea of agreement. The appeal of this notion lies in the liberal idea that cooperation ought to be based in the individuals' consent and ought to be for their mutual benefit. Social contract views differ according to how the idea of agreement is specified: Who are the parties to the agreement? How are they situated with respect to one another (status quo, state of nature, or equality)? What are the intentions, capacities, and interests of these individuals, and what rights and powers do they have? What is the purpose of the agreement? Is the agreement conceived of in historical or nonhistorical terms? Since these and other parameters have been set in different ways, it is difficult to generalize and speak of the social contract tradition. Hobbes's idea of agreement differs fundamentally from Rousseau's, just as Gauthier and Buchanan conceive of agreement very differently than Rawls and Scanlon.

Rather than being a particular kind of ethical view, the general notion of agreement functions as a framework for justification in ethics. This framework is based on the liberal idea that the legitimacy of social rules and institutions depends on their being freely and publicly acceptable to all individuals bound by them. If rational individuals in appropriately defined circumstances could or would agree to certain rules or institutions, then insofar as we identify with these individuals and their interests, what they accept should also be acceptable to us now as a basis for our cooperation. Seen in this way, the justificatory force of social contract views depends only in part on the idea of agreement; even more essential is the conception of the person and the conception of practical reason that are built into particular views.

In this paper, I discuss the concept of practical reason and its relation to the idea of social agreement in two different kinds of social contract views. My ultimate concern is to address a criticism, often made of Rawls, Rousseau, and Kant, that because of the moral assumptions made, the principles or institutions sought to be justified are not the product of a collective choice or agreement at all; the appeal to a social contract is an unnecessary shuffle that masks the true character of these views. This criticism has been formulated in more than one way. I shall focus on a version given by David Gauthier, directed against Rawls.[1] I will show (in secs. III through V) that Rawls's idea of agreement is not spurious but is closely tied to his conceptions of practical reason, justification, and autonomy. To do this, I need first to examine the different ways reasons are conceived of in social contract views (sec. I) and to consider the structure of Gauthier's own version of the social contract (sec. II).

I. Two Kinds of Social Contract Views

Let us begin with a rough distinction between Hobbesian, or purely interest-based, and right-based contract views.[2] Both take the idea of reciprocity—the idea that social cooperation should be for mutual advantage—as fundamental. They differ, however, in their characterization of this basic idea. In Hobbesian views, cooperation for mutual advantage involves no irreducible moral elements. Hobbesian views aim to show that morality is a subordinate notion, grounded in individuals' antecedent desires and interests. Each person's basic desires or interests are seen as definable without reference to any moral notions, and normally in terms of certain states of the person. The objective is to demonstrate that (1) moral principles are among the rational precepts necessary to promote one's prior and independent ends; (2) any sentiments we might have for such principles are conditioned by these ends; and (3) compliance with precepts that promote everyone's antecedent purposes is the most rational course of action for each individual to take in order to realize his interests, whether in himself or in other particular persons or objects.[3]

So construed, the conception of cooperation that Hobbesian views employ is one of efficiently coordinated activity for each person's benefit. The task is to show that, from among several modes of cooperation that might appear to be mutually advantageous when compared to the status quo or a noncooperative baseline, there is a unique set of institutions which will ensure cooperation on

1. David Gauthier, "The Social Contract as Ideology," *Philosophy & Public Affairs* 6, no. 2 (Winter 1977): 139n; see also Gauthier's "Bargaining and Justice," in *Ethics and Economics*, ed. Ellen Paul, Jeffrey Paul, and Fred D. Miller, Jr. (Oxford: Blackwell, 1985), 40–45. Jean Hampton develops a similar but more sympathetic argument in greater detail in "Contracts and Choices: Does Rawls Have a Social Contract Theory?" *Journal of Philosophy* 77 (1980): 315–38.

2. Rawls used the term "interest-based" in his lectures on political philosophy to indicate a contract conception like Hobbes's that is based in a nonmoral account of a person's good; he attributes the term to Joshua Cohen. I use the term "right-based," not in the sense of individual rights but in Rawls's sense of principles of right. A moral conception that is based in a conception of individual or natural rights would be right-based, but so, too, is a position like Rawls's, which is based in other principles of right. Rawls refuses to accept Ronald Dworkin's suggestion that justice as fairness is based in a natural right to equal concern and respect. He says, instead, that his position is "conception-based" or "ideal-based" insofar as it works from an ideal conception of persons and society. "Rights, duties and goals are but elements of such idealized conceptions." See Rawls, *Collected Papers*, ed. Samuel Freeman (Cambridge, MA: Harvard University Press, 1999), 400–401n (cited in text as *CP*).

3. This description represents a particular kind of moral conception often attributed to Hobbes and captures the central elements of Gauthier's view. Whether Hobbes himself actually held such a

stable terms and which is acceptable to everyone. The primary modern proponents of this view are David Gauthier and James Buchanan, both of whom argue for a form of laissez-faire capitalism.

Major representatives of right-based social contract views are Locke, Rousseau, Kant, and, among contemporaries, Rawls and Scanlon. The common feature of these accounts is not that they base the agreement primarily on an assumption of prior moral or "natural rights." (Locke, Kant, and Rousseau may make this assumption, while Rawls and Scanlon do not.) It is, rather, that principles of right and justice cannot be accounted for without appeal to certain irreducible moral notions.[4] This assumption affects the conception of social cooperation employed. It has a dual aspect: in addition to a conception of each individual's rational good, the idea of social cooperation has an independent moral component (characterized in Rawls by the notion of fair terms and what is reasonable and in traditional views by an assumption of innate moral rights). Moreover, right-based views ascribe to persons a basic interest defined in moral or social terms. Consequently, in contrast to Hobbesian views, social relations are not defined as a rational compromise among conflicting interests. This affects fundamentally the way right-based conceptions interpret the social contract. These contrasts have the following consequence: if we see the role of a unanimous collective agreement as an account of what we have reason to do in our social and political relations, then, according to right-based views, these reasons are not sufficiently accounted for in terms of what it is rational to do to promote our prior and independent ends. There are reasons that apply to us without reference to our antecedent desires and interests. What is the nature of these independent reasons, and where do they originate?

Consider the skeptical thesis, advanced by Hume, that moral considerations do not give each individual a reason for acting, whatever his ends or situation.[5] Philippa Foot once argued for a similar position.[6] She contended not that moral judgments have an automatic reason-giving force but that they "give reasons for

view is open to debate. For a different interpretation, see Keith Thomas, "Social Origins of Hobbes' Political Thought," in *Hobbes Studies*, ed. K. C. Brown (Oxford: Blackwell, 1965).

4. "Right-based" refers to, then, principles of right, and is to be distinguished from "rights-based." Among the principles of right relied on by right-based conceptions, there may be certain moral rights, as in Locke's and Kant's versions of the social contract. Rawls, however, denies that his view is a rights-based conception. See Rawls, "Justice as Fairness: Political not Metaphysical," *Philosophy & Public Affairs* 14, no. 3 (Summer 1985): 236n (cited in text as JF), where Rawls claims that "justice as fairness is a conception-based, or . . . an ideal-based view," since it works from certain fundamental intuitive ideas that reflect ideals implicit in the public culture of a democratic society. Certain principles of right are, Rawls aims to show, implicit in these ideals.

5. I use "skeptical" here to refer not to moral skepticism (which Hume did not hold) but to a skepticism about the reason-giving force of moral judgments independent of desires and nonmoral interests. See David Hume, *A Treatise of Human Nature*, ed. L. A. Selby Bigge and P. H. Nidditch, 2nd ed. (Oxford: Clarendon Press, 1978), bk. 2, pt. 3, sec. 3; and bk. 3, sec. 1, 1.

6. Philippa Foot, "Morality as a System of Hypothetical Imperatives," *The Philosophical Review* 81 (1972): 305–16; see also Foot's *Virtues and Vices and Other Essays* (Berkeley: University of California Press, 1978), chap. 11. Foot expands her position in chapters 10 and 12. Foot's position in these essays is not characteristic of her earlier or subsequent work.

action in ordinary ways."[7] What we have reason to do depends upon our ultimate purposes, as given by our desires, interests, and affections. Whether one
has reason to act on moral considerations is contingent upon whether it is in her
prudential interests to do so, or upon her having a benevolent disposition, a love
of justice, or some other moral motivation. Thus, it is not always irrational to be
amoral and act against moral requirements. One who rejects morality may be
villainous but is not necessarily acting contrary to reason.[8] We might look upon
the Humean position as presenting a challenge which is taken up by both kinds
of social contract views but which they respond to in different ways. Hobbesian
contract views attempt to meet this challenge on its own ground. They share
with the Humean view a conception of reasons that I shall refer to as "agent-centered."[9] Agent-centered conceptions approach the notion of reasons by focusing
on the deliberations of single agents with given desires and interests in fixed circumstances in which they face a range of options from which they must choose.
Reasons are then interpreted in instrumental terms by reference to the agent's
desires and interests as an individual. Given this conception of reasons, Hobbesian contract views seek to defeat the skeptical argument on the basis of certain
empirical assumptions. They posit a noncooperative situation in which persons
are described as fundamentally self-centered and individualistic, and they interpret morality as the cooperative norms that all can rationally accept in this situation. Other-regarding sentiments and our sense of duty are then explained as,
at best, secondary motivations that effectively promote our basic interests in ourselves (self-preservation and the means for "commodious living" in Hobbes, or
utility maximization in Gauthier and Buchanan). A leading problem in moral
philosophy then becomes how to demonstrate that the amoral or noncooperative
person fares worse in cooperative contexts, in terms of the satisfaction of his self-
regarding interests, than he would have fared had he steadfastly observed moral
requirements and cultivated social preferences and dispositions.

Right-based contract views accept the Humean premise that we have primary
desires not focused on the self and reject the Hobbesian approach to moral inquiry
from the point of view of isolated individuals abstracted from social relationships.
Their response to the skeptical argument is directed at the contention that all reasons must refer to the antecedent ends of particular individuals. The ultimate aim
is to show that moral principles and our sense of duty, while not derivable from
given desires and interests conjoined with principles of rational choice, still have a
basis in reason. Where does this conception of reasons come from?

7. Foot, *Virtues and Vices*, 154. Foot does not hold that desire is a condition of having a reason.
She departs from Hume in contending that there are prudential reasons for acting that are independent of an agent's existing desires (148). But she states that there are no independent moral reasons of
this kind that require us to take others' interests into account or act for their good (153–56).

8. Foot, *Virtues and Vices*, 152, 161–62.

9. I use the term "agent-centered" because, on this conception, all reasons center on the desires
and interests of particular agents. The term is not meant to imply egoism; the content of one's desires
and interests is left open. I aim to encompass a wide range of views. The rough idea is to represent
what Kant had in mind by the Hypothetical Imperative. Besides Foot, many others, including Williams, Harman, and Gauthier, contend that reasons are adequately characterized in this way.

If we focus on reasons solely from the perspective of single agents under conditions of choice, and interpret this notion purely by reference to their desires and interests as individuals, then the skeptical question, "Why should I be moral?" is a natural one to ask. And from that perspective it would appear that the only kind of considerations that can supply an answer to particular persons are instrumental ones about what promotes their antecedent ends. But these considerations are too narrow. They leave no place for the intuitive sense that practical reasons are not just normative considerations that must motivate an individual but also have a justificatory aspect extending beyond the individual's particular concerns. To account for this intuition, suppose we approach reasons differently, from the standpoint of our membership in a social group. When we ask for people's reasons in social contexts, we are not concerned simply with their intentions and motives, and we may not be interested at all in their having adopted effective means to realize their ends. Instead, our primary concern is whether their ends are legitimate and their means justified, as measured by the system of norms generally accepted within the group or by society as a whole.

Every social group has norms of cooperation, certain practices and procedures that regulate interaction and are necessary to sustain the life of the group. The norms do not simply characterize accepted constraints on conduct. They also serve a social role in providing a public basis for justification. Members of the group assess one another's activities and pursuits in terms of its system of norms. When someone's conduct departs from standard practices, he is subject to criticism according to these standards and is expected to justify his actions by reference to them. The system of norms has a central place in the public life of the group: certain rules and institutions are seen as providing reasons for and against people's actions and ends, whatever their desires and interests may be.[10]

Seeing reasons in a social context, as those considerations that count in public argument and structure public justification and criticism, is very different from seeing them as purely instrumental considerations taken into account by single individuals concerned to advance their particular ends. For, it is just the function of reasons in this social sense to provide a commonly accepted basis for assessing individuals' ends and desires and the courses of conduct they adopt in order to realize them. A separate dimension is added to the normative considerations that motivate particular individuals.

This implies a certain ambiguity in the notion of practical reasons. This ambiguity is often reflected in the structure of our individual deliberations. Practical reasoning normally involves (as agent-centered views correctly point out) clarifying our ends, making them consistent, and deciding on the most effective

10. The sense in which I use "reasons" here comes out in such claims as, "The Supreme Court's reasons for curtailing abortion rights were rather weak," and, "That slavery involves the domination of humans and holding them as property is sufficient reason for condemning it." The fact that an act is deceptive, coercive, or involves the breach of a promise or other commitment functions as a reason in the context of argument or assessment of a person's actions. In political debate, the fact that a law would violate individuals' constitutional rights, create unemployment, increase poverty, or undermine national security constitutes a reason against that law. These are examples of what I call "public reasons."

means to achieve them. But in our private deliberations we take for granted a background of social norms, which manifests itself in the following way. When some doubt arises as to the legitimacy of our ends or proposed actions, the question we normally confront is not whether abiding by these norms will effectively promote our purposes. It is, rather, whether our ends and proposed actions can be publicly justified to others according to the system of norms generally accepted within the group. We appeal to certain social norms to appraise our claims and expectations, and to assess the instrumental means that we have already determined effectively promote our purposes. The practice of public justification is in effect reflected in our private deliberations. In this way, certain social rules and institutions occupy a privileged position in the course of practical reasoning; they provide special reasons that subordinate the reasons that are instrumental to realizing our particular ends and concerns.

Being an adult member of a social group requires that one has developed the capacities to understand, apply, and act on these "public reasons" (as I shall call them). These capacities are, on the face of it, different from the abilities of individual agents to deliberate about their particular ends and the most effective means for realizing them. For, what is involved is a social capacity, an ability to assess critically and justify the pursuit of one's ends according to the requirements of a different kind of norm.

Hobbesian views need not deny that we have such a capacity, nor must they deny the social role of reasons in public justification. They contend, however, that since social principles are but an extension of principles of rational individual choice, whatever justificatory force public reasons have, they must have by virtue of their instrumental relation to each agent's more particular concerns. So the capacities to understand and apply social norms, and justify our actions by reference to them, are still subordinate to each individual's abilities to deliberate about the effective pursuit of his own particular ends. One of the primary points of Rousseau's *Second Discourse* is to show the shortcomings of Hobbes's conflation of these independent capacities and the two kinds of reasons they support.[11]

Rousseau maintains, contrary to Hobbes, that as an isolated being, man is a "stupid and shortsighted animal,"[12] tranquil by nature, and driven only by sensation and instinct. Being asocial, he is without language, and so also without reason and the realized capacities for rational choice. He is not moved by a concern for satisfying his future appetites (Hobbes's desire for "power after power"[13]), for without reason he has no conception of himself or his future. He has no need for reason, language, or prudential concerns; in his isolated condition, his needs are wholly satisfied by natural instinct. His capacities for reasoning are not activated until he enters into cooperative circumstances. Reason is the instrument of adap-

11. Jean-Jacques Rousseau, *Discourse on Inequality* [*Second Discourse* (1755)], in *Rousseau's Political Writings*, ed. Alan Ritter and Julia C. Bondanella (New York: Norton, 1988).

12. Rousseau, *On Social Contract or Principles of Political Right* (1762), in *Rousseau's Political Writings*, ed. Ritter and Bondanella, bk. 1, chap. 8, 95. See also his *Discourse on Inequality*, 15.

13. Thomas Hobbes, *Leviathan* (1651), ed. C. B. MacPherson (New York: Penguin, 1968).

tation man acquires to deal with social environments, as instinct is his mode of adaptation to the state of nature. And as a socially adaptive capacity, its primary role is to enable him to understand, apply, act on, and, if necessary, devise the norms of cooperation necessary for social life. It is in conjunction with the development and exercise of this social capacity, and not prior to it, that man is able to apply his rational capacities to the task of adopting and adjusting his individual ends and deliberating on effective means for realizing them.

Rousseau's state of nature is an analytical device, designed to show what we owe to society: the development and exercise of our capacities for reasoning according to both prudential and moral norms.[14] Being a member of a social group, recognizing and accepting that group's cooperative norms, and understanding how these norms function as public reasons within the group are conditions of our realizing our capacity for reasoning in agent-centered terms. This says nothing about the moral content of a group's cooperative norms; they may be quite perverse. It simply brings out their separate function, and shows the artificiality of Hobbesian attempts to use the instrumental aspect of practical reasoning as a sufficient basis for accounting for social cooperation and our capacities for reasoned justification. By defining reasons purely by reference to isolated agents with given desires, Hobbesian views start out by ignoring the public role of reasons in enabling us to justify our conduct to one another, and then explain our choice of ends according to norms that are a condition for the existence of the social group.

One way to look at right-based contract views is as views that begin with this other conception of reasons by focusing on the social role of norms in public justification. If we think of morality and justice in this way, and if our aim is to formulate principles that serve this social role, then the question is not whether members of society can be given reasons, as individuals, to comply with the norms of the group on the basis of their given ends. It is, rather, whether they can freely accept and abide by the normative system that provides the primary basis for public reasons, or whether they are entitled to complain. Unlike Hobbesian views, right-based views do not seek a set of rules that it is rational for every individual to comply with whatever that person's prior purposes. Basic norms of justice need not connect instrumentally with everyone's given desires and interests.[15] This fact is reflected in the starting assumption of right-based views; they do not take individuals' desires as given, or as having value on their own terms. Instead, they seek to provide a notion of our legitimate interests, defined by reference to what can serve as a common basis for public agreement, and supply standards for critically assessing people's desires and expectations. Given the necessity of social coopera-

---

14. Rousseau, *Discourse on Inequality*, 9–10. On the role of the state of nature in traditional social contract views, see Jean Hampton, *Hobbes and the Social Contract Tradition* (Cambridge: Cambridge University Press, 1986), chap. 9.

15. Compare Rawls, *A Theory of Justice* (Cambridge, MA: Harvard University Press, 1971; rev. ed., 1999), 576/505 rev. (cited in text as *TJ*; sometimes referred to as *Theory*); and T. M. Scanlon, "Contractualism and Utilitarianism," in *Utilitarianism and Beyond*, ed. Amartya Sen and Bernard Williams (Cambridge: Cambridge University Press, 1982), 105, 119.

tion over a lifetime, the requirement imposed on social norms is that no one can reasonably object when social norms are enforced against them.

That certain considerations count as reasons in public discussion and argument is a claim about our justificatory practices. By itself, it does not establish anything about the content of moral principles, or even that there are any. What is established is an additional basis upon which to build such principles. The idea is to give the notion of public reasons some kind of representation in theory. Accordingly, right-based views assume that the ability to understand and apply such reasons involves an independent capacity of practical reason;[16] further, they assume that agents have an interest in cooperating with others on terms that are publicly justifiable. The aim of a conception of justice is to specify principles that respond to this capacity and interest, that is, principles that provide a public basis for justification all can accept, in order to sustain willing social cooperation.

The problem is to show that there are principles that meet these specifications. This is where right-based views diverge in several ways: in their account of our moral capacities for practical reasoning, their conception of justification, and the role assigned in them to the social contract.[17] I shall later discuss these aspects of Rawls's view. First, however, notice how the focus of the skeptical conclusion must change once we conceive of reasons as having an independent role in public justification. The question whether there are reasons for us to accept and act on requirements of justice is no longer simply the question whether justice is compatible with our preexisting ends. That issue may remain, but it is not the primary concern of right-based views. Instead, a different question arises, the question whether there exists a set of principles that is capable of serving as a public basis for justification and that all individuals can reasonably affirm and accept as providing the basis for the social norms that regulate individuals' pursuits of their particular ends. It is an open question whether there are such principles; therefore, it is an open question whether there are moral reasons with a basis in considerations independent of individuals' antecedent desires and interests conjoined with principles of rational choice. The important point

---

16. See *TJ*, where Rawls defines moral theory as an account of our moral capacities (46–47/40–42 rev.) and defines justice as fairness as "a theory of the moral sentiments . . . setting out the principles governing our moral powers, or more specifically, our sense of justice" (50–51/44 rev.). Also, Thomas Scanlon offers that one of the capacities for agency is the ability to reason about what could be justified to others. See Scanlon, "The Significance of Choice," in *The Tanner Lectures on Human Values* (Salt Lake City: University of Utah Press, 1988), 8:173ff.

17. For example, Locke sought the ultimate basis for public justification in religion, in the self-evidence of God's natural laws. The basic moral capacity was thus represented epistemologically, as a capacity for rationally intuiting these laws and drawing inferences from them. In Kant, moral principles were seen as part of the structure of practical reason, which enabled us to conceive of ourselves as free. For Locke and Kant, the social contract had a reduced role; it was primarily a device for testing the legitimacy of existing political constitutions. Their agreements assumed, and were not designed to prove, a natural right of equal freedom, which was seen as justified on separate grounds. Rawls's social agreement has a more significant role since he seeks principles for designing basic social institutions, not just for testing constitutions. See John Locke, *Two Treatises of Government* (1660–1662), ed. Peter Laslett (New York: Cambridge University Press, 1988), and Immanuel Kant, *On the Common Saying: That May Be Correct in Theory, but It Is of No Use in Practice*, Ak 8:297.

is that we cannot answer this question a priori or on purely metaethical grounds. The relationship between morality and reason becomes a question of substantive moral theory.

Now let us return to Foot's concerns. Foot is perhaps right in saying that there is nothing rationally inescapable, in her sense of reasons, about morality whatever one's purposes or situation. What is inescapable, however, is one's being a member of a social group, recognizing the group's system of norms, and understanding how the norms function as reasons in public argument. Though that requirement does not involve endorsing all the norms of the group, whatever they may be, it does mean that one who is unwilling to cooperate with others on any terms except those most conducive to achieving his own particular ends is being unreasonable. The amoral man, however rational he may be (in agent-centered terms), is unreasonable just because he is not convinced or moved by any considerations except those that best promote his antecedent ends. He refuses to accept as authoritative any system of public reasons. This amounts to a refusal to acknowledge others as having claims of their own which warrant his recognition on some grounds independent of his particular purposes. And right-based contract views proceed on the assumption that moral reasons of justice involve the independent claims of other persons.

It is a fact about the vast majority of people that we acknowledge each other as independent sources of claims. (Indeed it is hard to take seriously anyone who says he does not see others in this way.) In large part, it is because of this recognition that we desire to justify our conduct and cooperate with others on terms that can be publicly accepted.[18] There may be exceptions—certain people without such sentiments. In their case, Foot is again right: there is little to be said to the man who cares nothing for justice to convince him to act justly.[19] But the absence of this moral motivation cannot be taken to show that his conduct is not contrary to reason. There is something more fundamental than one's given purposes underlying this assessment. And we need to discover it in order to comprehend why those of us who have moral motives and a desire to justify our actions have these motivations.[20]

II. Agent-Centered Reasons and the Social Contract

Let us now consider the relationship of the idea of a unanimous collective agreement to the different conceptions of practical reason in the two kinds of social contract views. I shall focus on Rawls's and Gauthier's views, beginning with Gauthier's Hobbesian account, as set forth in *Morals by Agreement*.[21] Gauth-

---

18. See Scanlon, "Contractualism and Utilitarianism," 116–17, on the significance of the desire to be able to justify one's actions and institutions.

19. Foot, *Virtues and Vices*, 166.

20. In Rawls, it is our conception of ourselves and our relations as democratic citizens that account for the moral sentiments of justice. See sec. V of this chapter.

21. David Gauthier, *Morals by Agreement* (Oxford: Oxford University Press, 1986) (cited in text as *MA*).

ier's purpose is twofold. First, he seeks "to defend Western market society by representing its ideal nature in relation to reason" (MA, 353). Second, there is a more traditional Hobbesian project, to give a "rational reconstruction" not only of morality but also of human sociability and all social sentiments (including love, friendship, and the sense of justice) (MA, 339; cf. 193). To carry out these tasks, Gauthier assumes a "natural man" who is fundamentally asocial, individualistic, and self-interested (MA, 310). Given these assumptions and the nature of his project, practical reasons are not going to be represented as having an independent social role of public justification.[22] Reason is interpreted purely in agent-centered terms, as individual utility maximization,[23] where the objects of a person's desires are specified "non-tuistically," or purely by reference to oneself (MA, 311). Gauthier places these persons in a noncooperative state of nature, which is Lockean to the extent that private property and rights in one's person are recognized, albeit on self-interested rather than (as in Locke) moral grounds. Each sees that his best response to others is to leave them to the quiet enjoyment of their powers and possessions, on the condition that they respond in kind. By a kind of Humean convention, individuals come to recognize each other's personal and property rights.

If persons and their initial endowments are conceived of in this way, only two possible modes of interaction are open to them: (1) hostility and (2) cooperation on the basis of contractual bargains (MA, 319). Accordingly, rational agents would enter into contractual relations with those with whom cooperation promises a Pareto improvement, and would dominate all the rest; the weak and handicapped, presumably, would be weeded out. Social cooperation is the result of a general contractual extension of this baseline. Justice is the set of constraints on market behavior and the direct pursuit of individual utility that rational agents would collectively agree to because it promises them a Pareto improvement. Gauthier sees no need for a coercive state to enforce these constraints or preexisting rights among rational beings; in contrast to Hobbes, that is not the purpose of his social contract.

Given Gauthier's assumptions, we might ask, what need is there for a social contract, a uniform public rule applying equally to all persons? Why could society (and, if need be, a coercive state) not arise out of a series of private contracts, as in Robert Nozick's view? Gauthier appeals to a collective agreement to deal with problems of market failure and externalities.[24] His contract is described as an

---

22. This is not to say that Gauthier would have to deny what I call public reasons. But he would explain and justify the system of public reasons in agent centered terms: something counts as a public reason in a society only if it ultimately advances the desires of agents as nonmembers.

23. "Practical rationality is the maximization of utility and so the maximization of the satisfaction of present preferences" (MA, 343). Of the maximizing view, Gauthier says he agrees "with economists and others that there is simply nothing else for practical rationality to be" ("Morality, Rational Choice, and Semantic Representation," Social Philosophy and Policy [1988]: 174).

24. MA, 84, 128ff., 223. "Morality arises from market failure" (MA, 84). The market failures Gauthier discusses are standard in economics: nuisances such as pollution, the provision of public goods, and economic rent. Gauthier does not discuss the need for political institutions to administer the requirements of justice or to decide on public goods. His account is extremely apolitical.

idealized economic bargain in which property-owning utility maximizers agree on a principle that corrects the inefficiencies of markets.[25] In the absence of this principle, Gauthier argues, rational agents would not all accept market outcomes and distributions. These are not problems for Nozick, since he rejects economic efficiency as the basis for the social order.

Regarding his conceptions of reasons and persons, Gauthier has argued that they are the only appropriate basis for justifying appeal to a social contract. For this reason he claims that Rousseau's and Rawls's views are not genuinely contractarian. Rawls's appeal to a social agreement is spurious, he says; the moral assumptions made are the real legitimating principles behind Rawls's view. "The real character of the theory emerges when one asks for the grounds of the legitimating principles."[26]

Gauthier's objection should be distinguished from Ronald Dworkin's. Dworkin says that, because Rawls's agreement is not an actual agreement, it would seem to be nonbinding and of no significance. This is not an objection to Rawls's idea of agreement but to its hypothetical nature. As such, it applies to the use of any hypothetical decision model in ethics—not just to Rawls's but also to Gauthier's and Kant's, and to Ideal Observer theories. A short answer to this objection (which I discuss below) is that agreement in the original position is heuristic; it is a thought experiment designed for purposes of self- and political clarification.[27] It helps us understand what the combined force of certain generally accepted intuitive ideas and firmly held moral convictions that shape public reasoning commit us to. Gauthier's hypothetical agreement has a different role. It operates from conceptions of practical reason and of the person that Gauthier contends are part of the best explanatory theory in the social sciences and seeks to develop a stable conception of justice consistent with these theoretical constructs (MA, 8).

---

25. Gauthier's principle of "minimax relative concession" (MRC) holds that "in any cooperative interaction, the rational joint strategy is determined by a bargain among the cooperators in which each advances his maximal claim and then offers a concession no greater in relative magnitude than the minimax concession" (MA, 145). In effect, this principle holds that individuals are to enjoy the benefits of cooperation, and share in the burdens, in proportion to their contributions to what Gauthier calls the "cooperative surplus" (MA, 224). MRC is an attempt to carry through the basic idea of the Marginal Productivity Theory of Just Distributions that underlies Gauthier's conception of justice and social cooperation: assuming private property in the means of production, to each according to his contribution to final output, as measured by the value of his marginal product. Cf. MA, 91, 97, 110–12, 140, 152, 154, 254.

26. Gauthier, "Social Contract as Ideology," 139n. See also his "Bargaining and Justice," 40–45.

27. For Dworkin's objection, see Ronald Dworkin, Taking Rights Seriously (Cambridge, MA: Harvard University Press, 1976), chap. 6, sec. 1. Dworkin's objection seems to be in part rhetorical, for he recognizes that the original position is a "powerful mechanic" for clarifying the requirements of equality. Here, too, it is relevant that Dworkin also appeals to hypothetical insurance choices under conditions of uncertainty to decide the appropriate level of social insurance a society should provide. If Rawls's hypothetical choice model is not binding, how can Dworkin's be? For Rawls's response to Dworkin's objection, see JF, 236ff. Compare Rawls's remarks on the "Socratic" nature of reflective equilibrium: "It is a notion characteristic of the study of principles which govern actions shaped by self-examination" (TJ, 48–49/omitted in rev.). See also Joshua Cohen, "Democratic Equality," Ethics 99 (1989): 750–51.

To lay the background for a discussion of the role of agreement in Rawls's view, we might focus more closely on certain features of Gauthier's account. For example, there is nothing about agent-centered reasons that requires that they be self-interested. But once we suppose (as all social contract theorists do) that justice and social cooperation have a basis in reason, then on an agent-centered view it is hard to resist an assumption of what cooperation-free interaction would look like for purposes of determining terms of social cooperation and the division of social benefits and burdens. For, that picture provides a baseline from which to compare the advantages of cooperating with persons with ends different from one's own, and allows one to assess how various modes of cooperation promote one's own given purposes. Social relations are then naturally portrayed as a contractual compromise among essentially conflicting interests. This marked tendency toward some form of Hobbism is characteristic of agent-centered views when applied to social questions.[28]

For Rawls, there is no place for comparing the benefits and burdens of cooperation with cooperation-free interaction; nothing like the state of nature plays a significant role in his view. One reason for this is that (as Rawls says) noncooperation is not a viable option for us. So the "take it or leave it" attitude implicit in bargains is inappropriate as a model for social relations. But that does not explain the more particular features of Rawls's agreement. Here it helps to focus on the structure of Gauthier's contract and recognize just how limited it actually is. Gauthier conceives of the social contract as an idealized economic bargain. Given his noncooperative baseline, some noncontractual basis must be provided for the preexisting claims that are needed to carry that idea through. So there is no justification in terms of justice and the social contract of absolute property, contractual bargains, the price system and unregulated market exchange, or prohibitions on coercion and deception. None of these rules and institutions rests on mutual consent. Gauthier does not see these crucial mechanisms for distribution and establishing claims as forms of cooperation; rather, they define or are an extension of the natural state of man.[29] They are necessary conditions for, not the product of, his social contract (cf. MA, 222, 295). Agreement on principles of justice is called for only to deal with problems that arise within this natural scheme of distribution.

Suppose, however, that Gauthier's parties had come together and agreed on principles, not after they had staked their property claims, but much earlier, shortly after their creation as intelligent beings. Then they would have to agree

---

28. See, for example, Gilbert Harman's version of conventionalism, which, though an explanatory project inspired by Hume, is also a kind of Hobbesian contract view as I use that term. Unlike Gauthier's hypothetical agreement, Harman argues that the moral principles that apply to a person are the result of actual agreement, in the sense of the implicit conventions people have accepted in dealing with each other. Harman, "Moral Relativism Defended," *Philosophical Review* 84 (1975): 3–22; Harman, *The Nature of Morality* (Oxford: Oxford University Press, 1977), chap. 9; and Harman, "Rationality in Agreement: A Commentary on Gauthier's Morals by Agreement," *Social Philosophy and Policy* 5 (1987): 1–16.

29. "Market freedom [is] conceived as an extension of the natural freedom enjoyed by a Robinson Crusoe" (MA, 276; see also MA, 90).

on a lot more than the limited principle Gauthier defines. They would have to settle on standards regarding how property rights are to be defined; how extensive they can be; how claims are to be initially acquired and then transferred; conditions on exchange, gifts, and inheritance; and many other things. Had they made such an agreement, would this make, in Gauthier's view, cooperative institutions of the resulting forms of property, markets, and so on? In any event, it seems that his parties would acknowledge principles defining property and distribution that are quite different from those Gauthier argues for on noncontractual grounds; at least it is an open question. What the possibility of an earlier agreement shows is the peculiar way in which the purpose and results of Gauthier's contract are dependent on historical conditions, that is, on when the agreement is made in the state of nature. Moreover, it shows how dependent his notion of social cooperation is on these contingencies.

I do not mean to suggest here that Gauthier's parties should come to an earlier bargain (based, say, on knowledge of their natural endowments) but rather that it is arbitrary when they do. For, cooperation will always be mutually advantageous whatever temporal point we choose in the noncooperative baseline, and the time at which the agreement occurs significantly affects the terms of cooperation agreed to. Fortuitous circumstances and decisions in the state of nature determine the content of Gauthier's account of justice.

As it is, given the way Gauthier sets up the state of nature and conceives of the social contract as an idealized bargain between persons with initial property endowments, the question whether these institutions need, or even can have, a justification in terms of a social agreement cannot arise for him. But this is just the issue that Rawls aims to address with his version of the social contract. Property, contracts, markets, and other forms of transfer (gift, bequest, inheritance, taxation, and so on), he sees as social institutions that can be designed in many different ways. How they are individually designed and combined into one social scheme deeply affects individuals' characters, the development of their abilities, and their desires, plans, and future prospects. Given the deep-seated effects of these institutions on the kinds of persons we are and can come to be, the first question of social justice for Rawls is, what are the appropriate principles for designing these basic social institutions? Rawls aims to show that there are noninstrumental principles implicit in what we accept as reasons in public life that have an important bearing on this question.

If we understand the problem of justice as a question about the proper design of the social institutions Gauthier takes for granted, and see the social contract as a response to that question, then the structure and significance of that agreement must differ markedly from those assigned to it in Gauthier's view. To begin with, the idea that the appropriate point of view from which to assess institutions and decide on principles is a noncooperative state of nature in which a certain form of private property already exists is wholly out of place. Second, the idea that an idealized economic bargain is the proper model for the social agreement must also drop out of view, since it is the legitimate scope of these kinds of agreements and the justice of the desires, claims, and expectations they take for granted that we are concerned with. Third, the kinds of persons who take an interest in the justice of absolute property, unregulated exchange, and so on are going to be very different from Gauthier's rational appropriators for whom these institutions are unproblematic. Rawls's parties conceive of themselves as free, not in the sense that they may act on any desire they happen to have but in the sense that they are able to control, revise, and take responsibility for their final ends and desires by acting on and from reasonable and rational principles. Recognizing the deep-seated effects of basic social institutions on these capacities and on their interests, they have a basic concern for how such institutions are designed. Not satisfied with the idea that these institutions answer to their desires for the accumulation of objects, Rawls's parties have a deeper interest in whether the institutions are structured so as to enable them to realize their reasoning capacities and whether the principles supporting these institutions can serve as a basis for public justification among persons like themselves.[30]

Both Rawls's and Gauthier's agreements are hypothetical. But unlike Gauthier's, Rawls's is also nonhistorical; it does not arise out of the status quo or a state of nature but requires that individuals abstract from all knowledge of their situation, abilities, particular ends, existing rights, and everything else about their own history and point of view. The gist of Gauthier's objection to Rawls is that there can be no nonhistorical contracts, or, what comes to the same thing, no genuine social agreements regarding the social institutions that constitute the basic structure. This argument is the natural consequence of Gauthier's conceiving of the social contract as an idealized bargain between persons with essentially conflicting interests and preexisting property claims. This is a very restricted (and perhaps overly legalized) interpretation of the idea of agreement. Not only does it severely limit the range of interpretations of the values of freedom and equality that underlie all social contract views but it also views justice and cooperation as exceedingly narrow notions, as if they had to do only with resolving certain problems that arise within private-propertied, market economies.

The consequence of such a narrow interpretation is that there is no place in Gauthier's conception of the social contract for a collective decision regarding social worlds. It is as if the kind of society in which Gauthier's agents live and set their ends were imposed upon them by forces beyond their collective control.[31] It is a separate question to what extent this follows from his agent-centered conception of reasons (as opposed to his assumptions regarding the prerequisites of the contract and the self-centered content of people's final ends).

---

30. Rawls denies, at least implicitly, that the set of institutions argued for by Gauthier can satisfy this condition (see *TJ*, sec. 12). Given the publicity condition, those who are worse off in society could not reasonably accept and give their support to a system of property and distribution that defines entitlements and contributions according to the principle of Pareto efficiency, especially since it is compatible with virtually any distribution. My concern, however, is not Rawls's rejection of economic bargains and Pareto efficiency as the major method of distribution but his rejection of them as the model for his social agreement.

31. Another reason for Rawls's focus on the basic structure, which I shall only allude to here, is raised by Gauthier's mistaken contention that Rawls denies individuals any return on their contributions to society or social productivity (*MA*, 248–50). Gauthier's argument is guided by the underlying premise given in note 25: assuming private property in the means of production, to each according to his contribution, as measured by his marginal product. But we have no well-defined notion of one's

Agent-centered views ultimately must take certain desires and interests as given and beyond rational assessment. Simultaneously, then, they must take as beyond rational assessment the background conditions that underlie and support people's primary ends.

To sum up, it is true that Rawls's social contract does not involve any kind of bargain in Gauthier's sense. This is because the question that underlies his view is not: Given individuals' ends (actual or presocial), is there a single set of norms that each has agent-centered reasons to comply with? It is, rather: Given our conception of ourselves as free and equal, how can the principles that specify the basic social institutions determining the ends and agent-centered reasons people have be defined so as to serve as a basis for a system of public reasoning within which individuals can justify their pursuits to one another consistent with their self-conception? The focus of Rawls's agreement on the basic structure follows from his conception of public reasons and their independence—what we accept as public reasons, and what we can accept as justifying a system of public reasons, cannot be reduced to what rationally promotes each individual's antecedent concerns.[32]

III. Public Reasons and Social Agreement

But does Rawls's response to his question still warrant talk of a social agreement? I shall argue that there are at least three ways in which an idea of social agreement functions in Rawls's view. The first follows from the conception of the person that he employs (discussed in this section). The second is implicit in his practical conception of justification (sec. IV). And the third is informed by Rawls's Kantian account of autonomy (sec. V).

Rawls's theory arrives at the social contract through its specification of the democratic conception of persons as free and equal. Beginning with the idea that society is a fair system of cooperation for mutual advantage, how should terms of social cooperation be specified among free and equal persons with different conceptions of their good? Given their self-conception, it would be inappropriate to see these terms as given by a higher moral authority distinct from the persons cooperating (for example, God) or even by a prior and independent moral order of values (such as natural law). For, in both instances the ultimate

contributions to society, or what he is entitled to in return, independent of the social institutions within which contributions are made. That owners of capital produce or contribute something as owners is simply an institutional fact (some would say a legal fiction) that follows from the way certain institutions assign rights and powers over things. Rawls's point in focusing on the basic structure is just that we need a public standard by which to assess and decide between different institutional systems defining entitlements and contributions (cf. *TJ*, secs. 47–48).

32. This accords with Rawls's stipulation that one of the reasonable (as opposed to rational, in his sense) constraints represented in the original position is that the parties are to agree on principles for the basic structure. See Rawls, "Kantian Constructivism in Moral Theory: The Dewey Lectures" (1980), in *CP*. Rawls assumes that a concern for "background justice" is implicit in our sense of justice.

source of public reasons would involve elements upon which free individuals with different ends and worldviews cannot agree. The most appropriate way to determine such principles, Rawls contends, is by an agreement among the persons cooperating, in light of their self-conception and each person's conception of his own rational good.

This is the first function of the idea of social agreement in Rawls's view. It is a way of working out terms of cooperation that all can accept and that can serve as a basis for public justification among persons with different ends who conceive of themselves as free and equal. There would seem to be little problem here, so far as Gauthier's objection is concerned. Gauthier is bothered, however, by Rawls's next move, establishing the nature and scope of the moral conditions placed on the agreement. Because free and equal persons are specified as persons having a higher-order interest both in the justice of the basic structure of society and in how their interests are influenced by it, a suitably independent perspective is needed that abstracts from existing conditions. This perspective cannot be defined by a state of nature, as we have seen, since its accidental contingencies would also distort the purpose of the agreement. So, Rawls specifies a now familiar point of view, the original position, to extend the idea of fair agreement to the basic structure. The veil of ignorance is a representation of strict equality (*CP*, 337). Since parties behind the veil do not know their particular ends, abilities, or anything about their endowments or situation, there is no room for a bargain in Gauthier's sense (*TJ*, 139/120 rev.). So there is no assurance—indeed it is highly unlikely—that the principles agreed to will improve each person's starting position in society. This is the basis for Gauthier's objection: Rawls's agreement is not a contract because it is not modeled on an economic bargain. The stringency of Rawls's equality condition precludes this.

The question raised by Gauthier's objection is whether there is room for a different kind of contract or agreement once we conceive of reasons in a noninstrumental way. Contracts are legal devices, and the conditions of valid contracts have been defined differently in different legal systems. Gauthier's conception of a contract recalls nineteenth-century Anglo-American law in which the same conditions were specified to accommodate an expanding market economy. Still, at no time have contracts ever been legally defined so as to constitute an equivalent of Gauthier's idealized bargain. All sorts of promises and commitments that do not involve anything resembling an economic bargain have been deemed enforceable as contracts.[33] Furthermore, background moral constraints

---

33. In fact, few contracts today are bargains in Gauthier's sense; the great majority (consumer purchases) involve acceptance of determinate offers not subject to revision by negotiation. The basic elements of a legal contract are a promise (or offer and acceptance), and what is called "consideration" in the common law and "sufficient cause" in civil law. "Consideration" is often defined by legal scholars as something that is bargained for or given in exchange for a promise, but there have always been promises enforced as contracts that do not involve either, for example, promises to charities and promises made under seal prior to the nineteenth century. The legal definition of "consideration" is relatively recent. Its source was not the courts but the American Law Institute, which noted that many other factors count as consideration in law to make promises enforceable in the absence of bargains or exchange—for example, reliance on a promise or commitment by the promisee to a third

are a condition of any legal contract; contracts are deemed "unconscionable" for a number of reasons, and no court would enforce a contract by which one party consented to alienate his constitutional rights. And, too, the condition of finality that is part of social contract views has never been a part of any valid legal agreement.[34] Finally, even if we concede that the idea of a contract connotes a fundamental conflict of interests and lack of mutual concern, that does not mean that there is not a place for some kind of social agreement in Rawls's view. Not all agreements are like economic bargains.

To begin with, there is a perfectly good sense in which a group of persons can agree to some joint activity (for example, to play basketball tomorrow) that all want to take part in for its own sake. Each commits himself by his word, thereby decreasing the likelihood that someone will later change his mind. There are also other means we use to bind ourselves by such friendly agreements, such as setting into motion certain practices or institutions that limit the range of future options open to those who participate (as in marriage agreements or joint commitments by members of the same religious association). Here again, the agreement is not a compromise among essentially conflicting interests. Instead, it represents a joint commitment to certain shared ends or ideal modes of interaction which each desires as regulative of his own pursuit of his particular purposes. The parties rely upon one another in order to achieve these shared norms or ends. The point of the agreement is not to resolve disagreement or conflict, for there may be none. It is, rather, to tie down the future, to keep the parties from later changing their minds and deviating from the shared norms or purposes of the association. These agreements are akin to the idea of rational precommitment,[35] except that they involve a joint precommitment among several persons, since the shared norms or ends of the association's members cannot be achieved in the absence of wide-spread compliance.

A general precommitment best expresses the kind of social agreement at work in the natural rights theory of the social contract tradition. Locke, and at times Rousseau, might be read as expressing this idea when they call their agree-ments a "social compact" (rather than a "contract"). And the idea of general precommitment indicates a significant way in which collective agreement plays a role in Rawls's view. Free and equal moral persons all have, in addition to their diverse ends and worldviews, a fundamental social interest (their sense of justice) in cooperating with one another on publicly justifiable terms that express their

---

party, detriment incurred by a promisee, and benefit received by the promisor. In actual practice, the notion of consideration is a way of expressing the idea that not all promises are legally enforceable; they will be enforced as contracts only if there is (to use the civil law term) sufficient cause. See Arthur L. Corbin, *On Contracts* (Minneapolis: West, 1951), chap. 5.

34. The condition of finality, as described by Rawls, is the condition that the terms of the contract are ultimate and conclusive in practical reasoning, overriding all other considerations (*TJ*, 135/116–17 rev.). Since it refers to the finality of reasons, it implies that the social contract, unlike any legal contract, is without excusing conditions.

35. See Jon Elster, *Ulysses and the Sirens*, rev. ed. (Cambridge: Cambridge University Press, 1984), chap. 2, esp. 37–47.

conception of themselves as free and equal (cf. *TJ*, 561/491 rev.).[36] This interest
is social, since it cannot be achieved by single individuals but requires coordination of activities. It is shared in that each individual desires the same object, a
background of just institutions.

To realize this shared social interest, free and equal citizens mutually precommit themselves (through their representatives in the original position) to
principles, appropriate to their self-conceptions, for the design of institutions and
the regulation of their individual pursuits. They commit themselves to, and rely
on each other to maintain, a status as equals in the free pursuit of their ends and
in the considerations that will be recognized as public reasons. The principles
create and sustain the conditions needed to realize their equal status and their
fundamental interest in cooperation based on mutual respect. Since these principles answer to a shared social interest, they are not (unlike Hobbesian views) a
compromise but rather everyone's best response to this situation. The usual compliance problems that bedevil Hobbesian views do not apply.[37]

In committing themselves to these principles, free and equal citizens willingly impose upon themselves certain constraints on future decision making at
all levels of choice, individual and collective. This precommitment is general,
because it is made by and applies to everyone. It is shared, since each depends
upon the others to hold him to his decision by maintaining an environment of
just institutions. And it is mutual, in that each gives his consent only on the condition that others do. Otherwise the coordination of activities necessary to each
citizen's realizing his basic interest in justice could not be achieved. These features warrant talk of a social agreement.

Members of a democratic society make this general precommitment, not
the parties in the original position. The parties choose from interested motivations and have no basic concern for justice and equality. Here Rawls's argument
from the "strains of commitment" plays an essential role (*TJ*, 145/125–26 rev.,
176–77/153–54 rev.). Because the parties conceive of themselves as free and able
to control their futures, each sees himself as responsible to the future claims of
the self (*TJ*, 422–23/371 rev.). Each knows that he will be held to his decision by
the others, so each aims to commit himself once and for all to principles that he
will not reproach himself for choosing even should the worst transpire. Commit-

36. The claim that practical principles "express" our self-conception is common among Kantians.
See, for example, Thomas Nagel, *The Possibility of Altruism* (Oxford: Oxford University Press, 1970), 18,
where it is part of his definition of "interpretation." Rawls gives sense to the claim via Kantian constructivism, discussed in sec. V of this paper (see esp. note 52 below on Rawls's constructivism).

37. Rawls describes this social interest as a highest-order interest in realizing one's capacity for
an effective sense of justice (*CP*, 312). We might look upon free and equal citizens' desire to realize
this interest as a metapreference for justice, that is, a preference that all one's future preferences meet
the conditions of reasonable principles. By agreement on the two principles, citizens in effect decide
to make themselves into the kinds of persons who will not make trade-offs between justice and their
particular ends. They will that they become persons whose preference structure is (in terms of rational choice analysis) lexicographic. Since lexicographic preference structures cannot be represented
by a utility function (see Elster, *Ulysses and the Sirens*, 124–27), we might see their choice as a decision not to be rational utility maximizers in Gauthier's sense.

ment by the parties to principles that secure equal citizenship and enable each freely to pursue his own good corresponds to the precommitment of free and equal citizens in society.

Still, does Rawls really need to talk of an agreement in the original position? Given the veil of ignorance, it might seem, as Jean Hampton says, that "there is no theoretical reason to posit more than one party in the original position."[38] One reason Rawls insists on an agreement is to carry through the contrast with utilitarianism. (See *TJ*, sec. 30.) The original position is not set up like Ideal Observer theories, where a single judge with full knowledge of all but its own identity impartially represents and sympathetically identifies with the interests of everyone.[39] As against the conflation of interests involved from this point of view, an agreement among many persons concerned to advance only their own interests emphasizes the distinctness of persons and the plurality and incommensurability of their conceptions of the good. More importantly, the contract condition is essential to Rawls's strains of commitment argument. Were there but one party choosing principles, there would be no one for him to commit himself to. Agreement, unlike individual choice, implies a joint undertaking where each is held by the others to his decision, thereby ensuring the perpetuity and irrevocability of the principles agreed to.[40]

Perhaps the best answer to Hampton's objection is that the agreement in the original position is designed to mirror the agreement of the members of a well-ordered society on public principles of justice. The hypothetical choice of the original position makes sense only in the context of free and equal persons trying to come to a social agreement on terms of cooperation and standards for public justification that all can accept, whatever their particular situations.[41] The veil

38. Hampton, "Contracts and Choices," 334. This objection voices the view of many who say that Rawls's original position merely depicts the rationally self-interested choice of one individual. See Gauthier, "Bargaining and Justice," 44; and Scanlon, "Contractualism and Utilitarianism," 124.

39. Gauthier's noncontractarian argument for his position in "The Archimedean Point" (MA, chap. 8), although it involves interested choice like Rawls's original position, still resembles Ideal Observer theories in that it is choice by a single agent with knowledge of everyone's preferences but not of his own identity. This resemblance is due to the fact that both utilitarianism and Gauthier's contract view take individuals' desires for granted and seek to maximize utility. The difference is that Gauthier refuses to aggregate utility, which in part explains why his ideal actor's choice is self-interested rather than sympathetic.

40. Hampton argues that the finality condition (see note 37) already implies irrevocability of the principles selected and that this renders Rawls's strains of commitment argument and the contract constraint on which it relies unnecessary (Hampton, "Contracts and Choices," 330). But although finality may imply that excusing arguments will not be entertained (perhaps ensuring a kind of irrevocability), it still does not bring out the idea that the parties are making a good faith commitment to one another, which they can rely on as citizens and cite to each other to justify holding one another to the terms of the agreement. Nor does finality (or irrevocability) imply the perpetuity of the undertaking, which, as Rawls indicates, has its basis in the "Agreement Condition" (*TJ*, 146–47/126–27 rev.).

41. Compare Rawls, "Reply to Alexander and Musgrave," *Quarterly Journal of Economics* 88 (1974): 651, where he says that "the reason for invoking the concept of a contract in the original position lies in its correspondence with the features of a well-ordered society." A well-ordered society is partially defined as a society in which everyone accepts, and knows that others accept, the same principles of justice.

of ignorance is imposed just as an extension of that basic contractarian idea. It corresponds to the fundamental equality of moral persons in agreement on the basic structure. Even if the parties are symmetrically situated by that condition,[42] Rawls needs to maintain the idea of distinct individuals coming to an agreement to make the main idea of his theory go through. So the most that one can say (although Rawls denies even this)[43] is that agreement among parties is the same choice as would be made by a single individual in the original position. But there is no reason to describe the choice in this way. This description misrepresents the conditions of choice in the original position; there is no way to arrive at it given the way Rawls sets up the situation.[44]

To sum up, if we conceive of reasons as having an independent social role of providing a public basis for agreement, then a social agreement is the most appropriate way to ascertain principles that serve this role among free and equal democratic citizens with different conceptions of their good. And this procedure, while not a contractual bargain, is still an agreement in that it embodies their shared precommitment to maintain their status as free and equal in the structure of institutions and system of public reasons. Interested agreement from the original position models this situation.

IV. Social Agreement and Practical Justification

We have considered how the social contract plays a role within Rawls's conception of justice, from the point of view of free and equal persons and from the perspective of the parties in the original position. Let us now consider a second way

---

42. Hampton says that the parties are completely identical in all their characteristics; hence, by Quine's principle of the identification of indiscernibles, we are forced to "construe the indistinguishable parties as one person" (Hampton, "Contracts and Choices," 334). But the parties are not described as having all the same properties (e.g., they have different conceptions of their good); instead, they share the property of not knowing any general properties about themselves that might give them evidence of their chances under social schemes structured by various principles of justice.

43. Rawls's denial is based on grounds that the class of things that can be agreed to is included in and is smaller than the class of things that can be rationally chosen (Rawls, "Reply to Alexander and Musgrave," 651–52).

44. Hampton also argues not only that a contract is uncalled for but also that the contract device is too weak to yield the irrevocable commitment Rawls needs. For, contracts are always revocable if all the parties agree. The parties might then count on the possibility of a revocation of the agreement once they enter society. So they might take risks, thereby changing the way they reason and endangering Rawls's argument for the two principles (Hampton, "Contracts and Choices," 331–32). But Rawls's argument assumes that members of society will enforce the agreement not out of self-interest but out of their sense of justice (*TJ*, 145/125 rev.). This moral motivation makes it highly unlikely that they would be willing to revoke and renegotiate the agreement. But even if they did, a revocation, or "rescission," of a contract is a separate contract. See Corbin, *On Contracts*, secs. 1236–37. And since they affect the basic structure, any rescission or renegotiation among Rawls's parties would also have to take place behind the veil of ignorance. But this rules out any grounds the parties might have in the original agreement for taking risks in hopes of later rescission and renegotiation. Finally, if this is not enough, Rawls stipulates that the principles agreed to are perpetual and irrevocable and that the

in which agreement plays a role, implicit in a third perspective in Rawls's view, that of ourselves as members of a democratic society.[45]

Rawls identifies the aim of political philosophy as a practical one: to define a conception of justice that can "provide a shared public basis for the justification of political and social institutions."[46] Its task is to locate a basis for agreement in a culture that all can affirm and accept and that can serve as a basis for public reasoning and stable social cooperation. The practical aim of a political conception is to be contrasted with what we might call the "theoretical aim" of a moral conception, which is truth. "Justice as fairness . . . presents itself not as a conception of justice that is true, but one that can serve as a basis of informed and willing political agreement between citizens" (JF, 230). This does not mean that Rawls is not interested in objectivity or truth (clearly Rawls thinks that the general facts assumed by his theory and the parties are true [TJ, 547/481 rev.]). Rather, there is a difference between the primary objects of a practical versus a theoretical inquiry. Whether Rawls's principles are or can be true, in the sense that they satisfy a metaphysical account of truth, is a separate issue which Rawls does not address. He thinks it important to "avoid the problem of truth and the controversy between realism and subjectivism" if justice as fairness is to achieve its practical aim in a democracy (JF, 230). This point is essential to Rawls's version of liberalism, as well as to understanding the sense in which his is a social contract view.

The practical aim of a political conception does not by itself seem to imply any form of a social contract. For, we might imagine a society in which appeals to religious authority, or to self-evident truths about good reasons, provided the basis for public justification and agreement (cf. CP, 343). Rawls's point is that such appeals cannot work in a democracy. For, given that democratic citizens have different and competing philosophical conceptions of the nature and bases of truth, objectivity, and so on, a basis for public reasoning and agreement cannot be achieved by a conception of justice that relies on such premises. Here the idea of social agreement comes in; such an idea is implicit in what I will call the "practical conception of justification" that Rawls sees as appropriate for a democratic society.

For a justification to be practical (as opposed to theoretical), it must satisfy the following conditions:

1. It must have a practical aim: addressed to those who disagree, it is designed to yield principles that all can accept and affirm as a basis for public justification and agreement (Rawls calls this the "social role" [CP, 305] or "public role" [CP, 426–27, 5–6] of principles).

---

parties know this. The stipulation is not arbitrary given that from our perspective principles of justice are to be the outcome of the agreement. It is entirely appropriate that moral principles of justice be perpetual and irrevocable.

45. On the three different perspectives and their significance, see CP, 321–21.

46. Rawls, "The Idea of Overlapping Consensus" (1987), in CP. See also JF, 230; CP, 328, 330; and TJ, 44/39 rev., 583/511 rev.

2. It must have a practical basis: it proceeds from considerations that count as public reasons in the culture, and so relies on premises and methods of reasoning that all can agree on and endorse (*TJ*, sec. 87; *CP*, 429). Our "considered moral convictions" of justice are primary among such premises.
3. It must meet a motivational requirement: practical justification assumes that members of a culture have a desire to give reasons that justify their institutions to one another (a common "desire for free and uncoerced agreement" [*JF*, 231; *CP*, 306]) — more generally, a willingness to cooperate with others on terms they can freely accept (a sense of justice).[47]
4. It must exhibit moral coherence: the principles yielded by it should accord with our considered moral convictions at all levels of generality, on due reflection and after considering alternative views, so that these principles and our convictions best fit together into one coherent scheme (what Rawls calls "general and wide reflective equilibrium" [*CP*, 321]).

These conditions identify the sense in which Rawls's view is contractarian from the point of view of those who are considering this conception of justice. None of these conditions, by itself, warrants talk of a contractarian justification. The mere fact that condition 2 is satisfied — that we can agree on certain precepts and methods of reasoning — does not by itself justify anything; contractarianism is not conventionalism. Hence, the importance of satisfying condition 4 — reaching reflective equilibrium. Then again, we might imagine a single individual trying to achieve equilibrium of all the moral convictions and ideas that stem from his conception of the good and his philosophical and religious views. (So we might interpret traditional philosophical arguments for comprehensive moral theories.) Others who do not share this individual's views would not be able to accept all his conclusions, although he might see them as authoritative for everyone. Rawls uses reflective equilibrium in a more public way, as a method of justification appropriate for political agreement on principles all can endorse; hence the significance of condition 1. It relies only on the considered convictions on which we all can agree (condition 2) and so excludes considered beliefs peculiar to our conceptions of the good or our metaphysical views. Reflective equilibrium, then, is "general": everyone should be able to accept the same conception.

Rawls's conception is social contractarian in that it seeks principles with which to provide a public basis for justification and agreement that reflectively cohere with the considered convictions and beliefs that we hold in common and that serve for us as public reasons. It is an agreement in that it is a mutual accommodation of different philosophical, religious, and moral views, reached by "reconciliation through public reason" (JF, 230). This reconciliation depends on public understanding that certain considerations — those that stem from individuals' particular worldviews and on which we cannot all agree — will not be offered as arguments or as a basis for public claims. The original position and

47. Rawls says that the sense of justice "implies the desire on the part of individuals and groups to advance their good in ways which can be explained and justified by reasons which all can and do accept as free and equal moral persons" (Rawls, "Social Unity and Primary Goods," in *Utilitarianism and Beyond*, 184).

other elements of Rawls's view model this situation: the bases for justification from which we actually proceed in trying to justify our social institutions to one another.[48] And the conception of justice that results incorporates these bases for justification. As such, it attempts to give standards for public deliberation where only the reasons specified by that conception—those that can be justified practically—count as reasons in arguments on constitutional essentials.

The agreement or reconciliation that Rawls's conception of justice represents is not a bargain, in the Hobbesian sense, between essentially conflicting views. It does not proceed from people's given ends and conflicting worldviews and seek to strike a compromise. Instead, it works from shared political convictions, and happens to meet individuals' different moral views at the point at which they converge (Rawls's "overlapping consensus" (PL, lect. IV). It does not, then, require one to compromise his basic convictions; or, if it does, it is only because they are incompatible with what that person accepts and relies on as public reasons. Here condition 3, the motivational requirement, is important. The purpose of this requirement is not to define what count as public reasons, but rather to ensure that citizens will act on principles so that the practical aim of the political conception can be carried through. Given Rawls's assumption that we have a shared sense of justice which is effective independent of our particular conceptions of the good, there is not the same concern, as in Hobbesian theories, that citizens are always prepared to pursue their goals at the expense of others and will depart from justice whenever circumstances allow.

Since he explicitly avoids claims to truth and objectivity according to epistemological and metaphysical criteria, Rawls's practical justification is open to the objection that it is not really a justification but rather a kind of complicated accounting method that unifies the underlying concepts and principles of a political culture.[49] But there is a stronger sense in which Rawls seems to characterize his principles as practically justified, based on the Kantian features of his view. Let us now return to the perspectives internal to Rawls's conception, and see the role that social agreement plays in defining autonomy and a practical conception of objectivity.

V. Reason, Autonomy, and Agreement

The purpose of the state of nature, according to a Hobbesian view, is to provide a perspective from which to rationally assess existing social arrangements. (Gauthier's assessment, however, is quite limited, since he incorporates into the state of

---

48. For this reason, Rawls describes the conditions defining the original position as a representation of reasonable restrictions on arguments for principles of justice (TJ, 18/16 rev., 120/103–4 rev., 138/119 rev., 516/453 rev.; JF, 237–38). They are general convictions that "we do in fact accept" (TJ, 21/19 rev.) insofar as they incorporate our considered convictions regarding the kinds of considerations that are and are not acceptable as reasons in arguments for principles of justice.

49. This raises the question, which Rawls mentions but avoids, whether his conception of justification is sufficient (CP, 437) or at least necessary (Rawls, "The Independence of Moral Theory" [1974], in CP, 295–301) for justification in the theoretical sense.

nature the very institutions many feel to be most in need of appraisal.) But this does not free the view from its anchor in antecedent desire; it only relocates the basis for the agent-centered reasons people have in certain natural tendencies and inclinations. Suppose, however, that we seek a basis for reasoned assessment in something other than existing social arrangements and natural inclination. Following Kant, Rawls appeals to our capacities for practical reasoning.

The moral powers of free and equal moral persons are the two separate capacities for practical reasoning as applied to matters of justice. The moral powers are (a) "the capacity for an effective sense of justice, i.e., the capacity to understand, to apply and to act from (and not merely in accordance with) the principles of justice," and (b) "the capacity to form, to revise, and rationally to pursue a conception of the good" (CP, 312).

These are, Rawls says, "executive" capacities (CP, 320) (one might add "judicial"), since they enable individuals both to regulate and to justify the pursuit of their ends by means of reasonable and rational principles. Our concern is the source of reasonable principles and their connection with a social agreement. Here Kantian constructivism and full autonomy come in; they develop the idea that the moral powers are not only executive but also collectively legislative.

The idea of constructivism works on two levels in Rawls's theory. First, it applies at the most general level of justification, reflective equilibrium. From certain considered convictions on which we agree, Rawls "constructs" the conception of justice that can best serve as a basis for public justification in a democracy. Here the notion of construction gains sense by contrast with appeals to linguistic or self-evident moral intuitions. Rather than raising certain considered convictions to the level of first principles because they are thought to be implicit in language or accurate reports of a prior moral order, Rawls seeks principles that best cohere with all our shared convictions of justice (what we rely on as public reasons), revising and, if necessary, discarding recalcitrant ones along the way. No specific level of generality is assumed to carry the burden of justification. Other moral conceptions can be construed as constructivist in this sense, so long as they rely on this method of justification.[50]

"Kantian constructivism" is a more specialized notion that works within this constructive model of justification; it explains why we may find some of our considered convictions recalcitrant. It aims to show that the principles that best cohere with our convictions are not questionable accidents of culture but are objective in that they have a basis in our capacities for practical reasoning. These capacities, Rawls presumes, underlie many of our considered convictions, including our political conception of ourselves as free and equal (JF, 233; TJ, sec. 77). Rawls seeks to capture this self-conception with an idealization, the "model conception" of free and equal moral persons. To construct, in our first sense, principles of justice appropriate for us, Rawls constructs a social world modeled on the self-conception and practical capacities of free and equal moral persons. The purpose of this second kind of construction is to give content to

50. For a discussion of this sense of construction, see Dworkin, *Taking Rights Seriously*, 159–68.

Kant's enigmatic idea of autonomy as reason legislating principles for itself. In the absence of some kind of procedure that shows the relationship between our capacities for reasoning and moral principles, such phrases are difficult to make sense of. Agreement from the original position serves this role; it is a "procedural interpretation" of practical reason in matters of justice (CP, 345–46; TJ, 256/226 rev.) or, more exactly, of a conception of persons as both reasonable and rational. Since this procedure is designed to "model" the moral powers,[51] the content of the principles chosen from that point of view will be determined by these reasoning capacities and the conception of the person to which they give rise (CP, 303, 306).[52] In this sense, moral principles are "constructed" on the basis of reason.

The objectivity that Rawls ascribes to his principles rests on his claim that they would be willed and agreed to from a shared point of view, which is objective in that everyone abstracts from their particular (subjective) aims, beliefs, and perspectives to view society on an equal footing (TJ, 516–19/452–55 rev.). This conception of objectivity is practical, as opposed to theoretical, in the following sense: Rawls's claim is not that, being impartially situated, we all have a clear, undistorted view that allows us to make true judgments about a prior and independent moral order. In constructivism, Rawls says, there is no order of moral facts, prior to human reasoning, for our moral judgments to be true of (CP, 354). This does not mean that Rawls must deny that a prior order of moral facts or principles can exist, for that metaphysical commitment would conflict with his practical aim. Rather, it means that if there is such an order, it is not because certain principles are true of it that we are bound, as democratic citizens, to follow them. What commits us, as citizens, to these principles is that they are "most reasonable for us" (CP, 340), in that they best accord with our capacities for practical reason-

51. Rawls's claims—that the original position "models," "mirrors," and "represents" the moral powers—are somewhat obscure. He seems to have in mind the following: the parties to the original position represent the capacity for rationality in that they judge according to the principles of rationality set forth in TJ, chapter 7, and desire to obtain an adequate share of the primary social goods. It is rational to want the primary goods, since these goods enable free and equal persons to realize their fundamental interests in the exercise and development of their moral powers and their particular conception of the good. This is all part of "the Rational" (CP, 315). The moral conditions of the parties' rational choice (or "the Reasonable") represent our capacity for justice in that, in exercising that capacity, we would judge these conditions to be fair and reasonable restrictions on arguments for principles of justice for the basic structure (TJ, 18–19/16–17 rev.; JF, 237–38). More particularly, the veil of ignorance embodies our conception of ourselves as equals in matters of justice. The publicity condition follows from our concern to know the underlying bases for laws and social institutions as well as from Rawls's aim to arrive at principles that will provide a basis for public reasoning and justification in a democratic society. The condition of finality conveys our conviction that considerations of justice are conclusive in public affairs; they override all other public concerns. For Rawls's account of how Kant's Categorical Imperative involves a procedure of construction, see Rawls, "Themes in Kant's Moral Philosophy," in Kant's Transcendental Deductions, ed. Eckart Forster (Stanford: Stanford University Press, 1989), 81–113.

52. To show how the content of Rawls's principles relates to his conception of the person would require a separate discussion. For Rawls's discussion of the first principle, see Rawls, "The Basic Liberties and Their Priority," in Political Liberalism (New York: Columbia University Press, 1993, paperback ed. 1996 and 2004 [cited in text as PL]), Lecture VIII. Briefly, the basic liberties are seen as "fully

ing in the circumstances of a democratic society. The conception of objectivity that informs this claim is practical, since the shared point of view from which we would agree to these principles is designed not to give us privileged access to a prior moral order but to represent our powers of practical reasoning in a way appropriate to our democratic conception of ourselves as free and equal.[53]

But what relation is there between the moral powers, autonomy, and a social agreement? Why is the procedural representation of "reason giving principles to itself" conceived as a collective decision instead of, as in Kant, the ideal choice of a single individual? One might say that agreement emphasizes "autonomy" in the sense of devising principles of justice for ourselves cooperatively and not as individuals. But moral principles, unlike positive laws, cannot actually be legislated or chosen, either by groups or by individuals. Nor is "autonomy" meant to imply that they are. Autonomy in both Kant and Rawls involves the justification of moral principles by reference to a conception of persons as both reasonable and rational, where the content of principles is determined by these persons' reasoning capacities and not their particular ends, their innate psychological tendencies, or an antecedent moral order. We judge and act autonomously, not by choosing our moral principles but by proceeding from and regulating our activities according to principles that reasonable and rational persons would freely accept and agree to from a shared point of view modeled according to these powers.

But although we do not choose, individually or collectively, principles of justice, we do devise basic social institutions. We cooperatively decide, through laws and willing acceptance of social and legal conventions, how the constitution, the economy, property, and so on are designed and fit together into one social scheme. Here the significance of social agreement comes in. These basic institutions fundamentally affect our final ends, our basic affections, our character, and the direction of our moral sentiments. So in cooperatively making and supporting laws and voluntarily complying with the existing rules of these institutions, we are deciding what kinds of persons we are and can come to be. In doing that,

---

adequate" to the development and exercise of the moral powers and to each person's pursuit of his rational good. Moreover, they provide the external freedoms that enable moral persons to realize their conception of themselves as free — that is, as self originating sources of claims with the rational capacities to have a conception of the good and who take responsibility for their ends (CP, 330ff.; JF, 240ff., PL 291–324). Finally, an equal right to the basic liberties accords with the equality of moral persons based in their all having the moral powers needed to engage in social cooperation (TJ, sec. 77). The difference principle ensures the fair value of the basic liberties for all and embodies an egalitarian conception of reciprocity (TJ, 102–3/87–88 rev.).

53. In this connection, it is important to note that Rawls's use of the term "reasonable" is ambiguous (CP, 340, 535–36). In its narrower use, it contrasts with "rational" (in the sense of each person's rational good) and expresses the idea of fair terms of cooperation (CP, 315–16). In its broader sense, used here in connection with his conception of objectivity, it is a stand-in for truth in Rawls's practical account of justification. The "principles most reasonable for us" are those that best fit with our capacities for both reasonable and rational deliberation, where "best fit" is ultimately decided by the two stages of Rawls's argument for justice as fairness: (1) the argument from the original position, and (2) Rawls's argument for stability and the congruence of the principles of justice with our rational good in a well-ordered society (TJ, pt. 3).

we deeply affect the kinds of considerations that count for us as good reasons. We are, in cooperatively devising and maintaining basic social institutions, indirectly shaping ourselves and defining practical reason.[54] The question is whether we are going to design basic institutions that enable us to realize our legislative and executive capacities for practical reasoning and thereby take responsibility for our characters and final ends; or whether we are going to sustain institutions that create in us desires and states of character that keep us in a state of heteronomy, or subjugation to forces that, although we (often unwittingly) create them, are beyond our direct control.

The significance here of a social agreement for the basic structure is three-fold. First, it emphasizes the social nature of practical reasoning, how what we accept as reasons in both public and private life is largely influenced by a shared public culture, primarily, the basic institutions we create and sustain. This accounts for the primary importance of our coming to a public understanding regarding the basic structure. That problem affects our personal and associational relations as well as our political relations; its resolution is a precondition of our resolving other deep-seated moral differences.

Second, agreement implies the social conditions necessary for autonomy. Rawls does not hold (as Kant sometimes seems to suggest) that we can realize moral autonomy under any circumstances. We need a background of social institutions of a certain kind (cf. CP, 339–40). A cooperative effort is required to create these institutions just as a cooperative effort is needed to sustain those we now have. Full autonomy presupposes a joint effort and a collective decision. It requires our cooperatively altering existing institutions and devising others so that they conform to our moral powers and our conception of ourselves as free and equal.

These two points underscore the importance of Rawls's full publicity condition (CP, 324), which suggests the final significance of social agreement. Again, unlike Kant, Rawls does not hold that first moral principles or the conception of ourselves as autonomous is implicit in individual moral consciousness. We must be educated about this conception of persons and their relations. Full publicity of principles and their justification makes possible an awareness and understanding of ourselves as autonomous beings. And social agreement on principles, unlike impartial individual decision, implies the publicity condition. Full publicity is important because it ensures that the process of public justification can be carried through completely. Everything that counts as a reason and a basis for claims in the public culture can be fully justified; there is no need to keep anything hidden from public view.

Let us return now to Gauthier. He specifies a conception of the autonomy of utility maximizers that involves critical reflection on means and clarification of ends but that denies that "reason affords substantive grounds for choice or action" (MA, 344). The significance of Gauthier's account of rationally autonomous beings is that it, too, seeks to capture a conception of persons and their

---

54. Compare CP, 347, where Rawls says that the moral powers are not fixed but are shaped and developed by a shared public culture.

social relations that is latent in a part of our culture: the pure capitalist ideal of fundamentally self-centered and acquisitive individuals whose relations are all based in contractual bargains (MA, 318–19). Gauthier's autonomous beings not only are moved ultimately by self-interest but also are under no illusions about it. They publicly affirm self-interest as fundamental to their social relations and the system of public reasons. It is a separate question whether Gauthier's principles and conception of the person can serve as a public basis for justification or provide for stable social relations even among his rational egoists. Still, Gauthier has latched onto an understanding of persons and a source of public reasons in our culture that stem from the institutions we willingly sustain and that provide a sufficient basis for public justification for many who are especially favored by those institutions.

Both conceptions of the person—Rawls's notion of the fully autonomous democratic individual and Gauthier's idealized conception of "economic man"—represent types engendered by our basic institutions. These conceptions reflect a fundamental tension at work in our culture and perhaps in ourselves. The ultimate justification of one or the other moral view cannot be (as Gauthier would have it) which conceptions of reasons and persons best approximate the model relied on in the social sciences (MA, 8, 316), for that account is designed to deal with entirely different problems. It is, rather, a practical question: What kind of persons can we most closely identify with and do we finally want to come to be—individuals whose institutions and basic relations are ultimately imposed upon them by their socially created desire for unlimited acquisition; or persons who can take responsibility for their desires, characters, and social relations by patterning institutions to help them realize their capacities for practical reasoning?

I am grateful to John Rawls for his helpful discussion and comments on a draft of this essay. I am also indebted to Joshua Cohen, John Carriero, R. Jay Wallace, and the editors of *Philosophy & Public Affairs* for many valuable suggestions that led to subsequent revisions.

2

Utilitarianism, Deontology, and the Priority of Right

This chapter ultimately aims to elucidate the role of an important distinction in moral and political philosophy, that between deontology and teleology. The real issue between teleological and deontological views, I argue, is the appropriateness of the idea of a single rational good in practical deliberation and in the formulation of moral and political principles. Teleologists see one rational good as essential to practical reasoning; without it, moral and political reasoning are often indeterminate and provide no guidance as to what we ought to do. Abandoning a completely rational morality, if we must, is for deontologists an acceptable price to pay to avoid the morally counterintuitive results of teleology; moreover, for Kantians such as Rawls, it is necessary and even desirable in order to provide a secure position for a plurality of intrinsic goods and for political freedom, equality, and individual autonomy.

I. The Issue

It is perhaps a moral truism to say that people ought to do what they can to make the world as good a place as possible. But construed in a certain way this becomes a highly controversial thesis about morality: the right act in any circumstance is one most conducive to the best overall outcome (as ascertained, say, from an impersonal point of view that gives equal weight to the good of everyone). This is consequentialism.[1] More simply, it holds that right conduct maximizes the good. G. E. Moore held this thesis self-evident. Nonconsequentialists argue nothing could be further from the truth. So far as they do, it appears (to consequentialists at least) they are committed to the indefensible idea that morality requires us to do less good than we are able to.

---

1. Here I follow, with some revision, Samuel Scheffler's definition. See Scheffler, ed., *Consequentialism and Its Critics* (Oxford: Oxford University Press, 1988), 1.

John Rawls's teleological/deontological distinction is different. Teleological views affirm the consequentialist thesis that the right maximizes the good. But they hold an additional thesis: "the good is defined independently from the right," or, as Rawls often says, independent of any moral concepts or principles.[2] To see how this view differs from consequentialism, consider a thesis once proposed by T. M. Scanlon.[3] A standard objection to consequentialist views like utilitarianism is that they are indifferent to the distribution of the good; this is purportedly a necessary feature of such views, since they define right and justice as what maximizes overall, or aggregate, good. Scanlon argued there should be a way to incorporate distributive concerns into a two-level consequentialist view. If we treat fairness or distributive equality as a good in itself, then it must be considered along with other goods, like net aggregate satisfaction, in determining the value of overall outcomes that are to be maximized. Rights could then be introduced at the level of casuistry, to promote the good of equitable states of affairs.

The two-level consequentialist view Scanlon suggests would not be teleological on Rawls's account; it would be deontological. As Rawls says:

> If the distribution of goods is also counted as a good, perhaps a higher-order one, and the theory directs us to produce the most good (including the good of distribution among others) we no longer have a teleological view in the classical sense. The problem of distribution falls under the concept of right as one intuitively understands it, and so the theory lacks an independent definition of the good. (*TJ*, 25/22 rev.)

Rawls's thought may be this: in order to define the distributions (e.g., equal states of affairs) that are intrinsically good, and then practically apply this definition to determine what we ought to do, we must appeal to some process of distribution that can only be described by antecedent principles of right or justice. But once we do that, then it is no longer the case that the right is exclusively defined in terms of what maximizes the good. For example, suppose fairness or the equal capacity of persons to realize their good is among the intrinsic goods in a consequentialist view: we are to act in ways that best promote fairness or equality of capacity for all persons. It is difficult to see how such vague ends can be specified for practical purposes without appealing to principles or procedures defining people's equal basic rights, powers, and entitlements. But once this specification is incorporated into the maximand, the right is no longer simply a matter of maximizing the good. For, the concept of the good itself, in this instance, cannot be described without an antecedent nonmaximizing moral principle of right: that people ought to be treated fairly, afforded certain basic rights and powers, and so on. Such a view by Rawls's definition is not only nonteleological but also not consequentialist, if by this is meant that to maximize the good is the sole funda-

2. John Rawls, *A Theory of Justice* (Cambridge, MA: Harvard University Press, 1971; rev. ed., 1999), 24/21–22 rev. (cited in text as *TJ*; sometimes referred to as *Theory*).

3. T. M. Scanlon, "Rights, Goals, and Fairness," in *Public and Private Morality*, ed. Stuart Hampshire (Cambridge: Cambridge University Press, 1978), 93–112.

mental principle of right. Incorporating rights or other moral dictates into the maximand is incompatible with this very idea.[4]

Phillipa Foot has said that what makes consequentialism so compelling is "the rather simple thought that it can never be right to prefer a worse state of affairs to a better."[5] But deontological theories, suitably construed, can account for this "simple thought" just as well (for reasons I discuss in sec. VI). The force of consequentialism must then lie elsewhere: it embodies a powerful conception of practical reason. If we assume that rationality consists in maximizing something, and that in ethics it involves maximizing overall good, then we are able to say that there is a rational choice between any two alternative actions, laws, or institutions. Therefore, under all conceivable conditions there is a uniquely rational, hence right, thing to do. Granted, it may not be knowable by us, but the idea of maximizing the good provides a way to assign a truth value to any statement about what persons or groups ought to do. No other conception of rationality offers such practical completeness. Sidgwick, well aware of the force of the idea of maximizing an aggregate in enabling a completely rational morality, used this idea quite effectively to argue that hedonism must be true and that rational egoism and utilitarianism were the only two "rational methods" in ethics.[6] He could not decide which of the two was more rational, but assuming that egoism is not a moral conception at all, then, given Sidgwick's premises, utilitarianism prevails without opposition.

These introductory remarks supply background I later refer to. My aim is to elucidate the teleology/deontology distinction. I begin with the contention that teleological theories are not moral theories at all. Will Kymlicka argues that the teleological/deontological distinction relied on by Rawls and others is misleading. Not only does the morally right act not maximize the good, any view which defines the right in this way is not a moral conception.[7] Right actions, Kymlicka says, concern our duties, and duties must be owed to someone. But if moral duty is defined as maximizing overall good, "Whom is it a duty to?" (*LCC*, 28). Kym-

---

4. A question I can only raise here: What role can rights and other distributive concerns really play once incorporated into the maximand in a theory that says we ought always to act in a maximizing fashion? That basic principle occupies all prescriptive space. If so, then by acting on nonmaximizing precepts made part of the maximand (by, for example, aiming to respect others' rights), how can we (except accidentally) avoid violating the basic principle of right—that we are always to act to maximize the good? This raises problems for "rights-consequentialism" as a moral theory as well as the "utilitarianism of rights" Robert Nozick suggests in *Anarchy, State and Utopia* (New York: Basic Books, 1974), 28.

5. Phillipa Foot, "Utilitarianism and the Virtues," *Mind* 94 (1985): 196–209. Against this, Foot argues that the idea of "the best state of affairs" (202–3), impersonally construed, has no reference or applicability in ordinary moral experience. Also see Scheffler, ed., *Consequentialism and Its Critics*, 227.

6. Henry Sidgwick, *The Methods of Ethics* (1907), 7th ed. (Indianapolis: Hackett, 1981), 406 (cited in text as *Methods*).

7. Kymlicka, *Liberalism, Community, and Culture* (Oxford: Oxford University Press, 1989) (cited in text as *LCC*). "To define the right as the maximization of the good . . . is to abandon the moral point of view entirely to take up a nonmoral ideal instead" (40). Most references to *LCC* in the text are to chap. 3, which is almost identical to Kymlicka's article "Rawls on Teleology and Deontology," *Philosophy & Public Affairs* 17 (Summer 1988): 173–90.

licka argues for the (Kantian) claim that morality concerns respect for persons, not the good impersonally construed. And the most credible moral conceptions, the only ones worth attending to, hold that "each person matters equally" and deserves equal concern and respect (*LCC*, 40).

Kymlicka's aim here is not to attack teleological views but to show that Rawls's teleological/deontological distinction cannot do the work Rawls wants; indeed, it is "based on a serious confusion" (*LCC*, 21). For utilitarians, Kymlicka claims, are just as committed to equality, equal respect for persons, and fair distributions as everyone else. The difference is that they interpret these abstract concepts differently. Here Kymlicka follows Ronald Dworkin's suggestion that "Rawls and his critics all share the same 'egalitarian plateau': they agree that 'the interests of the members of the community matter, and matter equally'" (*LCC*, 21). Utilitarians like Hare and Harsanyi, nonutilitarians like Rawls, Nozick, and Dworkin, and even many Perfectionists (Kymlicka mentions Marx), all accept that equal concern and respect is the fundamental moral principle. "All these theories are deontological in that they spell out an ideal of fairness or equality for distinct individuals" (*LCC*, 26). If so, Kymlicka argues, the dispute between utilitarians and their critics cannot be depicted in terms of Rawls's misleading distinction or in terms of the priority of the right or the good. At issue in these debates are different conceptions of the political value of equality.

I shall argue (in secs. II and III) that Kymlicka, not Rawls, is culpable of "serious confusion." He confuses deontology—a claim about the content of principles of right—with the principles that are invoked in justifying and applying the substantive content of a moral conception. Moreover, he confuses deontology with a related idea, the priority of right. The priority of right has received a great deal of attention from Rawls's communitarian critics. This is surprising in view of the fact that Rawls has so little to say about it in *A Theory of Justice*.[8] What accounts for this attention, I suspect, is Michael Sandel's misreading. He identifies the priority of right with deontology and says that both mean that Rawls's

---

8. Rawls specifically elaborates on the priority of right on pages 30–32/27–30 rev., and does not take up the idea again until part 3, "Ends," 449–50/394–96 rev. The priority of right is once again discussed at the end of *TJ*, in Rawls's account of "The Unity of the Self" (sec. 85). Later, Rawls elaborated on this idea in lecture 5 of *Political Liberalism* (New York: Columbia University Press, 1993; paperback edition, 1996, 2004) (cited in text as *PL*; references are to the paperback edition). Lecture 5 initially appeared as "The Priority of Right and Ideas of the Good," *Philosophy & Public Affairs* 17 (Fall 1988): 251–76. In this lecture, Rawls distinguishes between the "general meaning" and the "particular meaning" of the priority of right. "The priority of right means (in its general meaning) that the ideas of the good used must be political ideas, so that we need not rely on comprehensive conceptions of the good but only on ideas tailored to fit within the political conception. Second, the priority of right means (in its particular meaning) that the principles of justice set limits to permissible ways of life: the claims that citizens make to pursue ends transgressing those limits have no weight" (*PL*, 209). My discussion will be limited to the priority of right in its "particular meaning," which is the form of the idea as it appears in *A Theory of Justice* and which is at issue in discussions by Kymlicka, Sandel, and others. The priority of right in its general meaning concerns changes to Rawls's conception subsequent to *Theory*, and will not be discussed here.

argument for justice as fairness relies on no account of the human good or our interests.[9] Kymlicka rightly argues that Rawls does not seek "to derive principles of justice without any idea of people's essential interests" (LCC, 36). But he persists in identifying deontology and the priority of right.[10] In sections IV to VI, I argue that the priority of right is a different notion, one that is central to Rawls's liberalism and the Kantian structure of his deontological view

My primary aim in this chapter is not to attack Kymlicka's otherwise fine treatment of Rawls and liberalism; nor is it simply to expound Rawls's view, though I do a good deal of that. By so doing, however, my ultimate purpose is to elucidate the role of the very important distinction in moral and political philosophy between deontology and teleology. I criticize Kymlicka's understanding of this distinction only because he presents an influential and especially well-formulated alternative interpretation, one that I believe obscures the central issue.

II. Utilitarianism and Equality

Kymlicka distinguishes two interpretations of utilitarianism: teleological and egalitarian. According to Rawls's teleological interpretation, the "fundamental goal" (LCC, 33) of utilitarianism is not persons but the goodness of states of affairs. Duty is defined by what best brings about these states of affairs. "Maximizing the good is primary and we count individuals equally only because that maximizes value. Our primary duty isn't to treat people as equals, but to bring about valuable states of affairs" (LCC, 27). It is difficult to see, Kymlicka says, how this reading of utilitarianism can be viewed as a moral theory.

> Morality in our everyday view at least, is a matter of interpersonal obligations —
> the obligations we owe to each other. But to whom do we owe the duty of maximizing utility? Surely not to the impersonal ideal spectator . . . for he doesn't exist. Nor to the maximally valuable state of affairs itself, for states of affairs don't have moral claims. (LCC, 28–29)

Kymlicka says, "This form of utilitarianism does not merit serious consideration as a political morality" (LCC, 29).

---

9. Michael Sandel, *Liberalism and the Limits of Justice* (Cambridge: Cambridge University Press, 1982). Sandel says: "In its foundational sense, deontology opposes teleology; it describes a form of justification in which first principles are derived in a way that does not presuppose any final human purposes or ends, nor any determinate conception of the human good" (3); and, "The priority of right means that, of the two concepts of ethics, the right is derived independently from the good, rather than the other way around. This foundational priority allows the right to stand aloof from prevailing values and conceptions of the good, and makes Rawls's conception deontological rather than teleological" (18). These sentences are simply false, as we shall see.

10. "It has become a commonplace that most contemporary liberal theory is 'deontological'; that is, it gives priority to the right over the good" (LCC, 21). "Rawls calls such theories, which give priority to the right over the good, 'deontological'" (LCC, 23).

Suppose we see utilitarianism differently as a theory whose "fundamental principle" is "to treat people as equals" (*LCC*, 29). On this egalitarian reading,

> utilitarianism is a procedure for aggregating individual interests and desires, a procedure for making social choices, specifying which trade-offs are acceptable. It's a moral theory which purports to treat people as equals, with equal concern and respect. It does so by counting everyone for one, and no one for more than one. (*LCC*, 25)

So construed, utilitarianism interprets this notion of treating people with equal consideration by giving equal weight to each person's preferences, regardless of what they are preferences for. This supplies the basis for the utilitarian decision procedure. When we act on this procedure, "then utility is maximized. But maximization of utility is not the direct goal. Maximization occurs, but as a by-product of a decision procedure that is intended to aggregate people's preferences fairly" (*LCC*, 25).

Kymlicka argues that his egalitarian reading of utilitarianism is superior to Rawls's teleological one. For, on the egalitarian reading, our fundamental duty—equal consideration—is owed to persons, not to impersonal states of affairs; the problem of characterizing utilitarianism as a moral theory goes away. Moreover, this reading better accords with how utilitarians see their theories.

> It is the concern with equal consideration that underlies the arguments of Bentham and Sidgwick, and is explicitly affirmed by recent utilitarians like Harsanyi, Griffin, and Singer. And while this is not his preferred method, Hare too claims that one could defend utilitarianism by reference to a foundational premise of equal consideration. (*LCC*, 25)

Later (in sec. III), I consider whether Kymlicka's egalitarian interpretation appropriately depicts utilitarianism. But for now I aim to focus on Rawls's teleological/deontological distinction. Kymlicka says, once utilitarianism is construed as based in a fundamental principle of equal consideration, it cannot be seen as teleological; it becomes, "in Rawls's classification, a position that affirms the priority of the right over the good" (*LCC*, 26).

> In this more compelling form, utilitarianism is a "deontological" theory in that the right is not defined as the maximization of the good . . . and each individual is considered to have a distinct claim to equal consideration. (*LCC*, 32)

These claims and arguments are based on a misunderstanding of the role in ethics of the teleology/deontology distinction.

Distinguished here are four different levels at which some notion of equality might play a role in a moral conception:

1. At the stage of justification of substantive moral principles, which involves appeal to some account of practical rationality for its basic principles, and the nature of moral reasoning

2. In the content of substantive moral principles purportedly justified, which provide the ultimate practical standards according to which acts and institutions are right or just
3. In the application of these substantive moral principles to decide which acts are right and which rules and institutions are just
4. As a subordinate moral rule, required by 2 and 3[11]

To illustrate, take justice as fairness: the content (level 2) of Rawls's principles of justice provides that certain liberties are to be equally distributed, that social positions are to be open to all under conditions of fair equality of opportunity, and that income and wealth are to be equally distributed unless an unequal distribution would improve everyone's share (in which event institutions are to be designed so as to maximize the share that goes to the worst off). Here equality is a feature of each of Rawls's substantive principles of right; it is shown on their face. To justify these moral principles (at level 1), Rawls appeals to ideals of social cooperation and of free and equal persons presumed to be implicit in our conception of ourselves as democratic citizens; on this basis, he then models a procedure (the original position) that situates them equally behind a "veil of ignorance." His argument is that the egalitarian principles of justice would be agreed to from this equal position. Here, equality is a feature of a procedure that plays a central role in the justification of moral principles. Next, these principles are to be applied (level 3) in a separate decision process by legislators, judges, and citizens, who take up various positions of equality derivative from the original position (part of Rawls's "four-stage sequence"). In applying these principles, they determine the egalitarian laws and institutions (level 4) that supply the rules individuals are to observe in their day-to-day activities. Some conception of equality is invoked at each of these levels of Rawls's argument.

Now, at which levels do utilitarians invoke equality and, in particular, the principle of equal consideration of equal interests?

1. Justification: Sidgwick appeals to two sets of "philosophical intuitions," each of which incorporates a notion of equality-as-impartiality among persons, to justify the principle of utility: the self-evident Principles of Justice and Impartial Benevolence.[12] These "axioms of practical reason," together with other assump-

---

11. A fifth level can be distinguished here: equality might be part of a metaethical account of the subject matter of morality. For example, Scanlon's contractualism asserts that morality is the set of principles that free and informed persons, equally situated and suitably motivated, could not reasonably reject, as a basis for public agreement. By contrast, "philosophical utilitarianism" holds that morality's subject matter is individual welfare. See T. M. Scanlon, "Contractualism and Utilitarianism," in *Utilitarianism and Beyond*, ed. A. K. Sen and Bernard Williams (Cambridge: Cambridge University Press, 1982).

12. Sidgwick's Principle of Justice says: "It cannot be right for A to treat B in a manner in which it would be wrong for B to treat A, merely on the ground that they are two different individuals, and without there being any difference between the natures or circumstances of the two which can be stated as a reasonable ground for difference of treatment." Or, as he says, "individuals in similar conditions should be treated similarly" (*Methods*, 380). The "maxim of Benevolence" reads: "Each one is morally bound to regard the good of any other individual as much as his own, except in so far

tions, provide "a rational basis for the Utilitarian system" (*Methods*, 387). Similarly, R. M. Hare argues that universalizability is part of the meaning of moral terms; along with other assumptions, this provides a basis for an impartial decision procedure in which equal consideration is given to equal interests. The results of this procedure are equivalent to the requirements of the principle of utility.[13] Equality is here a property of the derivation of utilitarianism.

2. Principle of Utility: The content of the principle of utility is that we are to maximize aggregate utility or welfare. There is, on the face of this principle, no place for equality. Indeed, no independent position is assigned to any distributive concern (which is not to say the principle of utility is not to be used as a principle for deciding distributions). This follows from the fact that the principle of utility is a maximizing-aggregative principle. It tells us to maximize a sum, not to share a distribution (or even to maximize a distribution, whatever that may mean). Equality plays no role in defining the substantive content of the principle of utility.[14]

3. Application: Assume that the principle of utility is justified. To apply this principle to decide what we ought to do, we are to give equal weight to the equal interests of everyone. Here equality is a property of a decision process through which we decide our duty by reference to the principle of utility. Notice that our primary aim (as conscientious utilitarians) in adopting this procedure is not to give equal consideration to everyone's interest. It is to maximize overall utility; that's just what the principle directs us to do. Indeed, there is something peculiar in saying (with Kymlicka) that we are under a "duty" to give equal consideration in this procedure; equal consideration is just what is involved in applying the utility principle to decide what we ought to do. If we fail to do that, it is not that we have violated a duty to anyone; instead, we have applied the principle incorrectly.

4. Rules: Almost any utilitarian view will provide a place for equal consideration via the precept of formal justice—treat similar cases similarly—in the ordinary administration of law (e.g., Sidgwick in *Methods*, 380). And other requirements of fairness (equal rights of certain kinds, etc.) may be argued for on the basis of utility. These rules will occupy a central position in casuistry and common-sense moral reasoning on most utilitarian views.

Now return to Kymlicka's claim: utilitarianism "spells out" an idea of fairness or equality for distinct individuals and thus incorporates the priority of right and "is as 'deontological' as any other" view (*LCC*, 26). Utilitarianism provides a place for some notion of equality on three of the four levels I have designated, and it is by reference to utilitarians' claims with respect to one or more of these levels (particularly 1 and 3) that Kymlicka grounds his argument against Rawls.

as he judges it to be less, when impartially viewed, or less certainly knowable or attainable by him" (*Methods*, 382).

13. Hare, *Moral Thinking* (Oxford: University Press, 1981), 42–43, 111.

14. The exception is the rare occasion where two alternatives result in equal utility. Then, as Sidgwick argues on the basis of the axiom of justice, utilitarianism requires the more equal distribution. James Griffin makes the same point in *Well-Being* (Oxford: Oxford University Press, 1986), 208–15.

It does not incorporate any conception of equality into the substantive content of the principle of utility itself. But it is just the substantive content of moral principles—not their justification, application, or derivative rules—that Rawls is referring to in his teleological/deontological distinction, and when he claims that (classical) utilitarianism is teleological.

To explain: Any plausible moral conception must incorporate an account not just of what we (singly and collectively) ought to do but also of the final ends we ought to realize (directly or indirectly) through our actions. The former specifies a moral conception's account of right; the latter, its conception of the good. Rawls, along with Sidgwick, Kant, and many other philosophers, make such claims. Deontological views are often discussed as if they have no account of the good and are not concerned with the consequences of our acting on the principles advocated. But this surely is a misinterpretation of Kant and modern Kantians such as Rawls and Scanlon. (I doubt it even applies to W. D. Ross, Prichard, or any other serious Intuitionist view usually cited in support of this claim.) Any deontological theory that does not take consequences into account in formulating its principles, or in applying them to reach moral judgments, is not due serious attention.[15] That is simply not the issue between deontological and teleological (or consequentialist) views.

Rawls defines moral conceptions as teleological when their substantive moral principles hold that actions and institutions are right and just only if, given available alternatives, they most effectively promote the greatest amount of the good as defined independently of any moral concepts or principles. There are three noteworthy features of this definition. First, right conduct is defined as nontrivially instrumental. Second, the goodness of states of affairs promoted by right conduct is independently specified, describable purely in terms used in the natural or social sciences. Third, the good is uniquely defined as a dominant end.

Many moral views can admit that right acts in some sense promote the good. In Kant, for example, all have a duty to promote the Realm of Ends; each person's doing so is, we might say, instrumental to realizing this ideal community. But here the goodness of this end is not an independent state of affairs that is being promoted; this good is just defined as the state of affairs in which conscientious moral agents all freely act on and from the Moral Law. By acting and willing according to this principle, all treat the humanity of others as an end-in-itself. Moreover, to say this good (the Realm of Ends) is "maximized" when everyone does his or her duty really adds nothing; and it misleads us as to the structure and content of Kant's principle of right. By contrast, teleological views (1) define the good independent of any moral concepts and then (2) define the right purely in instrumental terms of principles of expedience, that is, as the course of action that most effectively and most probably realizes the greatest amount of good.

It is characteristic of teleological views, so defined, that they rely on a "dominant end" (as opposed to an inclusive one),[16] or what Rawls later came to call

15. As Rawls says: "All ethical doctrines worth our attention take consequences into account in judging rightness. One that did not would simply be irrational, crazy" (*TJ*, 30/26 rev.).

16. On dominant ends, see *TJ*, 552–54/484–486 rev., 565–67/495–96 rev.

a conception of "the one rational good." The need for a single, dominant end stems from the fact that teleological views depict right conduct in terms of what maximizes an aggregate. If one is to give any real content to that idea, then some basis must be provided for comparing different goods and diverse activities. Since one cannot maximize more than one thing, there must be one ultimate end that supplies this standard for comparison and therewith the final object of all right activity.

So defined, teleological views occupy a narrow position within the spectrum of possible moral conceptions. Yet Rawls contends this position has dominated the history of ethical thought. The teleological doctrine of the one rational good is to be found, in his judgment, in the perfectionist ethics of Plato, Aristotle, Augustine, Aquinas, Loyola, Leibniz, Wolff, and Nietzsche, and in the classical utilitarianism of Bentham, Edgeworth, Sidgwick, and their modern disciples.[17] Indeed, odd as it may seem, Rawls sees classical utilitarianism as the culmination of this tradition. Earlier I said the real attraction of teleological views is that they provide a way to make sense of the idea of how there can be a uniquely rational course of action under all conditions. Given that aspiration, Rawls says that hedonism is the symptomatic drift of teleological theories insofar as they try to formulate a clear and applicable method of moral reasoning" (TJ, 560/490 rev.). Here Rawls echoes Sidgwick's argument that pleasurable consciousness is the only reasonable "Ultimate Good" if we are to "systematize human activities."[18] For Sidgwick, like Mill and Bentham, it is not a concern for equality (contra Kymlicka, LCC, 25), but concern for a completely rational morality with which to resolve conflicting norms and combat appeals to intuition and sentiment, that historically provided the impetus to teleology and ultimately to utilitarianism.[19]

17. See Rawls, "Social Unity and Primary Goods," in *Utilitarianism and Beyond*, 160; reprinted in Rawls, *Collected Papers*, ed. Samuel Freeman (Cambridge, MA: Harvard University Press, 1999), chap. 17 (cited in text as *CP*). See also *TJ*, 553–54/483–85 rev. on Aquinas and Loyola, 556/487 rev. on Sidgwick; and *PL*, 134–35.

18. Sidgwick says: "If however [hedonism] be rejected, it remains to consider whether we can frame any other coherent account of Ultimate good. If we are not to systematize human activities by taking Universal Happiness as their common end, on what other principles are we to systematize them? It should be observed that these principles must not only enable us to compare among themselves the values of the different nonhedonistic ends which we have been considering, but must also provide a common standard for comparing these values with that of Happiness; unless we are prepared to adopt the paradoxical position of rejecting happiness as absolutely valueless. For, we have a practical need of determining not only whether we should pursue Truth rather than Beauty or Freedom or some ideal constitution of society rather than either, or perhaps desert all of these for the life of worship and religious contemplation; but also how far we should follow any of these lines of endeavor, when we foresee among its consequences the pains of human or other sentient beings, or even the loss of pleasures that might otherwise have been enjoyed by them" (*Methods*, 406).

19. J. S. Mill claims, near the end of his essay "Bentham": "We consider, therefore, the utilitarian controversy as a question of arrangement and logical subordination rather than of practice; important principally in a purely scientific point of view, for the sake of systematic unity and coherency of ethical philosophy . . . to [Bentham] systematic unity was an indispensable condition of his confidence in his own intellect. And there is something further to be remarked: whether happiness be

Kymlicka does not deny that utilitarianism, when complied with, maximizes overall utility. He does not even deny that happiness is a good for utilitarians.[20] So, in some sense, he seems to concede that for utilitarians, right conduct maximizes the good. What he wants to deny is Rawls's (purported) claim that, for utilitarians, acts are right "because" they maximize the good. On the egalitarian interpretation, acts are right not because they maximize the good but because they are required by an egalitarian decision procedure that requires giving equal weight to everyone's interests. Equal consideration, not maximum utility, is the "fundamental goal" of these egalitarian utilitarian theories (LCC, 31). Maximum utility is merely the state of affairs that happens to be realized by giving equal consideration to everyone's interests in this required procedure. What Kymlicka means here is that because utilitarians incorporate in some fashion equal consideration as a major premise in their arguments for the principle of utility, this makes their view nonteleological. Kymlicka is then resting his case against Rawls by appealing (as he says) to the "justification of utilitarianism" (LCC, 25), "the ultimate ground of the theory" (LCC, 29), that is, how utilitarians view the requirements of practical reasoning. But we must distinguish principles of right conduct from principles of moral reasoning. (In Rawls's view this marks a distinction between what he calls the right and the reasonable.) The former are a subset of the latter in any complete moral theory. That is, once their validity has been established, principles and precepts of right conduct are to be used in moral reasoning by conscientious moral agents, but not all principles of moral reasoning supply standards for right conduct. Instead, they serve a different role in helping us discover, justify, or apply those principles of right that we appeal to, to decide what it is right to do. The utilitarian principle of equal consideration is, in this sense, not a principle of right conduct at all. It is a principle of moral deliberation. It specifies no duty that moral agents can act on, nor does it provide a substantive standard by which to assess whether acts and institutions are right or just.

To see this, it is easy to imagine that there may be several ways to argue for the principle of aggregate utility, some of which incorporate egalitarian premises, others not. This all depends upon the foundational assumptions of a moral view: its account of the nature of morality, practical reasoning, and moral motivation. For example, egalitarian premises are not invoked in the argument that the principle of utility is self-evident, relied upon by some of his predecessors and by

---

or not be the end to which morality should be referred—that it be referred to an end of some sort and not left in the domain of value feeling or inexplicable internal conviction, that it be made a matter of reason and calculation, and not merely of sentiment, is *essential to the very idea of moral philosophy*; is, in fact, what renders argument or discussion on moral questions possible. That the morality of actions depends on the consequences which they tend to produce, is the doctrine of rational persons of all schools; that the good and evil of the consequences is measured solely by pleasure or pain, is all of the doctrine of the school of utility which is peculiar to it" (Mill, *Essays on Politics and Culture*, ed. Gertrude Himmelfarb [Garden City, NY: Doubleday, 1963], 114–15; emphasis added). For Rawls's reconstruction of this history, see *TJ*, 554–60/486–91 rev.

20. "Utilitarians do, of course, believe that the right act maximizes happiness, under some description of that good" (LCC, 23).

Sidgwick himself at one point (*Methods*, 507). Nor do they play a significant role in earlier attempts to justify utilitarianism by natural theology and divine commands (as in Paley), or in the argument recited by Mill (see note 19).[21] Moreover, as Kymlicka recognizes, equal consideration is not a major premise in the sympathetic spectator arguments Rawls appeals to, purportedly to show that utilitarianism is teleological (*LCC*, 27ff.). But the fact that some arguments for utilitarianism might appeal to egalitarian premises and others do not has no effect on the content of the principle of utility or our duties under that principle. Utilitarian philosophers with different justifications could still agree in their moral assessments of the world and people's actions within it. They could agree (and would, given the same information, etc.), because the substantive standard they apply to assess acts and institutions is the same moral principle, which says that right acts maximize aggregate utility. What makes these acts right is not equal consideration. That is an epistemological requirement, appealed to as part of the justification of the principle of utility or to apply it to assess the rightness of actions and states of affairs in the world. Acts are right or wrong independent of the actual or hypothetical assessments of moral reasoners giving equal consideration to the interests of everyone. They are right "because" they maximize the good, not "because" equal weight is given to equal interests in justifying or applying that aggregative standard of right.

Why is Kymlicka so averse to the teleological interpretation of utilitarianism? It is because he thinks the "fundamental principle" of a moral theory must specify a duty to persons, not impersonal states of affairs. On this test, teleological utilitarianism is not a moral theory but a "quasi-aesthetic" one, since it provides no answer to the question, Whom is maximizing utility a duty to? But whom is Kant's categorical imperative, or Rawls's difference principle, a duty to? (Persons? Is it specific persons, the class of all persons, or what?) These questions have no answers, since these principles, like the principle of utility, are not themselves duties to anyone but state standards we are to apply to decide the rules that specify our duties to people. A better test of moral principles, to decide whether they specify duties and therefore principles of right conduct, is the question, Whom is this principle a duty for? In the case of the principle of utility, the answer on direct utilitarian views is, "Everyone capable of understanding and acting on it." But what about the principle of equal consideration of everyone's interests? As a subordinate moral rule (at level 4) this principle states a formal precept of fairness we are to observe in certain settings. But in the abstract decision procedures Kymlicka relies on to ground his argument, there is no answer to the question, Whom is giving equal consideration to everyone's interests a duty for? The reason is that, in this form, this principle is not a principle of right conduct at all; instead, it is a deliberative principle that is part of a (hypothetical) procedure which serves as a criterion for appraising whether or not individuals' and institutions' conduct is right, as measured by the principle of utility. What leads Kymlicka to so misconstrue the point of the teleology/deontology distinction? It may be that

---

21. See an account of the early utilitarians by J. B. Schneewind, *Sidgwick's Ethics and Victorian Moral Philosophy* (Oxford: University Press, 1977), 122–29.

he uncritically accepts utilitarians' standard defense against the claim that their doctrine is insensitive to distributions. The standard rejoinder here (an argument Mill attributes to Bentham) is that utilitarianism is concerned with fairness and distributions, since the principle of utility respects all men as equals by observing the rule "Everybody to count for one, nobody for more than one."[22] Rawls says utilitarians fail to take seriously the distinction between persons (*TJ*, 27/24 rev.). But, Kymlicka says, this "utilitarian principle of distribution does recognize the distinctness of persons" (*LCC*, 32). It is only because Rawls conceives of utilitarianism as teleological that he is unable to recognize equal consideration as a principle of distribution and appreciate that utilitarians do see persons as distinct, with "distinct claims to equal consideration" (*LCC*, 31).

What kind of "principle of distribution" is equal consideration? Is it a principle of right conduct, or of "right" deliberation? What good is being distributed here, and by whom is it being distributed? Again, equality or fairness can be distinguished as a feature of the following:

1. Distributions of goods (happiness, or resources such as liberties, opportunities, and income and wealth)
2. Actual decision processes we use to distribute those goods (e.g., markets, majority rule, trials)
3. A hypothetical decision process that tells us how we ought to distribute these goods, or rights of participation in actual decision procedures

The "utilitarian principle of distribution" Kymlicka and utilitarians rely on to claim utilitarianism is sensitive to questions of justice and fair distribution is *not* a principle for the distribution of goods. It is not even a principle that is to be incorporated into any actual decision process we use to determine the distribution of goods. It is a formal principle that is part of a hypothetical decision procedure that (on many accounts) no one may ever actually apply or appeal to but which serves as the standard that determines if actual distributions of goods, and of rights of participation in actual decision procedures, are right and just. This is not what critics have in mind when they claim that utilitarianism "puts no value on the distribution of good" and "gives no weight to distribution" (Rawls); or that utilitarianism "is much too hooked on the welfare sum to be concerned with the problem of distribution" (Sen); or that, for utilitarians, "questions of equitable and inequitable distribution do not matter" (Williams).[23] They have in mind distributions of good(s), namely, of happiness or of the resources and opportunities that enable people to achieve happiness and lead a good life. Equal consideration in a hypothetical decision process is not a good in this sense. It is a purely procedural

22. Mill, *Utilitarianism*, in *On Liberty and Other Essays*, ed. John Gray (Oxford: Oxford University Press, 1991) 199, chap. 5, paragraph 36.

23. Rawls, "The Independence of Moral Theory," *Proceedings and Addresses of the American Philosophical Association* 47 (1974–75): 19 (also in *CP*, chap.15); A. K. Sen, *On Economic Inequality* (Oxford: Clarendon Press, 1973), 23; Bernard Williams, "A Critique of Utilitarianism," in *Utilitarianism: For and Against* (Cambridge: Cambridge University Press, 1973), 142.

prescription that provides no guarantee of substantive equal treatment. Indeed, it puts no substantive restrictions whatsoever on the distributions of goods. It is in this sense that utilitarianism is insensitive to distributions. Its substantive principle of distribution directs that we maximize aggregate good, letting shares fall where they may. Division of goods is simply instrumental to overall utility. This is precisely the sense in which utilitarianism is a teleological view.[24]

To sum up, though utilitarianism incorporates equality as a property of the justification of the principle of utility and of the decision process through which that principle gets applied, it does not leave any place for equality in the content of that principle. On its face, this standard of right conduct directs that we maximize an aggregate. As a result neither equality nor any other distributive value is assigned independent significance in resulting distributions of goods. Kymlicka claims that, because Rawls sees utilitarianism as teleological, he misdescribes the debate over distribution by ignoring that utilitarians allow for equality of distribution too. But the distribution debate Rawls is concerned with is a (level 2) debate over how what is deemed good (welfare, rights, resources, etc.) within a moral theory is to be divided among individuals. It is not a (level 3) debate over the distribution of consideration in a procedure which decides the distribution of these goods. Nor is it a (level 1) debate over the principles of practical reasoning that are invoked to justify the fundamental standard of distribution.

III. The Justification of Utilitarianism

Now I consider Kymlicka's argument on its own terms, to assess whether it is correct to interpret utilitarianism as egalitarian. Kymlicka argues utilitarianism is "deontological" because it is based in a "fundamental goal" of equality, made manifest through the principle of equal consideration incorporated into utilitarian procedures. Kymlicka speaks here as if it were pure coincidence that utilitarian procedures maximize the good. He says that on his egalitarian interpretation utility is maximized. "But maximization of utility is not the direct goal [but the] by-product of a decision procedure that is intended to aggregate people's prefer-

---

24. I do not mean to claim that Kymlicka is wholly in error. With respect to Harsanyi's average utilitarianism, his assertion of its deontological status may be correct. But this does not advance his case against Rawls. For, Rawls explicitly says that average utility "is not a teleological doctrine, strictly speaking, as the classical view is, and therefore it lacks some of the intuitive appeal of the idea of maximizing the good" (TJ, 166/143 rev.). But the reason he says this has nothing to do with the reasons Kymlicka argues, namely, the fact that Harsanyi assumes universality in his justification of average utility. For, classical utilitarians like Sidgwick and Hare appeal to universality too. Average utility is nonteleological, on Rawls's account, because the content of that principle directs that we maximize a state of affairs which incorporates a distributive standard, namely, average utility (per capita), which is the average share of each existing person, not the total utility summed across existing and future beings. It is only aggregate utility doctrines (classical utilitarianism and the co-ordinal utilitarianism of Arrow, Kolm, et al.) that Rawls claims are teleological. See Rawls, "Social Unity and Primary Goods," in *Utilitarianism and Beyond*, 173–83, on co-ordinal utilitarianism.

ences fairly" (*LCC*, 25). But surely the appropriate question here is, why are we to aggregate preferences, and then maximize, in the first place? I argue that this has little to do with equal consideration, or occupying a universal or objective point of view. It is only because utilitarians make certain fundamental assumptions, explicitly or implicitly about rationality and the ultimate good, that they are led to maximize the aggregate.

In a separate presentation of his argument, Kymlicka says:

> The requirement that we maximize utility is entirely derived from the prior requirement to treat people with equal consideration. So the first argument for utilitarianism is this:
>
> 1. People matter, and matter equally; therefore
> 2. each person's interests should be given equal weight; therefore
> 3. morally right acts will maximize utility.[25]

Kymlicka's reconstruction matches R. M. Hare's assertion that his argument for utilitarianism is based in a general "right to equal concern and respect . . . a precept which leads straight to Bentham's formula and to utilitarianism itself."[26] As Hare interprets this right, it requires "equal weight to equal preferences, counting everybody for one,"[27] and it is this requirement that purportedly leads "straight to" maximizing aggregate utility.

Now, what is peculiar about the Kymlicka/Hare claim here is that, though both present utilitarianism as grounded in equal respect for persons, classical utilitarian doctrine has been far more generous. It is not just the desires and interests of persons that are to be given equal consideration, but those of all sentient beings. Hare himself, in the same article, speaks of utilitarianism as a "morality of universal equal concern for all sentient beings."[28] If so, it is misleading to claim that utilitarianism seeks to treat people as equals; in a Pickwickian sense perhaps, namely, along with many other animal species in the universe. Kymlicka's premise 1 should read: "Sentient beings matter, and matter equally." For, being a person is not a necessary condition for equal consideration of one's interests in classical utilitarian procedures.

Why do so many utilitarians (Bentham, Sidgwick, Hare, Singer) hold this striking thesis? Because they make certain assumptions about the nature of the good. As Sidgwick argues, the "ultimate good" is pleasurable consciousness. It is a good no matter where it occurs. Beings other than persons experience this good. And, as the second principle of Impartial Benevolence directs, "As a rational being I am bound to aim at good generally . . . not merely at a particular part

25. Kymlicka, *Contemporary Political Philosophy* (Oxford: Oxford University Press, 1990), 31 (cited in text as *CPP*).

26. Hare, "Reply to Mackie," in *Utility and Rights*, ed. R. G. Frey (Minneapolis: University of Minnesota Press, 1984), 107. Kymlicka relies on this article to support his claim that Hare's view can be construed as egalitarian.

27. Hare, "Reply to Mackie," 110.

28. Hare, "Reply to Mackie," 116.

of it" (*Methods*, 382). It follows that, in utilitarian decision procedures, the experiences or welfare of all sentient beings must be weighed in the balance equally along with those of persons in deciding what we ought to do.

The inclusion of all sentient beings in the calculation of interests severely undermines the force of any claim that utilitarianism is an "egalitarian" doctrine, based in some notion of equal concern and respect for persons. But let us assume Kymlicka can restore his thesis by insisting that it concerns not utilitarianism as a general moral doctrine but as a more limited thesis about political morality. (Here I pass over the fact that none of the utilitarians he relies on to support his egalitarian interpretation construes the doctrine as purely political. The drift of modern utilitarian theory is just the other way: utilitarianism is not seen as a political doctrine, to be appealed to by legislators and citizens, but as a nonpublic criterion of right that is indirectly applied [by whom is a separate issue] to assess the nonutilitarian public political conception of justice.) Still, let us assume it is as a doctrine of political morality that utilitarianism treats persons, and only persons, as equals. Even in this form it cannot be that maximizing utility is "not a goal" but a "by-product," "entirely derived from the prior requirement to treat people with equal consideration" (*CPP*, 31).

Kymlicka says, "If utilitarianism is best seen as an egalitarian doctrine, then there is no independent commitment to the idea of maximizing welfare" (*CPP*, 35). But how can this be?

1. What is there about the formal principle of equal consideration (or, for that matter, occupying a universal point of view) which would imply that we maximize the aggregate of individuals' welfare? Why not assume, for example, that equal consideration requires maximizing the division of welfare (strict equality, or however equal division is to be construed); or, at least maximize the multiple (which would result in more equitable distributions than the aggregate)? Or, why not suppose equal consideration requires equal proportionate satisfaction of each person's interests (by for example, determining our resources and then satisfying some set percentage of each person's desires)?[29] Or finally, we might rely on some Paretian principle: equal consideration means adopting measures making no one worse off. For reasons I shall soon discuss, each of these rules is a better explication of equal consideration of each person's interests than is the utilitarian aggregative method, which in effect collapses distinctions among persons.

2. Moreover, rather than construing individuals' "interests" as their actual (or rational) desires, and then putting them all on a par and measuring according to intensity, why not construe their interests lexically, in terms of a hierarchy of wants, where certain interests are, to use Scanlon's terms, more "urgent" than others, insofar as they respond to more basic needs? Equal consideration would then rule out satisfying less urgent interests of the majority of people until all means have been taken to satisfy everyone's more basic needs.

---

29. For a similar account of equal justice, see W. K. Frankena, "Some Beliefs about Justice," in *Perspectives on Morality*, ed. K. E. Goodpaster (Notre Dame: University of Notre Dame Press, 1976), 93–106.

3. Finally, what is there about equal consideration, by itself, that requires maximizing anything? Why does it not require, as in David Gauthier's view, optimizing constraints on individual utility maximization? Or why does it not require sharing a distribution?

The point is just that, to say we ought to give equal consideration to everyone's interests does not, by itself, imply much of anything about how we ought to proceed or what we ought to do. It is a purely formal principle, which requires certain added independent assumptions, to yield any substantive conclusions: (1) concluding that utilitarian procedures maximize is not a "by-product" of equal consideration but stems from a particular conception of rationality that is explicitly incorporated into the procedure; (2) concluding that individuals' interests are construed in terms of their (rational) desires or preferences, all of which are put on a par, stems from a conception of individual welfare or the human good—a person's good is defined subjectively as what he wants or would want after due refection; and, finally, (3) concluding aggregation stems from the fact that, on the classical view, a single individual takes up everyone's desires as if they were his own, sympathetically identifies with them, and chooses to maximize his "individual" utility. Hare, for one, explicitly makes this third move. Just as Rawls says of the classical view, Hare "extend[s] to society the principle of choice for one man, and then, to make this extension work, conflat[es] all persons into one through the imaginative acts of the impartial sympathetic spectator" (TJ, 27/24 rev.).

If these are independent premises incorporated into the justification of utilitarianism and its decision procedure, then maximizing aggregate utility cannot be a "by-product" of a procedure that gives equal consideration to everyone's interests. Instead, it defines what that procedure is. If anything is a by-product here, it is the appeal to equal consideration. Utilitarians appeal to impartiality in order to extend a method of individual practical rationality so that it may be applied to society as a whole (cf. TJ, 26–27/23–24 rev.). Impartiality combined with sympathetic identification allows a hypothetical observer to experience the desires of others as if they were his own and to compare alternative courses of action according to their conduciveness to a single maximand made possible by equal consideration and sympathy.

The significant fact is that, in this procedure, appeals to equal consideration have nothing to do with impartiality between persons. What is really being given equal consideration are desires or experiences of the same magnitude. That these are the desires or experiences of separate persons (or, for that matter, of some other sentient being) is simply an incidental fact that has no substantive effect on utilitarian calculations.

This becomes apparent from the fact that we can more accurately describe the utilitarian principle in terms of giving equal consideration not to each person's interests but instead to equally intense interests, no matter where they occur. Nothing is lost in this redescription, and a great deal of clarity is gained. It is in this sense that persons enter into utilitarian calculations only incidentally. Any mention of them can be dropped without loss of the crucial information one needs to learn how to apply utilitarian procedures.

This indicates what is wrong with the common claim that utilitarians emphasize procedural equality and fairness among persons, not substantive equality and fairness in results. On the contrary, utilitarianism, rightly construed, emphasizes neither procedural nor substantive equality among persons. Desires and experiences, not persons, are the proper objects of equal concern in utilitarian procedures. Having in effect read persons out of the picture at the procedural end, before decisions on distributions even get underway, it is little wonder that utilitarianism can result in such substantive inequalities. What follows is that utilitarian appeals to democracy and the democratic value of equality are misleading. In no sense do utilitarians seek to give persons equal concern and respect.

To conclude this part of my discussion: Kymlicka says that what gives utilitarianism its "plausibility," what "motivates" it, is a concern to treat others as equals. But then he himself goes on to argue persuasively how implausible utilitarianism is as an interpretation of equality (*CPP*, chap. 2). I have argued the egalitarian account of utilitarianism is implausible and that the force of that doctrine must lie elsewhere: in defining right conduct as what maximizes the one rational good, utilitarianism provides a way to understand how there can be a rational moral choice under all circumstances. That is the very feature of utilitarianism which makes it a teleological view. Later I discuss how deontology combined with the priority of right are important concepts in defining the structure of a Kantian view. By denying that these notions are of any consequence, Kymlicka would obscure the difference between Kantian and other moral conceptions. The attitude encouraged by his proposal—"We are all Kantians" (utilitarians, perfectionists of all kinds, and philosophical liberals, alike)—impoverishes moral theory. Nowhere is this more evident than in his treatment of Rawls's account of the priority of right.

IV. The Priority of Right and Utilitarianism

Throughout his discussion of utilitarianism, Kymlicka, like Michael Sandel and others, identifies deontology with the priority of right.[30] But these are different concepts. Like deontology, the priority of right describes the structure and substantive content of a moral conception, not its procedural justification.[31] It is not then a claim about the order of justification of a moral conception. (So, contrary to Sandel, the priority of right does not aim at justifying a moral conception "aloof from prevailing values and conceptions of the good."[32] And contrary to Kymlicka, a moral conception does not achieve the priority of right simply because it relies on assumptions of equality in the argument to principles of right.) Unlike deontology, the priority of right does not describe how moral principles of right internally relate the concepts of the right and the good. Rather, it describes, in the

---

30. See notes 9 and 10.

31. That the priority of right presupposes the justification of principles is indicated by Rawls's claim: "Once the conception of justice is established, the priority of right guarantees the precedence of its principles" (*TJ*, 564/494 rev.).

32. See note 9.

first instance, the place of principles of right in the practical reasoning of moral agents motivated by a sense of right and justice, how they singly and collectively are to apply principles "given from the first a definite content" (*TJ*, 32/28 rev.), in deciding their good and what they ought to do. The "priority" of the priority of right refers to the lexical ordering of principles of right and justice in individual and social deliberation. It is but one among several priorities Rawls assigns to those principles (along with the priority of justice over efficiency, the priority of basic liberties over the difference principle, and the priority of moral worth over nonmoral values). In each case, Rawls means the serial ordering of principles of right conduct over considerations of a different kind (see *TJ*, 42–43n/37–38n rev.; 302–3/266–67 rev.).

What, then, is the priority of right? Almost any moral conception holds that in the deliberations of moral agents, moral principles and the reasons they provide are to take precedence over other considerations. Utilitarians, for example, hold that reasons of overall utility override what any individual or group may do in order to realize their desired ends. But the priority of right is not simply a formal claim about the overridingness of moral reasons. It refers to the substantive limits placed on the kinds of considerations that can count as reasons in practical deliberation, which stem from the content internal to principles of right. The priority of right is a claim about how the substantive content of a (Kantian) moral conception restricts the desires and interests moral agents can take into account, individually and collectively in formulating their purposes and rationally deciding what they ought to do. Principles of right and justice are prior and therefore govern our deliberations, not just about what we may do, but also about the ends and interests that individuals and societies may legitimately pursue. As such, the priority of right defines a notion of permissible ends and (morally) admissible (or reasonable) conceptions of the good. Reasonable conceptions of the good are those whose ends and activities accord with the requirements of the principles of right.[33]

To illustrate, take standard accounts of practical rationality (for example, utility maximization, or Rawls's deliberative rationality [*TJ*, sec. 64]). Whatever their differences, most contemporary accounts agree that practical reasoning basically involves reflecting on our ends as given by our desires and interests, ranking their priority and making them consistent, and then deciding the most rational means (effective, likely, inclusive, pleasurable) for realizing them. Call this "ordinary deliberation." Now the priority of right implies that there is something about the content and structure of moral reasoning that cannot be captured by ordinary deliberation alone, as guided by principles of rational choice or utility maximization. In the practical deliberations of conscientious moral agents—persons with an effective concern for right and justice—their moral motives are not given parity with other desires and interests and balanced off against them in ordinary

33. In *Theory*, Rawls says, "The principles of right, and so of justice, put limits on which satisfactions have value; they impose restrictions on what are reasonable conceptions of one's good" (*TJ*, 31/27 rev.). Rawls also uses the term "admissible conceptions of the good" in this connection in "Fairness to Goodness," *Philosophical Review* 84 (1975): 536–54, at 549, *CP*, 279.

ways. This does not mean moral motives and the reasons they provide are simply to be assigned an added weight in ordinary deliberation according to their importance or their intensity. They are assigned no weight at all in the ordinary sense; indeed, they do not even figure into our ordinary calculations where we balance one set of interests off against others to decide the most rational thing to do. To seek to incorporate moral desires into one's deliberations or utility calculations in ordinary ways simply misconstrues what moral desires are desires for. Moral desires (according to Kantian views) are (highest-order) desires with a certain content: namely, that all our other desires, interests, plans, and activities (as captured by say a utility function) meet the requirements of principles of right.

The priority of right asserts, then, that the reasons supplied by moral motives—principles of right and their institutional requirements—have absolute precedence over all other considerations. As such, moral motives must occupy a separate dimension in practical reasoning. Suppose, then, a supplementary stage of practical reasoning where the interests and pursuits that figure into ordinary deliberation and which define our conception of the good are checked against principles of right and justice. At this stage of reasoning, any ends that directly conflict with these moral principles (e.g., racist ends or the wish to dominate others), or whose pursuit would undermine the efficacy of principles of right (e.g., desires for unlimited accumulation of wealth whatever the consequences for others), are assigned no moral value no matter how intensely felt or important they may otherwise be. Being without moral value, they should count for nothing in deliberation. Consequently, their pursuit is prohibited or curtailed by the priority given to principles of right.

The priority of right then describes the hierarchical subordination in practical deliberation of the desires, interests, and plans that define a person's rational good to the substantive demands of principles of right and justice.[34] Purposes and pursuits that are incompatible with these principles must be abandoned or revised. The same idea carries through to social and political deliberations on the general good. In political deliberative procedures, the priority of right means that desires and interests of individuals or groups that conflict with the institutional requirements of principles of right and justice have no legitimate claim to satisfaction, no matter how intense people's feelings or how large the majority sharing these aims. Constitutional restrictions on majority rule exhibit the priority of right. In democratic procedures, majorities cannot violate constitutional rights and procedures to promote, say, the Christian religion or any other aspect of their good that undermines others' basic rights and opportunities. Similarly the institutional requirements of Rawls's difference principle limit, for example, property owners' desires for tax exemptions for capital gains and the just savings principle limits current majorities' wishes to deplete natural resources. These desires are

34. As Rawls says, ordinary practical reasoning is to be "framed within definite limits. The principles of justice and their realization in social forms define the bounds within which our deliberations take place" (TJ, 563/493 rev.). This claim is echoed in PL, where Rawls says: "The priority of right gives the principles of justice a strict precedence in citizens' deliberations and limits their freedom to advance certain ways of life. It characterizes the structure and content of justice as fairness and what it regards as good reasons in deliberation" (209).

curtailed in political contexts, no matter how intense or widely held, because of the priority of principles of right over individual and general good.[35]

The priority of right enables Rawls to define a notion of reasonable conceptions of the good: of those desires, interests and plans of life that may legitimately be pursued for political purposes. Only reasonable conceptions of the good establish a basis for legitimate claims in political procedures (cf. *TJ*, 449/394 rev.). That certain desires and pursuits are admissible, and political claims based on them are legitimate, while others are not, presupposes antecedently established principles of right and justice. Racist conceptions of the good are not politically admissible; actions done in their pursuit are either prohibited or discouraged by a just social scheme, and they provide no basis for legitimate claims in political procedures. Excellences such as knowledge, creativity, and aesthetic contemplation are permissible ends for individuals so long as they are pursued in accordance with the constraints of principles of right. Suppose these perfectionist principles state intrinsic values that it is the duty of everyone to pursue. (Rawls leaves this question open; cf. *TJ*, 328/288 rev.) Still, they cannot supply a basis for legitimate political claims and expectations; they cannot be appealed to in political contexts to justify limiting others' freedom or even the coercive redistribution of income and wealth (cf. *TJ*, 331–32/291–92 rev.). This is because of the priority of right over the good.

Now return to Kymlicka's argument. Kymlicka says both Rawls and utilitarians agree on the premise of giving equal consideration to everyone's interests, and that because utilitarians afford equal consideration, "they must recognize, rather than deny that individuals are distinct persons with their own rightful claims. That is, in Rawls's classification, a position that affirms the priority of the right over the good" (*LCC*, 26). Since "Rawls treats the right as a spelling-out of the requirement that each person's good be given equal consideration," there is no debate between Rawls and utilitarians over the priority of the right or the good (*LCC*, 40).

On the contrary, Rawls denies equal consideration of interests, and he denies it because of the priority of right.[36] To explain: A central feature of utility-maximizing views is the homogeneity of desires. In applying the principle of utility, (rational) desires are (1) taken as given, and (2) their satisfaction is taken as having value, no matter what they are desires for; to decide what is right to do, then, all desires are (3) put on a par in deliberation and (4) assessed according to their intensity. These four features describe what it is to give equal consideration to equal interests in utilitarian calculations. The priority of right rejects each of them: (1) Desires are not taken as given; their content must be compatible with principles of right. (2) If they conflict with principles of right, desires are not, to

---

35. See *TJ*, 449–51/394–96 rev. See also *PL*, where Rawls says, "The fact that we have a compelling desire in such cases [of constitutional essentials and basic justice] does not argue for the propriety of its satisfaction any more than the strength of a conviction argues for its truth" (190).

36. Rawls, "Fairness to Goodness," 536–54. Here, see Rawls's distinction between being fair to persons and being fair to interests or conceptions of the good: "We should not speak of fairness to conceptions of the good, but of fairness to moral persons . . . it is fairness to persons that is primary and not fairness to conceptions of the good as such" (554), (*CP*, 284–85).

use Kant's term, "worthy" of satisfaction;[37] therefore, their satisfaction is to be assigned no value whatsoever in political decisions. (3) Desires are not put on a par in deliberation and assigned importance according to intensity; instead, certain interests are deemed of greater urgency than all others.[38] In Rawls's account, then, moral persons are said to have "highest-order interests" in developing the moral powers necessary for social cooperation (the capacities to be reasonable and rational); the primary social goods needed to realize these powers take priority over their desire for other goods in political deliberation.[39] (4) As for the sheer intensity of a majority's desires and convictions, it has no independent moral weight; only if majority preferences accord with prior principles of justice do they establish a basis for legitimate laws and social policies.[40]

There is nothing equivalent to these restrictions in utilitarianism. Granted, in the deliberations of conscientious utilitarian agents, the principle of utility is to override all other considerations.[41] Moreover, once the principle of utility has been applied and the balance of satisfactions decided, utilitarians even have a basis for encouraging some ends and traits of character and discouraging others. But we have no way of knowing beforehand what these admissible and inadmissible ends and traits are. Whether toleration of diverse religious confessions, or nondiscrimination against racial minorities, is desirable or not is a factual question, wholly contingent on the content and weight of people's desires at the time. Nothing internal to the substantive content of the principle of utility restricts the ends that make up individual and collective good. Restrictions on ends that subsequently do arise are just those needed to maximize aggregate utility. This is a consequence of giving equal weight to equally intense interests. No concept of impermissible ends is defined, from the outset, by the utilitarian principle of right.

The priority of right then describes how the content internal to principles of right is to regulate the individual and collective deliberations of moral agents.[42] It puts limits from the outset on their decisions about individual and collective

---

37. See the essay "Theory and Practice," in *Perpetual Peace and Other Essays* (Indianapolis: Hackett, 1983), 63 (Ak. 8:273).

38. On the notion of urgency of interests, see T. M. Scanlon, "Preference and Urgency," *Journal of Philosophy* 82 (November 1975): 655–69.

39. Moreover, the primary goods themselves are ranked in order of relative importance by the principles of justice (the basic liberties have priority over all the rest, and fair opportunities have priority over income and wealth). See "Social Unity and Primary Goods," in *Utilitarianism and Beyond*, 166.

40. Rawls says as much in defining the priority of right: "The principles of right, and so of justice, put limits on which satisfactions have value; they impose restrictions on what are reasonable conceptions of one's good. In drawing up plans and in deciding on aspirations men are to take these constraints into account. Hence in justice as fairness one does not take men's propensities and inclinations as given, whatever they are, and then seek the best way to fulfill them. Rather, their desires and aspirations are restricted from the outset by the principles of justice which specify the boundaries that men's systems of ends must respect. We can express this by saying that in justice as fairness the concept of right is prior to that of the good. A just social system defines the scope within which individuals must develop their aims. . . . [I]nterests requiring the violation of justice have no value" (*TJ*, 31/27–8 rev.; see also *TJ*, 450/395 rev.).

41. See Hare, *Moral Thinking*, 50–61.

42. *PL*, 209, quoted in note 32.

ends and the measures that are needed to realize them. Principles of right define the range of admissible and reasonable conceptions of the good. This means Rawls does not share with utilitarians the principle of equal consideration. To give equal consideration to equal interests does not, as Kymlicka claims, "affirm the priority of the right over the good" (*LCC*, 26); it is its repudiation.

V. Perfectionism and the Priority of Right

The priority of right is further clarified by contrasting it with perfectionism. My aim here is to show how essential the priority of right is to the Kantian liberalism argued for in *A Theory of Justice*. Kymlicka contends the priority of right is ambiguous: Rawls uses this notion, not just (1) in a "teleology-versus-deontology sense" but also (2) in an "anti-perfectionistic sense," to argue "that our legitimate entitlements are not tied to the promotion of any particular view of the good life" (*LCC*, 35). But this cannot be an issue of the priority of right, Kymlicka says, for perfectionists affirm that priority in so far as they too give "equal weight to each person's interests" in devising a scheme of distribution (*LCC*, 34). Consequently, "Rawls and a perfectionist do not disagree over the relative priority of the right and the good. They just disagree over how best to define and promote people's good" (*LCC*, 35).

The priority of right, I have argued, is not a claim about giving equal consideration to persons or interests in deliberative procedures. It concerns the structure of the practical reasoning of moral agents who affirm the principles of right and justice that are part of Kantian views. Now deontological principles, by definition, do not direct us to maximize one rational good. Moreover, on Kantian views, these principles are expressly designed to leave persons free rationally to determine, revise, and pursue their good, so long as it conforms to certain moral conditions. Conscientious moral agents are then to appeal to deontological principles to monitor the ends and regulate the pursuits that are to be a part of their rational good as determined via ordinary practical reasoning. "The idea is to approximate the boundaries, however vague, within which individuals and associations are at liberty to advance their aims and deliberative rationality has free play" (*TJ*, 566/496 rev.).

Now, practical reasoning does not have "free play" in any sense under teleological perfectionism (as Rawls defines it), nor are its principles of right designed to provide "boundaries" within which persons are to deliberate on and pursue their good.[43] That is because the principle of perfection uniquely

43. In *A Theory of Justice*, Rawls distinguishes teleological, or "strict perfectionist theory," which holds that we are to maximize the one rational good, from "perfectionism [of an] intuitionistic form," which is a pluralistic doctrine holding that a teleological principle of perfection is but one among several moral principles and is to be balanced off against them. Rawls says the latter doctrine is "a far more reasonable view." See *TJ*, 326/286 rev. The bulk of his criticisms are directed against teleological perfectionism. The perfectionism Kymlicka attributes to Marx (correctly or incorrectly) would be classified as intuitionistic perfectionism on Rawls's account, since it incorporates an equality principle along with a principle of perfection.

defines people's ultimate good and defines for each individual what it is always rational, hence right, for him or her to do. It is rational, hence right, to maximize the one rational good (be it contemplation as in Aristotle, the Vision of God in Aquinas and Loyola, or whatever). Instead of envisioning two separate dimensions of deliberation in which first rational, then reasonable, principles are applied to determine our ends and what we ought to do, teleological perfectionism says there is but one standard for deliberation: each person's ascertaining the most effective means under one's circumstances for realizing the one rational good. According to perfectionism, rational principles to determine one's good, and reasonable principles of right, are one and the same. As such, the principle of perfection completely occupies all deliberative space. That is because "the dominant end of a teleological theory is so defined that we can never finally achieve it, and therefore the injunction to advance it always applies" (*TJ*, 566/495 rev.). Consequently (as Rawls says of the principle of utility), the principle of perfection "is not really suitable for a lexical ordering" of the very kind defined by the priority of right. Strictly construed, reasoning according to the principle of perfection provides no place for the regulation and monitoring of our free rational decisions about our ends and pursuits by reasonable principles of right. As a result, no place is left for free deliberation on our final ends, for a plurality of intrinsic goods, or for the autonomy of practical reason.

This contrast between justice as fairness and teleological perfectionism suggests why deontology and the priority of right are central to Rawls's liberalism. Among the assumptions integral to Rawls's liberalism (at least as presented in *Theory*) is, first, that there are a plurality of intrinsic goods and a plurality of ways of life that are rational for individuals to pursue. Deontology is a reasonable consequence; given the diversity of intrinsic goods and ways of life that affirm them, justice is not definable in terms of what maximizes one rational good. Assume now that a person's good is the way of life he/she would rationally choose from the ideal perspective Rawls calls "deliberative rationality." A second feature of Rawls's liberalism is the assumption that, whatever a person's rational good is (so defined), having the freedom to deliberate on, revise, and rationally pursue a conception of the good is a part of each person's good; it is a precondition of our living a good life. But if so, then an account of practical reasoning is needed that incorporates deontological principles of right into people's deliberations about their good. This is the role of the priority of right; it establishes that these moral principles have absolute precedence in deliberation over all other reasons, and so circumscribe individuals' freedom to choose and pursue a plan of life. Reasoning in this way enables a person to satisfy a third feature of Rawls's liberalism: that a condition of anyone's realizing one's rational good (at least in a "well-ordered society") is that his/her ends and pursuits be consistent with institutional requirements of justice. By deciding on and pursuing a rational plan from within the range of admissible plans defined by the priority of right, a person's good is reasonable and legitimate and so respects the limits of justice, satisfying this precondition of living a good life. This brings us to the final issue.

VI. The Priority of Right and the Full Theory of the Good

To conclude, I indicate how the priority of right plays a role in the definition of individual and social good in justice as fairness.[44] This will convey a better idea of how deontology and the priority of right come together in a Kantian view. The priority of right is a defining feature of Rawls's "full theory of the good."[45] The basic idea of the full theory is that the good of moral persons—conscientious moral agents motivated by a sense of right and justice—cannot be defined independently of principles of right and justice. Acting not just on but also from (for the sake of) these principles and their institutional requirements is an essential aspect of their good. Now there is nothing unusual about the idea that justice, as a virtue or an end, can be part of a person's good. But in Rawls's Kantian account, this idea is worked out in several distinctive ways, each of which presupposes a background structure supplied by the priority of right.

How does the priority of right figure into the full theory? According to Rawls's "thin theory of the good," a person's good is formally defined in terms of a rational plan of life, the plan of life a person would choose under the ideal conditions of "deliberative rationality."[46] Rawls assumes a partial similarity in free and equal moral persons' rational plans: whatever else their conception of the good may be, they all have a "highest-order" interest and corresponding desire to develop and exercise the moral powers that enable them to engage in social cooperation (the capacities to understand and apply fair terms of social cooperation, and formulate, revise, and pursue a rational plan of life).[47] On the basis of the account of rational plans, together with these essential interests, Rawls argues for the primary social goods as a necessary ingredient of the rational plans of free and equal moral persons. This is the "thin theory of the good," and it constitutes the aspect of Rawls's argument that he calls "the Rational." Contrary to Sandel's misreading, it is not so thin that it does not involve substan-

44. My account here relies on Rawls's account in A *Theory of Justice*. Certain subtleties are introduced in *Political Liberalism* which I cannot discuss in detail. See note 8. I omit a fuller discussion here, primarily because it is the account in *Theory* that has been the focus of discussion and criticism of Rawls's account of the priority of right (by Kymlicka, Sandel, and others). For a discussion of how *Political Liberalism* departs from the account of the good set forth in *Theory*, see chap. 6 of this volume, "Political Liberalism and the Possibility of a Just Democratic Constitution."

45. "I have supposed first that rational plans satisfy the constraints of right and justice (as the full theory of the good stipulates)" (*TJ*, 550/482 rev.).

46. Roughly a plan of life is rational for a person if it incorporates the primary desires, interests, and pursuits that are of fundamental significance to him (taking into account the Aristotelian Principle); involves a scheme of activities that enable him to realize these ends and pursuits in an effective manner (as defined by the principles of rational choice); and would be freely chosen by him under the ideal conditions of deliberative rationality (involving critical reflection on his ends, making them consistent, full information, etc.). See *TJ*, 408–9/358–59 rev.; see also, *PL*, 176–78.

47. To say these are "highest-order interests" means they are to be supremely regulative of each person's pursuit of his good. It does not mean the moral powers are worth realizing for their own sake. That has to be argued for, which is the role of Rawls's congruence argument (*TJ*, chap. 9). See also *PL*, chap. 5, secs. 7 and 8.

tial claims about the good of moral persons (e.g., realizing their moral powers, which includes the free development and successful execution of a rational plan of life). Combining the thin theory with the set of moral assumptions Rawls calls "the Reasonable" (the veil of ignorance, the formal constraints of right, etc.), we have the argument from the original position. And contrary to Kymlicka's misreading, these reasonable principles do not constitute the priority of right. That idea can enter in only after the principles of justice have been established, as part of the full theory of the good.

The priority of right, we have seen, is in the first instance a claim about the structure of practical reason of conscientious moral agents motivated by an effective sense of justice. In drawing up their rational plans to decide their good, these moral agents are not to balance their sense of justice off against other desires and interests but are to assign it a special place in their deliberations. The objects of this desire—principles of right and justice—are assigned a supremely regulative position so that they come to regulate decisions about all other ends and pursuits that make up one's conception of the good. As such, reasonable principles of justice come to guide, complement, and comprise the good of moral persons motivated by an effective sense of justice:[48]

1. Principles of justice guide the framing of the good when they regulate the deliberations of moral persons with an effective desire to act on these principles. This means that the good of moral persons comes to be defined as the rational plan of life a person would freely choose in deliberative rationality from among the range of morally admissible conceptions of the good; those schemes of ends, pursuits, and activities that satisfy the limits of principles of justice. Any desires and interests that conflict with or undermine these principles must be abandoned, or revised and brought into accord with them. This is one way in which principles of right conduct have priority within moral persons' conceptions of the good.

2. With the principles of justice in place, Rawls defines the concept of moral worth. A good, or morally worthy, person is one who has to a high degree the qualities of moral character that it is rational for persons in a well-ordered society to want in one another. Primary among these qualities are the virtue of justice and the various political virtues that go along with it. The virtue of justice for Rawls is a firmly settled highest-order disposition to act on and from principles of justice for their own sake. People who have this virtue effectively restrict their deliberations and aims, and draw up their claims so that they respect the priority of principles of right. They want not only to be reasonable and have an admissible conception of the good for its own sake, but also to have these desires effectively regulate all their activities. Whether or not this virtue is a good thing for the person who has it (i.e., fits with his rational plan), it is a good; hence, it is rational for each person in a well-ordered society to want others to have the virtues of

---

48. The three ways develop Rawls's claim regarding the priority of right (*TJ*, 32/28 rev.): "Thus certain initial bounds are placed upon what is good and what forms of character are morally worthy and so upon what kinds of persons men should be."

justice and to be firmly disposed to honor institutional requirements. In this way, principles of right complement each person's conception of the good: that others have these virtues is among the background conditions of realizing one's own admissible conception of the good.

3. Finally, the priority of right enables Rawls to argue that justice is itself rational, a good not just for others but also for the person who has the virtue of justice: justice (being a just person, having moral worth, and promoting just institutions) is a final end that is worth pursuing for its own sake, whatever one's admissible conception of the good. Or, we might say, being effectively disposed to respect the priority of principles of right in one's deliberations, sentiments, and actions is itself an intrinsic good for moral persons. A person whose rational good incorporates the priority of right in these ways acts with "full autonomy." For that person, the right and the good are "congruent." There are several strands to Rawls's congruence argument as presented in A *Theory of Justice* (the argument from the capacity for justice and the Aristotelian principle, and the argument from social union being the most noteworthy). It would take us too far afield to discuss any of them here (for further discussion, see chap. 5), but the basic idea behind congruence is to show that it is rational to be reasonable for its own sake. Exercise and development of one's capacity for justice, having the virtues of justice, promoting just ends and institutions, and being a member of the well-ordered society of justice as fairness are all intrinsic goods; they are among the final ends affirmed in the rational plans of free and equal moral persons in a well-ordered society.[49] In this way, principles of justice come to comprise the rational good of moral persons.

Now, finally, we can bring together deontology and the priority of right. Recall Rawls's definition of a deontological theory: "One that either does not specify the good independently from the right, or does not interpret the right as maximizing the good" (*TJ*, 30/26 rev.). Rawls says justice as fairness is deontological "in the second way" (ibid.). I assume he omits the first because of the central role of the thin theory. But the thin theory is what it says it is, namely, a partial account of the human good that is part of Rawls's procedural argument to the principles of justice. It is not intended to be a complete account of our good or of the good of moral persons in a well-ordered society. Once the principles of justice are established, then, given the priority of the right, it is part of Rawls's full theory of the good that justice as fairness is deontological also in the first way. That is: (1) The good of moral persons with an effective sense of justice is the reasonable plan of life that is rational for them to choose in deliberative rationality. Here, what plans of life are reasonable (or legitimate) cannot be defined independently of Rawls's principles of justice. (2) The same is true of the moral worth of persons—justice and the political virtues, the qualities of character it is rational to want in others, cannot be defined without reference to principles of right. (3) And assuming the congruence argument can establish that it is rational to want to exercise one's own capacity for justice, to have moral

---

49. On the intrinsic good of a well-ordered political society, see *PL*, 207–8.

worth and the virtue of justice, to support just institutions, and to promote the realization of a well-ordered society, all for their own sake, then justice is an intrinsic good of moral persons, one that cannot be defined independently of these principles of right.

As part of Rawls's full theory of the good, the priority of right reveals the Kantian structure of his view. Kant refers to a "paradox of method" that follows from his "critical examination of practical reason."

> The paradox is that the concept of good and evil is not defined prior to the moral law to which, it would seem, the former would have to serve as foundation; rather the concept of good and evil must be defined after and by means of the law.[50]

This is the very passage Rawls refers to when introducing the priority of right (*TJ*, 31n/28n rev.), and it brings together the priority of right and deontology. Rawls's view is Kantian because (among other reasons) it envisions that the good of moral agents is (partially) "constructed," built up, as it were, out of principles of right in the three ways I have mentioned. This implies we cannot completely define the good (of moral persons) without referring to nonmaximizing principles of right. That is one kind of deontological view, and the priority of right enables Rawls to make sense of it. Nothing comparable to this is found in utilitarianism and perfectionism, even if they do allow in some form, as Kymlicka maintains, for equal consideration of each person's good. This is because they take the good as the independent and prior notion, and define the right as maximizing this good and therefore as subordinate to it. The priority of right reverses this order: in deciding their good moral persons subordinate their rational ends and pursuits to the requirements of deontological principles of right; their rational good then comes to be partially defined by reference to these antecedent moral principles.

VII. Conclusion

I conclude with some general remarks about teleology/deontology. What, in the end, is the point of this distinction? Three things, commonly taken to be at issue in debates over consequentialism, are not at issue.

First, the teleology/deontology distinction does not mark a contrast between moral conceptions that take consequences into account and those that do not.

---

50. Immanuel Kant, *Critique of Practical Reason*, trans. Louis White Beck (Indianapolis: Bobbs-Merrill, 1956), 65 (Ak. 5:62–63). See also Kant's claim: "Had one previously analyzed the practical law he would have found . . . not that the concept of the good as an object of the moral law determines the latter and makes it possible, but rather the reverse, i.e., that the moral law is that which first defines the concept of the good—so far as it absolutely deserves this name—and makes it possible" (66 [Ak. 5:64]).

No significant position has ever held consequences do not matter in ascertaining what is right to do. (I simply assert this here, for it would take a good deal of historical exegesis to demonstrate.)

Second (as argued in secs. II and III), teleology/deontology is not a distinction regarding the principles invoked in justifying a moral conception or substantive moral principles. It concerns rather the substantive content of moral and political principles, how they relate the concepts of the right and the good.

Third, teleology/deontology is not a distinction between views that require occupying an objective and impartial standpoint in moral judgment versus those that rely simply on a personal point of view. Kantian views, like Rawls's, require judgment from an impartial, objective perspective as much as any teleological view and distinguish different kinds of reasons (public and nonpublic) on this basis; where they differ is in their accounts of this objective perspective and the principles it is appropriate to reason from in this point of view.[51]

Now, the distinction that proponents of this third approach draw between (objective) agent-neutral versus (objective) agent-relative reasons touches on, but in the end obscures, the real issue between teleology and deontology. For, the idea of agent-neutral reasons, defined as ascertainable from an impersonal perspective, assumes from the outset the appropriateness of the idea of the one rational good in defining what we have reason to do. This just presupposes what deontologists, like Kant and Rawls, refuse to admit. This is the real issue between teleological and deontological views.

The importance of the teleology/deontology distinction, then, is that it marks a division between views that rely on some idea of a single rational good and those that do not. That idea plays a fundamental role in the formulation of moral principles and in our conception of moral and political deliberation.[52] Once specified, the one rational good enables us completely to define right and justice in maximizing terms, as those courses of conduct that ultimately are most conducive to causing this independently specifiable state of affairs to obtain. This simplifies moral and political deliberation: all conflicts between prevailing norms and disparate ends are resolvable by ascertaining which combination of ends and courses of action promote the greater overall balance of good. And this in turn provides a rational morality, one that defines for all choices a uniquely rational thing to do.

Deontologists deny that there is but one rational and ultimate good in terms of which all other values and activities are to be ordered and justified. Morality cannot, then, be reduced to an overriding duty (such as impartial benevolence) to maximize the sum total of good in the world without regard to how it gets distributed. This complicates deliberation, requiring a plurality of principles,

51. Again, I simply assert this, without detailed argument against sophisticated depictions of the issues. See Derek Parfit, *Reasons and Persons* (Oxford: Oxford University Press, 1984), 143; see also Thomas Nagel, *The View from Nowhere* (Oxford: Oxford University Press, 1986), chaps. 8 and 9.

52. I am grateful to Joshua Cohen for suggesting this particular way of emphasizing the distinction between teleology and deontology and its importance.

which must be balanced off against one another in intuition or (as in Rawls's case) assigned priority rankings over limited domains. The complete rational systematization of conduct is thereby relinquished. But systematization of conduct is not, for deontologists, such a desirable end that it warrants abandoning the plurality of intrinsic goods, political freedom, equality of basic rights and opportunities, and the autonomy of individuals.[53]

53. Compare Rawls's claim: "Although to subordinate all our aims to one end does not strictly speaking violate the principles of rational choice . . . it still strikes us as irrational, or more likely as mad. The self is disfigured and put in the service of one of its ends for the sake of system" (*TJ*, 554/486 rev.).

3

Consequentialism, Publicity, Stability, and Property-Owning Democracy

This chapter reflects further upon aspects of Rawls's intricate relationship with utilitarianism and other consequentialist positions. It is divided into three separate and self-sufficient parts. In sections I and II, I discuss further why Rawls regarded utilitarianism as such a powerful moral conception, namely, its potential for providing a completely rational morality and systematically ordering conflicting claims. To retain this desirable feature of utilitarianism and yet avoid objections of its potential for injustice, some contemporary consequentialists have proposed incorporating reasons of justice into the good consequences to be promoted by rational action. Starting from some remarks of Rawls's, I explore potential problems with these proposals, focusing on A. K. Sen's version.

In sections III and IV, I discuss Rawls's arguments from the publicity and stability conditions, which he uses quite effectively against utilitarianism. Rawls's quest for a conception of justice that is publicly knowable and generally acceptable under conditions of a feasible and enduring "well-ordered society" has been criticized for its incorporation of facts about human nature into the justification of first moral principles. I begin here a discussion of the reasons Rawls sees general facts about psychology, economics, and social and political relationships as essential to justifying principles of justice: namely, to show the compatibility of justice with human nature and therewith the human good. We have reason to question the validity of a moral conception such as utilitarianism if it demands conduct of us that is beyond our normal capacities to regularly comply with. The problem is not simply the unfairness of imposing duties that are overly demanding or run counter to human nature ("ought implies can"). In addition, for morality and justice to impose such unattainable demands suggests that they are incompatible with the human good. I contend that one of the driving ambitions in Rawls's work, early and late, is to show that morality and justice are consistent with, if not part of, the human good. (Rawls's account of the good of justice is discussed in greater detail in chap. 5 of this volume.)

The stability of a conception of justice does not by itself speak for its full publicity among members of society; as Sidgwick argued, utilitarianism provides a basis for a stable society when employed as an "esoteric morality" that is hidden from "the vulgar" and known only by an elite few.[1] Rawls's argument for the greater relative stability of justice as fairness over utilitarianism presumes that each doctrine is publicly known and part of public political awareness, providing a public basis for justification. Clearly, utilitarians and others will question the relevance of publicity, so conceived, to the justification of a conception of justice. In section IV, I discuss the reasons for Rawls's publicity requirement.

Finally, in section V, I discuss the alternative liberal societies that Rawls saw as justified by utilitarianism and by justice as fairness. Many see A *Theory of Justice*[2] as a philosophical justification of the contemporary welfare state.[3] It may come as some surprise, then, that Rawls rejects the welfare state, certainly in its current form. One reason is that he saw the welfare state as closely tied to a utilitarian framework that simultaneously supports a nearly unfettered capitalism aiming for maximization of aggregate social wealth. Rawls has been criticized (by G. A. Cohen) for justifying capitalist accumulation as compatible with and perhaps even required by the difference principle. In these criticisms, the difference principle is read as an instrument to round off capitalism's rough edges by redistributing to the poor sums sufficient to justify "buccaneer" capitalists' rapacious practices. In section V, I suggest why this is a misunderstanding of how the difference principle applies to economic institutions, beginning a discussion of Rawls's account of distributive justice which is further discussed in chapters 4, 8, and 9 of this book.

I. Rawls and Utilitarianism

Rawls had a complicated position towards utilitarianism.[4] In addition to being one of utilitarianism's most effective critics, he also provides a conception of justice designed to supplant utilitarianism's position as the primary moral conception of justice and philosophical basis for a democratic society.[5] On the other hand, Rawls regards utilitarianism as the most intellectually powerful position in the history of moral and political philosophy. He thought there was nothing that could compare with its sophistication and comprehensiveness and its systematic clarity. He regarded utilitarianism as a continuously developing three hundred–year tradition extending back to Shaftsbury and Hutcheson; developing through Hume and Adam Smith, and the classical utilitarians Bentham, Edgeworth and

---

1. Henry Sidgwick, *The Methods of Ethics*, 7th ed. (Indianapolis: Hackett, 1981), 490 (cited in text as *Methods*).

2. John Rawls, *A Theory of Justice* (Cambridge, MA: Harvard University Press, 1971; rev. ed., 1999) (cited in text as *TJ*; sometimes referred to as *Theory*).

3. For example, Michael Sandel, in *Liberalism and the Limits of Justice* (Cambridge: Cambridge University Press, 1982), 66.

4. For a thorough discussion of Rawls's attitudes toward utilitarianism, see Samuel Scheffler, "Rawls and Utilitarianism," in *The Cambridge Companion to Rawls*, ed. Samuel Freeman (Cambridge: Cambridge University Press, 2003).

5. See *TJ*, vii–viii/xvii–xviii, rev.

Sidgwick; then surviving J. S. Mill's revisionism; and finally moving into twen-tieth-century academic thought, where utilitarianism is further evolving in phi-losophy, and also welfare economics, social choice theory, cost-benefit analyses, in the law and economics movement, and in other areas.

Sidgwick's influence on Rawls was enormous. Rawls says Sidgwick's *The Methods of Ethics* is the most "philosophically profound" work by any utilitar-ian.[6] Its originality resides in Sidgwick's recognition that the justification of a moral conception must proceed holistically, namely, from "a full knowledge and systematic comparison of the more significant moral conceptions in the phil-osophical tradition" (*Methods*, vi). This provides the impetus for Rawls's own comparative assessment of conceptions of justice from the original position. Here Rawls follows Sidgwick's classification of moral theories into utilitarian-ism, intuitionism, and perfectionism; but unlike Sidgwick, Rawls regards Kant as originating a distinct kind of moral conception—moral constructivism—and he rejects Sidgwick's position that rational egoism is among the "methods of eth-ics" (*Methods*, 89–95). Further, Sidgwick's requirement that a moral conception take into account and justify the considered intuitions of common sense morality also influenced Rawls's account of justification and reflective equilibrium. More-over, like Sidgwick, Rawls puts forth certain criteria that any moral conception of justice must meet, and he then compares and assesses different conceptions by assessing how closely each realizes these prerequisites.

For Rawls, among the "formal" criteria that a conception of justice must meet is the "ordering" condition. Rawls says, "It is clearly desirable that a concep-tion of justice be complete, that is, able to order all the claims that can arise (or that are likely to in practice)" (*TJ*, 134/115 rev.). The real philosophical drawing card of utilitarianism for Rawls (as for Sidgwick) lies in its ordering capacity—its potential capacity to provide, in principle, a determinate answer to the question, What, all things considered, is the most rational thing for individuals and groups to do morally speaking? For Rawls, classical utilitarianism is unique among tradi-tional moral conceptions in providing a model for a completely rational moral-ity, capable of determining for any situation the most rational and morally best course of action. Rawls was under no illusion that his theory of justice could match the ordering capacity of utilitarianism. But he aspired to come as close to it as he could, compatible with other conditions he imposes on moral principles and our considered moral convictions in reflective equilibrium. The main objec-tion Rawls has to various forms of intuitionism is that they leave the ordering of conflicting claims to the balancing of moral considerations in intuition.

At the same time, it is utilitarianism's strongest feature—its rationaliza-tion of conduct—that proves its undoing for Rawls. For, in order to completely rationalize morality, classical utilitarianism presupposes a dominant end—"the single rational end," Rawls says (*TJ*, 556/487 rev.), or "the one rational good" (*CP*, 360)—that is to be the ultimate purpose of all human activities. "Grant-ing that rational choices [always] are possible," Rawls says, "such a [dominant] end must exist" (*TJ*, 555/486 rev.). For Sidgwick, that there be such an "ultimate

6. Rawls, foreword to *Methods*, v–vi.

good" to order rationally all conduct was a requirement of practical reason; the only reasonable end—reasonable in that it avoids obscurantism, fanaticism, and inhumanity—capable of serving as the ultimate purpose for all conduct is pleasurable experience (*Methods*, 400–407).

Taking Sidgwick's argument as the exemplar, Rawls contends that it is the ambition to completely rationalize human conduct that explains the force of hedonism throughout the history of moral philosophy. "Hedonism is," he says, "the symptomatic drift of teleological theories insofar as they try to formulate a clear and applicable method of moral reasoning" (*TJ*, 560/490 rev.).

However, Rawls contends, any dominant end conception is misguided.

> Human good is heterogeneous because the aims of the self are heterogeneous. Although to subordinate all our aims to one end does not strictly speaking violate the principles of rational choice . . . it still strikes us as irrational, or more likely as mad. The self is disfigured and put in the service of one of its ends *for the sake of system*. (*TJ*, 554/486 rev.; emphases added)

But why can't hedonism overcome the potential fanaticism and madness implicit in other teleological views, since people find their pleasures in many different kinds of ends and pursuits? Rawls recognizes that "the subjective nature of the classical utilitarianism conception of the good" seems to offer "a way of adapting the notion of the one rational good to the institutional requirements of the modern state and pluralistic democratic society."[7] But he suggests this is misleading, for hedonism still means that the sole reason for doing anything and pursuing any aim is for the sake of its pleasant aftereffects. This strikes Rawls to be as wrongheaded, if not as equally mad, as the single-minded pursuit of any other end, be it freedom, truth, power, the Vision of God, or anything else. The idea that pleasure, regarded as a measurable quality of feeling, should be the only intrinsic good and the ultimate end of all human conduct does not fit with our "considered judgments of value" (*TJ*, 432 /379 rev.)—it is incapable of explaining and justifying the many final ends that we find intrinsically good and about which we build our lives.

Here utilitarians respond that our considered judgments of value are unreliable or simply mistaken. But what argument could convince us that love and friendship, philosophical and scientific knowledge, artistic creativity and the appreciation of beautiful objects, and self-determination of one's actions and aims are not worthwhile activities for their own sake? It is at this very point that Sidgwick appeals to the "practical need" for the complete ordering and systematization of conduct as a requirement of practical reason (*Methods*, 406). As J. S. Mill puts the same point in his essay on Bentham:

> The utilitarian controversy [is] a question of arrangement and logical subordination rather than of practice; important principally in a purely scientific point of view, for the sake of systematic unity and coherency of ethical philosophy. To

---

7. Rawls, "Social Unity and Primary Goods" (1982), in *Collected Papers*, ed. Samuel Freeman (Cambridge, MA: Harvard University Press, 1999), 384 (cited in text as *CP*).

[Bentham], systematic unity was an indispensable condition of his confidence in his own intellect. . . . Whether happiness be or not be the end to which morality should be referred—that it be referred to an end of some sort and not left in the domain of value feeling or inexplicable internal conviction, that it be made a matter of reason and calculation, and not merely of sentiment, is essential to the very idea of moral philosophy.[8]

Ultimately, the argument (between Rawls and Sidgwick or other classical utilitarians) comes down to a judgment about how much significance to assign to the complete rational ordering of human conduct as compared with the importance to be assigned to other purported constraints of practical reason (such as publicity) and to our considered moral judgments and judgments of value. Clearly, Rawls assigns greater significance than Sidgwick both to considered moral judgments and considered judgments of value. He accepts with Sidgwick that to be a rational agent involves rational pursuit of one's good, and that a person's good is to be identified with the plan of life that is rational for an agent to desire under ideal conditions. (This is implicit in Rawls's account of deliberative rationality [*TJ*, 416/366 rev.], which he says follows Sidgwick's account of a person's good [*Methods*, 111–12].) But Rawls assigns little if any weight to Sidgwick's self-evident "philosophical intuition," the "axiom of Rational Benevolence," which says that practical reason requires us to maximize a single rational good, the good of all individuals impartially construed (*Methods*, 387, 382). This fundamental principle underlying Sidgwick's utilitarianism conflicts too often with our considered moral judgments; it also, Rawls contends, conflicts with the heterogeneity of value and plurality of goods we affirm in our considered judgments of value. The systematic ordering of moral judgments is but one desideratum of practical reason, and it should not take priority over all others as well as our considered moral and evaluative convictions. Given the force of these considered convictions plus other desiderata (among these, publicity and stability of a moral conception), practical reason can achieve at most a partial ordering and systematization of moral judgments and judgments of value.[9]

There are ways to define "utility" other than hedonistically which are advocated by contemporary utilitarians. The satisfaction of people's preferences, or, alternatively, their rational preferences, are preferred understandings of utility among many contemporary utilitarians. Rawls argues, in "Social Unity and Pri-

8. Mill, "Bentham," in *Essays on Politics and Culture*, ed. Gertrude Himmelfarb (Garden City, NY: Doubleday, 1963), 114–15.

9. Here it is to be noted that Rawls did not think that classical utilitarianism could provide a full systematization of moral judgments and conduct. In his lecture notes on Sidgwick, Rawls discusses why classical utilitarianism is not an appropriate principle for determining population policies, but must be supplemented by some other principle. The idea that we should continue increasing population (whether human beings or other species) to the limit, until aggregate pleasure in the world is maximized, strikes Rawls not just as irrational but genuinely mad. He conjectures that this explains why many utilitarians have been attracted to average utility, which Rawls sees as a different sort of view from classical utilitarianism, since it no longer involves maximizing aggregate good. See Rawls, *Lectures on the History of Political Philosophy*, ed. Samuel Freeman (Cambridge, MA: Harvard University Press, forthcoming 2007), lecture 3 on Sidgwick.

mary Goods" (responding to Kenneth Arrow and S. C. Kolm), that even these conceptions must in the end rely on pleasure as a dominant end for the sake of which individuals must be willing to revise their preferences, if utilitarianism is to provide a first-person decision procedure that can systematically order all human conduct.[10] Most contemporary moral philosophers would accept that utility, however construed, is not an adequate account of intrinsic value, since it does not satisfactorily account for the plurality of human goods. They reject a dominant end teleological moral conception—the idea that there is one ultimate good that ought to be maximized in all that we do—as the appropriate framework for a moral conception. But many moral philosophers—perhaps a majority—still want to hang on to the remnants of a dominant end teleological conception, particularly the idea that all that matters in deciding what is right to do are the consequences of our actions, and that right actions are those that effectively produce the best consequences overall. In the next section, I discuss Rawls's attitudes towards some non-utilitarian consequentialist conceptions.

II. Plural and Mixed Consequentialist Conceptions

One way to avoid some of the unacceptable consequences of classical utilitarianism regarding the ends that morality promotes is to retain the consequentialist principle for its systematizing potential but incorporate a plurality of goods into the consequences to be optimally promoted. Some of these plural goods may be subjective (such as pleasurable experience or satisfaction of preferences), while others are objective, for example, knowledge and other excellences, creation and contemplation of beauty, love and friendship, and so on. G. E. Moore's "ideal utilitarianism" is such a pluralist doctrine. Rawls regards such views as teleological forms of intuitionism, since they require the intuitive balancing of intrinsic goods in deciding what is right and just to do (*TJ*, 40/35 rev.). While such plural consequentialist accounts fit better with our considered convictions of value, they often are still subject to the objections of justice that are leveled at utilitarianism. (For example, it is easier to rationalize inequality and oppression of an uncultured few, or even an uncultured majority, on a teleological perfectionist view than under classical utilitarianism.) One way that plural consequentialists have sought to address these objections is to incorporate values of justice into the good consequences to be promoted. This goes beyond "two-tiered" positions, which

10. See Rawls, "Social Unity and Primary Goods," in *CP*, 374–85, where Rawls says Kolm's idea of a "fundamental preference" presupposes "bare persons" with no character or attachment to their ends, who are driven solely to maximize agreeable feelings (382–83). Rawls contrasts the utilitarian conception of bare persons with the account of free and equal persons with determinate but incommensurable goods that is presupposed by justice as fairness. Here it is ironical how much Rawls's criticism of Kolm's co-ordinal utilitarianism resembles Michael Sandel's criticism of Rawls's conception of the person as "shorn of all its contingently given attributes" and detached from all particular ends and commitments, a claim which Rawls says is a mistaken conflation of his account of persons with the parties in the original position. See Sandel, *Liberalism and the Limits of Justice*, 93–95, esp. 94; see also Rawls, *CP*, 403n.

regard principles of justice as second-order rules instrumental to achieving such goods as freedom, equality, autonomy, and so on.[11] Instead, certain principles of justice, such as equal rights and fair procedures, are directly incorporated into the ultimately good consequences that are to be maximized or otherwise promoted by individual or institutional conduct.

A. K. Sen has recently proposed a sophisticated version of this sort of view. He says: "Consequential evaluation that takes note of freedoms, rights, and obligations—and their violations—would argue that bad things have happened *precisely because* someone's freedom has been breached, and some rights and duties have been violated."[12] And: "The fulfillment of rights is a good thing to happen—the more the better—as it would be seen in a consequential perspective" (CE, 498). Sen goes on to suggest as part of consequential evaluation a "consequentialism of rights," which says that (1) "the badness of the violation of rights, or the goodness of their fulfillment" are to be "included among the consequences"; (2) there can be "'trade-offs' between rights"; and (3) there can be "'trade-offs' between the goodness of rights fulfillment and other good consequences" (CE, 499, 499n).

It is not altogether clear how Rawls would regard these mixed consequentialist positions, as I will call them—"mixed" because they include both natural states of affairs and moral principles among the good consequences to be maximized, optimized, or otherwise promoted. I suspect he would construe them as some version of deontological intuitionism. Consider first the ultimate good of equality of (desirable) goods: Rawls says that distribution is normally considered under principles of right; as such, questions of equality of distributions would involve non-teleological principles. But if the goods that are to be promoted and equalized on a pluralist consequentialist position are naturally definable, in terms used within the natural or social sciences (equal happiness or welfare, or some account of equal capabilities for action, for example), then it is not so clear why Rawls need think that equal distribution of some natural good cannot be part of a teleological end-state that is to be maximized.[13] In such a position we would no longer be maximizing simply an aggregate of goods; we would also have to make sense of maximizing an aggregate's distribution. But such judgments often can be made; we often can know when one state of affairs is "more equal" than another, even if it is more difficult to assign relative importance to equality as compared with other goods under the circumstances.[14] Deciding how

11. In an article predating his contractualism, T. M. Scanlon outlined a "two-tiered" consequentialist approach that regards rights and other norms of justice as second-tier principles that promote such final ends as freedom, equal distributions of certain goods, and individuals' ability to control significant aspects of their lives. See Scanlon's collection of papers in *The Difficulty of Tolerance* (Cambridge: Cambridge University Press, 2003).

12. A. K. Sen, "Consequential Evaluation and Practical Reason," *Journal of Philosophy* 97 (September 2000): 477–502, at 494 (emphasis added) (cited in text as CE).

13. This seems to be Larry Temkin's position. See, for example, Temkin, *Inequality* (New York: Oxford University Press, 1993).

14. Is $100,000 more equally divided when (a) 90 of us have $1111 and 10 have nothing than when (b) 50 of us have $440 and 50 have $1560? The 10 with nothing in "a" have only $1111 less

much weight to assign to equal distributions is a different issue. Sidgwick claimed that when there is a tie between optimal states of affairs, the principle of equity requires choosing the state with the more equal distribution of utility (*Methods*, 416–17). But this is compatible with classical utilitarianism (since equality is not part of the maximand). By contrast, a pluralist position assigns more weight to equality and includes equality in the maximand. Then the problem is to construct an index assigning an appropriate weight to equal distribution, compared with other intrinsic goods.

But even if equal distributions of natural states can be incorporated into a consequentialist position, the incorporation of fair procedures, human rights, equal rights, or moral duties renders a position not just a form of intuitionism but also non-teleological on Rawls's account. Such mixed consequentialist conceptions contain within the ultimate good to be promoted principles of right and justice that specify fair procedures, or equal distributions of rights, or fulfillment of individuals' duties. As part of the ultimate good, fair procedures, respect for rights, and fulfillment of duties are regarded not simply as instrumental to some other good; they and the principles of right they incorporate are regarded as good for their own sake.

A potential problem with mixed consequentialism, so conceived, is that it can no longer maintain that maximizing the good, or promoting the best consequences, is the *sole* ultimate principle of right. For, there are already non-consequentialist moral principles that are partially constitutive of the ultimate good, which must be balanced off against other ultimate goods and the measures that instrumentally promote them. What are we to do when required to instrumentally promote fair procedures or respect for rights themselves? What if doing so requires that we violate these same rights and procedures (e.g., violate the rights of a few to protect similar rights enjoyed by the many). Which principle, then, has priority? If the moral principles that are part of the maximand are to be given any weight at all, then it appears that we have in effect two (or more) separate moral principles—one that tells us to maximize aggregate goodness and another that tells us to follow fair procedures, respect individual rights, or achieve a fair distribution for its own sake. These separate principles must somehow be weighed off against one another to decide what is right to do. If this is done intuitively, without priority rules and in response to particular circumstances, then mixed consequentialism is really a deontological form of moral intuitionism (in Rawls's sense).

My own view (Rawls's too, I believe) is that we might as well give up any pretense of maximizing the good or promoting the best consequences in mixed consequentialism and face the fact that once principles of right (such as fair pro-

than the rest, while those in "b" with $440 have $1120 less. So, in a sense, there is greater inequality in "b." But are our concerns for equality really reflected in an administrative decision that favors the first alternative "a" requiring less absolute inequality but complete destitution for a minority? My own view is that nothing speaks in favor of preferring "a" over "b," even in a position, like Temkin's, which says that equality of distribution is but one good to weigh in the balance against other goods. This sort of example raises questions about the wisdom of the idea that equal distributions are goods that ought to be maximized for their own sake. See Temkin, *Inequality.*

cedures, or equal rights, respect for human rights, or fulfillment of duties) are themselves regarded as ultimate intrinsic goods, we have a full-fledged intuitionist position requiring the balancing of both teleological with deontological principles. It is only in an attenuated sense that such a mixed pluralist position can be said to aim to maximize or promote the best consequences overall. It can be said of most any moral conception that it promotes the best consequences in an attenuated sense of requiring that people do the best thing overall. For example, W. D. Ross's intuitionism might be said to promote the best consequences. Ross requires balancing a prima facie teleological principle of benevolence along with prima facie deontological principles of justice, fidelity, gratitude, and so on, to come up with a judgment "all things considered."[15] It does not seem that Ross's position differs in any significant way from mixed consequentialist positions (other than perhaps incorporating more deontological principles than normal). But Ross's intuitionism is one standard example of a deontological moral conception.

Here it is important to see that in his account of consequentialist evaluation, Sen's use of "maximize"—which he says is drawn from set theory and contemporary axiomatic economic analysis (CE, 484)—is not the same sense used by classical utilitarians or by Rawls in his account of teleological conceptions. Sen's maximizing framework seems to involve ordinal rankings of states of affairs, and moreover "does not demand completeness of ranking" (CE, 483). Among the considerations Sen would have us take into account in ranking states of affairs as better or worse are the degree to which individuals' rights are respected and their duties fulfilled, and, more generally, the extent to which justice is done. Now, to choose the highest ranked option from among an ordinal ranking of states of affairs, some of which may be incommensurable, is quite different from maximizing aggregate goodness, conceived as a measurable state of affairs. There are, of course, different ways to "maximize" outcomes in the sense of achieving ordinal rankings of them. There are also different ways to represent people's valuations by choice functions of the kind Sen envisions.

In his lectures on Sidgwick, Rawls laments the fact that the terms "maximize" and "utility" have been taken over by decision theory and economic analysis from classical utilitarianism, and used in an entirely different way. Rather than "utility function" or "welfare function," he says that economic analysis and rational choice theory should use such terms as "multiple-objective function," which indicates the manner in which peoples' preferences over states of affairs incorporate multiple aims. Rawls says:

> Anyone's moral or political judgments can . . . be represented by some mathematical function. In terms of this function, one can say: they judge as if they think that in each case society should maximize this function, promote the *best consequences* (as defined by this function). . . . [But] mathematically speaking, the representation-function may be such that there is no natural sense in which it describes the agent as *maximizing anything*. E.g., there may be multiple objectives; or lexical orderings (no continuous representative function). . . . This way

15. W. D. Ross, *The Right and the Good* (Oxford: Clarendon Press, 1939), pp. 18–33, 41–42.

of speaking [maximizing something] implies *no specific* political conception. The question then is: what is the *shape*, or what are the *special features* of this function; and what conceptions and principles stand behind it in the thought and judgments of agents (individuals and society)?[16] (italics in original)

Rawls's suggestion here is that no specific political conception, consequentialist or deontological, is implied by maximizing a "multiple-objective" function. It depends upon what the aims or objectives are that are being pursued or "maximized." A deeper implication, I believe, is that once we uncover these aims and objectives, including the reasons and moral principles underlying judgments of good consequences and rankings of states of affairs in mixed consequential conceptions, we should see that we no longer have a view which says that maximizing good states of affairs is the sole ultimate moral principle. For, if we assign any independent weight at all to the moral considerations of justice, respect for rights, etc., that are to be maximized, then it follows that there are moral reasons that constrain the maximization of total goodness. And if we do not assign them any independent weight, then it seems they serve no real purpose in the maximand, but only obscure the good consequences that really inform our judgments about what is the best thing to do.

It is for these reasons perhaps that Rawls never used the term "consequentialism" as referring to a distinct kind of moral conception: he did not see consequentialists' use of the idea of promoting or maximizing the best consequences overall as sufficiently well-defined to serve as the foundation for a distinct family of moral conceptions. Instead, Rawls distinguished deontological conceptions from teleological conceptions. What is really distinctive about classical utilitarianism and other teleological conceptions (such as teleological perfectionism) is that they require us (a) to maximize the sum total of ultimate good and (b) to define the good *without* reference to any moral concepts or principles and in natural terms, or in terms otherwise appropriate in the natural and social sciences. Rawls seems to have thought (along with Sidgwick) that only if the good is defined in this manner can we make sense of the idea of the complete systematization of conduct according to principles of rational choice.

> I have all along assumed that the proposed dominant end belongs to a teleological theory in which by definition the good is specified independently from the right. The role of this end is in part to make the conception of right reasonably precise. (*TJ*, 565/495 rev.)

The implication is that, once we give up the non-moral specification of the good that is to be maximized, as do the consequentialisms suggested by Sen and others, then it appears that the major benefit of a teleological position—"to make the conception of the right reasonably precise" (*TJ*, 565/495 rev.)—has been abandoned. We are then left with the task of trying to make sense of the idea of

---

16. Rawls, *Lectures on the History of Political Philosophy*, from Sidgwick lecture 3, final sec. Compare *TJ*, 558/489 rev., where Rawls voices similar thoughts.

maximizing both an aggregate and a distribution of an assortment of goods, some of which are morally defined as the fulfillment of rights and duties and whose weights are not fixed once and for all, but which must be decided as circumstances permit by appeals to intuition. At this point, it is no longer clear what the real points of dispute are with traditional intuitionist forms of non-consequentialist conceptions (such as Ross's intuitionism) that also provide a mix of consequentialist and deontological principles.

Moreover, there is a serious question whether it is coherent to include rights, fairness, duties, and other moral concepts in the maximand of a consequentialist conception. For, if we understand consequentialism as a distinct kind of moral conception which says that the ultimate principle of right and justice is to maximize good consequences, then it would seem that there is no conceptual space left for the claim that we ought independently to respect others' rights, or that states of affairs where rights and fair procedures are respected and duties are fulfilled ought to be promoted for their own sake. Insofar as requirements of right and justice *are* incorporated into the ultimate good to be promoted and are given any weight independent of their consequences at all, it is no longer the case that the *sole* ultimate principle of right action is that we maximize the good. For, among the good consequences to be maximized are people acting according to these antecedent non-maximizing moral principles (of fairness, or respect for others' rights, and so on). If we inquire why people ought to conform to these principles, their justification for their doing so cannot be *simply* that compliance with these principles (respect for rights, fairness, etc.) promotes good consequences, for then the argument becomes circular. ("We should respect others' rights in order to maximize good consequences, which include respecting others' rights.") To avoid this circle, the mixed consequentialist would seem to have to concede that respecting these principles of right is good for its own sake ("precisely because," as Sen says, rights and duties are to be respected [CE, 494]). In this case, the ultimate good itself cannot be described in the absence of an antecedent non-maximizing principle of right; principles of right are part of its very definition. But then it seems no longer the case that maximizing the good is the sole ultimate principle of right, and thus we do not have a consequentialist view.

Moreover, if we assume these antecedent principles of right can ever provide sufficient reasons to act independently of their consequences, and we act on them at all for their own sake, then we are no longer acting in order to maximize good consequences—as such, we no longer satisfy the consequentialist requirement that we *always* act so as to maximize good consequences. Rather, these non-consequentialist principles (respect for others' rights for example) are sufficient justification and we act upon these principles for their own sake—not for the sake of further good consequences they promote. To say that we then maximize the good by acting on these very non-maximizing principles of right is empty.

Here proponents of the mixed consequentialist approach might distinguish two different notions of rightness: (a) there is, first, the conception of rightness as a substantive moral value, roughly equivalent with justice, and cashed out in terms of notions of individual rights, fair distributions, and so on; then (b) there is, second, the general notion of rightness at work when we speak of something as being the "right thing to do," in the sense of the action that is required by practical reason and the balance of reasons. It might then be open to the consequentialist to try to avoid the problem by saying that it is the "a"-type value, respect for rights and requirements of justice, that is included in the maximand, while claiming that the consequentialist principle of maximizing the good is the "ultimate principle of right" in the sense given by "b," namely, the ultimate principle of practical reason. If we accept a distinction between different notions of right along the lines just sketched, then there would seem to be room to say that acting for the sake of substantive values such as justice and human rights might sometimes also be acting in order to maximize good consequences, namely, when those substantive values weigh heavily enough to make acting so as to respect them the best outcome overall.[17]

It may be that this is what Sen has in mind in suggesting a "consequentialism of rights." But I am not sure that distinguishing two senses of "principles of right" would help much in resolving the problem I've raised. For, clearly, the individual rights and considerations of justice that are covered by "a" must themselves imply certain correlative duties on the part of individuals and social and political institutions, and these duties *already* provide instructions as to the right thing to do. Once these rights and duties of justice are incorporated into the maximand, then it should follow that an intrinsic good to be promoted by our action is that we respect others' rights and comply with duties of justice in the sense of "a." But this suggests that at least sometimes *the right thing for people to do*, in the sense of "b," is to respect individuals' rights and comply with other duties and requirements of justice, all for their own sake. But this is a different and potentially conflicting ultimate principle of right from the "b"-principle of right that people should always act to maximize good consequences.

Another way to pose this problem: let's assume that it is intrinsically valuable that rights are respected, material resources are fairly distributed, and other values of justice are enforced. Outcomes of actions are better when these conditions are realized, independently of any further consequences. Now assume that this is the sole valuable state of affairs—that justice be done according to these principles. (Admittedly this may be a peculiar position, but still it makes enough sense for our purposes.) Given that justice or people complying with justice is the sole intrinsic good, the clear implication is that people at least sometimes, if not always, have a moral duty to respect others' rights, fairly distribute resources, and so on. Doing justice is then the *right thing to do*, and since justice is an intrinsic good, it must be *ultimately* the right thing to do. Now a consequentialist comes along and says that, if doing justice is the sole intrinsic good, then we ought *always* to promote or maximize as a good outcome justice and states of affairs where people respect others' rights, and so on. Moreover, promoting or maximizing this state of affairs is *ultimately* the right thing to do. Given the nature of the consequentialist principle and its role within a consequentialist conception—which says we ought always to maximize good states of affairs—it seems

---

17. I am indebted to Jay Wallace for this suggestion as to how a consequentialist might reply to my objection.

that we now have a contradiction. The contradiction stems from the role of the consequentialist principle within a consequentialist conception—"the injunction to [maximize the good] always applies." (*TJ*, 566/495 rev.) Granted, if the consequentialist principle were a prima facie duty to promote just outcomes, then (as with Ross's consequentialist principle of beneficence) it would not contradict the claim that respecting others' rights and the requirements of justice for their own sake is also an ultimate principle of right. In that case, we would have two principles of right to weigh off against one another to decide what is right to do all things considered. But that is not how consequentialists conceive of the consequentialist principle: it is the *sole* ultimate principle of right. If we give up that claim, then we no longer have a consequentialist moral conception.

Now what makes mixed consequentialist positions like Sen's appear feasible, I believe, is that they are also pluralist: they (sensibly) recognize that there are a plurality of intrinsic goods that ought to be promoted, justice being but one among these. This means that sometimes we may have to compromise principles of justice to achieve other still-greater goods, to achieve the greater good of justice itself, or to prevent a horrendous state of affairs (nuclear holocaust, for example). So considerations of justice can only be a part of the ultimate good that is to be maximized or optimized. It is only one among the multiple objectives that are to figure into the "multiple-objective function" (Rawls) that is to be maximized or optimized. This position sounds sensible, but the problem is that the view still contains the hidden contradiction mentioned above, namely, part of the overall good that is to be maximized according to the ultimate consequentialist principle of right still contains competing ultimate non-consequentialist principles of right and justice. These ultimate non-consequentialist principles (e.g., afford equal liberties for all and distribute resources fairly) demand that we do justice for its own sake, even if it results in less goodness in the aggregate. To make sense of this plurality of ultimate principles of right, one might do what Ross does and say that the conflicting principles impose prima facie duties that are to be weighed off against one another under the circumstances to decide what is right to do all things considered. It is something like this non-consequentialist position, I believe, that mixed consequentialists must sign on to if they claim that doing justice for its own sake is intrinsically good. But if they want to maintain the integrity of a consequentialist position, with its claim that the sole ultimate principle of right is to maximize good consequences, then it would seem that they have to get rid of the claim we started with, namely, that respecting rights and distributing resources fairly are themselves intrinsically valuable and impose ultimate principles of right.

Finally, Rawls says, "All ethical doctrines worth our attention take consequences into account in judging rightness. One that did not would simply be irrational, crazy" (*TJ*, 30/26 rev.). This suggests that simply because a moral conception provides a place for consequentialist, namely, means-end, reasoning does not make it a consequentialist conception. For Rawls, a deontological conception can contain means-end reasoning and even *consequentialist (or maximizing) principles* so long as they are not given ultimate priority over all other principles. As suggested by my comments above, a distinction needs to be drawn between *consequentialist moral conceptions* on the one hand and moral conceptions that incorporate *consequentialist principles and consequentialist reasoning* on the other. For example, Rawls's difference principle is a rule-consequentialist principle of sorts that is part of a deontological moral conception, as is W. D. Ross's prima facie principle of beneficence. But the difference principle is limited in its domain to the distribution of certain primary goods, and its application is constrained by the priority of deontological principles insuring equal basic liberties, fair equal opportunities, duties of assistance to burdened peoples, and the duty to future generations. Another example is Rawls's duty of justice, which, in addition to a perfect duty to comply with the constraints of justice, imposes an imperfect duty to bring about just institutions where they do not exist. We satisfy this imperfect duty by taking measures that effectively promote just institutions and states of affairs—by rationally promoting the Reasonable (to use Rawls's terms). If the rational pursuit of justice were not itself regulated by constraints of justice and other reasonable principles, then the imperfect duty of justice would allow violating some people's rights for the sake of promoting rights of the same or greater importance for more people. In that case, the rational pursuit of justice would trump reasonable constraints of justice themselves, so long as "greater justice" (or perhaps some other greater good) is sufficiently realized in the aggregate. This is an option which Sen's mixed consequentialism seems to contemplate (CE, 499n.), but which Rawls rules out in his deontological view.

A consequence of my earlier claim regarding the circularity implicit in maximizing a good that incorporates moral principles is that not all consequentialist principles can sensibly serve as *fundamental principles* in a consequentialist moral conception. The duty to promote justice is a primary example, as is any other consequentialist principle that contains moral concepts or principles that are to be promoted (e.g., Sen's "consequentialism of rights" or Nozick's suggestion of a "rights utilitarianism"). This means that there is an asymmetry between consequentialism and deontology: while *deontological conceptions* can accommodate consequentialist principles (like the imperfect duty to further just institutions, or the duty of beneficence, or the difference principle) by priority rules or as prima facie duties, *consequentialist moral conceptions* cannot sensibly incorporate deontological principles. If consequentialism is to retain its claim that we are always duty bound to maximize or promote the good, it may not incorporate deontological principles either as an element of the good consequences to be promoted or as moral principles subject to priority rules and subordinated to the consequentialist duty to maximize the good. This asymmetry is due to the fact that consequentialist conceptions, even though they may incorporate a *plurality of ultimate goods*, can endorse but *one ultimate principle of right*, the requirement that good consequences be maximized. Given the priority assigned to this maximizing principle, there is no conceptual space left remaining for competing principles of right to weigh off against the maximization of good states of affairs. This, I believe, is the real reason Rawls insisted that teleological conceptions must specify the good to be maximized independent of moral concepts or principles and purely in naturalistic terms (broadly conceived).

This does not mean that mixed consequentialist positions like Sen's are incoherent. It suggests, rather, that they are not what they pretend to be. I have suggested that we can make perfectly good sense of what is going on in mixed consequentialism within a traditional intuitionist framework where consequential principles are weighed off against deontological principles as well as each other. Depending on the weights assigned to principles, sometimes individual rights may be traded off in order to promote greater rights-fulfillment in the aggregate, sometimes they may be traded off to promote other goods, and sometimes individual rights should be enforced simply for their own sake (as Sen suggests [CE, 499n]). But in striking a balance among these consequential and deontological principles, nothing is being maximized in any significant sense, certainly not in the sense of maximizing the "one rational good" that has driven teleological conceptions from Plato's perfectionism to the utilitarianism of the modern day.[18] The fact that we can describe what is going on by a mathematical function does not alter this fact, even if it might create an illusion to the contrary.

This is not simply an empty exercise in moral typology. The question is one of the structure of practical reasoning and the sorts of considerations that provide the final reasons in deciding what we ought to do. For Rawls, moral reasons of justice are the final arbiter in practical reasoning. Reasons of justice ultimately concern questions of rights and their fair distribution, and it is a mistake to think that these reasons can be explicated in terms of maximizing good states of affairs. Rawls says, "The structure of teleological doctrines is radically misconceived; from the start they relate the right and the good in the wrong way" (TJ, 560/490 rev.). I have contended that, if teleology is misconceived, there is something doubly misconceived about mixed consequentialism's efforts to characterize morality and justice in terms of maximizing the good of fulfillment of rights and duties. It may be an attractive idea, but it is of little genuine consequence for a consequentialism worth taking seriously.

To conclude this discussion, what moves many to consequentialism are "Pedro and the Indians" type problems of the kind Bernard Williams discusses.[19] The thought here is, "Surely we should shoot one innocent person to prevent nineteen people from being murdered, particularly when our intended victim will be killed by someone else anyway." It may well be that we *should* shoot him, but, if so, we do not need consequentialism to explain why we have that permission or even duty. Within Rawls's own framework of rational agreement behind a veil of ignorance, it would be rational for interested persons to agree to a range of circumstances that allow for, or even require, exemptions from perfect duties of justice to respect others' rights and claims, and to circumscribed rules that impose instead an exceptional permission or even imperfect duty to take measures that impinge upon one person's, or even a minority's, rights, in order to minimize equally serious violations to a far greater number. An example of this is to be found in Rawls's discussion of the supreme emergency exemption to the natural duty of justice not to kill civilians when waging war in a just cause.[20] This is a complicated and difficult topic; as Rawls says, "We must proceed here with

18. On the doctrine of the one rational good, see "Social Unity and Primary Goods," in CP.

19. Bernard Williams, *Utilitarianism: For and Against* (New York: Cambridge University Press, 1973), pp. 98–104.

20. Rawls, *The Law of Peoples* (Cambridge, MA: Harvard University Press, 1999) (cited in text as LP).

caution" (*LP*, 98). But in dealing with these kinds of "save the greater numbers" cases, we are not consigned to the consequentialist prescription that we maximize good consequences, which seemingly requires that we regularly violate the rights or integrity of some in order to achieve marginal improvements in the status of others.

III. Publicity, Stability, and the Principles of Justice

The Publicity Condition

One of the more controversial features of Rawls's account of justice, early and late, is his reliance upon the conditions of publicity and stability as criteria for justifying a moral conception of justice. Both criteria are implicit in the idea of a well-ordered society. One of the formal constraints on the parties' choice in the original position is that a conception of justice be publicly available and recognized by those subject to its requirements in a well-ordered society.[21] An important implication of the publicity condition is that principles of justice must be capable of being used in practical deliberation and public argument in a feasible social world that meets the requirements of a well-ordered society. A well-ordered society must then be achievable and "stable" (Rawls later adds, "Stable for the right reasons" [*PL*, xlii]): its principles of justice must describe a feasible social world in which everyone accepts and wants to comply with these principles of justice, and this society must instill in people a willingness to sustain its just institutions that enable them to endure from one generation to the next. In effect, stability requires that principles of justice be compatible with human nature, in the sense that institutions satisfying these principles engender in people subject to them a sense of justice, or a willingness and disposition to act on and from these principles and maintain the institutions they support.

Rawls says at one point that the stability condition is invoked to "confirm" the conception of justice chosen in the original position; but, in fact, stability serves more as a condition upon the parties' choice. For, the three arguments for the principles of justice that are in addition to the argument from the maximin criterion all appear to rely upon the stability requirement. These are the arguments from the strains of commitment, from publicity, and from the conditions of self-respect (see *TJ*, sec. 29). The strains of commitment require that the parties make an agreement in "good faith" and choose only principles of justice they are confident they can endorse and comply with, no matter what position they end up in within society. If the parties believe that they will not be able to respect just laws because such laws are too demanding should the parties end up in an unfavorable position, then they are not to choose those principles. The publicity

21. The other formal constraints of right are that principles be general in form, apply universally, provide an ordering of claims, and provide finality of reasons (*TJ*, sec. 23). On the ordering condition, see sec. 1 of this chapter. Rawls defines a well-ordered society as one whose regulative principles of justice are generally accepted by reasonable persons, are publicly known to be generally accepted, and are effectively embedded in institutions.

argument directs that principles chosen be stable under conditions where they are publicly known and recognized as the basis of social cooperation. Publicity assumes that principles of justice will provide a shared public basis for political discussion, criticism, and justification. Principles that cannot gain knowing, widespread support from reasonable and rational members of a well-ordered society are to be passed over in favor of those that do. Finally, the argument from self-respect enjoins that the parties choose principles they believe will affirm, or at least not undermine, their sense of self-respect as citizens; this condition, in turn, depends upon principles affirming citizens' conception of themselves as free and as deserving equal respect as citizens.

On all three counts, Rawls contends, the principles of justice would be preferred to both the classical and average principles of utility (and also, he later contends, to teleological principles of perfection).[22] Rawls maintains: (1) Because of its potential hardships, the principle of utility imposes greater strains of commitment than many willingly would bear in society, especially the least advantaged. Knowing that they might end up in a less-advantaged position, the parties in the original position cannot agree to the principle of utility in good faith, since they would be making an agreement they cannot comply with. (2) Since it requires that the less advantaged bear the adverse costs of greater benefits to those better off, the principle of utility could not serve as a public basis for justification among people who regard themselves as equals; hence the principle of utility would not engender the stability of well-ordered society. (3) The principle of utility is more likely to undermine the sense of self-respect and self-worth of the least advantaged, since in a utilitarian society they may be forced to accept inequalities of status and basic liberties, may face lesser prospects, and may be required to sacrifice their good for the sake of those better situated.

These arguments rely upon a number of empirical assumptions about human nature and social cooperation that Rawls sets out and defends in parts II and III of A *Theory of Justice*. Especially important here is the carefully elaborated moral

---

22. A guiding idea in each of these three arguments is already set forth in the second and third steps of Rawls's argument in *TJ*, sec. 26, from the maximin criterion. There, Rawls contends that the principle of utility potentially imposes such intolerable hardships upon some members of society — particularly those who are least advantaged — that it would be irrational to accept it if there were a better alternative. Rawls contends that it would be irrational to jeopardize the benefits guaranteed by the principles of justice, especially the basic liberties, for the sake of additional but unpredictable social and economic advantages that might be gained by choosing the principle of utility. See also Rawls, *Justice as Fairness: A Restatement*, ed. Erin Kelly (Cambridge, MA: Belknap Press, 2001) (cited in text as *Restatement*). In *Restatement*, Rawls says that the maximin argument largely depends on these two features, and relies less if at all upon the controversial claim that, because the parties in the original position have no basis upon which to form probability assessments, it would be irrational to apply the principle of insufficient reason and assume an equiprobability of being any member in society. "The first condition has a relatively minor role. As we shall see, what is crucial is that the second and third conditions should obtain to a high degree" (99). I conjecture that the reason Rawls later minimizes the role of the claim that "the concept of probability does not even apply" (98) in the original position is connected with his political liberalism. He wants to avoid a philosophical controversy on the wisdom of Bayesianism under conditions of complete uncertainty since this kind of dispute is not resolvable on the basis of public reason.

psychology in chapter 8 of *TJ*, the account of a person's good set forth in chapter 7, and the account of feasible social institutions set forth in part II of *TJ*. I want to focus here on the argument from publicity to highlight the ways the ideas of publicity and the stability of a well-ordered society are central to Rawls's argument against utilitarianism and to his entire view.

Consider the reply to Rawls's argument from publicity, that public knowledge of the principle of utility would not be a problem in a society of sincere and conscientious utilitarians. For, if they accept that maximum aggregate utility is the ultimate good and that they ought always to promote it, then public knowledge that the principle of utility provides the basis for their social relations should pose no real problem (barring perhaps certain coordination problems). If not, then it is not clear why a utilitarian well-ordered society should not instill in its members a desire to maintain utilitarian institutions and thus be stable "for the right reasons."

To reply to this: the argument from publicity cannot be the trivial claim that the principle of utility is publicly acceptable to conscientious moral agents, all of whom already accept overall utility as the ultimate good to be maximized in all that they do and are capable of abiding by its demands. That argument would be of little probative value. The publicity argument rather addresses the question: What principles of justice are publicly acceptable to (reasonable and rational) people who regard themselves as free and equal, given the inevitable fact that they will pursue, and think themselves justified in so doing, a plurality of ends and commitments that potentially conflict with others' ends and pursuits? The inevitability of a plurality of pursuits among people who are free and equal is among the facts Rawls appeals to. Here the utilitarian might respond: "Assuming the inevitability of plural pursuits due to the subjective circumstances of justice, still, insofar as people regard their particular aims as having priority over aggregate utility, they act upon false evaluative beliefs. And why should people's false beliefs be taken into account and serve as a test for assessing principles of justice? It is better to dispense with the publicity condition altogether in assessing principles of justice."

Here, then, to see what is at issue with the publicity condition, we need to consider why Rawls thinks the public knowledge of principles of justice is morally important. Rawls says that the publicity condition "arises naturally from a contractarian standpoint," and that it is also "implicit in Kant's doctrine" (*TJ*, 133/115 rev.). In general, Rawls appeals to two kinds of considerations in justifying the publicity condition. First, stemming from his contractarianism, he appeals to ideas about what is reasonable in light of our status as free and equal persons; second, from within the Kantian interpretation, he justifies publicity as a condition of realizing the ideal of free and equal moral persons and their achieving the good of autonomy in various forms. I start with the former.

Publicity, Reasonableness, and Mutual Respect: "The contract conception introduces the publicity conditions. . . . one of the most characteristic aspects of contract theory" (CP, 249). The thought here seems to be that to conceive of principles of justice as the product of an agreement implies that they are publicly known and accepted by members of society. Why regard principles of justice as the product of an agreement? Rawls says that justice as fairness provides a "rendering" of the ideas of respect for persons, human dignity, and the inherent worth of persons, "the value of persons that Kant says is beyond all price" (*TJ*, 586/513 rev.). Among the conditions of mutual respect is that people be able to justify their conduct, their claims, and their relative social positions to one another, on conditions that all can (in some relevant capacity) accept. "Among other things, respect for persons is shown by treating them in ways that they can see to be justified" (ibid.). The publicity of moral principles, and the moral conception of which they are part, is necessary if these justifications are to be completely carried through "to the limit, so to speak" (cf. *TJ*, 582/510 rev.). There are reasons that social and political relations are structured as they are, and publicity insures that these reasons are made available to everyone in ways that they can understand.

T. M. Scanlon's contractualism develops this aspect of Rawls's thought, and extends it more generally. Scanlon's idea is that the morality of "what we owe to each other" involves recognition of others as persons, which requires that we be in a position to justify our actions and institutions that profoundly affect others' lives, and do so in terms of reasons and rules that they "cannot reasonably reject."[23] Similarly for Rawls, part of respecting others as persons and as equal citizens is that we be in a position to justify our conduct and institutions on terms that they can reasonably accept and endorse in their capacity as free, equal, and reasonable and rational persons (or in their capacity as democratic citizens, as Rawls later holds in political liberalism) (cf. *TJ*, 586/513 rev.). This does not mean that we are "literally" to justify ourselves to a person, whatever "the conscience of an individual" and whatever he or she wants to do. Rather, we justify ourselves to others in their capacity *as* free and equal persons, by appealing to "the principles we would both acknowledge [in the original position]" and treat them as these principles require (*TJ*, 519/455rev.). I'll call this the "contractualist" justification of the publicity condition, due to its resemblance to Scanlon's position, and because it captures the manner in which publicity "arises naturally from a contractarian standpoint" (*TJ*, 133/115 rev., cf.17/15 rev.). Here it is significant that this sort of justification for making principles public to those whose lives are constrained and regulated by them is a moral requirement based on considerations of what is reasonable if we are to recognize and respect others as free and equal persons. There is no reliance upon a conception of a person's good or fundamental interests in this account of publicity.

Related to these considerations of reasonableness is that full publicity of a moral conception is especially appropriate for a conception of political and social justice among free and equal people.[24] Rawls mentions two reasons. First, "some

---

23. T. M. Scanlon, *What We Owe to Each Other* (Cambridge, MA: Harvard University Press, 1998).

24. See "Kantian Constructivism in Moral Theory" (The Dewey Lectures, 1980) in *CP*, 325. Rawls says here: "No doubt publicity is less compelling for other moral notions." This raises the question whether indeed publicity is an appropriate condition for a more general moral conception, such as Rawls's proposed "rightness as fairness" (TJ, 17/15 rev.) or Scanlon's contractualism. When we discuss political liberalism (chaps. 5–7), we will see that Rawls has reservations about any "comprehensive moral conception" being able to satisfy a full publicity condition (*PL*, xviii).

machinery of coercion" is needed to enforce its principles even under favorable conditions. Second, the basic social institutions that political principles regulate have such major long-term effects and shape the aims and characters of members of society, "the kinds of persons they are and want to be" (*CP*, 325–26)[25] "It seems fitting, then, that the fundamental terms of social cooperation between free and equal moral persons should answer to requirements of full publicity. For, if institutions rely on coercive sanctions . . . and influence people's deepest aspirations, the grounds and tendency of these institutions [and sanctions] should stand up to public scrutiny" (*CP*, 293, 326). Rawls's thought here seems to be that the duty to justify ourselves to free and equal persons would seem to apply especially when we coerce others, since coercion by its nature imposes a relation of inequality that restricts or denies individuals' freedom. The intuitive idea of the social contract doctrine is that free and equal persons should be in a position to accept and agree to the terms of cooperation that are politically enforced upon them, if they are to maintain their status as equals and as free.

Publicity, and Moral, Rational, and Political Autonomy: Now to turn to the Kantian background to the publicity condition. Rawls says: "I assume that each can understand these principles [of justice] and use them in his deliberations" (*TJ*, 132/114 rev.).[26] It is part of the legacy that Rawls accepts from Kant that moral principles should be capable of serving moral agents as principles of practical reasoning—having a role in guiding deliberation, both individual and public, and a role in public justification and criticism. The idea here seems to go beyond the concern that, to respect people, we have a duty to give them reasons for the ways in which our conduct and institutions profoundly affect their lives and interests. The emphasis, rather, shifts to our status as agents and our capacities for moral agency. What principles are we, as free and equal moral persons, to use in the exercise of our moral capacities, and more generally our capacities for practical reasoning? Like Kant, Rawls (at one point in his career) regarded moral principles of justice as somehow tailored to specifications provided by practical reasoning itself. This emerges in the Kantian interpretation of justice as fairness and later in the development of those same ideas in Kantian constructivism. (The Kantian interpretation will be discussed in more detail in chap. 5.)

The basic idea of the Kantian interpretation and Kantian constructivism is to show how moral principles of justice are an "expression" of our "moral personality" (our practical reason) as free and equal persons, particularly our moral capacities for a sense of justice. With regard to the publicity condition, the point is that to knowingly reason in terms of, and act for the sake of and according to public moral principles that are an "expression" of our capacities for a sense of justice, is a condition of our being free morally autonomous agents. To act with moral autonomy is to knowingly act upon principles that

25. See also "The Independence of Moral Theory" (1975), *CP*, 249.

26. Here Rawls adds a point I return to later: "This imposes an upper bound of sorts on how complex they can be, and on the kinds and number of distinctions they draw" (*TJ*, 132/114 rev.). Rawls makes these remarks not in his discussion of the publicity condition, but rather in his discussion of the formal condition that principles of justice should be universal in application. Evidently he builds publicity into this condition.

we "give to ourselves" out of our own capacities for practical reason where these capacities are "the decisive determining element" (*TJ*, 252/222 rev.). The Kantian interpretation demonstrates how principles of justice thus express our "nature as free, rational beings" (*TJ*, sec. 40). In order that we may be morally autonomous, we must be able to publicly acknowledge, endorse, and rely on our moral and political reasoning upon these principles of justice in structuring our political and social relations.

The point of Rawls's argument for congruence from the Kantian interpretation (as we'll later see) is to show that moral autonomy—acting on and from principles that originate in our moral capacity for a sense of justice—is an intrinsic good for all members of a well-ordered society. In this same connection, Rawls says later in Kantian constructivism that the exercise and development of the capacity to rationally form, revise, and pursue a plan of life is also a good for moral persons. This suggests that, in addition to our taking responsibility for the principles of justice that structure and regulate social relations, it is also an intrinsic good for persons that they take responsibility for their own good by rationally formulating and successfully executing a plan of life of their own choosing. This is "rational autonomy," and the conjunction of it with moral autonomy, Rawls calls "full autonomy" (*CP*, 308). Like moral autonomy, rational autonomy also has its condition in publicity. Because social institutions have such profound effects on people's characters, aims, and future prospects, it is important that we not be under any illusions about the normative bases of our social relations—the principles of justice that regulate social cooperation and within which people draw up their rational plans of life. Rawls does not say this for perfectionist reasons, that having true beliefs of this general kind is good for its own sake.[27] Rather, his reason is that knowledge of the moral bases that shape one's character and aims is a precondition of people being free agents who can take full responsibility for their conception of their good (*CP*, 326). When principles of justice are publicly known, people can know the real reasons for social constraints and expectations and can apply these reasons to plan their actions and pursuits. Moral grounds for action need not be occluded in individual deliberations. This is crucial to a person's being a fully responsible moral agent. Publicity is, in this regard, a condition of full autonomy and taking responsibility for a plan of life that one creates or otherwise assumes for oneself.

Finally, in *Political Liberalism*, Rawls abandons the comprehensive doctrine underlying the Kantian interpretation, which says that autonomy (i.e., rational autonomy regulated by a desire to do justice for its own sake) is a supremely regulative good.[28] But he still regards full publicity as a condition of the *political autonomy* of free and equal citizens. Because of reasonable pluralism, it is not

---

27. Rational autonomy resembles J. S. Mill's idea of Individuality, and it is often endorsed as a kind of perfectionist justification of liberalism. See, for example, Joseph Raz, *The Morality of Freedom*, (New York: Oxford University Press, 1986); also Ronald Dworkin, *Sovereign Virtue* (Cambridge, MA: Harvard University Press, 2000) (cited in text as *SV*).

28. Rawls, *Political Liberalism* (New York: Columbia University Press, 1993; paperback edition, 1996, 2004) (cited in the text as *PL*; references are to the paperback edition).

rational for free and equal democratic citizens all to want to be morally autonomous ("Many citizens of faith reject moral autonomy as part of their way of life"
[*PL*, xlv]). Still, Rawls contends that it is rational for them all to aim for political autonomy. Rawls defines "political autonomy" as "the legal independence
and assured political integrity of citizens and their sharing with other citizens
equally in the exercise of political power" (*PL*, xliv; *CP*, 586). Of "full political
autonomy" he says:

> Citizens gain full political autonomy when they live under a reasonably just
> constitution securing their liberty and equality, with all of the appropriate sub-
> ordinate laws . . . and when they also fully comprehend and endorse this consti-
> tution and its laws, as well as adjust and revise them as changing social circum-
> stances require, always suitably moved by their sense of justice and the other
> political virtues. (*PL*, 402)

The rationality (or good) of political autonomy stems from the desire of free and
equal citizens in freely pursuing their rational plan of life, and the fundamental
interests citizens have in the development and exercise of the moral powers that
are necessary for social cooperation. Regarding publicity, in this context Rawls's
idea seems to be that, *given* that democratic citizens conceive of themselves as
free and equal with higher-order interests in the moral powers, it is rational to
want to know the bases of social and political relations, and to want them publicly known by all, so that democratic citizens can protect their interests, assume
responsibility for their collective fate, and successfully realize their fundamental
interests and their individual conceptions of the good.[29] Here Rawls speaks of the
"educative role" achieved by the publicity of a political conception of justice, in
enabling citizens to come to awareness of the ideal of free and equal moral persons that is expressed in the basic structure of a well-ordered society.

I have gone over several reasons Rawls regards publicity of society's principles and conception of justice as required by a conception of justice. Some of
these relate to Rawls's conception of reasonableness and the contractarian basis
for principles of justice; others to his Kantian (or political) ideal of the person
and comprehensive (or political) account of an individual's rational good. To all
this, a utilitarian still may reply: "However important publicity of basic moral
principles is to achieving such values as mutual respect, responsibility for our
aims and characters, political autonomy, and even moral autonomy (assuming
constructivism makes sense), still, the demands of these values cannot outweigh

---

29. A further reason for publicity of principles of justice Rawls mentions is that it is a condition of the good of social union: "If we take seriously the idea of a social union and of society as a
social union of such unions, then surely publicity is a natural condition. It helps to establish that a
well-ordered society is one activity in the sense that its members follow and know of one another, that
they follow the same regulative conception; and everyone shares in the benefits of the endeavors of
all in ways to which each is known to consent" (*TJ*, 582/510 rev.). Social union is a complicated idea
I will not go into, but it is worth emphasizing that this reason for publicity, like rational and moral
autonomy above, appeal to what Rawls later calls "comprehensive reasons" regarding a person's good
(see *PL*, VI; esp. 251n).

the importance of the ultimate good, overall utility." Here Rawls's argument in part III of A *Theory of Justice* for the heterogeneity of the good plays an important role in responding to the utilitarian's skepticism about the appropriateness of publicity of basic moral principles. It may well be true that, if there is an ultimate nonmoral good by virtue of which anything else has its value, then the publicity to agents of that good, and people's knowledge of the moral principle designed to promote it, must be (trivially) of subordinate value. It is precisely for this reason that Sidgwick says that it might be better if utilitarianism remains an "esoteric morality," knowledge of which is confined to an "enlightened few."[30] But if there are a plurality of goods, and among these is the freedom of individuals to decide what goods to incorporate into the plan of life that is most suitable for themselves, then this utilitarian argument against the publicity of moral principles of justice loses its potency.

This suggests that a crucial aspect of Rawls's argument for the principles of justice from the publicity condition is his argument against the one rational good and for the plurality of values. But Rawls's account of the plurality of goods in A *Theory of Justice* is what he later calls a "comprehensive doctrine" in *Political Liberalism* (PL, xviii). If so, then the force of the publicity argument against utilitarianism (now conceived purely as a political conception) can no longer be made to depend on the pluralist account of value set forth in *Theory* (nor on arguments of the intrinsic good of rational and moral autonomy, and of social union). This is not to say that Rawls must give up the account of "goodness as rationality" in *Political Liberalism* (PL, 176), but he does have to abandon his earlier claim that it adequately provides a necessary account of a person's objective good. In *Political Liberalism*, he says that, rather than being a comprehensive account of value, goodness as rationality should be regarded as a conception of value that is appropriate for a conception of justice for the basic structure of a liberal society (PL, 176n). This seems to mean that, because people endorse different comprehensive doctrines, they cannot agree on such questions as the nature of value and the possibility of the objectivity of value, and whether there is one rational good or a plurality of intrinsic goods. In spite of those differences, however, Rawls assumes that reasonable people who regard themselves as free should be able to agree and appreciate the consequences of the fact that they inevitably will have different conceptions of their good—a result of the burdens of judgment and the fact of reasonable pluralism. This is simply a fact about the social relations of people who regard themselves as politically free and equal. Moreover, whatever we might think about the ultimate value of many people's conceptions of their good (many of us might assign negative value to many people's religious beliefs, for example), it is on a liberal conception more important that people have the freedom to pursue their conceptions of the good (so long as they are not unrea-

---

30. "It may be desirable that Common Sense should repudiate the doctrines which it is expedient to confine to an enlightened few. And thus a Utilitarian may reasonably desire, on Utilitarian principles . . . that the vulgar should keep aloof from his system as a whole, in so far as the inevitable indefiniteness and complexity of its calculations render it likely to lead to bad results in their hands" (*Methods*, 490).

sonable) than that they pursue all that is objectively good. It is against this background that Rawls contends that goodness as rationality is suitable as an account of the good within the context of a liberal conception of justice. This is not to say that it is adequate for all purposes, but it seems to require that Rawls's "thin theory of the good" (TJ, 396/347–8 rev.)—which says that it is rational for democratic citizens to exercise and develop the moral powers, including the power to decide and revise a conception of the good—not be incompatible with any reasonable comprehensive doctrine (including utilitarianism and other teleological conceptions); rather, the thin theory must be endorsable by all such reasonable doctrines in an overlapping consensus upon a politically liberal conception of justice within a well-ordered society.[31]

The Stability Requirement

What now about the idea of the *stability* of a well-ordered society—perhaps the most crucial assumption Rawls makes in his arguments against utilitarianism? Rawls suggests that, because of facts about human nature, there is not a feasible social world in which everyone can freely endorse and willingly commit themselves to act steadfastly on the terms of a utilitarian conception of justice. The utilitarian strains of commitment are just too great for people who end up less advantaged, and whose well-being is compromised or forfeited in order to advance the well-being of those better off. Moreover, a social world in which the principle of utility is publicly recognized would undermine the self-respect and sense of self-worth of many of its inhabitants. The strains of commitment argument is not that the worst-off can never learn to accept living in a society in which their happiness is sacrificed for the majority—for, of course, less advantaged people have had to learn to accept and live with the sacrifice of their well-being for someone else's sake in nearly all societies thus far in history. The argument is rather that people generally cannot be relied upon to develop a steadfast sense of justice which leads them to willingly act on and for the sake of moral principles and legal institutions that promote others' happiness at their own expense. Of course, some people might be able to do this—some people may be prepared to sacrifice their happiness so that other people unknown to them might gain marginal benefits. Whether their disposition to self-sacrifice or subservience is a healthy inclination to be encouraged, or a self-destructive attitude to discourage, is another question. But these people surely are exceptional, and the stability argument requires that all (or nearly all) reasonable and rational people in a well-ordered society be capable of knowingly developing a sense of justice that is shaped by utilitarian principles. The reciprocity principles that Rawls says characterize our psychological nature all say that we develop an attachment to persons and institutions that affirm, rather than deny, our sense of our good. The sense of justice is geared towards sustaining relationships and institutions formed

---

31. Here Samuel Scheffler raises the question whether this can be true of the classical utilitarianism of Bentham and Sidgwick. See "Rawls and Utilitarianism," in *The Cambridge Companion to Rawls*, 452.

on a basis of reciprocity, and not self-sacrifice. This suggests that the stability of a well-ordered utilitarian society is highly precarious. For, given human nature it is most unlikely that people could form the extensive bonds of sympathy and even impartial benevolence that would be required to inculcate in everyone a regulative sense of justice informed by the principle of utility.

Assume that Rawls's moral psychology is true. We are not, by nature, self-sacrificing beings reliably prone to extensive sympathy or impartial benevolence towards the general population as a whole. One response voiced by utilitarians, and also by non-utilitarians such as G. A. Cohen and Jürgen Habermas, is: "Why should human nature, or other empirical tendencies, be a condition of the truth or reasonableness of moral principles of justice? The empirical limits of human nature and unavoidable facts about social cooperation are certainly relevant to the *application* of moral principles, but they should not affect their truth value. This is a conceptual matter, not a question of fact—a matter of 'pure reason' (if you will). A condition upon the truth—or reasonableness—of a moral conception is that it be universally applicable, covering all possible (not just humanly feasible) circumstances; for this reason it cannot be influenced by human vulnerabilities."

This is a complicated objection and demands a more detailed response than can be given here. But briefly, Rawls's focus on the stability—or feasibility and endurance—of a well-ordered society is one of the more telling features of his position, early and late. It is the reason he made such substantial revisions to the argument for justice as fairness in A *Theory of Justice* that resulted in political liberalism. It is largely what explains what many find to be his enigmatic position in *The Law of Peoples*. The impetus for the stability condition can be traced to Rousseau's social contract and his idea of a "realistic utopia" (as Rawls terms it [*LP*, 6–7]). At the opening of *The Social Contract*, in a passage Rawls often cited, Rousseau says:

> My purpose is to consider if, in political society, there can be any legitimate and sure principle of government, *taking men as they are and laws as they might be*. In this inquiry I shall try always to *bring together what right permits with what interest requires* so that justice and utility are in no way divided.[32] (emphasis added)

"Men as they are" Rawls understood as a reference to our moral and psychological natures, and how that nature responds to and develops within a framework of social and political institutions. "Laws as they might be" refers to laws as they should, or ought to, be under the ideal conditions of a reasonably just and well-ordered democratic society (*LP*, 7, 13). So the first aspect of the stability issue is to discover principles of justice for the ideal circumstances (Rousseau says

---

32. Jean Jacques Rousseau, *On Social Contract or Principles of Political Right* (1762), in *Rousseau's Political Writings*, ed. Alan Ritter and Julia C. Bondanella (New York: Norton, 1988 [originally published 1762]), book. I, para. 1. This passage is quoted by Rawls in *LP*, 13, and discussed there and on 7.

"utopian") of a well-ordered society, principles which are nonetheless also to be "realistic"—that is, given human nature, principles that are within our reach and "workable and applicable to ongoing social arrangements" (*PL*, 13). It is primarily the role of chapter 8 of *Theory*, "The Sense of Justice," to show how Rawls's principles of justice are compatible with human nature and the potentials of human moral psychology.

The second aspect of the stability argument is suggested by Rousseau's phrase: "To bring together what right permits with what interest requires *so that justice and utility are in no way divided*." The combination of "justice and utility" calls for principles of justice that are responsive to the fundamental interests ("utility") of free and equal moral persons, and therewith are compatible if not "congruent" with the human good. Here it is the task of chapter 9 of *Theory*, "The Good of Justice," including the arguments from social union (sec. 79) and the congruence of the right and the good (sec. 86), to show that justice not only is possible for us given our nature but also is an essential element of the human good. This is where Rawls argues (as previously alluded to) that principles of justice are an "expression of the nature of free, rational beings," which we would ourselves choose in a procedure designed to represent our moral personality; and that for us to act on and from these principles is to realize our nature and therewith the intrinsic good of moral autonomy. (See chap. 5 of this volume for the details of this argument.)

There are, then, two general kinds of reasons that underlie Rawls's focus on stability.

1. *Justice and Human Nature*: First, if a conception of justice cannot be realized and endure in a feasible social world under the best of conditions—a well-ordered society, where people generally are made aware of that conception, it is generally accepted, and its terms are enforced—then that conception of justice is an "[un]realistic utopia" for Rawls. It is not, then, compatible with human nature, even under the most ideal of real world conditions. This is reason to say it is not reasonable, but instead utopian, to expect people generally to comply with the terms of a conception of justice that reasonable and rational people cannot all comply with. One might argue here that what is utopian is Rawls's expectation that reasonable people in *any* social world can agree on and generally endorse the same conception of justice—particularly justice as fairness; and, if so, then general acceptability is an unreasonable condition to impose on *any* moral conception. But Rawls was optimistic enough about the human condition to suppose that they could comply, however unlikely that will ever be: for there is nothing in human nature that requires that we are corrupt or wholly selfish and unable to respect others as justice requires for its own sake. It is true, however, that toward the end of his life, in "The Idea of Public Reason Revisited" Rawls recognized that in a well-ordered democratic society, because of the "burdens of judgment,"[33] a plurality of liberal conceptions will be endorsed by reasonable citizens. In this regard, he appears to concede that there is something unrealistic about his earlier hopes that justice as fairness in particular could be universally endorsed by

---

33. Rawls, "The Idea of Public Reason Revisited" (1997), in *CP*, 573.

reasonable people in a feasible social world. But even then, though all may not endorse the exact terms of justice as fairness specifically, Rawls thought that at least all reasonable people could endorse one or another similar liberal conception that provides for the priority of basic liberties, fair opportunities, and some kind of social minimum.

What is the alternative to the stability condition? One alternative is a conception of justice that people cannot generally comply with. But what could be the point in that? Its point or role as a moral conception of justice would have to be something different than Rawls's ambition to provide a basis for social cooperation that enables free and equal persons to live together on terms of mutual respect. (Perhaps its aim is maximizing the sum total of goodness in a world in which the freedom and equality of persons does not matter much.) Rawls assumes (with Kant and many other moral philosophers) that a condition upon the justification of any moral conception is that it be workable and within our reach, that it not demand the impossible of human nature. This is one way to understand Kant's adage "ought implies can."

Here the utilitarian may say: "But the principle of utility does not demand the impossible. It is adaptable to human nature and many different circumstances, no matter what kinds of beings we turn out to be — whether psychological egoists, as Bentham supposed, or limited altruists, as Hume holds, or even beings who are fully malleable and capable of impartial benevolence, as the most sanguine utilitarians might have it. A virtue of utilitarianism is that, no matter what kind of creatures rational beings turn out to be, the principle of utility can be applied to specify their rights and duties, whatever their circumstances."

It's true that utilitarianism can be adapted to provide norms of justice and morality for most any social world, regardless of human nature. This is taken to be one of its great strengths. And most any utilitarian society can be rendered stable, in the Hobbesian sense of "stability," if it has the right enforcement mechanisms. (In this sense, the Roman Empire was stable at least for a while.) But stability in the sense of a compromise among competing interests is not the kind of stability that interests Rawls; for as Hobbes showed, most any political conception can be made stable in that sense if there is absolute political power to back it up. The kind of stability Rawls is interested in, rather, is based upon reasonable persons developing a sense of justice and willingness to abide by the requirements of justice and support just institutions. The relevant question, then, is, can utilitarianism (or any moral conception) be *publicly* accepted and *freely* endorsed by *reasonable* people — reasonable in that they want to cooperate with others and act justly — who regard themselves as free and as equals and who inevitably have different and conflicting conceptions of their good? It is in this sense that Rawls aims to discover a stable conception of justice — stable under the (rather stringent) conditions of a well-ordered democratic society. His primary argument against utilitarianism is that it cannot meet these conditions — it cannot generate its own widespread support among free and equal persons — whereas justice as fairness can, better than any known alternative.

2. *Justice and the Human Good*: The second general reason for the stability of a moral conception addresses the relationship between justice and the human good. Why, for Rawls, should stability be "for the right reasons" (PL, lii), grounded

in citizens' settled disposition to comply with principles of justice? Why not simply stability as Hobbes conceived it, on the basis of compromise, coercion, and a modus vivendi among essentially conflicting interests? One of the primary "right reasons" that undergirds Rawlsian stability is the adequate development and full and effective exercise of people's sense of justice. Thus, among other things, stability for the right reasons is important because the development and exercise of a sense of justice is a higher order interest of free and equal democratic citizens, hence, an essential part of their good. In a society that is stable where people comply with laws simply on the basis of a modus vivendi, (or worse, either simply out of fear, if they are worse off, or because they are in a privileged position and especially benefit from society's terms), then people's sense of justice is not adequately engaged and developed; on the contrary, it may be distorted by attachment to unjust or exploitive conditions. They support and defend unjust conditions, believing that they are just. Moreover, for those who are worse off, and who must make sacrifices so that those who are better off may prosper, their sense of self-respect must suffer. Even if they did willingly accept the status quo—because they have been led to believe that they do not deserve to enjoy the benefits others do—their sense of self-respect is impaired simply because of the particular kind of stability their society enjoys.

Recall that development and exercise of one's sense of justice and achieving the bases of self-respect are two of the primary interests that motivate parties in the original position to choose the principles of justice. This suggests that one of the main reasons for Rawls's stability condition is that it insures that justice enables people generally to live in a society that furthers fundamental human interests, and, therewith, the human good. If it cannot be shown that a just society can be stable for the right reasons, then it cannot be shown that justice is congruent with the human good. (The congruence of justice and the good is the topic of chap. 5.)

For Rawls, what reason requires of a moral conception is conditioned by what is reasonable and what it is reasonable to expect of people. Return now to the objection considered above: that "the stability condition is an inappropriate measure of the truth or reasonableness of moral principles, but mainly plays a subordinate role in applying those principles to real world conditions." Is it reasonable to expect people generally to endorse and comply with principles that are incompatible with human nature? Is it reasonable to expect them to endorse and comply with principles that are fundamentally at odds with the human good? To conclude that it is unreasonable for principles to place these kinds of demands on people is to suggest that the stability of a moral conception of justice accords with the best of reasons.

IV. The Utilitarian Welfare State and Property-Owning Democracy

I conclude with some remarks on Rawls's view of utilitarianism's application to the modern conditions of a democratic society. In the 1987 introduction to the French edition of A *Theory of Justice*, Rawls says that the main reason he wrote the book was to provide an alternative conception of justice to utilitarianism, which he says is unable to satisfactorily account for the institutions of a constitutional democracy. Rawls sees two main shortcomings of utilitarianism. First, it is incapable of giving a satisfactory account of the basic rights and liberties and their priority that express the freedom of democratic citizens. Rawls says his "first objective" is to provide a philosophical account of these issues. Second, utilitarianism is unable to provide a satisfactory account of the democratic idea of equality. Utilitarianism's assumption of equal consideration of interests does not guarantee the substantive equality of citizens. Rawls's second objective is to integrate the liberal idea of basic liberties and their priority with an understanding of democratic equality that is geared towards providing fair and favorable conditions for the exercise of the basic liberties, in order that individuals can be suitably self-sufficient and independent and cooperate with others socially and politically while preserving a robust sense of their self-respect. This leads to the principle of the fair value of the political liberties, fair equality of opportunity, and the difference principle.

It's important to see that Rawls does not regard the classical utilitarians as insensitive to the values of freedom and equality, or to social policies addressing poverty, non-discrimination, and equal opportunities. In his lectures on Hegel (in *Lectures on the History of Moral Philosophy*), Rawls distinguishes between two kinds of liberalism: "liberalisms of happiness" and "liberalisms of freedom." Liberalisms of happiness are oriented primarily towards achieving the maximal welfare of citizens, while liberalisms of freedom are oriented primarily towards the freedom and independence of citizens.[34] Liberalisms of happiness are supported by the classical utilitarians Bentham, James Mill, and Sidgwick. Unlike liberalisms of freedom, liberalisms of happiness do not have as their first principle the freedom and equality of citizens but, rather, citizens' maximal happiness. Individuals' rights and the political values of freedom and equality are accounted for in utilitarian or welfarist terms (*Lectures*, 343). Proponents of the liberalisms of freedom that Rawls mentions are Kant, J. S. Mill, and his own positions in *A Theory of Justice* and *Political Liberalism* (ibid., 366; also, a reference is made to Hegel, 349). J. S. Mill is included because (1) his principle of liberty—and not the principle of utility—is regarded to be first among public political principles in a democratic society; (2) he emphasizes equal liberties and the equality of women; and (3) he regards Individuality as doing most of the work for the concept of utility in his political conception. Rawls says that liberalisms of freedom provide citizens with the all-purpose means needed to effectively exercise their freedoms; they do not however seek to guarantee citizens' happiness, "for that is a matter for citizens themselves" (ibid.).

One of the more interesting developments of Rawls's later reflections on justice as fairness is his disavowal of the welfare state, and his development of his

---

34. Rawls, *Lectures in the History of Moral Philosophy*, ed. Barbara Herman (Cambridge, MA: Harvard University Press, 2000), 366 (cited in text as *Lectures*). See also 330, 343,349 for further discussion of liberalisms of freedom, and 362–65 for Kant's liberalism of freedom.

earlier claim in *Theory* that justice as fairness and the difference principle would be best realized in a "property-owning democracy."

> To see the full force of the difference principle, it should be taken in the context of a property-owning democracy (or of a liberal socialist regime) and not a welfare state: it is a principle of reciprocity, or mutuality, for society seen as a fair system of cooperation between free and equal citizens. (*TJ*, xv rev.)

Rawls regards a property-owning democracy as one that puts into the hands of citizens generally, and not in the hands of a few, the productive means and equal political power needed to make them fully cooperating members of a democratic society. It is not a society that is largely divided into a class of owners who control production, and workers with no say in the productive process. There is widespread dissemination of productive resources, including human knowledge and skills as well as real capital. A property-owning democracy provides for basic economic needs when necessary insofar as they are not met by individuals' initiatives (mainly through earned-income supplements). But redistribution of wealth is not designed to promote individuals' welfare; instead, it is designed to promote individuals' independence and an environment in which citizens cooperate as equals. Rawls says that unlike the welfare state, the primary aim of a property-owning democracy

> is not simply to assist those who lose out through accident or misfortune (although that must be done) but rather to put all citizens in a position to manage their own affairs, on a footing of a suitable degree of social and economic justice. . . . The least advantaged are not, if all goes well, the unfortunate and unlucky—objects of our charity and compassion, much less our pity—but those to whom reciprocity is owed as a matter of political justice among those who are free and equal citizens along with everyone else. (*Restatement*, 139)

It is because the welfare state focuses on individuals' economic welfare, and on individuals' welfare levels as consumers rather than their economic powers as producers, that it can often lead to unemployment and a "discouraged and depressed underclass many of whose members are chronically dependent on welfare." As a result, "this underclass feels left out and does not participate in the public political culture" (*Restatement*, 140).

Justice as fairness works from the idealization that all citizens are normal and fully cooperating members over a complete life. "This assumption implies that all are willing to work and to do their part in sharing the burdens of social life" (ibid., 179). Part of the idea of reciprocity embodied in the difference principle, then, is that able-bodied individuals should do their fair share in contributing towards the cooperative social product. For this reason, Rawls rejects entitlements to lump sum welfare payments for the able-bodied who choose not to work ("Surfers must somehow support themselves" [ibid.]). Rawls favors instead income supplements for working people. This explains Rawls's insistence that government is the "employer of last resort," with an obligation to provide employment for those unable to procure private employment in civil society. It also explains why the "least advantaged" under the difference principle are not the handicapped or the most depressed but rather the least skilled workers in the lowest income class. Handicaps and other disabilities are regarded as special needs, which a society is obligated to respond to under the natural duties of assistance and mutual aid. As with the public provision of basic health care for the non-handicapped members of society capable of normal cooperation, the level of assistance for greater disabilities arising from handicaps and special needs is to be democratically determined at the legislative stage, where relevant information about the prevalence of handicaps and special needs and the availability of resources are on hand to inform decision (cf. *Restatement*, 173–76).

Given the common perception that A *Theory of Justice* is a justification of the welfare state,[35] it is surprising that Rawls does not think that justice as fairness, including the difference principle, is even capable of being realized through the welfare state (much less so by laissez-faire capitalism or state socialism with a command economy). Rawls regards the welfare state as a development of capitalism, which on the classical liberal view is oriented towards maximal economic growth and maximal productive output. He refers to "welfare state capitalism" (*Restatement*, 138) and directly contrasts a property-owning democracy with capitalism.[36] As an outgrowth of capitalism, the welfare state permits very large inequalities in the ownership of productive assets and natural resources, so that the control of the economy rests in the hands of an elite few. Largely because of its economic inequalities, the welfare state allows those who own and manage capital far-greater-than-equal influence within political democracy; the business class largely determines the political agenda (an all too familiar state of political affairs).

Rawls says that of the three democratic features of justice as fairness—the fair value of the political liberties, fair equality of opportunity, and the difference principle—none of them is realized within the capitalist welfare state. The great inequalities of wealth that are required by capitalism undermine both fair equality of opportunity and the fair value of the political liberties. To prevent this, Rawls calls for steeply progressive inheritance and gift taxes that prevent intergenerational transfers of large sums of wealth. On the other hand, Rawls seems to think that when the difference principle is conjoined with fair equality of opportunity, there will be less need for progressive income transfers to achieve and maintain a social minimum than there is in a welfare state.[37] Assuming fair equality of opportunity is in place, the gross disparities in ownership of capital

35. See, for example, Sandel, *Liberalism and the Limits of Justice*, 66, where he says Rawls is a "welfare state liberal."

36. "We think of such a [property-owning] democracy as an alternative to capitalism" (*Restatement*, 135–36).

37. See *Restatement*, 161. Rawls suggests the role of progressive income taxes, or better, expenditure taxes, should be mainly to prevent concentrations of wealth that undermine the fair value of political liberties and fair equality of opportunity. Otherwise, he suggests that a proportional tax on income (or expenditures) is more appropriate. For a criticism of proportional taxes, see Barbara Fried, "Proportionate Taxation as a Fair Division of the Social Surplus: The Strange Career of an Idea," *Economics and Philosophy* 19 (2003): 211–239.

and skill endowments that generate such gross income inequalities in the capitalist welfare state should be absent in a property-owning democracy. Rawls suggests (rather optimistically) that in a fully competitive labor market where all have been able to develop their talents and abilities, income level differences will not be so great. Rawls says that, unlike the welfare state, which seeks to redistribute income after it has accrued to redress the gross disparities of income and wealth within capitalism, a property-owning democracy avoids such disparities from the outset since it aims to put into the hands of citizens generally the human and real capital that enable them to be fully cooperating members of society on an equal footing. Since citizens have greater control over their lives and their relations, the dependency and despondency that is characteristic of the underclass in the welfare state, due to the fact they have been left out of participation in public culture, is avoided (cf. *Restatement*, 139–40). Moreover, unlike the welfare state, a property-owning democracy envisions that workers derive a portion of their income from ownership of capital (e.g., worker-owned and worker-managed firms). When joined with the social minimum that a property owning democracy guarantees, this means that workers are not forced to sell their labor to the capitalist class in order to survive.[38] There at least will be other alternatives.

But these measures still do not adequately respond to the left's objection that the best way to maximize income and wealth to the least-advantaged is indeed in a wage economy where capitalist "buccaneers" are allowed to have their way, and then we redistribute to the least advantaged the maximum amount allowable to make them better off without creating disincentives for the buccaneers. How can Rawls just assume that the difference principle underwrites a property owning democracy with less political and economic inequality than exists in a welfare state (*Restatement*, 159)? Perhaps most puzzling is his suggestion that the difference principle does not require a society devoted to ever-increasing prosperity and maximizing wealth.

> A feature of the difference principle is that it does not require continual economic growth over generations to maximize upward indefinitely the expectations of the least advantaged measured in terms of income and wealth. (*Restatement*, 159)

This claim by Rawls is puzzling. For, it suggests that in a property-owning democracy satisfying the difference principle, the least advantaged may indeed be economically worse off than will be the least advantaged in a welfare state that does aim, through continual economic growth, to maximize the income and wealth

---

38. A point made by R. Krouse and M. MacPherson. See "Capitalism, 'Property-Owning Democracy,' and the Welfare State," in Amy Gutmann, ed., *Democracy and the Welfare State* (Princeton, NJ: Princeton University Press, 1988), 91. They argue that Rawls may be overly optimistic about the minimal need for income transfers in a well-ordered property-owning democracy. He does not adequately take into account marginal differences in certain kinds of talents that result in enormous differences in income. Nor does he adequately take into account bad market luck. It should be noted here that Rawls clearly envisioned a mechanism for income supplements for the less advantaged, "a so-called negative income tax" (*TJ*, 275/243 rev., 285/252 rev.).

that go to the least advantaged; and perhaps Rawls's least advantaged will even be economically worse off than the least advantaged in a utilitarian welfare state that seeks to maximize aggregate utility. But how can this be, given that the difference principle requires us to maximize the position of the least advantaged?

Perhaps a clue can be found in Rawls's endorsement of J. S. Mill's "stationary state," which is not focused on maximizing wealth and where real capital income growth ceases, as well as Mill's idea of worker-managed firms and the diminishing influence of the wage relationship in a property-owning democracy.[39] Rawls says that the difference principle is to be understood in conjunction with equal basic liberties—which insures the fair value of the political liberties—as well as fair equality of opportunities, which for Rawls requires real opportunities for all income classes to control capital and their means of production (*Restatement*, 67). These two egalitarian features of justice as fairness have priority over the difference principle, and thus over the aim of maximizing the share of income and wealth that goes to the least advantaged. Rawls evidently conceived of the fair value of the political liberties and providing fair equal opportunities as a check upon the control of capital and concentration of economic power in the hands of a class of owners who stand in a purely wage relationship with workers who have no control over capital and the means of production. The widespread and fair distribution of the primary goods of powers and opportunities to control one's labor and the means of production require an economic system that is incompatible with capitalism, as traditionally understood. Rawls says in *Theory*, "What men want is meaningful work in free association with others, these associations regulating their relations to one another within a framework of just basic institutions" (*TJ*, 290/257 rev.). The fair equality of opportunity to acquire economic powers, including workers' control of capital and the means they employ in production, takes priority over maximizing the share of income and wealth that goes to the least advantaged under the difference principle.

Moreover, the difference principle itself does not simply enjoin us to maximize only the share of income and wealth to the least advantaged. Though Rawls says one's share of income and wealth is a reliable measure of how one fares under it, the difference principle enjoins that we maximize the total index of primary goods, including powers and opportunities available to the least advantaged (equal basic rights and liberties are already guaranteed by the first principle). If we include among the powers and opportunities that are to be maximized for the sake of the least advantaged greater worker control over their economic fates and increased opportunities to take part in the social production process, then we can see how a property-owning democracy might in the end provide less income and wealth to the least advantaged than the capitalist welfare state. But while least advantaged workers in a property-owning democracy may enjoy marginally less

---

39. See *Restatement*, 64, 159, 176, 178. "Mill's idea of worker-managed firms is fully compatible with property-owning democracy. Mill believed that people would much prefer to work in such firms; this would enable the firms to pay lower wages while being highly efficient. In due course these firms would increasingly win out over capitalist firms. A capitalist economy would gradually disappear and be peacefully replaced by worker-managed firms within a competitive economy" (178).

income than they would in the richest capitalist welfare state, they nonetheless have greater powers and opportunities, including greater and more equal political influence and more equal social status with those more advantaged. These powers and opportunities are among the primary bases of self-respect in a democratic society.

The main point of Rawls's contrast between the welfare state and a property-owning democracy seems to be this: by focusing its attention primarily on the level of welfare of members of society, the welfare state does not encourage its citizens to take control of their lives and be actively productive and equal participants in social and political life. Because it allows for such great inequalities, concentrations of enormous wealth, and control of the means of production by an elite class of corporate managers, welfare state capitalism does not provide citizens generally with sufficient means or fair opportunities to enable them to be fully cooperative participants in economic production. And because it does not—and perhaps cannot, due to gross economic inequality—provide for the fair value of the political liberties, the capitalist welfare state does not encourage equal and effective political participation among citizens generally.

It is noteworthy how Rawls's distinction between welfare state capitalism and a property-owning democracy parallels his distinction between liberalisms of happiness and liberalisms of freedom. Since welfare state capitalism is primarily oriented towards continual economic growth and promoting maximal welfare, Rawls implicitly associates it with liberalisms of happiness, and therefore with utilitarianism and welfarism. Here it is important to keep in mind that Rawls viewed utilitarianism primarily as a social conception of justice. He says in his lectures on political philosophy that the great utilitarians—Hume, Adam Smith, Bentham, J. S. Mill, Sidgwick, and Edgeworth—rather than being moral philosophers in the modern academic sense, were primarily social and political philosophers in addition to being economists as well. They regarded utilitarianism primarily as a conception of social justice to be applied by legislators and other political officials to determine the constitution, laws, and social practices. He associated utilitarianism with classical economics and later with modern welfare economics (from which the term "welfare state" derives). Utilitarianism was for him the traditional and still-primary justification for a capitalistic society that is oriented towards maximum productive output and perpetual economic growth—Adam Smith's "progressive state" with which Mill's "stationary state" is to be contrasted. As Rawls indicates in his lectures on political philosophy, it is no accident that the great classical economists—Adam Smith, David Ricardo, J. S. Mill, P. Y. Edgeworth—were all utilitarians. Of course, utilitarians, such as John Maynard Keynes and welfare economists, were also behind the modern welfare state, which sought to temper the gross discrepancies and poverty of laissez-faire capitalism. We might say that for Rawls, the capitalist welfare state is the contemporary institutional expression of the liberalism of happiness that is justified by utilitarianism. A property-owning democracy, because it is oriented to realizing the freedom, independence, and active participation of equal citizens in economic and political life, is the institutional expression of the liberalism of freedom that is realized by Rawls's justice as fairness.

V. Conclusion

One reason Rawls gives for his stability condition is that we cannot assess what conception of justice is most reasonable or appropriate for a democratic society until we work out its social implications and what it requires of human nature.

> We cannot tell solely from the content of a political conception—from its principles and ideals—whether it is reasonable for us. Not only may our feelings and attitudes as we work through its implications in practice disclose considerations that its ideals and principles must be revised to accommodate, but we may find that our sentiments prevent us from carrying it out. On reflection we cannot live with it. (*Restatement*, 136)

For Rawls, the reasons for taking the stability of a moral conception of justice into consideration reflect his reasons for seeking reflective equilibrium. It is a mistake to think that our philosophical intuitions and abstract reasoning alone can provide sufficient justification for a moral conception of justice, independent of an assessment of its practical and institutional implications. We have insufficient reason to give absolute priority to our most abstract philosophical intuitions in seeking to justify principles of justice. Considered judgments at all levels of generality bear on the justification of a moral conception. The conception of practical reason that says that empirical laws and tendencies of human nature are of no probative value in political philosophy is mistaken, as is the idea that practical reason demands one or more universal principles (such as Sidgwick's principle of impartial benevolence) that provide a justification for conduct in all possible worlds.

One of the reasons Rawls rejected utilitarianism as a conception of justice is that it has played such a major role as the primary ideology used to vindicate the institutional inequalities that are intrinsic to capitalism. His account of a property-owning democracy, however sketchy the account may be, is an attempt to show how his principles of justice support a private-propertied market economy that does not deprive equal citizens of their equal standing in the economic and political life of a democracy. As reciprocity occupies a space between mutual advantage and altruism, and as the difference principle seeks to find an appropriate position between equality and efficiency, a property-owning democracy aims to occupy a space between capitalism and socialism. As with Rawls's other medium positions, it aims to incorporate the strengths of each alternative without their moral weaknesses.

A shorter draft of this chapter was initially written for a session on Rawls, Utilitarianism, and Social Policy, at the 2004 Central Division meetings of the American Philosophical Association. I am grateful to Jay Wallace, Rahul Kumar, Samuel Scheffler, and K. C. Tan for their helpful suggestions and comments on this chapter.

4

Rawls and Luck Egalitarianism

The position that has come to be called "luck egalitarianism" is endorsed in some fashion by many of the most important contemporary theorists of distributive justice—Ronald Dworkin, G. A. Cohen, John Roemer, Phillippe van Parijs, and Richard Arneson, among others. It often is said that John Rawls commits himself to luck egalitarianism, but that he is inconsistent in its application. In this paper, I examine these claims and criticisms in hopes of showing them to be based in a misunderstanding of Rawls's account of distributive justice. I proceed from Susan Hurley's discussion of luck egalitarianism and some remarks she makes regarding Rawls.

The rough idea underlying luck egalitarianism is that in matters of distributive justice, society should try to equalize the effects of brute luck and misfortune in the distribution of the goods that a society effectively controls. Just as a person's prospects should not be determined by the social class she is born into, so too should a person's prospects not be determined by the natural talents (or lack thereof) that she has. Instead, the effects of these and other accidents of fortune should be equalized, or at least neutralized, in the distribution of benefits and burdens, for no one is responsible for, and no one deserves, the natural capacities (or handicaps) she is born with. In this regard, luck egalitarianism seems to generalize on the idea of equality of opportunity that is central to liberal and democratic thought. It suggests that if we are to take the idea of equality of opportunity seriously, we need to neutralize as best we can not only the effects of social class but also the effects of the distribution of natural talents and (dis)abilities and other accidents of fortune.

Susan Hurley, in her recent book *Justice, Luck, and Knowledge*,[1] contends that the fundamental intuition underlying luck egalitarianism does not warrant its conclusion. Simply because people are not responsible for their natural tal-

---

1. Susan Hurley, *Justice, Luck, and Knowledge* (Cambridge MA: Harvard University Press, 2003) (cited in text as *JLK*).

ents and may not deserve them, it does not follow that the effects of the natural lottery—the gains people enjoy or losses they suffer in exercising their natural talents—should be equally distributed. How benefits and burdens are to be distributed in a society depends not fundamentally upon facts about responsibility but upon moral considerations such as fairness and impartiality. Hurley advocates, in the end, a kind of maximin position according to which society should distribute benefits and burdens so as to maximally benefit its least advantaged members.

Hurley thus contends that responsibility does not play a fundamental role in determining *how* distributions should be made, or in determining the *"currency* of distributive justice" (*JLK*, 206–231), namely, the kind of good or benefit that is the primary object for distribution—whether it be resources of some kind (such as Rawls's primary social goods), or welfare (as utilitarians and other welfarists hold), or capabilities for functioning (as Sen contends), or some other good (opportunities for welfare, access to advantage, etc.). Still, she finds two legitimate roles for responsibility to play in distributive justice: the "incentive parameter role" and the "well-being role" (*JLK*, 267–269, 243–246). (I'll discuss the former in due course.)

I endorse, in general, Hurley's position, and my differences with the specifics of her arguments are few. Some of these differences concern her reading of Rawls; I will refer to these remarks to frame my discussion of the ways that Rawls's account differs from luck egalitarianism. First, I discuss John Rawls's enigmatic remarks regarding the natural lottery, often regarded as the source of contemporary discussions of luck egalitarianism. I contend that, understood correctly, these passages do not commit Rawls to a luck egalitarian account of distributive justice but that they are designed to do something quite different. Then I suggest an alternative basis to the one Hurley considers, for the luck egalitarian insistence that matters of luck should be neutralized in distributive justice. From there, I will discuss some of Rawls's reasons for the difference principle and examine their adequacy. In section III, I discuss the criticism that Rawls's account of responsibility for ends suggests a luck egalitarian commitment that is inconsistent with the difference principle. Here I discuss Rawls's similarities and differences with Ronald Dworkin's idea of responsibility for choice and raise some questions about Dworkin's use of the idea to support market distributions once compensation for brute luck has been made. This leads to a discussion in section IV of why luck egalitarianism by itself is radically incomplete; it does not respond to many of the most pressing questions at issue in an adequate theory of distributive justice. Section V proceeds from Hurley's discussion of incentives to address G. A. Cohen's criticism of Rawls's account of the role of incentives in distributive justice.

Overall, my discussion is designed to clarify Rawls's position on distributive justice and show how it differs from luck egalitarianism. I do not pretend to provide an adequate defense of the difference principle or an adequate argument against luck egalitarianism itself or Dworkin's or Cohen's powerful accounts of it. I do hope to have adequately responded to at least some of their criticisms.

I. Rawls and the Natural Lottery

Like many philosophers, Susan Hurley sees Rawls's purported egalitarianism in *A Theory of Justice* as based in a "luck-neutralizing emphasis." She notes a "fundamental tension in Rawls's attitude to responsibility" (*JLK*, 134). Hurley says:

> Suppose it is true that concepts of responsibility and desert play no significant role in a theory of justice at the level of fundamental principle. How then could it be fundamental to our conception of justice [as Rawls purportedly contends] that no one is responsible for or deserves his distribution of natural assets, or that it is unjust to allow distributive shares to be influenced by such morally arbitrary factors? . . . The motivating thought that natural assets are a matter of luck is not independent of the thought that people are not responsible for them. If the former is fundamental to justice, then so is the concept of responsibility. (*JLK*, 134)

Hurley goes on to say of Rawls:

> If you judge that no one is responsible for his natural assets, you make a negative judgment, true. But it is still a judgment about responsibility, which essentially employs the concept of responsibility. A negative application of a concept is not less an application of it than a positive application. If significant consequences for distributive justice flow from such negative applications, then this concept does indeed play a fundamental role in the theory of justice. (*JLK*, 135)

Hurley sides with John Roemer and Richard Arneson (against Sam Scheffler) in regarding Rawls "as containing the embryo of the later explicit egalitarian concern with responsibility" (*JLK*, 136n), that is later worked out by Dworkin, Cohen, Arneson, and Roemer. Arneson, Hurley says, "attributes the fundamental concern with compensating for misfortune or bad luck to Rawls. My view similarly reads Rawls as holding that people are not responsible for their natural assets, hence as employing the concept of responsibility, rather than holding that the concept of responsibility is incoherent" (*JLK*, 136n).

Fundamental to Rawls's conception of distributive justice (I believe) is the idea (or combination of ideas) of *reciprocity* among *free and equal democratic citizens* who are *socially productive* and engaged in *ongoing social cooperation* (which always includes political cooperation) on grounds of *mutual respect*. Assume that Rawls explicitly denies that responsibility and desert are fundamental to distributive justice. He also explicitly denies that effort and the contribution a person makes are fundamental.[2] Suppose that he had explicitly denied that considerations of need, the risks one bears, moral virtue, excellences of mind and body, merit, social class, and other criteria, also have a significant role at the level

---

2. See John Rawls, *A Theory of Justice* (Cambridge, MA: Harvard University Press, 1971; rev. ed., 1999), sec. 47, on "The Precepts of Justice" (cited in text as *TJ*; sometimes referred to as *Theory*).

of fundamental principle. It seems peculiar to say that, because of these denials, all these concepts are fundamental to his conception of distributive justice. It is true that some of these concepts (need, effort, contribution, taking responsibility for one's ends) are accommodated by Rawls in some manner, but this does not make them fundamental to his account of distributive justice.

I want to offer a different understanding of Rawls's much-discussed claims regarding the "natural lottery" and responsibility for natural assets (*TJ*, secs. 12, 17). The reason is not simply to correct what I take to be a widespread misunderstanding of Rawls on this point. More importantly, it is to situate Rawls's difference principle within the framework of a very different kind of account of distributive justice, one that is responsive to Hurley's criticism of luck egalitarianism.

I'll begin with four important claims, the first three of which involve attributions to Rawls of claims he did not make (initially attributed by Robert Nozick, but then they took on a life of their own). First, Rawls nowhere says that a person is not responsible for, or does not deserve, her natural assets.[3] Rather, he suggests that strictly speaking the concept of desert is out of place, and inapplicable, in ascriptions regarding natural assets. Rawls says that "moral desert always involves some conscientious effort of will, or something intentionally or willingly done, none of which can apply to our place in the distribution of native endowments, or to our social class of origin."[4] Here Rawls is using the term "desert" in the sense of moral worth of character or what one morally merits for something she has done. In this sense of "desert," the suggestion is that it makes little or no sense to say that a person deserves her natural assets. If so, then it would seem that this concept of (moral) desert can play no significant role in a theory of justice at the level of fundamental principle.

Second claim: Rawls nowhere says, nor does he commit himself to, the position that natural endowments should not influence or affect distributive shares, or that holdings "shouldn't [even] partially depend upon natural endowment," or that "differences in holdings stemming from differences in natural assets ought to be nullified."[5] Likewise, he nowhere says or commits himself to the claim that arbitrariness of natural endowments (or even social class) means that justice requires equality of primary goods. Nozick and many others contend that Rawls's claim—"the initial endowment of natural assets and the contingencies of their

---

3. Nozick, Gauthier, Sandel, and many others attribute this claim to Rawls. Robert Nozick's discussion of Rawls on natural endowments is (I believe) a major source of this common misreading of Rawls. Nozick, *Anarchy, State, and Utopia* (New York: Basic Books, 1974), 213–31, esp. 216, 224. Michael Sandel accepts Nozick's reading of Rawls and provides what he thinks is an explanation for it: "On Rawls's account all endowments are contingent and in principle detachable from the self." Sandel, *Liberalism and the Limits of Justice* (Cambridge: Cambridge University Press, 1982), 78. Sandel contends that, because the Rawlsian self is "disembodied" or shorn of all characteristics, people cannot "possess" or "own" their natural assets or attributes, and therefore cannot be said to deserve them (82–83). Also, David Gauthier says that Rawls holds that we do not deserve our natural assets, and that natural talents are, for Rawls, "to be considered a common asset." Gauthier, *Morals by Agreement* (Oxford: Oxford University Press, 1986), 219–21 (cited in text as *MA*).

4. Rawls, *Justice as Fairness: A Restatement*, ed. Erin Kelly (Cambridge, MA: Belknap Press, 2001), 74n (cited in text as *Restatement*).

5. Nozick, *Anarchy, State, and Utopia*, 215, 216, 218.

growth and nurture in early life are arbitrary from a moral point of view" (*TJ*, 311–12/274 rev.)—implies that natural endowments may not affect distributions, and their effects should be equalized. This is the luck egalitarian position, but it is not Rawls's, nor (so far as I can tell) does he endorse the intuitive idea at any point. Under the difference principle, clearly, people can benefit from their natural endowments, and the arbitrary distribution of natural talents can influence distributions and result in inequalities, so long as this maximally benefits the least advantaged. Here Rawls's critics contend that he is being inconsistent. But there is nothing inconsistent about Rawls's view (or so I will argue).

Third claim: Rawls nowhere says that natural endowments and natural talents are a "common asset" or are a "collective asset," or "that everyone has some entitlement or claim on the totality of natural assets (viewed as a pool)."[6]

Fourth claim: Rather than saying no one deserves (or is responsible for) her natural assets, what Rawls, in fact, says is: "It is one of the fixed points of our moral judgments that *no one deserves his place in the distribution of natural assets* any more than he deserves his initial starting place in society" (*TJ*, 311–12/274 rev.; emphasis added). It is then a particular inequality that Rawls says is not deserved: namely, one's relative position in the distribution of natural assets. Likewise, instead of saying that natural talents are a common asset, Rawls says, "The difference principle represents, in effect, an agreement to regard *the distribution of natural talents* as a common asset, and to share in the benefits of this distribution" (*TJ*, 101/87 rev.; emphases added. See also 179/156 rev.). Here again, it is the distribution of natural talents, the differences or natural inequalities among people, that are a common asset, not natural talents themselves. These are significantly different claims than the claims attributed to Rawls by his critics.

What does Rawls's claim regarding the arbitrariness of the distribution of natural assets mean? It means simply (as Rawls explicitly says) that "no one deserves his *greater* natural capacity nor merits a *more favorable* starting place in society" (*TJ*, 102/87 rev.; emphasis added). Rawls is concerned with the relative advantage or disadvantages a person has with respect to others. It's the *differences* in natural capacity, the inequality itself, that one does not deserve. Rawls took this point to be trivial. "Who could deny it?" he asks (*Restatement*, 74). "All this is perfectly obvious and has long been agreed to" (*TJ*, 311–12/274 rev.). "Do people really think that they (morally) deserved to be born more gifted than others?" (*Restatement*, 74).

There are numerous places in *Theory* where Rawls refers to either the "natural lottery" or deservingness with respect to natural assets, and in all these references he is quite explicit that it is the "distribution of natural assets" that is not deserved by anyone and that also is "arbitrary from a moral perspective" (e.g., *TJ*, 74/64 rev.).[7] Again, Rawls is not saying that a person's natural assets are morally

---

6. Nozick, *Anarchy, State, and Utopia*, 228. Cf. Sandel, *Liberalism and Limits of Justice*, 77–82; Gauthier, *MA*, 219–21.

7. See Rawls's index in *TJ* where the entries under "Natural assets" and "Natural lottery" are both devoid of references, saying instead, "See Distribution of natural assets," under which there are 15 separate page references.

arbitrary or are not morally deserved. What is morally arbitrary is the fact that one person is born *more or less* talented than another.

The point then is simply that no one deserves to be born with greater or less innate intelligence or ability, greater or less strength and health, or greater or less beauty or physical attractiveness, charm, and so on, than anyone else. This is different from saying that no one deserves or owns his/her natural features. In *some* sense of "desert," namely in the loose sense of what people have a fundamental right to, Rawls even seems to concede that people do "deserve" their native endowments. For, according to the first principle of justice and the protection it affords for the basic rights and liberties specified by the freedom and integrity of the person, people have complete rights of control over their capacities, including the freedom to decide when and how to use them.[8]

What is the implication for Rawls of our not deserving greater natural talents or our position in the distribution of natural assets? It is *not* (as many contend) that we should equalize, neutralize, or eliminate the effects of differences in natural capacities. ("But, of course, this is no reason to ignore, much less to eliminate these distinctions" [*TJ*, 102/87 rev.].) Nor is it that people may not gain from their natural assets. ("Those who have been favored by nature . . . *may gain from their good fortune*" [*TJ*, 101/87 rev.; emphasis added].) There is no hint, so far as I can see, of an explicit luck egalitarian commitment by Rawls to equalize the effects of arbitrary inequalities.[9] Rather the implication is simply that differences in natural talents by themselves are not a reason for *any* pattern of distribution. Other reasons must be invoked to decide that issue. Luck egalitarians take the moral arbitrariness of the natural lottery to mean that people cannot benefit from their exceptional gifts *at all*. But this is not the only conclusion one might draw. That some are born more gifted than others may also be taken to mean that they *can* benefit so long as others do too. As Rawls says, "Those who have been favored by nature . . . may gain from their good fortune only on terms that improve the situation of those who have lost out" (*TJ*, 101/87 rev.).

This is the same point that Rawls is making in the much-discussed reference to the "natural lottery" in section 12 of *TJ*. Of the position Liberal Equality, Rawls says that, because it relies on the principle of efficiency,

> distributive shares are decided by the *outcome of the natural lottery*; and this outcome is arbitrary from a moral perspective. There is no more reason to permit

8. Rawls on "owning" one's natural assets: "The question of ownership of our endowments does not arise, and *should it arise it is persons themselves who own their endowments*: the psychological and physical integrity of persons is already guaranteed by the basic rights and liberties that fall under the first principle of justice" (*Restatement*, 75; emphasis added). Rawls recognizes yet another sense of "desert" that applies to income and wealth—"desert as entitlement earned under fair conditions"— and says that in this sense of desert-as-entitlement people do deserve "the social position or offices we may hold in later life, or the realized skills and educated abilities we may have after we have reached the age of reason" (*Restatement*, 78).

9. In *TJ*, I have not found any assertion or indication by Rawls in sections 12 and 13 or anywhere else, that arbitrariness of natural endowments, or of social class, requires an equal distribution. Rather, what Rawls says is that the arbitrariness of natural endowments requires that we "mitigate the arbitrary effects of the natural lottery itself" (*TJ*, 74/64 rev.). Also, in Rawls's narrative in section 12,

the distribution of income and wealth to be settled by the *distribution of natural assets* than by historical and social fortune. (*TJ*, 74/64 rev.; emphases added)

But rather than concluding that the arbitrary distribution of natural endowments requires an equal distribution of its consequences, Rawls says "we may want to adopt a principle which mitigates the arbitrary effects of the natural lottery itself" (*TJ*, 74/64 rev.). Here Will Kymlicka replies that the difference principle "does not entirely 'mitigate the effects of natural accident and social circumstance.'"[10] But Rawls does not say he aims to "entirely mitigate" these effects, only to "mitigate" them. Obviously, to mitigate the effects of something does not mean that we must eliminate, equalize, or neutralize its effects. I may want to mitigate the effects of the sun, so I put on sunblock lotion. I could entirely mitigate them with clothing, but then I would lose the sun's beneficial effects in providing vitamin D. Similarly, it may be that the effects of undeserved natural inequalities can be arranged to serve the common good in some way and fairly benefit everyone. Then, it may be a mistake to "entirely mitigate" the effects of the natural lottery.

Rawls's point, then, in the famous "natural lottery" claim is not that we do not deserve or are not responsible for our natural assets; nor is it that we cannot benefit from differences in natural assets or that the effects of such differences must be equalized. It is, rather, (as he says in the case of birth into a social class) that we should not "[permit] distributive shares to be *improperly influenced* by these factors so arbitrary from a moral point of view" (*TJ*, 72/63 rev.; emphasis added). The "improper influence" of contingencies should not be taken to mean that people cannot gain from arbitrary features such as natural talents or social position at all. "The naturally advantaged are not to gain *merely* because they are more gifted" (*TJ*, 101/87 rev.; emphasis added). Clearly, this does not foreclose their gaining from their natural gifts altogether. It suggests, rather, that there has to be some other reason instead of the mere fact that a person is born more gifted than others, to support the claim that he or she is *entitled* to greater income and wealth. Perhaps there is no such reason; perhaps there are instead reasons that imply that an equal distribution is required. (Such reasons will be discussed in the next section.) But, in that case, it is not the arbitrariness of natural endowments that determines an equal distribution but these other moral reasons.

he uses the arbitrariness of social class to show why fair equality of opportunity is preferable to formal equality of opportunity. He does not say that the arbitrariness of social class requires equalization of primary goods, nor that fair equality of opportunity requires it either. Instead, he says that fair equality of opportunity requires such measures as "preventing excessive accumulations of property and wealth" and "maintaining equal opportunities of education for all" (*TJ*, 73/63 rev.). The idea of fair equal opportunity is rather narrow; it concerns the opportunities people have to compete for social positions and the legal powers they involve. We might, then, say it involves equal opportunity for powers and positions among "those who are at the same level of talent and ability, and have the same willingness to use them" (*TJ*, 73/63 rev.). This is quite different from the much broader distributive idea of equal opportunity for welfare endorsed by some luck egalitarians.

    10. Kymlicka, *Liberalism, Community, and Culture* (Oxford: Oxford University Press, 1989), 72 (cited in text as *LCC*). Kymlicka quotes *TJ*, 100/86 rev.

This resembles the argument that Hurley herself makes against luck egalitarianism. Her point, too, is that the fact of natural inequality is not reason enough for an equal distribution; instead, she says that there has to be something else, such as considerations of fairness, to justify an egalitarian pattern of distribution (JLK, 166–167, 182). But if Rawls makes a similar point, then we should question Hurley's own claim "for a luck-neutralizing view of the deep structure of Rawls's egalitarianism in A Theory of Justice" (JLK, 136). For, nothing said thus far by Rawls has anything to do with equalizing or neutralizing the effects of differences in natural talents, nor would it seem to imply it.

Turn now to the luck egalitarian claim that natural and social inequalities should be compensated. It is often argued that Rawls, if he does not explicitly endorse, is still committed to this position too. Will Kymlicka says of Rawls: "He endorses: (2) Social inequalities should be compensated and natural inequalities should not influence distribution. . . . But if natural and social inequalities really are equally undeserved, we should instead endorse (3): Natural and social inequalities should be compensated" (LCC, 72). But Rawls does not endorse either aspect of 2, and thus he rejects 3 in its entirety. As we have just seen, he does not hold the second clause of 2, that "natural inequalities should not influence distributions." He says, on the contrary, "Those who have been favored by nature . . . *may gain from their good fortune*" (and then immediately adds, "only on terms that improve the situation of those who have lost out") (TJ, 101/87 rev.). Nor does Rawls endorse the first clause of 2 and say that social inequalities should be compensated (at least not in the luck egalitarian sense). His response, rather, is that arbitrariness of social class should not "improperly influence" distributions, and that it requires fair (rather than formal) equality of opportunity.[11]

Most important, however, is that compensation (in the luck egalitarian sense) for social and natural inequalities and other accidents of fortune is not implicit in the difference principle. Rawls implicitly denies it. For, he says of "the principle of redress":

> This is the principle that undeserved inequalities call for redress; and since inequalities of birth and natural endowment are undeserved, these inequalities are to be somehow *compensated* for. . . . The idea is to redress the bias of contingencies in the direction of equality. . . . Now *the difference principle is not of course the principle of redress*. It does not require society to try to even out

---

11. Rawls does say of the difference principle: "The basic structure can be arranged so that these contingencies work out to the good of the least fortunate. Thus we are led to the difference principle if we wish to set up the social system so that no one gains or loses from his arbitrary place in the distribution of natural assets or his initial position in society without giving or receiving *compensating advantages* in return" (TJ, 102/87 rev.; emphasis added). But this is not the sense of compensation Kymlicka or luck egalitarians have in mind, for they criticize the difference principle since it does not compensate for, namely, equalize, the effects of chance. If this passage *is* taken to imply that Rawls in fact does seek to compensate for disadvantage, then it belies Kymlicka's claim that Rawls rejects but should endorse 3 and compensation for natural advantage, for what the above quote by Rawls, read in this way, says is that the difference principle itself "compensates" for both natural and social inequalities.

handicaps as if all were expected to compete on a fair basis in the same race. (*TJ*, 101/86 rev.; emphasis added)

Rawls then goes on to say, "Although the difference principle is not the same as that of redress, it does achieve *some* of the intent of the latter principle" (*TJ*, 101/87 rev.; emphasis added). What exactly does the difference principle achieve in common with the principle of redress and luck-egalitarianism? Significantly, Rawls does not say that the difference principle, like the principle of redress, compensates the less advantaged; he says instead, "It transforms the aims of the basic structure so that the total scheme of institutions no longer emphasizes social efficiency and technocratic values" (*TJ*, 101/87 rev.). How does it transform them? Rawls immediately adds here the frequently misconstrued "common assets" claim:

> The difference principle represents, in effect, an agreement *to regard the distribution of natural talents* as in some respects a *common asset* and to share in the greater social and economic benefits made possible by the complementarities of this distribution. Those who have been favored by nature, whoever they are, may gain from their good fortune only on terms that improve the situation of those who have lost out."[12] (*TJ*, 101/87 rev.; emphases added; see also 179/156 rev.)

The general point, then, is that the passages most commonly cited provide little, if any, evidence for the claim that Rawls is a luck egalitarian, or that he provides an embryonic version of luck egalitarianism, or that he is, in spite of himself, somehow committed to luck egalitarianism.[13] Instead, he denies that the difference principle aims to equalize or redress handicaps or other social, natural, and other accidental inequalities, and says that people can gain from accidental inequalities on terms that improve the situation of those who have lost out. This is not simply an exegetical point about the difference principle. It is important when we consider whether the difference principle is a more reasonable response to the "natural lottery" than is luck egalitarianism.

---

12. As a gloss on this passage, Rawls years later says: "It is not said that this distribution *is* a common asset: to say that would presuppose a (normative) principle of ownership that is not available in the fundamental ideas from which we begin the exposition. Certainly the difference principle is not to be derived from such a principle as an independent premise. . . . [Instead,] by agreeing to that [difference] principle, it is *as if* they agreed *to regard* the distribution of endowments as a common asset. What this regarding consists in is expressed by the difference principle itself. . . . What is regarded as a common asset is the distribution of native endowments and not our native endowments per se. It is not as if society owned individuals' endowments . . . To the contrary, the question of ownership of our endowments does not arise and *should it arise it is persons themselves who own their endowments*: the psychological and physical integrity of persons is already guaranteed by the basic rights and liberties that fall under the first principle of justice." (*Restatement*, 75; emphasis added).

13. Here I am in agreement with Samuel Scheffler's perceptive treatment of these issues in "What is Egalitarianism?" *Philosophy & Public Affairs* 31 (Winter 2003): 5–39, esp. 8–12, 24–31. He says that, rather than seeking to equalize the contingencies of natural endowment and social class, "Rawls's emphasis on the moral arbitrariness of natural attributes and social starting points is meant to undercut our tendency to treat those factors as morally authoritative, especially when doing so would compromise something morally fundamental," namely, maintaining the status of citizens as equals (26).

II. Responsibility and Luck Egalitarianism

What now of Hurley's argument against luck egalitarianism, that considerations of responsibility do not, by themselves, tell us much of anything about *how* we ought to distribute goods or resources? With regard to luck, she similarly contends that simply because something is a matter of luck does not mean it should be equally distributed (*JLK*, 151). One reason for this, she says, is that "the fact that people are *not responsible* for difference does not mean that they *are* responsible for *non-difference*. . . . people may not be responsible for either. If so, then equalizing no more neutralizes luck than maximining does" (*JLK*, 152; italics in original).

I think Hurley, here, is correct, that treating people equally does not, perhaps cannot, "neutralize" luck. The reason (if I understand her correctly) is that equality of position is itself (often) a matter of luck, and if that is the case, then luck is not neutralized by distributing the unequal effects of natural differences equally. What this seems to imply is that some other principle must be invoked to justify equal distributions. What might this principle be?

In defense of luck egalitarianism, I think what might be said is the following: Sidgwick says that it is a self-evident "fundamental principle that individuals in similar cases should be treated similarly." This principle—which he sees as among the "axioms of practical reason"—is "more or less clearly implied by the common notion of 'fairness' or 'equity.'"[14] Sidgwick earlier provides a variation of this "principle of equity" as a response to the question, What conditions must laws fulfill in order that they may be just in their distributive effects? (*Methods*, 266). He responds that "justice here is thought to resolve itself into a kind of equality" (*Methods*, 267) in that like cases are to be treated alike. Rawls, too, endorses this principle—similar cases ought to be treated similarly—as a formal requirement of justice. It is the basis for what he calls "formal justice," the rule of law and "justice as regularity" (*TJ*, sec. 38, 58–59/50–52 rev.).

Assume now that we all have the natural talents we do due to the "natural lottery," in the sense that our differences in natural endowments are all a matter of luck. The luck egalitarian might reason as follows: "Why shouldn't we be treated equally with regard to this natural distribution and its effects? For, after all, like cases should be treated alike. Why shouldn't the benefits and burdens that result from the exercise of our natural endowments be equally shared? This is not simply (as Hurley says) a 'default position' (*JLK*, 152). It is, rather, required by a fundamental principle of justice. It is clearly less arbitrary to treat equal cases equally, and distribute the products of luck equally, than any other distribution. This is true, even if, as Hurley claims, the ways in which we are by chance equal can also be a matter of luck. Of course this is true, but the point is that there is a fundamental moral principle that says that like cases ought to be treated alike regardless—*whether or not* likenesses or similarities are the result of luck or of effort.

---

14. Henry Sidgwick, *The Methods of Ethics*, 7th ed. (Indianapolis: Hackett, 1981), 380 (cited in text as *Methods*).

I do not see any "egalitarian fallacy" with this position. If so, then it would seem that luck egalitarians do not need to draw the faulty inference that Hurley assigns to them (*JLK*, 152). The inference of equal treatment and equal distribution they draw is based upon a basic moral principle.

Something very much like this "principle of equity" is the principle that Sidgwick, and many other utilitarians, appeal to in order to argue that equal consideration should be given to everyone's equal interests. If human beings are equals in all relevant respects, then they should be treated equally, at least in the absence of compelling reasons. On the assumption that happiness is the ultimate good, and that satisfying people's desires or promoting their welfare is the right thing to do, we should give equal consideration to everyone's equal interests. The result, presumedly, is that we should seek to maximize aggregate satisfactions or welfare.

"So too," the luck egalitarian might claim, "if human beings are equals in relevant respects, namely with regard to their lack of responsibility or desert for their natural talents (or for differences in natural talents), it should follow they should be treated equally with regard to the effects of their natural talents. Equal treatment is mandated because like cases (of non-responsibility in this case) ought to be treated alike."

This position might appear to resemble the "equality default" view that Hurley discusses (*JLK*, 153–54). She says of this position: "This view in effect helps itself to equality as the default position" (*JLK*, 154). But perhaps it does not help itself to equality wholly without reason: for equality is taken as the default position because of the principle of equity, that similar cases ought to be treated similarly. This is what is wrong with the "inequality-default view" Hurley discusses, that "aristocrats should have more than peasants, whether this is a matter of luck or not" (*JLK*, 154). There being no morally relevant difference between aristocrats and commoners at birth, it is simply not true that aristocrats ought to have more, for it violates the fundamental principle of justice: "Like cases should be treated alike."

It may be that Hurley is correct to say, "The specifically egalitarian character of the equality-default position owes nothing to the aim to neutralize luck" (*JLK*, 154). On my account, we should redistribute equally the effects of luck, not in order to neutralize luck but to treat similar cases similarly. I would conjecture that this Principle of Equity underlies the intuition of luck egalitarianism. If so, there is no egalitarian fallacy implicit in luck egalitarianism, at least not in the absence of some compelling reason to treat similar cases dissimilarly and distribute the effects of luck unequally.

It is important that the statement of Sidgwick's Principle of Equity and formal justice is accompanied by a *ceteris paribus* clause. Is there any moral consideration that would justify departing from the assumption that similar cases of non-responsibility ought to be treated similarly, and hence justify rejecting the luck egalitarian conclusion that the effects of natural differences ought to be distributed equally? Rawls raises a similar question when he initially provides an "intuitive argument" for the difference principle from the original position. He says:

The sensible thing [for the parties in the original position] is to acknowledge as the first step a principle of justice requiring an equal distribution. Indeed, this principle is so obvious given the symmetry of the parties that it would occur to everyone immediately. . . . [But] there is no reason why this initial acknowledgment should be final. Society should take into account economic efficiency and the requirements of organization and technology. If there are inequalities in income and wealth, and differences in authority and degrees of responsibility, that work to make everyone better off in comparison with the benchmark of equality, why not permit them? . . . Thus the basic structure should allow these inequalities so long as these improve everyone's situation, including that of the least advantaged, provided that they are consistent with equal liberty and fair opportunity. Because the parties start from an equal division of all social primary goods, those who benefit least have, so to speak, a veto. Thus we arrive at the difference principle. Taking equality as the basis of comparison, those who have gained more must do so on terms that are justifiable to those who have gained the least." (*TJ*, 150–51/130–31 rev.)

By the same token, just as it is rational to depart from equal distribution in the original position, one might argue that it is a good and sufficient moral reason to depart from distributing the effects of natural fortune equally when an unequal distribution would redound to the benefit of everyone, starting with the least advantaged position. For, in that case, not only does everyone benefit but the least advantaged benefit maximally, since under no other arrangement would they be in a better position. What could be the reasons against permitting an inequality of this kind? So long as the least advantaged maximally benefit from the inequality, there is no reason for them to be dejected or resentful simply because others are in a better position; for all has been done to secure added advantages to people in their position. And those who are more advantaged have little reason to complain either, since they are allowed to benefit from the accidental advantages of nature they enjoy much more than they otherwise would if the effects of the natural lottery were equally distributed. Seen in this way, luck egalitarianism might be regarded as the initial step of an argument for the difference principle. But it is an initial step in an argument, and not itself a stopping point or a conclusive position.

Is this a sufficient argument for the difference principle? Before going on, it should be noted that Rawls perhaps overstates the conclusion in his "intuitive argument" above. Perhaps the more advantaged do have *some* reason to complain about the difference principle. There are other ways that inequalities may improve everyone's situation without their maximally benefiting the position of the least advantaged. For example, suppose the economy is designed to provide the least advantaged with an adequate social minimum (adequate to the exercise and development of their moral powers) that well exceeds what they would obtain were strict equality the rule; but once all are provided with the adequate minimum (via income subsidies, etc.) and other social demands are met (public goods, meeting the needs of the handicapped, etc.), remaining income and wealth is distributed (for example) via market transactions and people's free choices, or to maximize average utility, or to maximize the amount of wealth in society. These are perhaps not unreasonable alternatives. After all, Rawls says above that the reason for departure from equality is to allow for economic efficiency and the effects of organization and technology. Given these reasons, why isn't one of these positions equally rational for the parties, if not more so, than the difference principle? Rawls says that the least advantaged have a veto over any departure from equality, but this is true of everyone else—the more advantaged as well as the less advantaged—since the argument from the original position requires unanimous agreement. Why, then, couldn't the parties in the original position reason that, once an adequate social minimum is guaranteed, no one needs to worry any longer about impoverishment or not having adequate resources to exercise their basic liberties and pursue their good? In this case, why isn't it rational to take a chance that one will be among the more advantaged, and choose a principle that permits greater advantages to the wealthy and greater inequalities than the difference principle? So we arrive at a prima facie justification for the capitalist welfare state, which guarantees minimal welfare for all, but allows the efficiency of markets and people's free choices to determine the further distribution of income and wealth. Rawls needs to say more to justify the difference principle from the original position than he says in the "intuitive argument" above. At most his intuitive argument justifies certain departures from equality that benefit everyone.

Nor is the argument Rawls gives in *TJ*, section 26, from the maximin rule of choice and the rationality of risk aversion behind the veil of ignorance adequate to justify the difference principle. For, among the conditions that make the maximin rule of choice appropriate is that there is no alternative choice that offers an acceptable minimum (*TJ*, 115–16/134 rev.). But the alternatives to the difference principle mentioned above all provide an adequate social minimum. As Rawls later says:

> Despite the resemblance between the difference principle as a principle of distributive justice and the maximin rule as a rule of thumb for decisions under uncertainty, the reasoning for the difference principle does not rely upon this rule. The formal resemblance is misleading. (*Restatement*, 94–95)

So even though the intuitive argument might justify a departure from equal division, we are still left in need of an argument for the difference principle specifically, as opposed to some other distributive principle providing an adequate social minimum. Neither the informal comparison of Democratic Equality with Natural Liberty and Liberal Equality (*TJ*, sec. 12), nor the intuitive argument above (*TJ*, sec. 26), nor the argument from maximin from the original position (Ibid.) are adequate or designed to supply that argument. Rawls subsequently provides a number of arguments for the difference principle; these appear in A *Theory of Justice*, section 49, "Mixed Conceptions," as well as in subsequent works, and offer the same alternatives to the difference principle mentioned above.[15] Among the

---

15. See also "Justice as Fairness" (1958), secs. 34–38, and "Some Reasons for the Maximin Criterion" (1974), in Rawls, *Collected Papers*, ed. Samuel Freeman (Cambridge, MA: Harvard University Press, 1999), 388, 225 (cited in text as *CP*).

reasons he provides for the choice of the difference principle over the alternatives mentioned are reciprocity among equal citizens, the publicity of the difference principle, maintaining citizens' bases of self-respect, the strains of commitment, and stability. Whether these arguments are successful would require an extended discussion, one which we need not undertake for purposes of this paper, which is to show that Rawls makes no commitment to luck egalitarianism.

III. Responsibility for Ends

Another aspect of Rawls's position that is pointed to in support of his commitment to luck egalitarianism is the idea that people are to be held responsible for their ends.[16] This is an aspect of individuals' freedom, Rawls says. Since moral persons have the capacities to form, revise and pursue a rational plan of life, they are presumed to be in control of their aims and the desires that motivate them, and can adjust their aspirations in light of the resources they can reasonably expect to acquire.[17] We do not regard one another as "passive carriers of desires" (PL, 186). A person's tastes and desires are then not to be treated like handicaps or other disabilities; they are not accidents of fortune or foisted upon us by nature or circumstance, but are regarded as freely assumed and part of a person's life plan. People therefore should take responsibility for and pay the costs of their free choices. They should bring their desires and tastes into line with the income and wealth they can reasonably expect under the difference principle. Hence, a person who has expensive tastes, no matter how he or she came about acquiring them, should be held responsible for them and cannot impose added demands upon society to subsidize choices that satisfy expensive tastes.

Here Kymlicka, Arneson, and others claim that Rawls's endorsement of responsibility for ends implies a commitment to luck egalitarian premises. Luck egalitarianism says that people should not be held responsible for "brute luck," the accidents of birth and fortune that beset them during their lives. The "flip side" of this is that a person is to be held responsible for her choices (LCC, 73) (including the contingencies that eventuate as a result of choice—which Dworkin calls "option luck").[18] Responsibility for ends means that a person is required to pay the costs of her choices that result from her ends. But (Kymlicka objects) Rawls's difference principle does not require the least advantaged to pay for the cost of their choices. Suppose someone chooses to play tennis or to surf all day, and does not work or otherwise produce any income. Without income, this indolent person and others like him will be among the least advantaged. But then working people who are born similarly endowed will be required to subsidize the indolent person's choice of a leisure life-plan. As Ronald Dworkin says, "It seems

16. See, for example, G. A. Cohen, "On the Currency of Egalitarian Justice," *Ethics* 99, no. 4 (1989): 906–44, at 914–15.

17. Rawls, *Political Liberalism* (New York: Columbia University Press, 1993; paperback edition, 1996, 2004), 33–34, 186 (cited in the text as *PL*; references are to the paperback edition).

18. Ronald Dworkin, *Sovereign Virtue* (Cambridge, MA: Harvard University Press, 2000), (cited in text as *SV*).

unfair wholly to ignore the impact of a welfare scheme on people who are not in the worst-off group . . . but who nevertheless must struggle to secure a decent living for their families, and who unsurprisingly feel resentment when part of their hard-won wage is taken in taxes and paid over to those who do not work at all" (SV, 331). It is unfair, presumably, because (Dworkin seems to think) the difference principle does not hold the least advantaged responsible for their choices; its "discontinuous character prevents it from taking account of choice and conduct in the right way" (SV, 330). If the indolent want to live a life of leisure, they should find some way to pay for it without expecting others to subsidize their indolence. This is yet another way, it is alleged, in which the difference principle contravenes the luck egalitarian assumptions underlying Rawls's position.[19]

Here it is important to recall that the difference principle is a reciprocity principle, designed to structure the fair cooperative norms of property and economic relations among free and equal persons. As a reciprocity principle, it assumes that all will do their fair share in maintaining the system of cooperation. This includes their making a contribution to productive output. Rawls takes for granted "that all are willing to work and to do their part in sharing the burdens of social life."[20] It is for this reason that the least advantaged, according to the difference principle, are defined not as the most indolent and non-productive class, or as the most handicapped, but as unskilled working people who make up the minimum income–minimum wage workers, in effect. What then does Rawls do with people who do not work at all, and who otherwise cannot support their lifestyle?

Begin with the handicapped: the complaint is often raised that the difference principle does not adequately respond to the needs of handicapped citizens. Again, Dworkin says the difference principle "seems insufficiently sensitive to the position of those with natural handicaps, physical or mental, who do not themselves constitute a worst-off group, because this is defined economically" (SV, 113). For a luck egalitarian, the prospects of the most handicapped should be of utmost concern for an account of distributive justice. But for Rawls, if people are so handicapped that they are prevented from working and "can never be normal contributing members of social cooperation" (Restatement, 170), then their disability is not to be regarded as a problem of distributive justice or the difference principle (cf. PL, 21). Rawls sees distributive justice as part of social justice (for reasons discussed at length in chap. 8 of this volume). For Rawls, social justice is a distinct kind of justice, different from humanitarian justice, global justice, and various forms of local justice (within the family and other associations). What makes social justice distinct is that its primary focus is setting the terms of social cooperation, including the basic structure of society. As part of social justice (rather than humanitarian justice or global justice), distributive justice concerns (in the ideal case) the regulation of economic relations and distribution of the product among socially

19. See LCC, 73–76, for a similar argument.
20. "We assume that all citizens are normally and fully cooperating members of society over a complete life. . . . Now this assumption implies that all are willing to work and to do their part in sharing the burdens of social life provided of course the terms of cooperation are seen as fair" (Restatement, 179).

productive free and equal citizens who are engaged in social cooperation. Partly for this reason, the difference principle is not an allocative principle which can be applied to divide up a preexisting supply of goods. Rather, it is designed to apply in the first instance to basic economic and legal institutions (to specify, among other things, the institution of property and other legal relations necessary to production, exchange, and consumption of goods and resources), in order that distributions of income and wealth may be decided by "pure procedural justice" (*TJ*, 86–88/75–77 rev.). These distributions go to those engaged in economic cooperation.

Insofar as those with handicaps are able to work and to do their part in sharing the burdens of social life, then they receive their fair share under the difference principle like everyone else. But their handicaps are addressed by other principles of justice. When cooperating citizens are impeded by illness, accidents, and resulting disabilities, the principle of fair equality of opportunity requires that they be provided with resources needed to enable them to take advantages of the opportunities within the normal range of functioning for people with their level of abilities and disabilities (*PL*, 184; *Restatement*, 174). "The aim is to restore people by health care so that once again they are fully cooperating members of society" (*PL*, 184). (Here Rawls follows Norman Daniels' suggestions [*PL*, 184n]). But when severely disabled or handicapped people are seriously hindered or altogether prevented from engaging in productive and cooperative activity, then what? Again clearly the difference principle does not apply to address their extraordinary needs. But Rawls does not say here just what principles should apply, though he clearly regards severe handicaps as a problem of justice that must be addressed (*PL*, 21). Perhaps the best way to approach the severely handicapped within Rawls's existing framework is a twofold approach: First, proceed by analogy with governments' duty of assistance to burdened peoples in the Law of Peoples and with the natural duty of mutual aid individuals owe to one another. Each society is obligated to apply an analogous principle of assistance to address and alleviate the mental and physical disabilities and special needs of its members who are without the capacities for social cooperation. They are to make these determinations after conscientious (democratic) deliberation and in consideration of the resources that society is able to employ given its other duties and responsibilities under the principles of justice, and its historical and economic circumstances. Here an appropriate guide in determining the level of medical assistance and educational benefits might be by analogy with the principle of fair equal opportunity: we should provide those incapable of social cooperation with a reasonable degree of medical care and training designed to enable them to develop and exercise their (diminished) capacities so that they can take advantage of whatever activities are available to people with their level of disability. The important point is that the aim of such remedies is not to try to compensate people in a vain effort to equalize natural fortune but to enable them so far as possible to exercise the abilities they have, whether or not they can become fully cooperating members of a democratic society (cf. *PL*, 184; *Restatement*, 175).[21]

---

21. See Scheffler, "What is Egalitarianism?" 29–30, on how Rawls's treatment of special needs and the handicapped differs from luck egalitarianism's.

Rawls does not say enough about the principles or mechanics needed to address special needs and handicaps (see, however, *PL*, 183–86; *Restatement*, 171–76), and he admits that further guidelines need to be developed for more extreme cases (*PL*, 21; *Restatement*, 176n). This is a particularly difficult problem for any conception of justice, given the virtually limitless needs of those severely handicapped. But given the priority of fair equality of opportunity (and perhaps the natural duties as well) over the difference principle, justice as fairness implicitly requires (I believe) that the basic needs of the handicapped be addressed (like the claims of future generations under the just savings principle), even if not fully settled, before the level of the difference principle's basic minimum income is determined.

Now what about healthy able-bodied citizens who voluntarily choose to forgo productive activity in favor of a leisure lifestyle, and are not otherwise wealthy enough to support themselves—full-time surfers and tennis players, and others? Contrary to the objections raised above, Rawls *does* hold them responsible for their life choices. "Surfers must somehow support themselves" (*Restatement*, 179). (This assumes that it is society's duty, under fair equality of opportunity, to insure full employment and make sure that opportunities for fruitful work are generally available.) There are two ways to hold the leisurely responsible for their leisure choices under the difference principle (Ibid).[22] First, leisure time itself might be treated as a primary social good, which is calculated into the index that determines who is least advantaged. Non-workers will then be deemed to have eight hours more leisure per day and regarded as that much better off than those who work and enjoy less leisure time. Second, assume that everyone works a standard eight-hour working day: then for those who are among the least advantaged because they voluntarily choose not to work (or work only part-time), we could subtract from the minimum income guaranteed them by the difference principle some measure of the income that they would have gained had they chosen to work eight hours (for example, an amount that equals the market income of the least skilled worker for a normal working day; or perhaps the amount that the surfer, given his past work history or level of skills, did or could earn from the market if he chose to work now).

Rawls does not go into the details here. In any case, either alternative can leave the able-bodied indolent with still some income supplements according to the difference principle, perhaps enough for them to sustain themselves indefinitely while enjoying their unproductive lifestyle. But why is this a problem? When unemployed, people still do their part in maintaining the scheme of cooperation in other ways: they perform their civic duties as well as social duties and charitable actions, they observe the laws, respect others' property, and so on. If free-riding is the fear, full-time surfers and others in the leisure class are paying the costs for their choice of lifestyle, as it is measured by the difference principle, for they have deducted from their guaranteed minimum income an amount

22. See also "Reply to Alexander and Musgrave" (1974) in *CP*, 253, for a discussion of leisure time as a primary good.

equal to the leisure time they enjoy. Incentive and free-riding-problems should then be adequately addressed.

Here a libertarian will object that the indolent do not pay their *full costs* and are still subsidized to some degree; no matter how valuable their cooperation may be otherwise, they do not produce *income or wealth* but still receive as subsidy a portion of the income normally guaranteed by the difference principle. But again, why is this a moral problem? People who are more advantaged and are the beneficiaries of gifts and bequests do not produce that income either and are subsidized (privately) to that degree as well. Are such gifts to the more advantaged any more deserved than income subsidies to the least advantaged? Here the libertarian no doubt will say that they do "deserve" it in the sense that they are the beneficiary of someone else's free choice, unlike the surfer. But that is a separate issue (addressed below) from the objection raised—that surfers do not pay their full costs. Neither pays.

Others will object that it is unfair for working people to be taxed to subsidize able-bodied indolence to any degree (see Dworkin's criticism of the difference principle above). This raises a larger question, namely, why should the baseline for a person's entitlements be set by the amount of income a person gains from labor and other market activity and by free gift from others? To begin with, the gifts and bequests a person receives are largely a matter of fortune, depending upon the social position of one's family and friends. Moreover, economic output is a social product that results from the participation of all who contribute to the process of production, and, more generally, by all who engage in social cooperation and respect others' claims and expectations as defined by law and other terms of cooperation. While allocation of the factors of production is most efficiently achieved by markets in labor and other resources, this is not justification for presuming that market distributions of income and wealth create entitlements and are just, or even for regarding markets as providing a presumptive measure for the just distribution of income and wealth that result from social cooperation. It should not, then, be simply assumed that the proceeds of taxation of those better off that are used to provide income supplements to the less advantaged implies that the more advantaged are subsidizing the poor. This presumes what has yet to be proved, namely, that all are entitled from the outset to all transfers to them from market activity. If taxation has any role at all in establishing just distributions, then it cannot be that people have a right to all transfers accruing to them through market activity, gifts, bequests, and gambling.[23]

Here Dworkin sees markets and the price system as justified since they measure the opportunity costs of a person's choices on others, and, for this reason, they provide the baseline for determining the costs of assuming responsibility for one's ends (SV, 69–70). But this does not justify using markets as the primary basis for determining the distributive shares people have at their disposal to pay for goods and services (after adding in the amount they may gain by compensation for natural and social misfortune). It only seems to imply that, however we

---

23. The role of taxation in establishing just distributions is discussed in Liam Murphy's and Thomas Nagel's *The Myth of Ownership: Taxes and Justice* (Oxford: Oxford University Press, 2002).

decide distributive shares, people should be required to pay the full costs of their choices as determined by their market price. So far as this goes, it does not conflict with using the difference principle to determine the distribution of income and wealth, including the income subsidies that are to go to the least advantaged. The least advantaged are held responsible for their ends in that they have to pay the full costs of their choices; they pay the same for goods and services as does anyone else. Moreover, even indolent surfers pay the full costs of their leisure choices, as measured by the difference principle, since the costs of their leisure is subtracted from their social minimum. But in their objection that the difference principle requires the diligent to subsidize the leisure choices of the indolent, it appears that Dworkin and Kymlicka (like Nozick and libertarians) rely upon market distributions and gifts as the baseline for the entitlements a person has (again, after taking into account what a person might also be due as compensation for inherited disadvantage), and then measure the costs that a person's choices impose upon others from this market distribution baseline.[24] It is this assumption about the distribution baseline for measuring entitlements and costs to others that requires justification, and I believe it must be done in terms other than taking responsibility for one's choices. For, to take responsibility for one's own choices does *not* mean that one must also take responsibility for *not being the beneficiary of others' choices*; nor does responsibility for one's choices imply that a person has the right to enjoy the full measure of others' market decisions or gifts if he is chosen by them.

The problem for any luck egalitarian in relying upon markets and the market wage in order to determine distributive shares resulting from people's choices is that prices (including the price of labor) and distributions resulting from market choices are, like being a beneficiary of others' gifts and gambling, often as much a matter of chance and even indirect brute luck as are accidents of social class and the natural lottery. An elderly couple retires to Palm Springs after selling for millions the family home in Palo Alto for which they paid a pittance in 1960, while

---

24. Dworkin says: "We must, on pain of violating equality, allow the distribution of resources at any particular moment to be . . . ambition-sensitive. It must . . . reflect the cost or benefit to others of the choices people make so that, for example, those who choose to invest rather than consume . . . or to work in more profitable rather than less profitable ways *must be permitted to retain the gains that flow from these decisions* in an equal auction followed by free trade. But . . . we must not allow the distribution of resources at any moment to be endowment-sensitive, that is, to be affected by differences in ability of the sort that produce income differences in a laissez-faire economy" (SV, 89; emphases added). The right to what one gains by market activity is also implicit in Dworkin's contention: "If . . . no one can earn movie star wages, people who wish to watch movies may perhaps find very different fare available which, rightly or wrongly, they will not regard as highly as what they now have" (SV,105); as well in his discussion of the similarities and differences between his position and Nozick's regarding the role of markets, and the Wilt Chamberlain example (SV, 111–12). In spite of their many differences, "both Nozick's theory and equality of resources . . . give a prominent place to the idea of a market, and *recommend the distribution that is achieved by a market suitably defined and constrained*" (SV, 111; emphases added). In Nozick's example, starting out with equal shares, "each of many people pays a small sum to watch Chamberlain play basketball, after which he grows rich and wealth is no longer equal. Equality of resources would not denounce that result, considered in itself. Chamberlain's wealth reflects the *value to others* of his leading his life as he does" (Ibid.; emphases added). I understand this to mean that people have a presumptive right to what they gain

a couple in the Rust Belt cannot afford to move since their same model home is now worth much less than they paid in 1960. One industry of workers receives a higher wage because of increased demand for the good they manufacture and a shortage of the labor supply in the region, whereas another group has its wages reduced or is laid off because decreased demand for their product and an over-supply of labor. One fashion designer gains riches and fame because fickle teen-age tastes prefer the culottes worn by Britney Spears to Angelina Jolie's miniskirts. Why should the fortunate owner, worker, or designer be entitled to the entire windfall, and others similarly positioned, or, more fittingly, the less advantaged, gain nothing? Here Dworkin says that, were the designer or the movie star not able to earn "movie star wages" (SV, 105), then the service they provide to others will go unperformed, thereby presumably frustrating some people's choices. This may be true to a degree at the margin depending on income effects (for example, Pavarotti might make 20 rather than 25 appearances one year—but then again, because of substitution effects he may make 30 appearances in order to buy a new villa in Capri). But this is a point about income effects and the wisdom of incentives in satisfying people's preferences, not a point about people taking responsibility for their choices.

It is true that the property owner's windfall or "movie star wages" may reflect, as Dworkin says, "the value to others" of movie stars' and fortunate real-estate owners' leading the life they do (or at least reflect the value to others of the prop-erty the real estate owners hold).[25] But, granting the point that others should pay the full market price in order to take responsibility for *their* choices, why should the fortunate recipients of the benefits of *others'* choices have a presumptive right to the entire income? Again, taking responsibility for *my* choices (regarding when and how much I work, for example) does not mean that I be the exclusive benefi-ciary from the *choices of others* who do business with me. By the same token, tak-ing responsibility for *my* choices does not entail that I must assume full respon-sibility for being neglected or ignored by *others'* choices should I lose out due to market contingencies and an oversupply of workers in the labor force.

Here, on Dworkin's account, it might be said the fortunate property owner, designer, worker, and movie star do not receive and are not entitled to the full amount of income their market activity stimulates, but must pay their fair share in taxes to fund public goods and the welfare programs that compensate the unfor-

---

on the market—"to each as they are chosen" as Nozick says (*Anarchy, State, and Utopia*, 160)—assuming, in the ideal case, that they start from an equal position and, in the real world, that they have been duly compensated for inevitable inequalities of natural and social position. Of course, all this assumes that people will pay their fair share to fund the social insurance scheme, public goods, and other requirements in Dworkin's account. See also SV, 70.

25. Query: Is "value to others" anything more than marginal product? In the case of the owner of property, his "value to others" or "marginal product" is not the result of *his producing* anything; rather he simply enjoys returns to ownership. Why should he have full rights to the income for "his," namely, the real estate's, marginal product? What does an owner's receiving the full marginal product of the value of real estate have to do with his taking responsibility for his choices? If he were aware beforehand that enormous capital gains would be taxed at 50% to pay income supplements for the less advantaged, isn't he just as responsible for his choice as if he had not been taxed at all?

tunate for the adverse effects of brute chance and circumstance. But this still leaves in the hands of economic agents a substantial surplus that is the product of market luck. Market prices and market choices—the mechanisms Dworkin and Rawls appeal to in holding people responsible for the costs of their choices—are suffused with the effects of good and bad luck. While it is understandable that a price system is used to determine what people must pay for goods and services, it seems peculiar for someone who puts so much emphasis upon neutralizing the effects of chance and fortune to ultimately leave distributions up to the chance and fortune of market trends.

Dworkin will reply that since market prices are the result of people's choices, this is "option luck," the combined result of people's choices, and not "brute luck," the kind that nature or circumstance inflicts upon us. And it is brute luck, not option luck, that should be compensated, for option luck is the combined result of other people's choices and defines "the parameters of justice" (SV, 298). But why should distributions to people that exceed the socially assured baseline be entirely the product of their option luck in the market (plus proceeds from gifts and gambles) any more than product of their brute luck? Like libertarianism (though clearly in a more humane way), Dworkin allows distributions after a point to be decided by the accumulated results of many separate and ostensibly fair transactions, social trends, historical contingencies, and the accidents of the sum of innumerable historical choices. This does not mean that "option luck" should not affect distributions—if a person wants to gamble away the social minimum she is entitled to under the difference principle, or spend all her income for some expensive good in high demand like champagne, she will be held responsible and will not be compensated for her foolishness or expensive tastes. It means, rather, that the benchmark for basic *entitlements* each is due (after compensation for brute luck) is not at any point to be determined by market contingencies and the accidents of how much one is chosen (or not), any more than by natural contingencies.

Rawls's difference principle seeks to maintain the "background justice" (*Restatement*, 10, 54) of the social institutions that provide the framework for market activity and within which people's choices are made. It maintains background justice so that the income and wealth that is jointly produced comes to be eventually distributed, not according to each person's "value to others" or their marginal product and the confluence of historical contingencies but on terms of reciprocity among free and equal citizens. The question the difference principle addresses is: How are the basic institutional norms of economic production and distribution to be structured among free and equal persons who are socially productive and who aim to cooperate with one another on terms of reciprocity and mutual respect? This establishes an altogether different focus and aim for distributive justice than a luck egalitarian distributive scheme that is designed to be "endowment insensitive" by compensating for natural and social inequalities, and "ambition sensitive" (SV, 89) by rewarding people according to their option luck in being chosen by others after making their career and investment choices.

It would require more discussion than can be given here to show why it is a mistake to base distributive justice upon any version of the luck egalitarian choice/circumstance (or "ambition/endowment") distinction.[26] The problem is not simply that we often should alleviate the consequences of people's bad choices and should not try to compensate the disadvantages resulting from many unchosen aspects of a person's life. Nor is the problem simply that there is no way to equalize, neutralize, or eliminate the effects of many natural misfortunes and handicaps by compensation (how does one "compensate" the autistic or those with fatal genetic diseases?).[27] Nor is the problem simply that the choice/circumstance distinction is so difficult to draw and is too often indeterminate. The main shortcoming of luck egalitarianism, I believe, is that principles of distributive justice must focus on far more than simply questions of compensation for undeserved inequalities, if these principles are to serve as a fair basis for economic production and distribution among free and equal citizens. This is a question to which we now can turn.

IV. A Problem with Luck Egalitarianism

I've argued that using markets and the price system to hold people responsible for their ends does not justify reliance on market prices to settle the distribution of income and wealth. Taking responsibility for one's own choices does not imply taking full responsibility for others' choices upon oneself. What further justification might a luck egalitarian offer for accepting a fundamental role for market distribution? Suppose, in the previous examples, it is said that those who benefit from market luck should be entitled to their market returns (once they have paid their fair share for social insurance, public goods, etc.) because this encourages more innovation, risk-taking, savings, and investment, and these benefits lead to greater overall productive output for all. This is a sensible response, though one still has to clarify just why increasing aggregate output is such a good thing

---

26. On the problems with the choice/circumstance distinction, see Scheffler, "What is Egalitarianism," 17–21. Scheffler says that the weight that luck egalitarians place on the choice/circumstance distinction is "both philosophically dubious and morally implausible" (p. 17). People's identity is in large part defined by unchosen personal traits and circumstances into which they are born, and their voluntary choices are deeply influenced by these and other unchosen features of their lives. Moreover, for many disadvantageous personal attributes, it is implausible to demand compensation (my examples: less-than-average attractiveness, wittiness, or charm); and it is equally implausible that we not compensate urgent medical needs that result from people's negligence, foolishness, or high-risk behavior, not to mention rational choices that simply turn out badly (such as bankruptcy, unemployment, and other calamities of "option luck"—again, my examples). In response to Scheffler, the luck egalitarian may reply that all medical needs and personal catastrophes, whether resulting from choice or circumstance, will be covered by social insurance provisions provided for all (universal health care might be justified, for example, by Dworkin's hypothetical insurance scheme [SV, chap.9]). But the fact that Dworkin's hypothetical deliberators would foresee the wisdom of compensating people for medical and living needs resulting from bad choices as well as misfortune seems to belie the luck egalitarian choice/circumstance dichotomy. For, it suggests that justice requires that we collectively take social responsibility for and alleviate after all not just individuals' disadvantages resulting from brute bad luck, but also from their free choices and bad "option luck" as well.

27. For similar reasons, Kymlicka himself recognizes that, "[g]iven these difficulties, Rawls's refusal to compensate for natural disadvantages makes sense" (LCC, 79).

for a society to seek to do. Is it for reasons of maximizing the sum of advantages or welfare, or is it because greater output redounds to the benefit of everyone starting with the least advantaged, or is it for some other reason? Whatever the reason, I conjecture it has little to do with considerations of responsibility for choice or compensation for circumstance. There are reasons other than choice and circumstance that must underlie an account of distributive justice; holding people responsible for their choices and compensating them for brute misfortune are not sufficient to specify a system of distribution and all that must go with it. The luck egalitarian framework is not set up to respond to these sorts of questions.

Consider here what Rawls says about the luck egalitarian thesis that disadvantages are to be redressed or compensated:

> The principle of redress has not to my knowledge been proposed as the sole criterion of justice, as the single aim of the social order. It is plausible as most such principles are only as a prima facie principle, one that is to be weighed in the balance with others. For example, we are to weigh it against the principle to improve the average standard of life, or to advance the common good. But whatever other principles we hold, the claims of redress are to be taken into account. (*TJ*, 101/86 rev.)

The point, I take it, is that the luck egalitarian intuition that we should redress (mis)fortune by equalizing the effects of brute luck cannot by itself serve as a conception of distributive justice. At most, it provides a necessary condition that any principle of distributive justice must meet, or one that should be weighed in the balance with other equally pressing concerns. Even if we compensate brute luck and hold people responsible for their choices, before questions of distributive justice can be settled, we still have to decide how much weight to assign to considerations such as effort, inventiveness, risk-taking, contributions to production, and to people's free choices, along with the role of the common good, economic efficiency, people's standard of living, and so on, in defining a just distribution. To focus simply on starting endowments and responsibility for choices is too narrow a basis for a theory of distributive justice. This is Rawls's point (I believe) in saying that the principle of redress is at best a prima facie principle. This suggests that the luck egalitarian intuition is not itself sufficient for a conception of distributive justice; rather, at most it sets conditions upon whatever the final theory of distribution might be.

This is not to say that luck egalitarians believe that all distribution questions are settled by considering matters of choice and circumstance. They differ among themselves regarding such questions as the "currency" of distributive justice (welfare, resources, or capabilities), and Dworkin supports market distributions in a way and to a degree that G. A. Cohen and John Roemer do not. Nonetheless, they seem to agree that, however the economic system of production, transfer, and ownership is designed, and no matter who controls the means of production, or who actually produces the product, the distribution of final product should be made so that the effects of brute luck are equalized and people are held responsible for their choices.

But there is a further claim implicit in Rawls's saying that the principle of redress is at most a prima facie principle: namely, that the primary role of a theory of distributive justice is not to distribute income and wealth without regard to how it gets produced. More crucially, its role is to structure the social system of property and economic relations, and to do so in such a way that it affirms the freedom and equality of citizens, preserves their independence, and maintains their self-respect as they do their fair share in contributing to production and to social cooperation more generally. To serve this multifarious role, a theory of distributive justice has to have some goal other than merely distributing income and wealth so as to equalize the effects of (mis)fortune and hold people responsible for their choices. As Rawls says in his discussion of distributive justice: "I have assumed that the aim of the branches of government is to establish a democratic regime in which land and capital are widely though not presumably equally held. Society is not so divided that one fairly small sector controls the preponderance of productive resources" (*TJ*, 280/247 rev.). Moreover, in a well-ordered society, "the worst aspects of [the] division [of labor] can be surmounted: no one need be servilely dependent on others and made to choose between monotonous and routine occupations which are deadening to human thought and sensibility. Each can be offered a variety of tasks so that the different elements of his nature find a suitable expression" (*TJ*, 529/464 rev.). One of the main roles of fair equality of opportunity in establishing distributive justice is to guarantee the wide dispersal of productive resources, including technical knowledge, so that all may develop their productive capacities and engage in "meaningful work in free association with others."[28] This is part of what Rawls means in saying that "we cannot possibly take the difference principle seriously so long as we think of it by itself, apart from its setting within prior principles" (*Restatement*, 46n). For, "the requirements of the prior principles," particularly fair equality of opportunity, "have important distributive effects" (ibid.). To understand Rawls's theory of distributive justice, we have to take into account the aim and distributive effects of all three principles of justice, and their role in shaping basic economic institutions.

The luck egalitarian idea that basic economic institutions ought to be arranged so as equalize brute luck and hold people responsible for their choices says nothing about who should control means of production, how widespread the distribution of land and capital should be, limits on accumulation of resources and concentrations of wealth, the degree to which private and social ownership of natural resources and real capital are each in order, or about government's role in ensuring full employment and providing the unemployed jobs when necessary, or about the kinds of property interests that are legitimate and their extent, permissible and impermissible uses of property, or about the relationship of distributive justice to the common good and to enabling individuals to effectively exercise their capacities and their basic rights and liberties, and so on. Other than questions of distribution of final product and its consumption, luck egalitarianism gives little if any guidance in resolving many of the crucial questions about the

---

28. "What men want is meaningful work in free association with others, these associations regulating their relations to one another within a framework of just basic institutions" (*TJ*, 290/257 rev.).

basic structure of economic life of a democratic society. It imagines people, not as socially productive and as doing their fair share in contributing to social cooperation, but in a passive role as recipients and consumers of output, and tries to provide a recipe for dividing up the social product without regard to how or by whom it gets produced and in exchange for what contributions. Luck egalitarianism, in this way, abstracts from the social relations that underlie the production of income and wealth, and says that no matter how wealth gets produced or who contributes toward its production and to what degree, wealth and income are to be distributed without regard to any other considerations, simply in order to equalize the effects of brute luck and reward and hold people liable for their choices. This is a truncated conception of the role of a theory of distributive justice.

Here luck egalitarians might reply that they are only working through the most important considerations in constructing a theory of distributive justice, and that, of course, these other considerations (the specification of property rights and permissible economic relations, control of capital, limits on concentration of wealth, permissible uses of property, etc.) have to be dealt with before distributive shares are settled. But this just seems to be Rawls's point, namely, that luck egalitarianism provides only a prima facie principle that must be balanced off against other considerations which themselves have serious distributive consequences; it is by itself incapable of serving as a conception of distributive justice.

V. Incentives and Responsibility

For luck egalitarians, inequalities are justified when they are the product of people's free choice. For Rawls, inequalities are justifiable so long as they benefit everyone while maximally benefiting the least advantaged. It is not my purpose here to discuss or examine the persuasiveness of Rawls's several arguments for the difference principle. Instead I examine one reason he discusses for distributive inequalities:

> The function of unequal distributive shares is to cover the costs of training and education, to attract individuals to places and associations where they are most needed from a social point of view, and so on. Assuming that everyone accepts the propriety of self- or group-interested motivation duly regulated by a sense of justice, each decides to do those things that best accord with his aims. Variations in wages and income and the perquisites of position are simply to influence these choices so that the end result accords with efficiency and justice. (*TJ*, 315/277 rev.)

This passage suggests that a reason for inequalities in income and wealth is that *incentives* are needed to induce people to expend the extra time, energy, or money, and so on, to produce, or train themselves to produce, or undertake risks enabling production, and such. If people are going to temporarily forgo income in order to educate their natural abilities, forgo consumption in order to save, live in less attractive environments, or work longer hours or in more arduous positions, it is (in most cases) unreasonable to expect them to remain satisfied with an equal share. Moreover, reasonableness aside, the basic fact is that most people simply will refuse to undertake these and other additional sacrifices without some kind of incentive.

What is the legitimate scope for and extent of permissible incentives? G. A. Cohen contends that most if not all the incentives allowed by the difference principle are unreasonable, especially when they are needed and designed to induce people with greater or rarer natural talents to exercise their talents to benefit those less advantaged. Since Rawls recognizes "the propriety of self- or group-interested motivation" (*TJ*, 315/277 rev.) ("duly regulated by a sense of justice," one should add), what is to prevent the naturally gifted from taking advantage of their fortuitous position, and extracting unreasonable rewards in exchange for contributions, even if the outcome is to the benefit of the least advantaged? After all, were the naturally gifted not to exploit their natural gifts and demand so much for their services, the least advantaged would benefit even more. But Rawls's difference principle applies primarily to institutions and is not designed to directly serve as a guide to people's everyday choices; Rawlsian justice does not presuppose an "ethos" that requires economic agents to structure their individual choices and plans so as to benefit the least advantaged. Instead, benefits accrue to the least advantaged as a result of an "invisible hand" guided by the basic structure. But, Cohen objects, the invisible hand of the difference principle encourages self-seeking and exploitation by the naturally fortunate of their undeserved talents.

In chapters 8 and 9 of *Justice, Luck, and Knowledge*, Hurley focuses on this important topic, and argues that one area in which responsibility plays a legitimate role in distributive justice is in helping to settle the issue of the appropriate limits on permissible incentive seeking. While she rejects Cohen's luck egalitarianism, she agrees that Cohen has touched upon a legitimate point here regarding incentives. Hurley suggests that the kinds of beliefs people have about responsibility can affect the level of incentives required to motivate them to do extra work. ("Different levels of incentive seeking are possible relative to different beliefs about responsibility" [*JLK*, 235]). For example, a talented physician who believes he is entirely responsible for his marginal product may think that he should gain this entire amount, and these beliefs about income will lead him to demand this (excessive) amount as incentive for him to work longer hours in his position. This is what the talented physician must be paid if the least advantaged are to benefit. So, too, Hurley conjectures, if an equally talented person (another gifted physician, let's suppose) has a "regressive" and highly restricted conception of responsibility, according to which one has no responsibility for work habits, levels of skill, and so on, this person is more likely to adopt a much more altruistic position regarding incentives, requiring virtually no incentives to induce her to put the extra hours for standard pay, if not for free. Finally, a "non-regressive reason-responsiveness view of responsibility would land us in middle of spectrum of levels of incentive seeking,", and is consistent with accepting the maximin view (*JLK*, 315).[29]

---

29. "Maximin argument for incentive inequality invokes middle of spectrum" (*JLK*, 313).

The general point, then, is that, because of beliefs regarding responsibility, the incentives required to benefit the worst off under the difference principle vary markedly from one person to another. But why should peoples' beliefs about their responsibility for product (frequently falsely informed) be the determining factor in society's decision of how much will be distributed to the least advantaged? This, I presume, is the legitimate aspect Hurley sees in Cohen's argument against Rawls. "What is right [about it] is that a theory of distributive justice should not treat beliefs about responsibility and associated normative expectations as exogenously fixed external constraints. The mere fact that certain normative views are prevalent does not immunize them if they compromise the demands of justice. Egalitarians can criticize and reject the beliefs and expectations that underwrite certain levels of incentive seeking, rather than tamely accepting them and operating within the limits they impose" (*JLK*, 238). Later, Hurley says: "A maximin rule is relatively empty of content in the absence of such constraints [on the acceptable parameters of incentive seeking]. This is the critically important message that derives from Cohen's arguments about incentive inequality" (*JLK*, 247).

Why are incentives needed under the difference principle to induce people to exercise their talents in ways that benefit not only themselves but also the least advantaged? In a well-ordered society of justice as fairness, where the difference principle is embodied in basic institutions and is generally endorsed by reasonable persons, the need for incentives is not due to people's (false) beliefs about their responsibility, for example, for their marginal product and their expectations that they are entitled to the full value thereof. For, in a well-ordered society where all accept the difference principle, reasonable people do not have false libertarian or other beliefs about justice (such as self-ownership of oneself and one's marginal product); rather, they all accept and endorse justice as fairness and have a settled disposition to support institutions and rules that embody it, including the difference principle. The need for incentives, then, should not be distorted by libertarian beliefs about ownership of one's marginal product or other beliefs about responsibility. Rather, incentives are needed, and presumably are justified, in a society that is well ordered by the difference principle because of *people's free adoption and pursuit of plans of life that incorporate a plurality of (objective) goods*.[30] Reasonable persons affirm different goods and have different convictions about what is of ultimate importance; they make different judgments about the relative significance of primary ends and how they are going to divide their time

---

30. Here, my account is indebted to Samuel Scheffler's idea that it is for reasons of moral pluralism that incentives are needed under Rawls's difference principle. See "The Division of Moral Labour: Egalitarian Liberalism as Moral Pluralism," *Proceedings of the Aristotelian Society, Supplementary Volume* 79 (2005): 229–53. One qualification that should be made is that in *Political Liberalism* (as opposed to *A Theory of Justice*), Rawls cannot rely upon a controversial philosophical claim regarding the plurality of objective values. Here instead, the claim must be that incentives are justified by the subjective circumstances of justice and the fact that people pursue a plurality of permissible conceptions of the good and endorse different reasonable comprehensive doctrines—no philosophical judgment being made regarding the possibility that their conceptions of the good or comprehensive doctrines incorporate objective values.

in pursuit. A gifted physician or lawyer has to make the decision whether to spend five more hours with his children each week, or playing music, working for Habitat for Humanity, or doing any number of other worthwhile non-professional activities, versus devoting another five hours at the hospital or law office (doing pro bono work for the least advantaged, let's assume). What justifies paying him "time-and-a-half" or more for overtime is not his false libertarian beliefs about his self-determinating responsibility and his right to his entire marginal product. It is, rather, what is needed to induce him to give up time that otherwise would be devoted to pursuing one or another of the freely chosen ends he endorses in addition to his professional commitments. The problem that Hurley alludes to, namely, false beliefs about responsibility that distort incentives under the difference principle, should not arise to any substantial degree in a well-ordered society of justice as fairness where, by definition, all have a sense of justice that incorporates the difference principle.

Does the physician's or lawyer's choice depend on self-interest? It could, depending upon his freely chosen plan of life. That plan may include what we may regard as self-interested ends, for example, the sheer desire to accumulate wealth, or to live as comfortably as possible. But none of the ends mentioned above are self-interested ends. Instead, they are socially or individually worthwhile activities that are worth engaging in for their own sake (caring for one's children, making music, building homes for the displaced, etc.). Why should the naturally advantaged be morally expected to devote their extra time exclusively to working for the interests of the economically least advantaged members of society, instead of to these and other equally worthy social activities (working for the A.C.L.U., or spending time helping autistic or other handicapped people, for example)? Simply because the economic framework of a well-ordered society is, for reasons of reciprocity among free and equal persons, structured so as to maximally benefit the economically least advantaged does not imply that their economic interests should have priority in individuals' choices and life plans over all other ends, even all other social ends.

If this is so, it is no longer so clear what the truth is in Cohen's critique of the maximin argument for incentive inequality. Is it that Rawls and liberals have a false view about permissible life plans, namely they think that it is permissible for people to pursue plans of life that incorporate a plurality of final ends and that do not directly incorporate as a primary end for individual pursuit maximizing the prospects of the least advantaged? Is it that the freedom to form, revise, and pursue a conception of the good is not itself an important human interest? Or is it the claim that only pursuits based on true beliefs about the human good are allowed to set the parameters on incentive seeking? None of these claims is reasonable. (The last claim might appear reasonable, but it involves an unduly arduous requirement since it implies that freely chosen ends which are not based on true beliefs [most if not all religious practices, for example], or which are not worthy of pursuit [watching many television programs and other forms of popular culture, instead of working overtime for the least advantaged] do not create legitimate claims for incentives under the difference principle.)

Cohen seems to commit to the position that justice requires that individuals adopt as an ethos or primary end the direct and conscious pursuit of the maximization of the position (welfare or primary goods) of the least advantaged. Let's assume that this aim is an aspect of Cohen's account of the sense of justice. This differs from the primary end that Rawls, in his account of the sense of justice, assigns free and equal citizens in a well-ordered society. For Rawls, the sense of justice involves, in part, a supremely regulative desire to support, maintain, and help bring about just institutions which over time work to maximize the position of the worst off (while also providing for everyone's basic liberties and fair equal opportunities). The Rawlsian sense of justice also includes a disposition to adhere to the natural duties of equal respect, justice, mutual aid, emergency assistance, and so on, discussed further below. The difference between Rawls's and Cohen's accounts of the sense of justice is that, whereas Cohen insists that it is a motivational requirement of justice that individuals *directly aim to promote* the welfare of the least advantaged, Rawls seeks to promote the position of the least advantaged *indirectly*, namely through everyone's compliance with the institutional requirements of principles of justice and other duties as we pursue our individual rational plans of life. Unlike Cohen, Rawls is not a welfarist. This might account for some of the motivational difference in their view. (It perhaps makes better sense that all should have as a primary end the direct promotion of the welfare of the least advantaged than that all should seek to directly maximize the share of income and wealth of those economically least advantaged.) But, more likely, it is because Rawls gives priority to the plurality of objective human goods and the free choice of one's ends and rational life plan over the aim of maximizing the welfare or resources of the least advantaged. For Rawls, it is an essential part of each person's good that he or she freely decide what goods constitute a rational life plan, and also successfully execute this plan. (This is what it means for the parties in the original position to have a "higher-order interest" in the exercise and development of the capacity to be rational.) For some people, their direct promotion of the position of the least advantaged is a good, part of their rational plan assuming this end is freely endorsed. For others, it may not be. They will have presumably other ends to pursue that are equally worthwhile (for example, helping autistic people and other mentally and physically handicapped). But Rawls contends that, whatever people's free choices might be, it is important, indeed it is also an essential part of their good, that all have a settled disposition to act on and from principles of justice which are designed to maximize the position of the least advantaged. (This is part of the parties' highest order interest in the exercise and development of the other moral power, the capacity for a sense of justice.)

Now, if a person has an effective sense of justice in Rawls's sense (and in a well-ordered society, all do), he or she should care about the prospects of the least advantaged to some degree. Just as a matter of human nature, a person who had a sense of justice (including a desire to act from the difference principle), but who cared not a whit for the prospects or welfare of the least advantaged, would be a psychological rarity (if not subject to some split brain condition). Moreover, while the first subject of justice is the basic structure, justice also imposes directly upon individuals natural duties and obligations. The Rawlsian sense of justice thus incorporates a desire to comply with the natural duties of mutual respect and mutual aid, not to mention the duties of justice, fairness, and fidelity. These individual duties surely must impose restrictions upon a person's readiness and willingness to take advantage of the position of those less advantaged, not to mention forbidding the exploitation of anyone's misfortune, ignorance, and so on, and requiring fair dealing and fair play (*TJ*, secs. 17–18, 51–52). Justice as fairness is not, then, without resources that would mitigate against the likelihood of many of the abuses that G. A. Cohen foresees in Rawls's system.[31] Take one example directly relevant to Cohen's claim regarding "buccaneers" and other scoundrels that he thinks Rawls sets loose. Rawls says, "The principle of fairness, on the other hand, binds . . . those who, being better situated, have advanced their aims within the system. There is, then, another sense of *noblesse oblige*: namely, that those who are more privileged are likely to acquire obligations tying them even more strongly to a just scheme" (*TJ*, 116/100 rev.).

But the more important point is that it is not the purpose of Rawls's focus on the basic structure as the primary subject of justice to provide space for capitalist self-seeking and aggrandizement. As Samuel Scheffler has well explained,[32] the difference principle applies primarily to the basic structure, not in order to unleash capitalist self-seeking but, on the contrary, to establish the background justice needed to rectify the excessive inequalities and unfairness that is the joint product over time of innumerable economic transactions that taken by themselves are each individually fair (as measured by obligations of fairness and fidelity.) This is part of the moral division of labor implicit in Rawls's separation between principles for institutions and principles for individuals.

To summarize, it is a serious misunderstanding of Rawls to regard his primary focus on the basic structure, and his recognition of the need for incentives under the difference principle, as part of a liberal attempt to justify the unrestrained pursuit of self-interest by individuals, the product of which is to be redistributed to benefit the least advantaged who lose out in a capitalist world of self-seeking. Rawls's focus on the basic structure and his recognition of the need for incentives have nothing to do with that. They are, rather, based in a number of primary sources: First, his effort is to make distributive justice a matter of pure procedural justice and to rectify the unjustifiable inequalities resulting from the contingencies of a market system in the allocation of capital and labor, and in the distribution of income and wealth. Second, there is his account of the pluralism of values—the recognition of a plurality of (objective) goods that are worth pursuing for their own sake (objective goods in *A Theory of Justice*, permissible goods in *Political Liberalism* given the aim of avoiding controversial philosophical claims there). Third, there is the liberal idea that part of each person's good is to have the freedom to form her own rational life plan and decide what (objective) values to incorporate therein from among the range of (intrinsically) valuable activities. Of course, some people are going to make unreasonable self-interested choices and pursue false values in a liberal society, like any other. There is no way to prevent this compatible with maintaining individuals' freedom. But a well-ordered soci-

31. On these matters, see Joshua Cohen, "Taking People as They Are?" *Philosophy and Public Affairs* 30 (Fall 2001): 363–86.

32. See Scheffler, "The Division of Moral Labour," 229–53.

ety of justice as fairness—unlike laissez faire capitalism or even the capitalist welfare state—is not designed to encourage such choices, even if it tolerates them.

Perhaps the way to rephrase Hurley's "important point" that Cohen's position implies is that, in a well-ordered society of justice as fairness, people's freely adopted conceptions of the good will inevitably influence the incentive parameter, and therewith the share that goes to the least advantaged. It is probably true, as Cohen argues, that if everyone in his ideal world were deeply committed to promoting as a primary end the position of the least advantaged, then the least advantaged would fare better than they do in Rawls's well-ordered society of justice as fairness. ("Perhaps true," since it may be that conscious pursuit by everyone of the well-being of the least advantaged is self-defeating and they would fare better if people chose to pursue instead other primary ends.) But the important question is whether Cohen's motivational demand can reasonably be said to be a requirement of justice. Why should we want to live in a society where everyone's utmost priority is to act in ways that maximize the economic position or even the welfare of the least advantaged, and where as a result all other important ends were deemed of secondary importance? More reasonable perhaps is a society where all are committed to promoting the position of the least advantaged until all have achieved a certain threshold of prosperity where they are suitably independent free and equal citizens. But why isn't this second alternative already achieved by justice as fairness?[33]

All this, I believe, supports my contention that in a well-ordered society people's judgments of individual responsibility do not have much of a role to play in "affecting the range of possible incentive-seeking behavior by the talented" (*JLK*, 280). Other factors, especially motivational factors stemming from people's conception of the good, play the more central role by far. Admittedly, in a society like our own that is not well-ordered, but where disagreements about distributive justice are the norm, and indeed where an "everyday libertarianism"[34] (as Thomas Nagel and Liam Murphy term it) is endorsed by many people, it may be true that judgments of responsibility (the belief that I alone am responsible for my marginal product) play some role in providing incentives to some people to work longer hours or take risks with their savings. They might also play a role in a more well-ordered society that applied the difference principle, but where many people did not accept it but instead had "everyday libertarian" or

---

33. Here it should be mentioned that even in a society where people believed that wealth and income should be equally distributed, there will surely be incentive problems in the absence of widespread impartial benevolence or overriding concern for the overall level of welfare. (It is Hume's point that in a world of equal distributions, all would be reduced to poverty because limited, not impartial, altruism is the normal circumstance of human life). Whether impartial benevolence among all is a feasible society, or a desirable society, is a question I will not address. The point, rather, is that, given that people regard their own interests and values as more important than other people's interests and values, incentives are a necessary fact of human life if we are to reasonably expect people, whether talented or not, to work longer or harder or to undertake training to develop their skills. Incentives are needed even if people value equality or seek to benefit the less advantaged. I don't think Cohen would deny this.

34. Murphy and Nagel, *The Myth of Ownership*, 31–38.

other views about distributive justice. Perhaps this is Hurley's point. If so, then perhaps we would have to take that into account in applying the difference principle in non-ideal circumstances and come to some decision about limits on the kinds of incentives it is permissible to offer (as Hurley says, "a floor on the level of incentive seeking" in applying the difference principle [*JLK*, 254]). This is, I believe, consistent with Rawls's view (it would be part of non-ideal theory).[35] But Cohen's incentive argument against Rawls is intended, as I understand it, to apply to a well-ordered society where the difference principle is generally accepted by everyone and is institutionalized. Here, Cohen claims, unnecessary and unreasonable inequalities would still exist because of people's distorted incentives and motivations. But what is the source of the distortion, assuming it is no longer people's false beliefs about (libertarian) justice and what they are due? Is it citizens' pursuit of primary ends other than maximizing the good of the least advantaged? Why should that create a distortion, if these ends are permissible and themselves worthy of pursuit? Is it, then, a fact that the gifted are able to demand unreasonable incentives because their talents are rare? What is the standard for unreasonableness here, so long as all have a sense of justice, all adhere to their natural duties and obligations, fair equality of opportunity is in place and all those with similar natural talents have the opportunity to develop their capacities and are in a position to compete with other exceptionally talented people? For Cohen and other luck egalitarians, no doubt, the standard for unreasonableness would stem from their preferred luck egalitarian theory. I have tried to raise some doubts (though, clearly, more needs to be said than I can here) about the wisdom of these views.

This chapter originated as a comment written for a session at the Pacific Division APA Meeting, March 2005, on Susan Hurley's *Justice, Luck, and Knowledge*. I am grateful for her remarks as well as for the critical comments of K. C. Tan and Samuel Scheffler.

---

35. On the other hand, such a floor would imply that the least advantaged are not as well-off as they otherwise might be if there were no such floor. So it is not altogether clear that Rawls would endorse such a floor under non-ideal circumstances where the difference principle is applied.

5

Congruence and the Good
of Justice

One of Rawls's guiding aims in the development and revision of his work has been to show how a well-ordered society of justice as fairness is realistically possible. Rawls thinks establishing the "stability" of a conception of justice and the enduring feasibility of a society patterned upon it is essential to justifying a conception of justice. My aim is to discuss the role and import of Rawls's stability argument. To do so, I will concentrate primarily on the second part of Rawls's discussion of stability in *Theory of Justice*, the argument for the "congruence of the right and the good."[1] This argument particularly exhibits Rawls's indebtedness to Kant in the justification of his view. After discussing the purpose of congruence (in secs. I and II), I outline in detail what the argument is (secs. III and IV), emphasizing the role of the Kantian interpretation of justice as fairness. Then (in sec. V), I discuss how problems with the Kantian congruence argument led Rawls to political liberalism.

I. Stability and Congruence: Outline of Issues

Rawls's congruence argument has been widely neglected in discussions of his work.[2] Reasons for this neglect are several. First, there is sheer exhaustion. The congruence argument begins in part III of *Theory of Justice*, is developed intermittently for over two hundred pages, and culminates (in sec. 86) at the end of a very long book. Second, there is Rawls's uncharacteristic lack of clarity in setting out the congruence argument: it is interrupted and intertwined with other argu-

---

1. See John Rawls, *A Theory of Justice* (Cambridge, MA: Harvard University Press, 1971; rev. ed., 1999) (cited in text as *TJ*; sometimes referred to as *Theory*).

2. Rawls once said (in conversation) that he thought the congruence argument was one of the most original contributions he made in *A Theory of Justice*, and that he was puzzled why it did not attract more comment.

ments that Rawls simultaneously develops. Finally, there is the feeling among some of Rawls's main commentators that the argument is a failure. As Brian Barry says, Rawls himself seems dissatisfied with the argument, but "his dissatisfaction does not seem to me to go anywhere deep enough. The only thing to do is to follow the course followed virtually unanimously by commentators on A *Theory of Justice* and forget about it."[3]

But it would be a mistake to forget about the congruence argument for a number of reasons. First, it is primarily Rawls's dissatisfaction with congruence that led him subsequently to recast the justification for justice as fairness, culminating in his account of political liberalism. It is then difficult to appreciate *Political Liberalism*[4] without first understanding what congruence is about and Rawls's reasons for dissatisfaction with it.

A second reason to focus on congruence is that it deals with a central problem in moral and political philosophy, a problem which Kant left hanging, or at least failed to resolve by turning to religion in his account of the Highest Good. The problem is a version of the ancient quandary, whether justice is part of the human good. Rawls argues that, under certain social conditions, justice can be part of the human good, and, indeed, must be if a just social scheme is to be feasible and to endure.

Rawls's congruence argument constitutes the second part of his account of the stability of justice as fairness. Concern for social stability is a common feature of social contract views. For Hobbes, stability was paramount—the primary subject for a conception of political justice. A just society for Hobbes is nearly identifiable with a stable social order. He conceives of justice as peoples' mutual compliance with the norms and institutions that are needed to establish peaceful social cooperation. Hobbes argues that nearly absolute sovereignty is needed to secure a stable state of peace. His modern followers think differently; some even contend that in order to minimize costs fully rational agents motivated only by their particular interests would see the wisdom of an absence of coercive political force.[5] Still, justice is conceived as the norms and institutions instrumental to achieving a stable state of peaceful and productive cooperation. Moreover, stability is achieved as the result of a practical compromise among essentially conflicting interests. These are two distinctive features of Hobbesian contract views.

The liberal and democratic social contract doctrines of Locke, Rousseau, and Kant conceived of stability differently. Stability does not define the first subject of political justice. For, by itself, a stable social order, however rational it may be, can be of little moral consequence if it does not rectify but only perpetuates gross injustice. So a conception of justice should be worked out beforehand by relying on independent moral considerations. Then the question of its stability

---

3. Brian Barry, "John Rawls and the Search for Stability," *Ethics* 105 (July 1995): 874–915, at 915n54 (cited in text as SS).

4. Rawls, *Political Liberalism* (New York: Columbia University Press, 1993; paperback edition, 1996, 2004) (cited in the text as PL; references are to the paperback edition).

5. Thomas Hobbes, *Leviathan* (1651), ed. C. B. MacPherson (New York: Penguin, 1968). The absence of coercive political institutions is noticeable in David Gauthier's *Morals by Agreement* (Oxford: Oxford University Press, 1984) (cited in text as MA).

is raised to test the feasibility of a just society conceived along the lines of this conception.[6] What is important is not the stability of cooperation per se but the justice of cooperation and its stability "for the right reasons."[7]

The structure of this argument is articulated by Kant.[8] Kant says that demonstrating how a just constitution is possible is "the greatest problem for the human species." To solve this problem three things are needed: first, the "correct concept" of a just constitution; second, "great experience during much of the world's course"; and third, "above all else a good will prepared to accept that constitution."[9]

The three parts of Rawls's *Theory of Justice* parallel Kant's framing of these issues. In part I, "Theory," Rawls sets forth what he sees as the most appropriate conception of justice for the constitution (or "basic structure") of a democratic society. Following the democratic social contract tradition, Rawls contends that a just constitution is possible only if it commands the reasonable agreement of free and rational persons who are equally situated. The original position is designed to situate people equally in a strict sense, purely in their capacity as rational and as free and equal persons. From the original position, Rawls makes his familiar argument for the principles of justice (the principles of equal basic liberties and fair opportunities, the difference principle, and the natural duties of individuals needed to support just institutions). These provide Rawls's account of the "correct concept" of the principles that define a just constitution.

In part II of *Theory*, "Institutions," Rawls provides an account of the political and social institutions needed to satisfy his principles. Taking into account the workings of social systems under modern conditions, he argues for the insti-

6. On different kinds of stability, see Rawls, *Justice as Fairness: A Restatement*, ed. Erin Kelly (Cambridge, MA: Harvard University Press, 2001), 185–86 (cited in text as *Restatement*). In *A Theory of Justice*, Rawls refers to the stability (1) of a society or "scheme of cooperation," (2) of a conception of justice, and (3) of "just schemes" of cooperation, or a well-ordered society. Rawls says a scheme of social cooperation is stable when it is "more or less regularly complied with and its basic rules willingly acted upon; and when infractions occur, stabilizing forces should exist that prevent violations and tend to restore the arrangement" (TJ, 6/6 rev.). For a scheme of cooperation to be stable, people need the assurance that everyone else has sufficient reason to comply with the rules. Hobbes's sovereign is designed to provide this assurance (cf. TJ 497/435 rev.), but it comes at the price of justice as Rawls conceives it. Rawls is concerned exclusively with 2 and 3, the problem of the stability of a conception of justice and a just well-ordered society. He applies "stability" in the first instance to a conception of justice. A well-ordered society is stable when the conception of justice on which it is based is stable and "citizens are satisfied . . . with the basic structure of society" (*Restatement*, 202). Rawls says, "To insure stability men must have a sense of justice or a concern for those who would be disadvantaged by their defection, preferably both. When these sentiments are sufficiently strong to overrule the temptations to violate the rules, just schemes are stable" (TJ, 497/435 rev.). Rawls later uses the terms "stability for the right reasons" to indicate that he is concerned with stability as grounded, not in coercive force, but in citizens' moral motivations, primarily a sense of justice (see note 7).

7. A term Rawls first uses in "Reply to Habermas," an essay included in the paperback edition of *Political Liberalism*, 388n, 390ff.

8. Here I draw on my paper "Political Liberalism and the Possibility of a Just Democratic Constitution," chapter 6 of this volume.

9. Immanuel Kant, "Idea for a Universal History," in *Perpetual Peace and Other Essays* (Indianapolis: Hackett, 1983), 33–34.

tutions of a constitutional democracy. They provide for constitutional rights that protect basic liberties, measures guaranteeing fair equality of opportunity, and a "property-owning democracy" (or a liberal socialist scheme) (*TJ*, 274/242 rev.) providing a social minimum that enables all citizens to exercise their basic rights effectively and realize fair opportunities, thereby achieving individual independence.

The third of Kant's issues, on the "good will," concerns the stability of a just constitution given prominent tendencies of human nature. This subject occupies Rawls throughout part III, "Ends." The problem is: Assuming we have accounts of the correct conception of justice, and of the institutions needed to realize it, how are we to motivate rational persons effectively so that they affirm and support these institutions and the conception of justice that informs them? This is not the Hobbesian stability problem of specifying justice by reference to individuals' private wills. If Rawls is correct, justice is already specified in *Theory* parts I and II by reference to a public will founded on considered moral convictions and knowledge of democratic institutions. Given that these principles and institutions are worked out and already in place, Rawls's stability argument aims to show how these expressions of the public will can engage each individual will—if not ours, then at least the wills of hypothetical agents living under the conditions of a "well-ordered society" of justice as fairness.[10]

There are at least two problems to address here. First, given natural human propensities, how do people come to care about justice to begin with? And second, why should they care about it sufficiently so that they have reason to subordinate pursuit of their ends to requirements of justice? Unless it can be shown that citizens, if not now then at least in a just and well-ordered society, can be regularly motivated to act as just institutions demand, then a just social order is unstable and for this reason utopian.[11]

These two parts of Rawls's stability argument are addressed respectively in chapters 8 and 9 of *Theory*. In chapter 8, he sets forth a moral psychology designed to show how people in a well-ordered society of justice as fairness can come to acquire the moral motivation Rawls calls a "sense of justice." Rawls defines the sense of justice as a normally effective desire to apply and to abide by principles of justice and their institutional requirements (*TJ*, 505/442 rev.).[12] He advances a social-psychological argument: individuals in a well-ordered society of justice as fairness will normally come to acquire a settled disposition to support institutions that benefit them. Rawls contends, on the basis of three psychological

10. Rawls defines a well-ordered society as an ideal social world where everyone agrees on and accepts the same conception of justice, and this is publicly known; moreover this conception is effectively realized in society's institutions. See *TJ*, 4–5/4–5 rev., and sec. 69. See also *Restatement*, 8–9.

11. Rawls explicitly indicates two parts to the stability argument in *PL*, 141, though he rephrases the issues there to fit with political liberalism.

12. After *Theory*, Rawls defines the sense of justice more broadly, particularly in *Political Liberalism*,: "A sense of justice is the capacity to understand, to apply, and to act from the public conception of justice. . . . [A] sense of justice also expresses a willingness, if not the desire, to act in relation to others on terms that they also can publicly endorse" (*PL*, 19).

laws of moral development, the "reciprocity principles," that the sense of justice is continuous with our natural sentiments and is a normal part of human life (at least in a well-ordered society).[13]

Then, in chapter 9, Rawls further argues how the sense of justice is compatible with, and can even constitute part of, a person's good. This is the congruence argument proper. Of this argument, Brian Barry says that it is not only unnecessary, but also wrongheaded (SS, 885–87). It is unnecessary because Rawls has already shown in chapter 8 how people normally come to acquire a sense of justice to support just institutions. This should be sufficient for stability. The congruence argument is wrongheaded since it stems from Rawls's rejection of the idea that a person can be motivated to do what is right and just out of a sense of duty. To support this reading of Rawls, Barry cites Rawls's rejection of W. D. Ross's doctrine of the "purely conscientious act" (TJ, 477/418 rev.). Rawls says this doctrine holds

> that the highest moral motive is the desire to do what is right and just simply because it is right and just, no other description being appropriate . . . . Ross holds that the sense of right is a desire for a distinct (and unanalyzable) object, since a specific (and unanalyzable) property characterizes actions that are our duty. . . . But on this interpretation the sense of right lacks any apparent reason; it resembles a preference for tea rather than coffee. Although such a preference might exist, to make it regulative of the basic structure of society is utterly capricious. . . . (TJ, 477–78/418 rev.)

Barry responds:

> I am inclined to think that this is a travesty of the thoroughly commonsensical idea represented by saying that people can do their duty out of a sense of duty and not in order to achieve some independently definable end. This does not have to mean that moral action is "utterly capricious," as Rawls has it. We can perfectly well tell a story about motivation that makes acting rightly appear as rational. The story that I would commend is that of T. M. Scanlon. According to this, the moral motive is the desire to act according to rules that could not reasonably be rejected by others similarly motivated. . . . It is therefore quite natural to say that the thought that something is the right thing to do is what motivates us to act rightly. I take this to be precisely the proposition that Rawls objects to. (SS, 884)

Moreover, it is because Rawls objects to this moral motive that he must make the congruence argument. Barry says:

13. See secs. 69–75 of TJ, especially secs. 72 and 74. The three reciprocity principles are set forth together at TJ, 490–91/429–30 rev. The third says: "Given that a person's capacity for fellow feeling has been realized by his forming attachments in accordance with the first two laws, and given that a society's institutions are just and are publicly known by all to be just, then this person acquires the corresponding sense of justice as he recognizes that he and those for whom he cares are the beneficiaries of these arrangements."

> Recoiling from "the doctrine of the pure conscientious act," Rawls commits
> himself in Chapter 9 of A *Theory of Justice* to the ancient doctrine that no act
> can be regarded as rational unless it is for the good of the agent to perform it.
> Thus, the problem is one of "congruence between justice and goodness." (ibid.,
> 884–85)

As Barry would have it, then, Rawls, by rejecting the idea that we do what is right
and just simply because it is right and just, also rejects the idea that people can
normally do their duty out of a sense of duty, or simply for the sake of the duty
of justice. And this is why Rawls thinks he must show, in chapter 9, that justice
must promote the human good. How, otherwise, could people be motivated to
do what is right and just given that, for Rawls (presumably), morality and justice
by themselves cannot supply a rational motivation?

   This reading misinterprets Rawls on several counts. First, Rawls does not
deny that people can act for the sake of duty—quite the contrary. In *Theory*,
Rawls says, simply as a fact about people, that moral principles "engage our affections" (*TJ*, 476/416 rev.), and that the sense of justice is "among our final ends"
(*TJ*, 494/432 rev.). In *Theory* and afterwards, he says on numerous occasions that
we can act not simply "on" but also "from" our sense of justice, and that we can
and do act simply for the sake of justice.[14] What Rawls is concerned to deny (in
the passage quoted) is a particular account of moral motivation held by rational
intuitionists, like W. D. Ross and H. A. Prichard. This view says that what motivates us in acting morally is our grasping of a simple unanalyzable, nonnatural
moral property, which is by itself sufficient to give rise to a desire to do what is
right. It is this motivation, the "desire to do what is right and just simply because
it is right, *no other description being appropriate*," that Rawls rejects (*TJ*, 477/418
rev.; emphases added). For, there is an appropriate description for the desire to
do what is right. It is, on Rawls's account, the desire to act on principles that rational individuals would agree to from a fair position of equality. Here Rawls agrees
with Scanlon.[15] Whereas Scanlon has defined the contractualist moral motivation that Barry himself endorses as "the desire to act according to rules that could
not reasonably be rejected by others similarly motivated" (SS, 884), Rawls defines
the contractualist motivation only somewhat differently, as a desire "to live with
others on terms that everyone would recognize as fair from a perspective that all
would accept as reasonable" (*TJ*, 478/418 rev.).[16]

   14. See *TJ*, 476/416 rev. See also *Political Liberalism* where the sense of justice is partially
defined as a capacity "to act from the public conception of justice" (19), and as a capacity "to be
moved to act from fair terms of cooperation for their own sake" (54). Rawls says, "Reasonable persons
. . . desire for its own sake a social world in which they, as free and equal, can cooperate with others
on terms all can accept" (50). This again comes out clearly in Rawls's extended discussion of moral
motivation where he examines principle-dependent and conception-dependent desires (81–88).
   15. Or, more correctly, Scanlon agrees with Rawls, since this is the historical order of influence. See *PL*, 50n2, where Rawls discusses the kinship of his account of motivation with Scanlon's:
"In setting out justice as fairness we rely on the kind of motivation Scanlon takes as basic."
   16. Elsewhere, Rawls says the sense of justice is "the desire to act in accordance with the principles that would be chosen in the original position" (*TJ*, 312/275 rev.).

Rawls then does not reject the idea that "people can do their duty out of a sense of duty and not in order to achieve some independently definable end" (SS, 884). But, if not, why does Rawls feel it is necessary to say anything more to prove that justice as fairness is feasible? Why the need for the congruence argument?

The reason is that having a sense of justice and acting for the sake of justice still is not sufficient to show that the sense of justice is compatible with human nature or our good—far less so that justice can be part of our good.[17] Having a sense of justice, then, does not mean people will consistently act justly and that a just society will be stable. It may be that meeting requirements of justice are just too demanding for most people given certain tendencies of human nature. Moreover, justice often conflicts with other primary motives people have, and, when it does, what is to assure that people will not often sacrifice justice for the sake of other primary ends? Or perhaps, as Nietzsche argued, a disposition to morality and justice is destructive of what is best in human character. These issues should come into better focus upon clarification of the structure of the congruence argument.

II. The Question of Congruence

The question addressed by Rawls's congruence argument is this: Assuming that people in a well ordered society of justice as fairness have an independent sense of justice, and so *do* want to do what is right and just for its own sake, what assurance do we have that they will consistently affirm and act upon this motive and regularly observe requirements of justice? Rawls assumes that people can be expected to consistently act on and from moral motives of justice only if justice is compatible with their good.

What does Rawls mean by a person's good? He formally defines it in terms of what is rational for a person to want under certain ideal deliberative conditions. Hence the label "Goodness as Rationality" (*TJ*, 345/347 rev.). Rationality is speci-

---

17. Scanlon recognizes this problem in "Contractualism and Utilitarianism," in *Utilitarianism and Beyond*, ed. A. K. Sen and Bernard Williams (Cambridge: Cambridge University Press, 1982), 106. Scanlon distinguishes two motivational questions. First, a theory of morality must make clear the nature of the reasons that morality provides. A satisfactory moral philosophy will not leave concern with morality as a simple special preference, like a fetish or a special taste, which some people just happen to have. It must make it understandable why moral reasons are ones that people can take seriously, and why they strike those who are moved by them as reasons of a special stringency and inescapability. This echoes Rawls's rejection of the purely conscientious act, for which Barry criticizes Rawls by citing Scanlon's account of motivation.

The second motivational question, Scanlon says, is "whether susceptibility to such reasons *is compatible with a person's good* or whether it is, as Nietzsche argued, a psychological disaster for the person who has it. If one is to defend morality one must show that it is not disastrous in this way, but I will not pursue this second motivational question here" (ibid.; emphasis added). Rawls pursues the question, and this is part of the congruence argument. Scanlon, then, seems to recognize the same two questions that Rawls does and sees the need for any moral theory to provide an answer to each.

fied in terms of certain principles of rational choice. Some of these are standard in most any account of practical rationality: taking effective means to one's ends, ranking one's ends in order of priority, and making one's final ends consistent; taking the most probable course of action to realize one's ends; and choosing the course of action that realizes the greater number of one's ends (*TJ*, sec. 63). These "counting principles," as Rawls calls them, are not controversial, so there is no need to dwell on them. More controversial is Rawls's assumption of the rationality of prudence, construed as no time preference—to give equal concern to all the (future) times of one's life. This assumption, found also in Sidgwick,[18] enables Rawls to incorporate the idea of a "plan of life" into the account of rationality, making it part of the formal definition of a person's good (e.g., *TJ*, 93/79 rev.). A plan of life consists of a schedule of the primary ends and pursuits a person values, and activities that are needed to realize them, over a lifetime. Each of us can imagine more than one such plan we might be satisfied with. The most rational plan of life for a person satisfies the counting principles, and is the plan the person would choose under conditions of "deliberative rationality" (*TJ*, sec. 64). These are hypothetical conditions where a person is assumed to have full knowledge of what it is like to live a life pursuing chosen ends, critically reflects upon this plan, and appreciates the consequences.[19] The account of the plan of life a person would choose in deliberative rationality provides Rawls's formal definition of a person's good.

The idea of a rational plan supplies the basis for Rawls's "thin theory of the good" (*TJ*, 396/348 rev.). It is presupposed in the argument from the original position; the parties are rational in this sense. With this formal outline of the thin theory in place, we can get a better idea of the congruence problem. There are two ideal perspectives in Rawls's conception of justice: the original position and deliberative rationality. The former provides the foundation for judgments of justice; the latter provides the basis for judgments regarding a person's good. The original position abstracts from all information particular to our situations, including the specific ends and activities constituting an individual's good. In deliberative rationality, all this information is restored: judgments of value, unlike judgments of right, are explained relative to individuals' particular ends and situations, so Rawls assumes they require full knowledge of one's circum-

---

18. Henry Sidgwick, *The Methods of Ethics* (1874), 7th ed. (Indianapolis: Hackett, 1981) (cited in text as *Methods*).

19. Rawls says a rational plan of life "is the plan that would be decided upon as the outcome of careful reflection in which the agent reviews, in the light of all the relevant facts, what it would be like to carry out these plans and thereby ascertains the course of action that would best realize his more fundamental desires" (*TJ*, 417/366 rev.). Deliberative rationality defines an objective point of view from which to assess a person's good and the reasons he/she has as an individual. The plan of life that a person *would* choose from this perspective is "the objectively rational plan for him and determines his real good" (ibid.). Perhaps we can never really occupy this position, given its idealizations and uncertainty about the future. But with the information we have, we can determine, Rawls says, a "subjectively rational plan" (*TJ*, 422/370 rev.), which defines our apparent good.

stances. The original position is a collective public perspective[20]—we occupy this position jointly, and judgment is common since we must all observe the same standards of justice. So Rawls characterizes it as a unanimous social agreement. Deliberative rationality, by contrast, is an individual perspective—the "point of view of the individual," to use Sidgwick's terms (*Methods*, 405). Judgments there are made singly, by each individual; because our ends and circumstances differ, Rawls assumes our individual goods must differ. There can be no thoroughgoing agreement on the human good, even under ideal conditions; pluralism of values is a fundamental feature of Rawls's view. Both perspectives are idealizations; neither takes individuals just as they are. Instead, both artificially control the information available and constrain the judgments of those occupying these positions by normative principles: by rational principles in judgments of one's good and by reasonable principles constraining rational judgment in case of judgments of justice. Finally, both perspectives purportedly specify objective points of view, providing a basis for judgments of objective reasons: public reasons of justice applying to everyone from the standpoint of justice, and individual reasons objectively defined for each person from the standpoint of the individual's good. The congruence argument purports to show that under the ideal conditions of a well-ordered society, the judgments that would be made from these two ideal perspectives coincide. Reasonable principles judged and willed as rational from the common perspective of justice are also judged and willed as rational from each individual's point of view. The basic question of congruence is, Is it rational in a well ordered society of justice as fairness for persons to affirm individually, from the point of view of deliberative rationality, the principles of justice they would rationally agree to when they take up the public perspective of justice? If so, then it is rational for the members of a well-ordered society to make their sense of justice a regulative disposition within their rational plans, and justice becomes an essential part of each person's good. If Rawls can show this, then he has gone a long way towards resolving Sidgwick's "dualism of practical reason" (*Methods*, 404, 506–9). For, then he will have shown that the point of view of the individual, defined by rational principles, and the impartial public perspective of justice, defined by reasonable principles, are not fundamentally at odds, as Sidgwick feared, but are "congruent" (*TJ*, 514/450 rev.).

The congruence problem is not to be confused with the traditional question whether it is rational to be just, *whatever* one's desires and situation. On the assumption that rationality involves clarifying one's ends, making them consistent, and taking effective means to realize them, Phillipa Foot, Bernard Williams, and others have argued, following Hume, that there is no necessary connection between rationality and justice. Given their supposition that rationality is taking effective means to given ends, their arguments must be correct. For, if it is assumed that rationality is the effective pursuit of one's desired ends, that

---

20. In *Political Liberalism*, Rawls distinguishes "the public point of view from the many non-public (not private) points of view" (xxi), which parallels his distinction between public versus non-public reasons.

people can want most anything, and that there may be people with absolutely no moral sentiments, then it is a truism that rationality does not require of them the pursuit of justice.

Rawls seems to agree (*TJ*, 575/503–4 rev.). But this has little bearing on his argument. For, Rawls has no interest in showing the rationality of justice whatever people's situations.[21] His argument applies to the favorable situation of a well-ordered society. And even then, it assumes that everyone in these circumstances already has an effective sense of justice, and so has prima facie reason to act on it.[22]

But if congruence already assumes so much, why should it be of any interest? This, again, is just Barry's objection, namely, that Rawls's argument that members of a well-ordered society normally have a sense of justice is already sufficient to prove stability within Rawls's framework (*TJ*, chap. 8). It is, Barry says, only due to Rawls's faulty moral psychology—his purported belief that it is irrational to do justice for its own sake—that Rawls thinks the congruence argument is needed (SS, 884). I have argued that Rawls is not culpable of the moral psychology Barry ascribes to him. Rather, for Rawls, the very fact that a self-sufficient sense of justice is "a normal part of human life" (*TJ*, 489/428 rev.) poses the very problem addressed by the congruence argument. For, nothing has been said yet that would show that our moral sense of justice is not "in many respects irrational and injurious to our good" (ibid.).

Several different problems arise once it is assumed that people have a desire to do what is just for its own sake.

1. What is to assure us that our sense of justice is not entirely conventional, a peculiar product of our circumstances with no deeper basis in human tendencies, or, what is worse, that the sense of justice may be illusional, grounded in false beliefs covertly instilled in us, either by those in power or by our circumstances and social relations? People's suspicion that their sense of justice is arbitrary or manipulated in these ways can only cause it to waver and subside, giving rise to social instability. The most forceful criticism of this kind is the Marxian

21. Note, however, that this does not imply for Rawls that justice is not required by practical reason. According to Rawls's account, not all reasons are desire- or even interest-based. On principle-dependent and conception-dependent desires, see *PL*, 85n and the accompanying text. Nor does the concept of rationality exhaust the kinds of reasons we have. Rawls's account of "the reasonable" implies there are reasons of justice that apply to us, whatever our particular ends or desires. These reasons are established independent of our desires and situations, ultimately by reference to our considered *judgments* of justice. (See chap. 1 of this volume.) In Kantian and Political constructivism, Rawls seeks to show how these judgment-based reasons are connected with our capacities for practical reasoning, the moral powers. On objectivity and the reasonable, see *PL*, 111–12, 115; see also "Constructivism and Objectivity," lecture 3 of "Kantian Constructivism in Moral Theory" (The Dewey Lectures, 1980), in Rawls, *Collected Papers*, ed. Samuel Freeman (Cambridge, MA: Harvard University Press, 1999), 340–58 (cited in text as *CP*).

22. "I am not trying to show that in a well-ordered society an egoist would act from a sense of justice. . . . Rather, we are concerned with the goodness of the settled desire to take up the standpoint of justice. I assume that the members of a well-ordered society already have this desire. The question is whether this regulative sentiment is consistent with their good" (*TJ*, 568/497–98 rev.).

argument that justice is ideological, even incoherent, and based on our affirming false values and living under distorting conditions.

2. Rawls himself concedes that justice developmentally has its origins in a "morality of authority" which we acquire from our parents and our upbringing (*TJ*, chap. 8). What guarantees that our sense of justice does not remain anchored in submission to authority and is simply an infantile abnegation of responsibility? Freud argues, for example, that our existing moral feelings may be in many ways punitive, based in self-hatred, and that they incorporate many of the harsher aspects of the authority situation in which these feelings were first acquired (cf. *TJ*, 489/428 rev.).

3. Conservative writers contend that the tendency to equality in modern social movements and democratic demands for redistribution are expressions of envy directed against those who are more gifted and successful at managing life and its contingencies. The desire for fair distributions and egalitarian justice then may mask a lack of self-worth and a sense of failure and weakness. Here Freud was more evenhanded. The sense of justice, he argued, has its origins not only in the envy of the poor, but also in the jealousy of the rich to protect their social advantages. As a compromise, the rich and the poor settle on the rule of equal treatment, and by a reaction-formation envy and jealousy are transformed into a sense of justice. What is to assure us that the sense of justice does not have its source in these undesirable characteristics?

4. In a similar vein, there is the Nietzschean argument that justice and morality are self-destructive sentiments, a kind of psychological catastrophe for us, requiring abnegation of the self and its higher capacities, and a renunciation of final human purposes and excellences of character by those capable of achieving them.

5. Finally, most people reflectively affirm the value of sociability and of community. The things that are worth pursuing are not simply private ends done for oneself. Common ends, where we cooperate and aim to accomplish the same object, can be private ends in this sense. But common ends can also be shared — ends which people not only hold in common and achieve jointly but also take enjoyment in the participation of others in the same activity. (Family life, at its best, might achieve these shared ends, as can many other joint activities.)[23] Now, achieving justice requires a common effort. But even if we want to do justice for its own sake, still, for all to act for the sake of principles of justice is not, on its face, the same as all acting for a shared end. Can justice also be a shared end where each recognizes the good of others as an end and enjoys participating in and accomplishing this joint activity? Is there any value in being a participating member of a just society? How, in other words, can an account of justice account for the values of community?

---

23. So members of a competitive team might have the common aim, not just of winning but winning with the successful participation of each teammate; even members of opposing teams can have a shared end of engaging in a worthy competition, and appreciate and even enjoy one another's expertise. Cf. *TJ*, sec. 79.

These are the kinds of problems that any theory of justice needs to address. It may be that we want to do our duty of justice for its own sake; still, if these moral sentiments are grounded in illusions, defeat our primary purposes, prevent us from realizing important human goods, or require ways of acting that it is not in our nature consistently to perform, then surely this is relevant to the justification of a conception of justice. This, I suggest, is how we should understand the peculiar array of arguments in chapter 9 of *Theory*. The argument that justice as fairness allows for the objectivity of judgments of justice is designed to defuse the instability that would result if people thought their moral judgments of justice were purely conventional, arbitrary, or grounded in illusion (sec. 78). The argument for autonomy shows that justice as fairness is not grounded in a self-debasing submission to authority (sec. 78). The argument that feelings of excusable envy will not arise sufficient to undermine a well-ordered society shows how justice as fairness does not encourage propensities and hopes that it is bound to repress and disappoint (secs. 80–81). And the account of social union aims to show how justice as fairness can account for the good of community (sec. 79). Here I will focus on a further argument for the congruence of justice with people's good, which responds to the Nietzschean objection mentioned in the preceding list of problems, that justice is a self-destructive moral sentiment.

But first, return to Barry's claim that there is no need for the congruence argument within a contractualist framework. There is in moral philosophy a phrase, deriving from Kant, which says that "ought implies can." Philosophers of all persuasions accept this as a requirement on moral principles, yet give it different readings. Hobbesians, like David Gauthier, contend that the Kantian requirement means that we cannot expect people to act on moral rules unless it can be demonstrated that these rules are rational, in the sense that they are compatible with people's existing preferences. Otherwise, how could people be motivated to act on these principles? This provides the basis for Gauthier's contractarian account of justice. Justice is the rules of cooperation that purely rational individuals, whatever their ends, would rationally agree to, to satisfy their known preferences.

The congruence argument interprets the requirement that "ought implies can" in a different way. Congruence does not require that moral principles be compatible with given preferences and conceptions of the good. Rather, it requires that principles of justice, derived on grounds independent of given preferences, be within the reach of human capacities and be compatible with a human good that affirms our nature. Seen in this way, the role of the congruence argument within a contractarian framework comes more clearly into view. For, the contractualist account of motivation that Barry himself subscribes to says the moral motive is a desire to justify one's actions to others on terms they could not reasonably reject. But surely others can reasonably reject any moral principles they are not capable of consistently abiding by, given human nature, and which undermine rather than affirm their good even under ideal conditions. If so, then congruence would seem to be a normal feature of a contractualist view.[24]

---

24. As Scanlon himself suggests; see note 17.

Return now to the argument that the sense of justice can be a psychological catastrophe. There are different ways to develop this argument. For example, take the claim that moral requirements of justice are overriding; they have priority over all other considerations and aims. In opposition, it has been argued that justice requires, it seems, a kind of self-effacement, namely, that we sacrifice pursuit of the ends, commitments, and capacities that define us whenever they conflict with the impersonal demands of justice.[25] To fully respond to this objection it needs to be argued that (1) justice and exercise of a sense of justice do not have such self-abnegating consequences; moreover, (2) there are intrinsic goods that can be realized only by acting for the sake of justice; and finally, (3) justice, rather than being self-destructive, is self-affirming. Rawls advances these three claims by way of several different arguments.[26] Because of its bearing on *Political Liberalism*, my focus here will be upon that part of the argument that invokes the "Kantian Interpretation" of justice as fairness.

As background to Rawls's Kantian congruence argument, let's consider briefly a psychological law Rawls puts forward, the "Aristotelian Principle." This principle involves a rather substantial claim about human nature. It says, basically, that we desire to exercise our higher capacities, and want to engage in complex and demanding activities for their own sake so long as they are within our reach.

> Other things equal, human beings enjoy the exercise of their realized capacities (their innate or trained abilities), and this enjoyment increases the more the capacity is realized, or the greater its complexity. The intuitive idea here is that human beings take more pleasure in doing something as they become more proficient at it, and of two activities they do equally well, they prefer the one calling on a larger repertoire of more intricate and subtle discriminations. For example, chess is a more complicated and subtle game than checkers, and algebra is more intricate than elementary arithmetic. Thus the principle says that someone who can do both generally prefers playing chess to playing checkers, and that he would rather study algebra than arithmetic. (*TJ*, 426/374 rev.)

Rawls does not imagine that the Aristotelian Principle states an invariable pattern of choice. It states a natural tendency that may be overcome by countervailing inclinations in various situations such as the desire for comfort and satisfy-

---

25. The objection does not assume that all other-regarding sentiments are self-destructive. Rather, part of the problem is just that the commitments we have to persons or associations are inevitably compromised by the purportedly overriding and impersonal claims of morality. See Bernard Williams, "Persons, Character, and Morality," in *Moral Luck* (Cambridge: Cambridge University Press, 1981), 1–19.

26. For example, to show justice is not self-abnegating, Rawls argues, in *TJ*, secs. 83–85, that while self-abnegation might result from a "dominant end" theory like utilitarianism, this charge cannot be leveled against a theory like justice as fairness, which recognizes the heterogeneity of the good, and the regulative role of moral principles in constraining the means we adopt to pursue our ends. His reasoning in "The Idea of Social Union" (sec. 79) constitutes part of the argument for the idea that there are intrinsic goods which can only be realized in acting for the sake of justice. I cannot discuss these arguments here.

ing bodily needs. But it does imply, first, that once a certain threshold is met in satisfying these "lower pleasures" (to use Mill's term), a disposition to engage in activities that call for the exercise of our higher capacities takes over; and second, that individuals prefer higher activities of a kind, the more inclusive they are in engaging their educated abilities.

While this principle, like any psychological law, seems of limited use in explaining people's choices on particular occasions, it is useful in explaining the more general aims and activities about which people structure their lives. Rawls's main contention is that, assuming the Aristotelian Principle characterizes human nature, then a plan of life is rational for a person only if it takes this principle into account. It is then rational for persons to train and realize their mature capacities, given the opportunity to do so. In conjunction with Rawls's account of a rational plan, this means that the plan of life rational persons would choose under deliberative rationality is one that allows a central place to the exercise and development of their higher abilities. As such, the Aristotelian Principle "accounts for our considered judgments of value. The things that are commonly thought of as human goods should turn out to be the ends and activities that have a major place in rational plans" (*TJ*, 432/379 rev.). This means that certain valued activities (earlier, Rawls mentions, as primary examples: knowledge, creation and contemplation of beautiful objects, and meaningful work [*TJ*, 425/373 rev.]) are valued and thought of as human goods largely because they engage and call for the development of aspects of our nature that permit complex development. We enjoy such activities for their own sake; that is what the Aristotelian Principle asserts. If so, then the exercise and development of at least some of one's higher capacities should be a part of most anyone's good, barring adverse circumstances.

III. The Good of Justice and the Kantian Congruence Argument

Now let us turn to Rawls's main argument for the good of justice.[27] A just person has the virtue of justice, which, for Rawls, is a normally "regulative desire" to abide by reasons of justice in all of one's actions. Rawls's main argument for the rationality of this virtue aims to show that it is an intrinsic good. For the virtue of justice to be an intrinsic good means that exercise of the capacities for justice in appropriate settings is an activity worth doing for its own sake. The primary bases for making such an argument within Rawls's theory derives from the account of rational plans in conjunction with the Aristotelian principle.

How, then, does the Aristotelian Principle fit into Rawls's congruence argument? In *Political Liberalism*, Rawls says that, in a well-ordered society, justice as fairness is a good for persons individually because "the exercise of the two moral powers is experienced as a good. This is a consequence of the moral psychology used in justice as fairness. . . . In *Theory* this psychology uses the so-called Aristotelian Principle" (*PL*, 203, 203n35). This makes it seem as if the congruence

---

27. Other arguments for the good of justice are suggested in sec. 86 of *TJ*, and include the argument from social union (sec. 79), and an instrumentalist argument (sec. 86).

argument involves a straightforward appeal to the Aristotelian Principle. The idea here would be that the capacity for a sense of justice is among our higher capacities. It involves an ability to understand, apply, and act on and from requirements of justice (cf. *TJ*, 505/443 rev.). This capacity admits of complex development and refinement. Since all have a sense of justice in a well-ordered society, it is rational for each to develop it as part of his or her plan of life.

Consider now two objections to this simplified argument: First, though all of us may have the same natural capacities, we have them to varying degrees. None of us can develop any capacity to a high degree without neglecting others. The capacities that are rational for people to develop will depend on their natural endowments, their circumstances, their interests, and other factors. All that follows from the Aristotelian Principle is that it is rational for each to develop *some* of their higher capacities. If so, then the range of abilities individuals ought to develop will differ. How, then, can it be inferred that the capacity for justice should occupy a place in everyone's rational plan?[28] In what way does this higher capacity differ from the capacity for dance or sport, or other highly coordinated physical activity? Some of us might aim to develop these capacities, but others understandably do not.

A second objection is, What warrants making the capacity for justice supremely regulative of *all* our pursuits? Suppose that, consistent with the Aristotelian Principle, I decide, like Kierkegaard's aesthete "A," to perfect my capacities for elegance and aesthetic appreciation.[29] I resolve to act in ways that are aesthetically appropriate, according to received rules of style and etiquette. Is there anything intrinsic to my sense of justice that would make it regulative of this disposition? Why could I not, consistent with the Aristotelian Principle, just as well make my sense of elegance supremely regulative, sacrificing justice when it conflicts with aesthetic norms? More generally, what is to prevent my giving weight to my sense of justice only according to its relative intensity, and subordinating it to stronger dispositions, weighing off my concern for justice against other final ends in ordinary ways?

The simplified argument from the Aristotelian Principle is not Rawls's argument for congruence. But it is extremely difficult to piece together what his argument is. The best way to uncover his argument is by seeing how he would respond to the two objections just stated. The answers he gives depend on the conception of the person built into Rawls's view.

According to the "Kantian Interpretation" of justice as fairness (*TJ*, sec.40), and what Rawls later calls "Kantian constructivism,"[30] justice is construed as

28. "We should like to know that this desire is indeed rational; being rational for one, it is rational for all, and therefore no tendencies to instability exist" (*TJ*, 567/497 rev.; also see 568/497 rev.) Rawls seems to allow, however, that there may be some in a well-ordered society for whom the sense of justice is not a good (*TJ*, 575–76/504 rev.). Barry notes this apparent inconsistency in "Search for Stability."

29. See Soren Kierkegaard, *Either/Or* (1843), vol. 1 (Princeton: Princeton University Press, 1944).

30. See Rawls, "Kantian Constructivism in Moral Theory" (The Dewey Lectures, 1980), in *CP*, chap. 16.

those principles that would be justified to, and accepted by, everyone under conditions that characterize them as "free and equal moral persons" (or "free and equal rational beings" [*TJ*, 252/222 rev.]). The original position specifies these conditions; it is a "procedural interpretation" of our nature as free and equal rational beings (*TJ*, 256/226 rev.).[31] Rawls says that, by acting from the principles that would be chosen from this standpoint,

> persons express their nature as free and equal rational beings subject to the general conditions of human life. For to express one's nature as a being of a particular kind is to act on the principles that would be chosen if this nature were the decisive determining element. . . . One *reason* for [acting from the principles of justice], for persons who can do so and want to, is to *give expression to one's nature*. (*TJ*, 252–53/222 rev.; emphases added)

Conjoining this conception of the person with the formal account of rationality and the Aristotelian Principle, we can identify the following focal points of Rawls's Kantian argument for congruence.[32]

1. On the basis of the Kantian interpretation, persons regarded as moral agents are by their nature free and equal rational beings (*TJ*, 252/222 rev.) (or, the same idea in *Theory*, "free and equal moral persons" *TJ*, 565/495 rev.).[33] Rational agents in a well-ordered society (WOS) conceive of themselves in this way "as primarily moral persons" (*TJ*, 563/493 rev.; see also *CP*, 309).

2. Rational members of a WOS "desire to express their nature as free and equal moral persons," (*TJ*, 528/462–63 rev., 572/501 rev.). (Rawls evidently sees this as a nonarbitrary rational desire.) Combined with the formal account of a person's good under the thin theory, this implies point 3.

3. Members of a WOS desire to have a rational plan of life consistent with their nature, which implies, in turn, a "fundamental preference . . . for conditions that enable [them] to frame a mode of life that expresses [their] nature as free and equal rational beings" (*TJ*, 561/491 rev.).

4. Having a plan of life compatible with the desire to express their nature as free and equal rational beings requires that persons act from principles that "would be chosen if this nature were the decisive determining element" (*TJ*, 253/222 rev.). According to the Kantian interpretation, the original position interprets or characterizes the nature of individuals as free and equal moral persons (*TJ*, 252/221 rev., 515/452 rev.); it is a "procedural representation" of human beings' nature, and for them to act from principles chosen

---

31. In "Kantian Constructivism," Rawls refers to the original position as a "procedure of construction." See *CP*, 340; see also 310–12.

32. Here I interpret the final argument for congruence Rawls suggests in *TJ*, sec. 86. See especially 572/501 rev., first paragraph, in conjunction with 445/390 rev., and then all of secs. 40 and 85, and other pages cited in the text. I provide here only the main strands of argument Rawls weaves together, without detailed elaboration.

33. "The nature of the self as a free and equal moral person is the same for all" (*TJ*, 565/495 rev.).

therein is to "express their nature as free and equal moral persons" and to be determined by it.[34]

5. According to its standard interpretation, the original position is designed to "make vivid to ourselves the restrictions that it seems reasonable to impose on arguments for principles of justice" (*TJ*, 18/16 rev.). It embodies fair conditions of equality that you and I (presumably) find appropriate for an agreement on principles to regulate the basic structure of society.

6. The normally effective desire to apply and act upon principles that would be agreed to from an original position of equality is the sense of justice (*TJ*, 312/275 rev., 478/418 rev.).

7. Taken together, points 4 through 6 suggest that the desire to act in ways that "express one's nature" as a free and equal rational being is, "practically speaking," the same desire as the desire to act upon principles of justice acceptable from an original position of equality (*TJ*, 572/501 rev.).[35]

8. Thus, for individuals in a WOS to achieve their desire to realize their nature as free and equal rational beings entails that they act from their sense of justice and as the principles of justice require (*TJ*, 574/503 rev.).

9. By the Aristotelian Principle, it is rational to realize one's nature by affirming the sense of justice. "From the Aristotelian Principle it follows that this expression of their nature is a fundamental element of [the] good" of individuals in a well-ordered society (*TJ*, 445/390 rev.).[36]

10. The sense of justice is, by virtue of its content (what it is a desire for), a supremely regulative disposition: it requires giving first priority to the principles of right and justice in deliberation and action (*TJ*, 574/503 rev.).

11. To affirm the sense of justice is to recognize and accept it as supreme by adopting it as a highest-order regulative desire in one's rational plan.[37]

12. To have justice as a highest-order end is the most adequate expression of our nature as free and equal rational beings, and is to be autonomous (cf. *TJ*, 515/452 rev.). Autonomy is then an intrinsic good for free and equal moral persons.

The role the Aristotelian Principle here (in point 9) is to establish that it is intrinsic to people's good to realize their nature (as free and equal rational

---

34. "Human beings have a desire to express their nature as free and equal moral persons, and this they do most adequately by acting from the principles that they would acknowledge in the original position" (*TJ*, 528/462–63 rev.). As Rawls makes clear in "Kantian Constructivism," the original position is designed as a "procedural representation" or "modeling" of central features of the conception of moral persons, so that the principles chosen there are determined by these defining features (*CP*, 308).

35. Rawls says there is a "practical identity" between these two desires (*TJ*, 572/501 rev.). Cf. "Properly understood, then, the desire to act justly derives in part from the desire to express most fully what we are or can be, namely free and equal rational beings with a liberty to choose" (*TJ*, 256/225 rev.).

36. Rawls also says: "When all strive to comply with these principles and each succeeds, then individually and collectively their nature as moral persons is most fully realized, and with it their individual and collective good" (*TJ*, 528/462–63 rev.).

37. Compare: "These principles are then given absolute precedence . . . and each frames his plans in conformity" (*TJ*, 565/495 rev.).

beings). Just why Rawls says this is not clear. It appears to stem from the difficult section 85, "The Unity of the Self." The basic idea there is that it is because of moral personality, the capacities for a sense of justice and a conception of the good, that a person sees himself as a free agent and is able to shape and follow a plan of life and "fashion his own unity" (TJ, 561/491–92 rev.). In this regard, moral personality grounds our capacity for agency. (More on this below).

Just as crucial for the argument are 7, identifying the sense of justice with the desire to realize one's nature, and 10 and 11, establishing the priority of the sense of justice in rational plans. Point 7 is important since, by connecting the sense of justice with our "nature" (I will discuss what this means), 7 establishes that the desire to act justly is not psychologically degenerative. Recall the criticism that the sense of justice is a compulsive desire which we subconsciously develop to either (a) mask our weakness (as Nietzsche held), or (b) as an outgrowth of envy and jealously (as Freud held) (cf. TJ, 539/472–73 rev.). Or suppose (c) the sense of justice were nothing more than a disposition furtively instilled in us by those in power, to insure obedience to rules designed to advance their interests (cf. TJ, 515/452 rev.). In each case, the sense of justice would not be worth affirming as an intrinsic part of our good. It might even be better not to have this desire if we could get along in society without it. But if the sense of justice can be shown to belong somehow to our nature, then Rawls can contend that, by affirming it, we exercise a capacity that is fundamental to our being. And since (by the Aristotelian Principle) for persons to express their nature as free and equal rational beings "belongs to their good, the sense of justice aims at their well-being" (TJ, 476/417 rev.).

The crucial question, then, is, Why does Rawls contend that the sense of justice "belongs to our nature," and what does this obscurity mean? In *Theory*, Rawls adopts Kant's position, that persons are by their nature as moral agents, free, equal, and rational and in the absence of distorting factors, in a WOS, they publicly conceive of themselves in this way. The "nature" of free, equal, and rational beings is their "moral personality" (TJ, secs. 77, 85). Moral personality is defined by the moral powers, which are, in effect, the capacities for practical reasoning as applied to matters of justice. These capacities include (a) a capacity for a sense of justice (the ability to understand, to apply, and to act on and from requirements and principles of justice) as well as (b) a capacity for a conception of the good (to form, to revise, and to pursue a rational plan of life).[38]

Why are these capacities so important? Rawls's idea seems to be that, from a practical point of view, when acting as agents (and especially in cooperative contexts) we normally see ourselves and each other not just in terms of our particular identities, ends and commitments; more fundamentally we conceive of ourselves and others as free moral agents capable of determining our actions, adjusting our wants, and shaping our ends—all according to the requirements of practical principles. And, "since we view persons as capable of mastering and adjusting their wants and desires, they are held responsible for doing so."[39]

---

38. TJ, 505/442 rev., 561/491 rev.; "Kantian Constructivism," in CP, 312–13.
39. Rawls, "Fairness to Goodness," CP, 284.

Now the bases for people's agency and their conception of themselves as free and responsible moral agents and as equals are the moral powers.[40] A person without these capacities is not recognized by others as answerable for his acts or ends (morally or legally) or deemed capable of taking an active part in social cooperation.[41] Moreover, we do not see our lives as a matter of happenstance simply imposed on us by our situations. Instead, within the limits of the circumstances we confront, we normally see our actions and our lives as under our control. It is by virtue of the capacities for moral personality that we are able to decide what ends and activities we should pursue and can fashion these ends into a coherent and cooperative life plan that accords with principles of rational choice and principles of justice. So it is by virtue of the moral powers as capacities to act upon rational and moral principles that we are able to give "unity" to our lives, and so to our selves, by adopting and pursuing a rational plan of life.[42]

It is because of their central role in making possible our agency that Rawls says that the moral powers "constitute our nature" as moral persons. "Moral person" and "moral personality," terms found in both Locke and Kant, are to be taken here in the seventeenth- and eighteenth-century sense: they refer to agents and their capacities for agency. To say these powers "constitute our nature" is not a metaphysical claim for Rawls; this is suggested by his account of "the independence of moral theory" from metaphysics and epistemology (CP, chap. 15). Rather, it means that, when we think of ourselves practically, from the point of view of agents engaged in planning our pursuits in the context of social cooperation, then what is most important to our being an agent for these purposes are the moral powers. Contrast thinking of oneself purely naturalistically, as a physical organism or object whose behavior is determined by a combination of forces. This is not how we see ourselves in practical contexts (though some might occasionally think of themselves in this way from a purely naturalistic point of view). That persons are free and responsible agents capable of controlling their wants and answering for their actions is something we just go on from a practical standpoint.[43] This belief provides our orientation in the realm of human activity. And it is hard to see how it could be any other way. For, otherwise, we must see ourselves and one another as natural objects beyond the realm of responsibility.[44]

So it is the centrality of the capacity for a sense of justice to the self-conception of moral agents that underlies Rawls's claim (in point 7) that the sense

40. See TJ, sec.77, "The Basis of Equality"; see also Rawls, "Kantian Constructivism," in CP, 330–33.

41. "The two moral powers [are] the necessary and sufficient conditions for being counted a full and equal member of society in questions of political justice" (PL, 302).

42. As Rawls contends in TJ, sec. 85, "The Unity of the Self," 561–63/491–93 rev.

43. Christine Korsgaard makes a similar point in "Personal Identity and the Unity of Agency: A Kantian Response to Parfit," Philosophy and Public Affairs 18 (1989): 101–32.

44. Similar considerations underlie Rawls's claim that he is not relying on a metaphysical conception of the person in the argument for justice as fairness. See "The Independence of Moral Theory" (1975), in CP. Perhaps to avoid a misconstrual of the Kantian elements in his view, Rawls, subsequent to Theory of Justice, ceases referring to persons' "nature as free and equal rational beings" and substitutes instead the "moral ideal" of "free and equal moral persons." See "Kantian Constructivism," in CP, 321.

of justice and the desire to express one's nature are "practically speaking the same desire." And this supports point 8, the conclusion that to realize one's "nature" (or practical self-conception) requires acting on, and from, the sense of justice. This addresses (if it does not fully respond to) the first objection (raised at the beginning of this section). This was the question, How can everyone have sufficient reason, even if the Aristotelian principle is assumed, to develop and exercise their capacity for justice? What distinguishes it from other capacities, which we may not have reason to develop depending on our circumstances? The answer is that development of the sense of justice (along with the capacity for a conception of the good) is a condition of persons being rational moral agents who are capable of assuming responsibility for their actions and taking part in, and benefiting from, social life. People who do not develop their capacities for music or sports, while they may miss out on worthwhile activities, can nonetheless lead good lives engaged in other equally worthwhile pursuits. But those whose moral capacities for justice (and the capacity to be rational) remain undeveloped are not capable of social life. They are not, then, in a position to achieve the benefits of society and will be hard pressed to learn and pursue most any worthwhile way of life.

IV. Finality and the Priority of Justice

Now turn to the second objection discussed previously: Even if we assume justice is a good, why should it be regulative of all other values and pursuits? That justice expresses our nature as free and equal rational beings on Rawls's Kantian interpretation (*TJ*, 252/222 rev.) should go some way towards responding to this objection. Still, people have ends and commitments which they believe are equally, if not more, important than justice or expressing their nature, and often they have more pressing desires to act for these ends. Rawls says, "A perfectly just society should be part of an ideal that rational human beings could desire more than anything else once they had full knowledge and experience of what it was" (*TJ*, 477/418 rev). But given the multiple aims and commitments that people care about, how could this be true?

The problem here is assigning the appropriate position to the sense of justice within rational plans of life of people who are morally motivated and who desire to be just persons. How should the sense of justice be situated in relation to other final ends and within the hierarchy or "system of desires" (*TJ*, 498 rev.)? Rawls says that, in drawing up a rational plan, final ends and fundamental desires need to be organized and combined into one scheme of conduct (cf. *TJ*, 410–11/360–61 rev). And, sometimes, after taking into account all relevant reasons and considerations (including the Aristotelian principle), critical deliberation might run out, at which point the rational choice may just be to decide according to the intensity of desire.[45]

---

45. "Sometimes there is no way to avoid having to assess the relative intensity of our desires" (*TJ*, 416/365 rev.).

> The real problem of congruence is what happens if we imagine someone to give weight to his sense of justice only to the extent that it satisfies other descriptions which connect it with reasons specified by the thin theory of the good. (*TJ*, 569/499 rev.)

I interpret this passage as follows: Suppose a person is morally motivated by a sense of justice and is trying to decide how to fit considerations of justice into her life-plan. She wants to be a just person yet also aims to be loyal to her family, successful in her career, devoted to her church, and an accomplished amateur musician. These are the primary ends that provide structure to her life. What happens if, after full deliberation, she assigns the sense of justice a position of importance alongside other final ends and weighs it off against them in ordinary ways, sometimes relying on the relative felt intensity of desires to resolve conflicts among her final ends? If people generally reasoned this way, and it were publicly known, then people could not have the kind of assurance regarding others' actions that is needed for a well-ordered society to be stable in Rawls's sense. Ultimately, the congruence argument, to succeed, must show that it is contrary to reason to weigh the sense of justice off against other ends. What needs to be shown is that it is rational to give the sense of justice a highest-order position in rational plans. It must have regulative priority over all other final ends and parts of rational plans.

One way to argue for assigning priority to a disposition is to establish that it is a desire to be a certain kind of person. Harry Frankfurt has argued that the desire to be a certain kind of person is a "desire of the second or of higher orders"; part of the content of this desire is that a person's first-order desires (desires for particular objects) conform to an ideal that person has set for himself.[46] Here it can be said that, given the content of this desire, one cannot satisfy it if it is balanced off against other desires in the course of practical reasoning. Rawls conceives of the sense of justice in a similar way.

> An effective sense of justice . . . is not a desire on the same footing with natural inclinations; it is an executive and regulative highest-order desire to act from certain principles of justice in view of their connection with a conception of the person as free and equal. (*CP*, 320)

Still Rawls needs to say more than this. For, so far as Frankfurt's argument goes, it could as well apply to the desire to be elegant. That, too, is a desire to be a certain kind of person, and it would seem compatible with Frankfurt's view that it could also be a highest-order disposition regulative of all one's other desires for someone (for example, Kierkegaard's aesthete) if he or she so chooses. But where does this leave the aesthete who also has a sense of justice? Frankfurt's view seems to imply that which of these two dispositions has primacy is to be settled in the end by that person's radical choice. This cannot be Rawls's view. The very ques-

---

46. Harry Frankfurt, "Freedom of the Will and the Concept of a Person," in *The Importance of What We Care About* (Cambridge: Cambridge University Press, 1988), 11–25.

tion he aims to raise is, By virtue of what powers are we capable of choice, and what do these capacities reveal about us and how we conceive of ourselves as free moral agents capable of responsible action and social life?

Rawls contends, in effect, that the desire to express one's nature is "highest-order," not because it is a general desire to be most any kind of person, but because it is a desire to be a specific kind of person, namely, one who is just. Unlike other desires, there is something special about the desire to be a just person that makes it supremely regulative of all other desires independent of a person's desires or choices.

> This is a consequence of the condition of finality: since these principles [of justice] are regulative, the desire to act upon them is satisfied only to the extent that it is likewise regulative with respect to other desires. . . . This sentiment cannot be fulfilled if it is compromised and balanced against other ends as but one desire among the rest. It is a desire to conduct oneself in a certain way above all else, a striving that contains within itself its own priority. Other aims can be achieved by a plan that allows a place for each, since their satisfaction is possible independent of their place in the ordering. But this is not the case with the sense of right and justice. (*TJ*, 574/503 rev.)

As a desire to act on the principles of justice, the sense of justice is subject to the condition of finality that defines these principles. Finality requires that considerations of justice have absolute priority over all other reasons in practical deliberation (reasons of prudence, self-interest, private and public benevolence, etiquette, and so on) (*TJ*, 135/116–17 rev.). Given this condition, persons cannot fulfill their desire for justice if they balance it off against other desired ends, even other final ends, according to their relative intensity or in other ways. To do that would compromise what this desire is a desire for. The sense of justice in effect is a desire that *all* one's desires, aims, and actions conform to the regulative requirements of justice. On its face, the sense of justice reveals itself as a supremely governing disposition. We can satisfy what this desire is a desire for only if we assign justice the highest priority in our activities. Moreover, given the practical identity of the sense of justice with the desire to express our nature (see point 6 in sec. III), we cannot "express our nature by following a plan that views the sense of justice as but one desire to be weighed off against others" (*TJ*, 575/503 rev.). Therefore, in order to realize our nature we have no alternative but to plan to preserve our sense of justice as governing our other aims (*TJ*, 574/503 rev.).

There is one final claim to consider (point 12 in sec. III) and the congruence argument is complete. What does it mean to realize the conception of the person as a free and equal rational being in one's rational plan? Rawls says, "Kant held, I believe, that a person is acting autonomously when the principles of his action are chosen by him as the most adequate expression of his nature as a free and equal rational being (*TJ*, 252/222 rev; cf. *TJ*, 584/511). In the Kantian Interpretation of justice as fairness, Rawls assumes that citizens in a well-ordered society "regard moral personality . . . as the fundamental aspect of the self" (*TJ*, 563/493 rev); as a result they desire to be fully autonomous agents. Autonomy, on Rawls's Kantian account, requires acting for the sake of principles that we accept, not because

of our particular circumstances, talents, or ends, or due to allegiance to tradition, authority, or the opinion of others, but because these principles originate in
and give expression to our common nature as free and equal rational beings (*TJ*,
252/222 rev., 515–16/452 rev.). (In *Political Liberalism*, Rawls uses the term "constitutive autonomy" to emphasize the Kantian idea that moral agents "constitute"
principles of justice on the basis of their practical reason and moral personality
[*PL*, 99]. It is the role of Kantian constructivism to show how principles of justice
can be construed as so constituted.) By affirming their sense of justice, members
of a well-ordered society accomplish their conception of themselves as free, that
is, as moral agents who are free from the eventualities of their circumstances, their
upbringing, and their social position. "Acting from this precedence [of the sense of
justice] expresses our freedom from contingency and happenstance" (*TJ*, 574/503
rev.). And this is what it is to be autonomous. So, "when the principles of justice .
. . are *affirmed* and acted upon by equal citizens in society, citizens then act with
full autonomy."[47] Full autonomy (as opposed to simply "rational autonomy") is
then the ultimate consequence of persons realizing their nature by making the
sense of justice a highest-order desire in their rational plans. And this means, given
the rest of Rawls's argument, that autonomy is an intrinsic good. Rawls concludes:
"This sentiment [of justice] reveals what the person is, and to compromise it is not
to achieve for the self free reign but to give way to the contingencies and accidents
of the world" (*TJ*, 575/503 rev.). It reveals "what the person is" practically, as a
moral agent and so to compromise it is to compromise one's free agency.

Before going on to discuss what Rawls himself sees as problematic about
this argument, let us consider a crucial step many will find especially controversial: Rawls's appeal to the finality of considerations of justice.[48] To understand
what the controversy over finality might be, we should clarify how Rawls views
it. Philosophers often talk about the "overridingness" of moral duties and moral
reasons, where this is meant to imply that moral duties and moral reasons outweigh all others. Some have rightly questioned whether duties of justice always
must override all other practical considerations. Sometimes it seems perfectly
permissible to breach duties of justice, even for the sake of prudential and self-
related ends.[49] Rawls's finality condition does not deny this. Finality is not the

---

47. Rawls, "The Basic Liberties and Their Priority," lecture 8 (*PL*, 305–6). Rawls distinguishes
two kinds of autonomy—in "Kantian Constructivism" (in *CP*) and later in *Political Liberalism*—each
of which is associated with one of the moral powers. "Rational autonomy" is acting on a rational plan
of life one has formed for oneself according to principles of rational choice and which incorporates
ends that are part of the plan of life one would choose in deliberative rationality. "Full autonomy"
seems to include rational autonomy but also involves acting on and from the principles of justice,
where justice is given highest order priority in regulating one's rational plan. In this regard, full autonomy involves the congruence of the right and the good. See "Rational and Full Autonomy," lecture 1
of "Kantian Constructivism," in *CP*, esp. 308; see also *PL*, 72–81. In later works, Rawls uses the term
"moral autonomy" to refer to full autonomy, and perhaps even rational autonomy, as the idea is found
in Mill's account of individuality. See *CP*, 586.

48. See, for example, Bernard Williams, "Practical Necessity," chap. 10 in *Moral Luck*.

49. For example, it may well be permissible sometimes to break certain nonsignificant promises (to meet with a student, say) in order to take advantage of an opportunity that is important to one's
career. Or consider what some may think a more serious breach: stealing to prevent one's starvation.

claim that any specific moral duty or consideration of justice outweighs all other practical norms and considerations on every occasion. Finality, rather, is about the position of considerations of justice within the *totality of practical reasons.* Considerations of justice taken together are "the final court of appeal in practical reasoning" (*TJ*, 135/116 rev.).

Imagine the totality of practical reasons—moral reasons of justice along with other moral reasons (of benevolence, etc.) combined with reasons of prudence, self-interest, law, custom, etiquette, and so on—that bear on the question what we ought to do and the respective weights of these considerations. Finality does not say that each and every reason of justice outweighs all other reasons of a different kind. It implies, rather, that (a) taken together, reasons of justice have a special position in the system of reasons in so far as they are regulative of all other reasons; and (b) once the course of practical reasoning has reached its conclusion, and all relevant reasons are considered, the question of what one ought to do is settled—no further question about what one within reason ought to do remains to be asked simply because one does not like the conclusion. Thus, when reasons of prudence and self-interest are outweighed by moral considerations, there is sufficient reason, and it is reasonable, to moderate the claims of interest. Likewise, if reasons of interest and prudence outweigh a specific moral duty of justice on a particular occasion (breaching a promise to take advantage of an extraordinary personal opportunity, for example), then this is because there is some moral reason that permits that exception. It is then reasonable, and not simply rational, to act for reasons of prudence or self-interest (e.g., to break a promise to further one's career) under those circumstances.

Finality, then, does not mean that we are always required to sacrifice the ends of the self to the impersonal claims of morality. But, if and when morality does not require such sacrifices, and if and when we are sometimes permitted to breach specific moral rules, then this must be because it is justified by the totality of moral reasons. It is not because there are practical reasons of a superior order to the totality of moral reasons. There are no such superior reasons; moral reasons are "the final court of appeal in practical deliberation" (*TJ*, 135/116 rev.).

The question now becomes, Why should moral reasons have such a special position in practical reasoning? Consider three kinds of arguments for the finality condition.

1. The finality of moral reasons (or of moral reasons of justice specifically) is part of our understanding of morality (or of justice); some might even say it is "analytic." In any case, it is in the nature of moral reasons (or specifically reasons of justice) that, taken collectively, they cannot be outweighed by other kinds of reasons. To take them into account at all is to give them regulative priority.
2. Finality, in the end, is a claim about the structure of practical reason of moral agents. For persons who take moral reasons seriously, practical reasoning, appropriately carried through, first involves deciding what is in their best interest by settling their ends and ascertaining what is the rational course of action (according to principles of rational choice and one's rational plan);

then, secondly, ascertaining whether their rational action (or plan) squares with moral requirements, or what is reasonable. Only deliberations reached in this way are final with respect to all the requirements of practical reason.

3. The finality of moral reasons is connected (in a way represented by the Kantian interpretation and Kantian constructivism) with autonomy and the unity of the self as a free and equal moral person. We are able to be free and fully rational agents who give shape and unity to our lives only by virtue of the moral powers (*TJ*, sec. 85). Only if we assign to the moral principles of justice that express these powers a supremely regulative position in our lives can we be fully rational and autonomous.

Each of these considerations may play a role in Rawls's finality condition. He may rely on additional considerations, but what these are is just not clear. Rawls initially stipulates that the finality condition is among the "formal constraints of the concept of right" (*TJ*, 130/112–13 rev.). Other than contending that it is reasonable to impose this condition on principles of justice, he has little directly to say about the basis of the finality condition. Rawls does not seem to hold that finality of moral considerations is analytically implicit in the concept of right or that it is part of the meaning of morality. As he says, "The merit of any definition depends upon the soundness of the theory that results" (*TJ*, 130/112–13rev). Within his justificatory framework, this means that finality is an appropriate ("reasonable") condition to impose on reasons and principles of justice since the conception of justice that results better fits with our considered moral convictions of justice (in wide reflective equilibrium) than any other theory (surely better than any theory that omits finality). Why this should be the case merits more discussion than I can give the matter here.

V. The Transition to Political Liberalism

Recall that the role of the Kantian congruence argument is to fill out the argument for the stability of justice as fairness and to show how a just constitution is realistically possible. If it can be shown that a well-ordered society describes conditions under which justice is an intrinsic good for each person, one that is supremely regulative of pursuit of all other goods, then it has been shown how justice can be supremely rational for each person. Being supremely rational for each, stability has been demonstrated in the strongest possible way, for justice is everyone's best response to their circumstances. Does this ambitious argument succeed?

The congruence argument contains many grand and controversial claims. It assumes that the ground for moral agency and "the unity of the self" reside in the capacities for practical reasoning, and not in any particular conception of the rational good. Also, implicit in its conclusion is the Kantian idea that the activity of practical reason in matters of justice is itself an intrinsic good. The argument further implies a Kantian thesis about the nature and constitution of morality and the realm of value: moral principles and the realm of value, rather than being given to us by a prior and independent order, have their origins in the activities of practical reason and the principles and ideas it constructs.[50] My concern here is limited to the question of whether the argument succeeds on its own terms.

Assume, then, that the congruence argument successfully shows that justice is an intrinsic and supremely regulative good for each person in a well-ordered society. Still, this does not show that each person in a well-ordered society will in fact recognize and accept justice as an intrinsic good. Unless a sizable proportion of them do, the Kantian congruence argument itself does not significantly advance the case for stability. For, only if people believe that justice is at least a significant value, if not an intrinsic good, will they be inclined not to compromise justice, and be assured that others will not, too, when it puts significant demands on their conception of their good.[51] Now it is true that, as part of the justification of justice as fairness, the Kantian congruence argument itself is, under the "full publicity" condition, publicly available and widely known (at least by those interested in this kind of thing.) Given full publicity, part of the public culture of a well-ordered society is the proposition or ideal that justice and autonomy are intrinsic to each person's good. This may be integrated into public education in a variety of ways, and accepted by the official culture of a well-ordered society. The problem is that, while these efforts might encourage many to believe that justice is intrinsic to their good, for others it might well have contrary, destabilizing effects.

In *Political Liberalism*, Rawls says that there is a "serious problem internal to justice as fairness [arising] from the fact that the account of stability in Part III of *Theory* is not consistent with the view as a whole" (*PL*, xv–xvi). He continues: "The serious problem I have in mind concerns the unrealistic idea of a well-ordered society as it appears in *Theory*" (*PL*, xvi). What is primarily unrealistic about the account in *Theory*, I conjecture, is the Kantian congruence argument. It fails to appreciate the extent of the "subjective circumstances of justice," or what Rawls later calls "the fact of reasonable pluralism" that characterizes a well-ordered society (*PL*, 66, 63). These circumstances imply that, while individuals might agree on principles of justice (as the idea of a well-ordered society assumes), under conditions where individuals have freedom of thought, conscience, and association (as liberal principles require), it is unrealistic to expect that they will ever all agree in their religious, philosophical, or ethical beliefs.[52] It is then unrealistic to expect that citizens in a well-ordered society will all agree on the ultimate justification of principles of justice that all accept, or on the supreme intrinsic good of autonomy, or even the intrinsic good of justice.

Imagine, then, a well-ordered society of justice as fairness, where there is widespread agreement and support for Rawls's liberal principles of justice. How is this general acceptance possible? Given liberty of conscience and freedom of thought and association, it must be because individuals affirm and support these

---

50. Compare Rawls's discussion of Kant's Moral constructivism. See *PL*, 99–101.

51. I am grateful to Milton Meyer for helping me clarify this point.

52. Rawls's reasons for the fact of reasonable pluralism rest on his account of "the burdens of judgment" (*PL*, 54–58), which were implicit in his initial account of the subjective circumstances of justice in *Theory* (*TJ*, 127/110 rev.).

principles for different reasons and from different points of view. For, it is unrealistic to suppose that everyone endorses the principles of justice for reasons specified by the Kantian interpretation. Liberal Thomists, then (to take one example), will affirm the principles of justice for their own specific reasons. They are seen as among the natural laws preordained by God and knowable by the natural light of our reason; in following these laws rational beings realize their essence and obtain the final end of their creation, the Beatific Vision.[53] On the basis of this comprehensive religious view, God alone, not human reason, is the ultimate origin of moral standards and the good. Justice and the human good are requirements of our created essence, not of unaided human reason. Moreover, moral autonomy is not an intrinsic good; instead it is a false value which conflicts with what the liberal Thomist sees as the only ultimate intrinsic good, the contemplation and enjoyment of God.[54]

Nothing about a comprehensive religious and ethical view like liberal Thomism is incompatible with compliance with requirements of justice as Rawls construes them. It is, then, a permissible conception of the good in a well-ordered society and presumably could gain many adherents. But, if so, then the content of this (and other) permissible conceptions of the good conflict with the Kantian conception of the good that is a part of public culture according to the Kantian interpretation. This may well have the effect of undermining many people's sense of self-respect; it might also cause resentment since, even though they accept the same principles of justice as everyone else, their most basic values are recognized as false values by the public culture. The problem here is that there is a kind of doctrinal intolerance of non-Kantian conceptions of the good that is built into the public culture of a well-ordered society of justice as fairness. Even if we assume that these religious and ethical views are false (on the assumption that the conclusion to the congruence argument is still sound) they are nonetheless permissible conceptions of the good according to the principles of justice. Their public rejection can only have the effect of undermining many people's allegiance and support for just institutions.

The problem may go even deeper than this. It may be that, given Rawls's account of a person's good in *Theory* (as the plan of life it would be rational to affirm in deliberative rationality), it cannot be said of non-Kantians that they are mistaken about their good. This would depend on features of Rawls's account of deliberative rationality he does not go into. According to this account, a person's good is the plan of life she would choose if she had full information of "all relevant facts," reasoned correctly, and imaginatively appreciated the consequences of choosing a plan of life. If the full information condition means that a person's good is what she would choose if she had no false beliefs, then we encounter the problem mentioned previously; namely, that many persons in a well-ordered

---

53. See Jacques Maritain, *Man and the State* (Chicago: University of Chicago Press, 1951), 84–101, on natural law, and his *Scholasticism and Politics* (New York: Macmillan, 1940), 121–22, on the Beatific Vision.

54. See Maritain, *Man and State*, 83–84, where he rejects Rousseau's and Kant's arguments that natural law is based in the autonomy of the will.

society will have mistaken beliefs (about God's creation of the universe, for example, including the realm of value), and so will not recognize that autonomy is an intrinsic good or that justice has its origins in moral personality. If so, then the congruence argument does not insure the stability of a well-ordered society. But if the full information condition expresses a weaker condition and means simply that everyone has access to all relevant evidentiary information, this would imply that many rational plans will be informed by false beliefs (such as God's creation of the realm of value). But if this is the case, then Rawls's Kantian congruence argument would simply fail on its own terms for large classes of people from the outset. For, then it would impute to all a conception of the good (to be morally autonomous) which many might not rationally endorse.

The general problem these objections raise is that we cannot expect large numbers of people in a well-ordered society to be motivated to comply with standards of justice for the Kantian reason that they realize their nature as free and equal rational moral beings and are thereby morally autonomous. But this is what the congruence argument sets out to prove in order to show how a well-ordered society can be stable and endure over time. The only way around this problem is to concede that the Kantian congruence argument is not needed to show the stability of a well-ordered society.[55] But this still leaves the problem the argument was designed to redress, namely, to show the effective rationality of justice in a well-ordered society. Stability then has to be satisfied by other means. This accounts for Rawls's development of the idea of overlapping consensus as well as other ideas central to political liberalism.[56]

Overlapping consensus means that people in a well-ordered society will normally act justly for many different reasons. Given reasonable pluralism of different philosophical, religious, and moral doctrines, what primarily motivates citizens in a well-ordered society to comply with public principles of justice is not a desire for autonomy or the intrinsic good of justice itself (though many may act justly for these reasons); rather, it is the many different values implicit in different comprehensive doctrines people subscribe to in a well-ordered society. Overlapping consensus is, in effect, a hypothesis about the kinds of conceptions of the good that will be fostered by a well-ordered society. It extends the reasoning behind the principles of reciprocity underlying development of the sense of justice in *Theory* (chap. 8) so that it applies to reasonable comprehensive doctrines and individuals' conceptions of the good.[57] As individuals tend to develop

55. This suggests that Barry's criticism that the congruence argument is unnecessary is at least partially correct, but not for the same reasons he discusses, that is, that having a moral sense of justice is sufficient to prove stability. For reasons discussed in the text, Rawls does not accept this; the problem of showing the rationality of justice still remains, and this is mainly the role of the idea of overlapping consensus in political liberalism.

56. See *PL*, xviii, where Rawls says that "all differences [between *Political Liberalism* and *Theory*] are consequences of removing that inconsistency" in the original stability argument. For a fuller account of how overlapping consensus and public reason respond to the problems implicit in the original congruence argument, see chapter 6 of this volume.

57. See *TJ*, 490–91/429–30 rev., for a concise statement of the reciprocity principles. See note 13 in this chapter for the third principle.

a desire to support just institutions that benefit them and those they care for, so, too, the main comprehensive doctrines in a well-ordered society should evolve doctrinally so as to accept liberal justice and its political values. (Rawls's example is the Vatican II reforms where the Catholic Church came to accept the values of constitutional democracy.) Thus, from among the many possible religious, philosophical, and ethical doctrines, those who will gain adherents and thrive in a well-ordered society will be reasonable and will endorse (or at least will be compatible with) the public principles of justice, each for their own specific doctrinal reasons. Unreasonable, irrational, or mad doctrines, though always present, will not muster sufficient support to gain sizable adherence. There will, then, be no widely accepted comprehensive view that rejects liberal principles of justice or which assigns an insignificant position to considerations of justice in its system of beliefs, values or moral principles. Assuming that this conjecture holds true in a well-ordered society, all will have sufficient reason to comply with liberal principles of justice for their own specific reasons. Justice will then be rational for each—instrumentally or intrinsically, depending on their particular conception of the good—and society will evince internal stability "for the right reasons" (PL, 388n.).

Overlapping consensus does not address all the issues the original congruence argument set out to. It does not claim, for example, that justice as fairness is true or objective according to universal criteria or that it will be publicly recognized as such. Given different philosophical views, such philosophical positions cannot be argued for on the basis of public reasons or resolved as part of the public conception of justice. They are part of ongoing, nonpublic moral and political debate among conflicting reasonable comprehensive philosophical views. The important point is that, if an overlapping consensus exists, such disputes should have little adverse effect on the stability of a liberal conception of justice. For, whether or not all citizens see liberal principles of justice as objective or true (moral skeptics do not, and they will always be present), all reasonable citizens (including skeptics) nonetheless should find these principles the most reasonable principles of justice for persons who conceive of themselves as free and equal democratic citizens. Moral skepticism and relativism are then effectively neutralized as threats to stability.

Overlapping consensus also does not imply that justice is supremely rational or is even an intrinsic good. So far as overlapping consensus goes, justice may be no more than an instrumental good for many people, a necessary means to what they believe to be the ultimate good, and hence subject to compromise when it conflicts with their final ends. Rawls's thought here may be that, since justice nonetheless occupies a significant position in each person's view, even if only as an instrumental good for many, conflicts between justice and their final ends will not be so frequent and entrenched to undermine stability.

So in a well-ordered society, it seems there is no assurance after all that justice will occupy a supremely regulative position in each person's conception of the good. This does not, however, deprive justice of its finality; rather, it shifts finality to a more restricted domain, the political domain of public reasons. Reasons of justice no longer may be taken to override all other reasons within all reasonable comprehensive doctrines or everyone's conception of the good. Still, justice does override all other reasons within the public political domain, for it provides the proper "content of public reason."[58]

I am grateful to R. Jay Wallace for his comments and discussion of earlier drafts of this chapter; to Andrew Levine, Harry Brighouse, and other members of the Philosophy Department at the University of Wisconsin; and to Susan Wolf, Henry Richardson, Douglas MacLean, Milton Meyer, Rahul Kumar, and other members of the Philamore Group for their helpful suggestions and criticisms.

58. Thanks to Gopal Sreenivasan for helping me to clarify this point.

Part II

Political Liberalism

6

Political Liberalism and
the Possibility of a Just
Democratic Constitution

Introduction

My aim in this paper is to provide an overview of John Rawls's project in *Political Liberalism*.[1] I sketch how this book is designed to respond to certain problems internal to Rawls's argument in *A Theory of Justice*.[2] *Political Liberalism* is a development and extension of Rawls's original project, as stated in *A Theory of Justice*, to work out "the most appropriate moral basis for a democratic society" (*TJ*, viii/ xviii rev.). *A Theory of Justice* itself invokes assumptions and arguments that are at odds with Rawls's egalitarian liberalism. It is to respond to these internal tensions that Rawls recasts not the substantive content of justice as fairness or its principles but how we are to conceive of their justification.

To say this recasting is internal to Rawls's original project means that *Political Liberalism* is not motivated by external criticisms.[3] There is a widespread perception that the revisions Rawls has made to *A Theory of Justice* leading up to *Political Liberalism* have come largely in response to communitarian criticisms.[4] Recall Michael Sandel's argument that Rawls's Kantian liberalism is saddled with a conception of the person as shorn of any substantive commitments

---

1. John Rawls, *Political Liberalism* (New York: Columbia University Press, 1993; paperback edition, 1996, 2004) (cited in text as *PL*; page references are to the paperback edition).

2. Rawls, *A Theory of Justice* (Cambridge, MA: Harvard University Press, 1971, rev. ed., 1999) (cited in text as *TJ*; sometimes referred to as *Theory*).

3. The exception is chapter 8 of *PL*, the 1982 Tanner Lecture "The Basic Liberties and Their Priority," which constructively and appreciatively responds to H. L. A. Hart's criticisms of Rawls's initial argument for the first principle of justice and the specification of the basic liberties. See also H. L. A. Hart, "Rawls on Liberty and Its Priority," *University of Chicago Law Review* 40, no. 3 (Spring 1973), 534–55.

4. Rawls alludes to this in *PL*, and says, "I do not believe there is a basis for saying this" (xix n. 6).

or deep attachments to persons or final ends.[5] It is as if Rawlsian agents are cold, bare, rational choosing machines, hardly worthy of the deep respect Rawls, as a Kantian, would claim for persons. Given Rawls's description of the agents in the original position,[6] one can see how this criticism might become so popular. (Still, to achieve this reading, one must ignore the account of the person Rawls gives in A *Theory of Justice* and substitute for it the account of the parties in the original position.)[7] It is also understandable why many would think that communitarian criticisms have prompted Rawls's recent changes. Rawls, after all, does alter his account of the role of the conception of the person, at least so far as to contend that it is only an account of our conception of ourselves in our political relations. It is not, then (as Sandel might have thought), a metaphysical account of the nature and identity of persons (a claim Rawls had already denied, long before Sandel's book).[8] Nor is the conception of the person even a more general normative conception, that stems from an account of human agency or which is part of a comprehensive ethical view (something Rawls evidently did think in A *Theory of Justice*).[9] Instead, the conception of the person as free and equal, and as defined by two moral powers (and a conception of the good), is said to be a purely "political conception," designed to capture our self-awareness as democratic citizens (*PL*, 29–35).

As I will discuss, there is in *Political Liberalism* a distancing from the Kantian foundations of justice as fairness Rawls relies on in A *Theory of Justice* and

5. See Michael J. Sandel, *Liberalism and the Limits of Justice* (New York: Cambridge University Press, 1982), 15–23; see also Bernard Williams, "Persons, Character, and Morality," in *Moral Luck* (New York: Cambridge University Press, 1981).

6. *TJ*, 17–22/15–19 rev. In the original position, rational, interested agents are without knowledge of their individual talents, social position, ends, or any other information about their particular situation. Rawls says: "This initial situation is fair between individuals as moral persons" (*TJ*, 12/11 rev.).

7. See *TJ*, secs. 63–64, on persons and rational plans. See also *TJ*, sec. 77 and 12/11 rev., 19/17 rev., 329/289 rev., 561/491 rev., on moral personality. Sandel ignores the role of the moral powers in defining the person, as well as Rawls's claims regarding the connection of persons with their conception of the good. See, for example, Rawls's statements in *Theory*: "Here I adapt Royce's thought that a person may be regarded as a human life lived according to a plan. For Royce an individual *says who he is* by describing his purposes and causes, what he intends to do in his life. . . . Royce uses the notion of a plan to characterize the coherent, systematic purposes of the individual, what makes him a conscious, unified moral person. . . . And I shall do the same" (408 n. 10/358 rev.; emphasis added). See also *PL*, 26–27 (addressing Sandel's criticisms).

8. See Rawls, "The Independence of Moral Theory" (1975), in *Collected Papers*, ed. Samuel Freeman (Cambridge, MA: Harvard University Press, 1999), 286–302 (cited in text as *CP*). Rawls argues why the conception of the person implicit in justice as fairness is normative, and not metaphysical, and thus is not susceptible to criticisms that have their basis in metaphysical accounts of personal identity. Rawls argues that his account of moral personality is not incompatible with a Humean account of personal identity, such as Derek Parfit's, that contends that there is no deep fact about the identity and individuation of persons, but that personhood is simply a matter of the continuity and connectedness of experiences and activities.

9. See Rawls, "The Unity of the Self," in *TJ*, sec. 85, as well as the widely misconstrued (e.g., by Sandel) paragraph on 560/491 rev., where Rawls says, "For the self is prior to the ends that are affirmed by it." This comes in the context of an argument against teleological moral views, which

"Kantian Constructivism in Moral Theory."[10] But none of the significant changes leading up to and through *Political Liberalism* have been designed with communitarians in mind.[11] This will not likely satisfy these critics for at least two reasons. First, while Rawls gives up certain Kantian foundations of his view, still, as far as the structure and content of justice as fairness is concerned, *Political Liberalism* affirms and develops certain Kantian features of the view more than ever. (Here I mean the idea of political constructivism, the conception of free and equal moral persons, the priority of right, etc.) Second, contrary to communitarian arguments that Rawls's Kantian liberalism incorporates no shared conception of the good, the fact is that A *Theory of Justice* did rely on what Rawls would now call a "partially comprehensive" conception of the good common to all persons in a well-ordered democratic society (*PL*, xviii, 13, 175). This was most prominent in Rawls's argument for stability in part III of A *Theory of Justice*, his "congruence" argument. One major change *Political Liberalism* makes is that it gives up this partially comprehensive conception, along with the general Kantian moral conception that grounded justice as fairness.

These are among the internal problems Rawls is addressing in *Political Liberalism*. "*Theory* . . . regards justice as fairness and utilitarianism as comprehensive, or partially comprehensive, doctrines" (*PL*, xviii). But "no comprehensive doctrine is appropriate as a political conception for a constitutional regime" (*PL*, 135). Now, it may be that these changes will make Rawls's view even more objectionable on some communitarian views. For, Rawls's argument, as we shall see, is just that egalitarian liberalism cannot incorporate, consistent with its own principles, any general moral doctrine or comprehensive conception of the good. This denies what seems to be a fundamental communitarian thesis: a comprehensive conception of the human good, politically endorsed and shared by the members of society, is a condition of social and political unity. Both A *Theory of Justice* and *Political Liberalism*, each in its own way, agree that some shared conception of the good of justice is a condition of social and political unity. But *Political Liberalism*, unlike the account in A *Theory of Justice*, requires that this good cannot be publicly recognized or affirmed as part of any comprehensive ethical view. If Rawls is right, this means that, insofar as communitarians aim for a view with egalitarian and liberal features, they fail to present a feasible alternative.

---

hold that form is given to our lives by nonmoral ends, or aims that are defined independently of any moral restrictions. Rawls's point here, I take it, is that as moral beings principles of justice are in some manner implicit in our moral awareness and in our conception of ourselves as moral agents. It is in large part the purpose of moral philosophy to uncover and clarify these principles. So far as this goes, Rawls's work in *Political Liberalism* leaves it unchanged except to limit this claim to political principles implicit in our self-awareness as democratic citizens.

10. Rawls's 1980 Dewey Lectures. See *CP*, 303–358.

11. Rawls does briefly reply to Sandel's criticism that Rawlsian agents are abstract and independent of any attributes such as final ends and attachments. He says this reading is "an illusion caused by not seeing the original position as a device of representation" (*PL*, 27). The original position is not an ontological statement of the nature of the self but an attempt to vividly represent and combine assumptions regarding the requirements of equality, rationality, freedom, etc., to see what they imply by way of principles of justice.

In section I, I review the problem in A *Theory of Justice* which prompts the changes that lead to the doctrine of *Political Liberalism*. In section II, I discuss the first major change in Rawls's view, the idea of overlapping consensus. In section III, I take up a second major alteration, the idea of public reason. Finally, in section IV, I discuss the relevance of public reason to the role of the courts in a constitutional democracy.

My overall aims in this article are to explain and clarify, rather than to criticize, Rawls's account of *Political Liberalism*. Often one has the feeling, in reading and rereading Rawls, that increments of understanding are accompanied by increased confusion. This stems from the complexity of Rawls's view and the interrelatedness of his main ideas. Increased understanding in one area often requires that one rethink what one feels is already understood. My efforts here are directed at diminishing the sense of confusion many (including myself) have in finding their way through *Political Liberalism*.

I. The Relationship of *Political Liberalism* to *A Theory of Justice*

In the introduction to *Political Liberalism*, in explaining the changes in his view, Rawls says:

> But to understand the nature and extent of the differences between *Political Liberalism* and *A Theory of Justice* one must see them as arising from trying to resolve a serious problem internal to justice as fairness, namely from the fact that the account of *stability* in Part III of *Theory* is not consistent with the view as a whole. I believe *all differences* are consequences of removing that inconsistency. Otherwise these lectures take the structure and content of *Theory* to remain substantially the same. (*PL*, xvii-xviii; emphasis added)

Rawls goes on to indicate that "the problem of stability has played very little role in the history of moral philosophy"; still, it is "fundamental to political philosophy" (*PL*, xix). The extent to which moral philosophy has neglected the problem of stability is reflected in the degree to which treatment of Rawls's work has neglected discussion of it. *A Theory of Justice* is one of the most discussed philosophical works of the twentieth century. But, of all the voluminous commentary on this work, very little of significance has been written on Rawls's argument for stability in part III of *A Theory of Justice*, and virtually nothing has been written on the central feature of that argument on "the congruence of the right and the good" (*TJ*, sec. 86). What is involved in the argument for stability?

In general, in Rawls's account in *A Theory of Justice*, to show that a social scheme is stable is to show that it will be regularly complied with and its basic rules willingly acted upon, and also that when deviations or infractions occur that upset the social scheme, stabilizing forces come into play that prevent further deviation and tend to restore the arrangement (*TJ*, 6/5-6 rev.). The primary example of this kind of argument is found in Hobbes's work. The primary role of government for Hobbes is to give everyone sufficient assurance that the laws will be enforced. By enforcing a public system of coercive sanctions, government removes the grounds for believing that others are not complying with the laws. Without this assurance, it is not rational for individuals to observe the rules themselves. Hobbes argues, given his bleak assumptions about the predominant self-interest of human nature, that the only way to solve this problem is to endow one (legal) person, the "sovereign," with nearly absolute political power.[12] External forces then supply the primary basis for stability in Hobbes's view. Rawls makes different assumptions about human nature. Rather than assuming that our sole primary motivations are interests in ourselves, he contends people normally have a sense of justice, including a desire to act on terms of cooperation that are fair and reasonable, and a desire to justify their actions to others on terms of mutual respect others can reasonably accept (*TJ*, 46–50/40–44 rev, 472–79/414–19 rev.). It is these moral motivations that Rawls mainly relies upon for the stability of a well-ordered society. Consequently, the stability problem for Rawls is structured differently than in Hobbes, and has a different solution. Rawls's aim is to show how a just scheme can elicit its own support and achieve inherent stability (*TJ*, 479/419 rev.).

One way to approach the stability problem, as Rawls deals with it, is by focusing on a passage from Kant. In his essay, "Idea for a Universal History," Kant raises the question: How is a just constitution possible? This is, Kant says, "the greatest problem for the human species."[13] The reason this question is so difficult is that it requires, Kant says, "the correct concept" of a just constitution, "great experience during much of the world's course, and above all else a good will prepared to accept that constitution."[14] Kant's question raises, then, three kinds of problems, each suggesting a host of more specific issues. First, there is the problem of conception: we need an account and justification of the principles that define a just constitution. Second, we encounter an institutional problem (Kant's problem of "experience"): how to describe the social and political institutions that are required to realize these principles in societies. And third, a motivation problem arises: to give an account of how people can acquire the will to do justice and the desire to support just institutions.

One way to look upon the structure of Rawls's A *Theory of Justice* is as an attempt to provide interconnected answers to these three general issues. Thus we find in part I, "Theory," an answer to Kant's first problem, namely, an account of the most appropriate conception of justice for the constitution (more generally, the basic structure) of a democratic society. In line with the democratic social contract tradition, Rawls contends that a just constitution is possible only if it commands the reasonable agreement of free and rational individuals who are ideally situated, from a position of equal right. Appealing to certain moral convictions implicit in our sense of justice, Rawls elicits certain considered convictions regarding reasonable restrictions on arguments for principles of justice (*TJ*, 18–21/16–19 rev.). This provides the basis for the original position, his version of

---

12. See Thomas Hobbes, *Leviathan*, pts. 1, 2 (1651).
13. Immanuel Kant, *Perpetual Peace and Other Essays*, trans. Ted Humphrey (Indianapolis: Hackett Publishing, 1983), 33–34.
14. Kant, *Perpetual Peace*, 33–34.

the appropriate standpoint of equality from which to achieve a reasonable social agreement. From there, Rawls makes his familiar argument for the principles of justice. This in large part is Rawls's account of the "correct concept" of the principles for regulating a just constitution.

Then, in part II of A *Theory of Justice*, "Institutions," Rawls responds to Kant's second problem. Taking into account the workings of social systems under modern conditions conjoined with facts about human nature, Rawls provides an account of the democratic institutions that satisfy his principles of justice. These are the institutions of a constitutional democracy which provide for a set of constitutional rights that protect basic liberties, laws that guarantee fair equality of opportunity, and a "property-owning democracy" (*TJ*, 274/242 rev.), or perhaps some liberal socialist scheme (*TJ*, 280/247–48 rev.), which provides a social minimum that enables each citizen to effectively exercise these rights and achieve individual independence.

The third of Kant's issues is the one he considers most difficult. (That Rawls, too, considers it most difficult is suggested by his returning to the problem in *Political Liberalism*, and revising his initial account of the stability argument). Assuming we have the correct conception of justice and have in place the institutions needed to achieve it, how are we to motivate individuals who are members of this social scheme, to affirm and support these institutions and the conception of justice that underlie them? This is not simply a problem of engaging peoples' moral beliefs about justice. If Rawls is right, this has been achieved already in the argument for a conception of justice and a just constitution that best fit with our considered moral judgments. The problem Rawls addresses in part III of A *Theory of Justice*, "Ends," is largely that of showing how this conception can engage the will of those who live under a just social scheme (a "well-ordered society" of justice as fairness). Assuming that citizens in a well-ordered society have public knowledge and agreement on justice and just institutions, how do they come to care about them? Rawls contends from the outset that all have a sense of justice and a desire to justify their activities to others as just. In the moral psychology set forth in chapter 8 of A *Theory of Justice*, he shows how people can come to acquire this disposition to abide by the principles of justice and their requirements in a well-ordered society. This is the first part of the argument for stability in A *Theory of Justice*.

But then a second problem arises: even assuming that each person has a sense of justice, why should they sufficiently care about justice, to the degree that they recognize and are willing to respect its demands even when these demands conflict with or impede individuals in the pursuit of their conceptions of their good? Even assuming we can get all in a well-ordered democratic society to agree in their judgments on the principles of a just constitution and the institutions needed to support it (*TJ*, pts. I and II), and even assuming that all citizens have a sense of justice and a desire to be just (*TJ*, chap. 8), there remains this significant problem of consistently engaging their will. It must be shown why people have sufficient reason, from within their individual perspectives, to observe and act on requirements of justice when these requirements constrain or oppose other ends and commitments they have. A just constitution is possible only if it sufficiently engages each person's will, and to do this it must promote or affirm their good (*TJ*, 398–99/350 rev.). To show that something promotes or affirms one's good is, on Rawls's account, to show that it is rational to desire (*TJ*, chap. 7). And this requires ultimately an argument that shows an activity, in this case the activity of justice, is compatible with human nature, such that it would be rational to incorporate this activity as a primary feature of one's conception of the good (or "rational plan of life" as Rawls says in A *Theory of Justice* [*TJ*, 408/358–9 rev.]).

This basically is the problem of stability as it is set up within Rawls's view. This is not the same problem that confronts Hobbes or the Hobbesian. A just constitution is possible only if its requirements harmonize with each person's good. On this, both Hobbesian contract and democratic social contract views agree. But for Hobbesian views, no sharp distinction is made between the conceptual and motivational problems Kant delineates (hence no sharp distinction is made between what is "reasonable" and "rational" as Rawls uses those terms). There is in Hobbesian views no attempt to define justice independent of individuals' particular perspectives and conceptions of the good, from an impartial point of view. Hobbesians define a just constitution basically in terms of agreement on those principles that are instrumental to each person's given desires and interests, given the desires and expectations of others (as specified under cooperation-free circumstances and independent of any moral notions). Justice is then reduced to a rational compromise among essentially conflicting interests, or (in Kant's terms) a "coalition of private wills."[15]

Rawls's Kantian account employs both a different structure and a different moral psychology than Hobbesian views. Structurally, justice is articulated independent of individuals' particular desires and interests, by reference to reasonable moral convictions. These then come to be articulated in terms of what everyone would jointly will as free and equal from an impartial public perspective. The stability problem then becomes: How can persons come to have a will to do the public will, as defined by the social contract? "Stability is secured by sufficient motivation of the appropriate kind acquired under just institutions" (*PL*, 142–43). Here Rawls's alternative moral psychology comes into play. Unlike Hobbes and Hobbesians, for Rawls, "motivation of the appropriate kind" is not some external mechanism (positive or negative sanctions) that induces people with no independent interest in justice to comply with social rules.[16] Instead, Rawls aims to show how the principles and institutions of a constitutional democracy, justified as reasonable on grounds independent of each individual's particular point of view and conception of the good, are or can be internalized and incorporated into their desires, so that doing justice becomes a part of and even affirms each person's particular good. A just constitution is possible only if its citizens can freely endorse it, and it affirms their good. This requires ultimately an argument that shows that justice is compatible with human nature, such that it would be rational to incorporate this activity as a primary feature of one's conception of the good (or ratio-

15. Kant, *Perpetual Peace*, 77.
16. *PL*, 143. "The problem of stability is not that of bringing others who reject a conception to share it, or to act in accordance with it, by workable sanctions."

nal plan of life). Is it rational, integral to one's good, to develop and exercise one's sense of justice by doing justice? Is it rational to be reasonable? Or, alternatively, is the sense of justice irrelevant to, or (as Nietzsche held) even destructive of, our well-being? That is how Rawls conceives the question of stability.

This is only a sketch of the stability problem Rawls confronts, but it should be sufficient to enable us to understand Rawls's enigmatic claim that the problem he is addressing in *Political Liberalism* is that the "account of stability in Part III of *A Theory of Justice* is not consistent with the view as a whole" (*PL*, xvii–xviii). Rawls says the problem is that in *A Theory of Justice*, justice as fairness is a "partially comprehensive doctrine" (*PL*, xviii). It is not immediately evident, from my description, how the argument in *A Theory of Justice* dealt with the stability problem by invoking a (partially) comprehensive doctrine. In part I of *A Theory of Justice*, Rawls does mention, in passing, that, "the contractarian idea can be extended to the choice of more or less an entire ethical system. . . . Obviously if justice as fairness succeeds reasonably well, a next step would be to study the more general view suggested by the name 'rightness as fairness'" (*TJ*, 17/15 rev.). There is no suggestion here that justice as fairness must be considered as part of such a more comprehensive ethical system, and no intimation this is required for stability. Indeed, from a reading of the first five hundred pages (chaps. 1–8) of *A Theory of Justice*, it is hard to see exactly where Rawls thinks he had to invoke a more comprehensive ethical doctrine to justify justice as fairness.[17] And some of this material (especially chap. 7 on rational plans, and the moral psychology of chap. 8) contains much of Rawls's argument for stability. It is only when we reach chapter 9, and the second stage of the argument for stability, from "congruence," that the deeper bases of the view in Kantian ethics become really apparent. The argument for "the congruence of the right and the good"(*TJ*, 572/501 rev.) aims to show that, under the circumstances of a well-ordered society, it is rational to be reasonable, not just by acting on requirements of justice, or even incorporating them into one's rational plan (or conception of the good). Justice is not simply an instrumental or even essential good in a well-ordered society of justice as fairness (though showing that is also a part of Rawls's argument for stability). In addition, the congruence argument seeks to show that (1) justice is an intrinsic good, an end that is worth pursuing for its own sake; moreover, (2) by its nature, justice is the supreme good, in that, whatever else one's final ends may be, the requirements of justice are to take priority over them in the sense that the pursuit of other intrinsic goods is to be steadfastly regulated by requirements of justice. As a good, justice is "supremely regulative"; it has "absolute priority" over all other goods (*TJ*, 570–75/499–504 rev.).

If Rawls's congruence argument could go through, then one can see how justice as fairness could specify a stable social scheme. For, it would mean that under the ideal circumstances of a well-ordered society, where justice as fairness is in force, it is almost never rational for citizens to act in ways that violate requirements of justice, because by acting unjustly, they would be acting con-

17. Here one must exclude section 40, "The Kantian Interpretation of Justice as Fairness," where Rawls argues how his principles can be seen as part of a more general Kantian moral doctrine.

trary to their (supreme) good. This ambitious argument is made in A *Theory of Justice* primarily on the basis of the "Kantian Interpretation" of justice as fairness (cf. Rawls, *TJ*, sec. 40): by acting not simply in accordance with but also from a motive of justice, we realize our nature as free, equal, and rational beings, and are therefore morally autonomous.

The Kantian congruence argument says, roughly, that justice as a virtue and an end is worth pursuing for its own sake, because by so doing we fully realize our capacity for a sense of justice. But then the sense of justice is a settled disposition to act on principles of justice, and "the desire to act justly and the desire to express our nature as free moral persons turn out to specify what is practically speaking the same desire" (*TJ*, 572/501 rev.). So to develop and exercise the desire to act on principles of justice for their own sake is to realize one's moral power of justice; and (by parallel with Kant's notion of a good will), to realize one's moral powers is to be morally autonomous. And according to Rawls's "Aristotelian Principle,"[18] it is rational, indeed essential to our good to realize the higher powers implicit in our nature (*TJ*, 572/501 rev.). Moral autonomy is then an intrinsic good. Moreover, given its nature, it is not just one intrinsic good among others; because of the content of principles of justice, autonomy is a "supremely regulative" intrinsic good that is necessary if we are to realize "our nature" as "free and equal rational moral beings."[19] If so, then it is rational to be reasonable for its own sake and to consistently subordinate one's ends and regulate one's pursuits according to justice. So we have the "congruence of the right and the good" (*TJ*, sec. 86).

This is barely a sketch of Rawls's complicated Kantian congruence argument.[20] It must suffice for our purposes. The important point to gain from it is that the central aspect of Rawls's argument for stability relies upon a general moral doctrine, one that specifies a partially comprehensive conception of the human good in terms of individual moral autonomy. Note, however, that this deep Kantian argument plays no central role in solving the problems, dealt with in parts I and II of A *Theory of Justice*, of (1) eliciting the reasonable principles of a just constitution, and (2) deciding the institutions that satisfy them. In Rawls's view, even in A *Theory of Justice*, we can elicit the "correct concept" and the institutions of a just basic social structure, by appealing to the considered convictions of justice that we commonly share, along with our knowledge about the

---

18. This psychological principle of motivation basically says: Other things equal, human beings enjoy the exercise of their realized capacities (their innate or trained abilities), and this enjoyment increases the more the capacity is realized, or the greater its complexity. The intuitive idea here is that human beings take more pleasure in doing something as they become more proficient at it, and of two activities they do equally well, they prefer the one calling on a larger repertoire of more intricate and subtle discriminations (*TJ*, 426/374 rev.). This principle Rawls invokes to explain the rationality of developing and exercising the sense of justice.

19. Here I mean that Rawls sees the desire to act justly as a highest-order desire, that all one's other desires or ends conform to principles of justice. Given this content, justice is not the kind of end that can be scheduled in alongside other ends, to be pursued when one has the time for it. The only way to successfully realize the object of the supremely regulative desire is by constantly observing requirements of justice. See Rawls, *TJ*, 574/503 rev.

20. The specific details of this argument are set forth in the preceding chapter of this volume.

workings of social institutions.[21] For these purposes, there is no need, even in *A Theory of Justice*, to appeal to deeper philosophical claims about the nature and conditions of human agency, and the intrinsic good of such agents. These kinds of considerations really come into play only in part III of *A Theory of Justice*, in order to show that the scheme of moral principles justified as right and reasonable on independent grounds in part I are also good and rational to conform to and pursue, and that, therefore, justice as fairness evinces not only justice but also inherent stability (*TJ*, 498/436 rev.).

What now, according to *Political Liberalism*, is the problem with the argument for stability in *A Theory of Justice*? Rawls says the "fundamental question about political justice in a democratic society" is: "How is it possible for there to exist over time a just and stable society of free and equal citizens, who remain profoundly divided by reasonable religious, philosophical, and moral doctrines" (*PL*, 4). We have here, in effect, Kant's original question—How is a just constitution possible?—phrased so as to apply to democratic citizens with conflicting comprehensive views and conceptions of the good. Rawls contends that in any democratic scheme in which individuals are regarded as equally free and as capable of formulating and pursuing their own conceptions of the good, it is inevitable that there will be a plurality of potentially conflicting religious, philosophical, and moral views, each of which is legitimate from the point of view of justice. This "fact of reasonable pluralism" is a permanent feature of a democratic system that recognizes free institutions, as individuals freely exercise their reason to formulate religious, philosophical, and moral views (*PL*, 4, 36, 55).[22]

Consider now the well-ordered society of justice as fairness, as defended in *A Theory of Justice*. Because of the protection of the basic liberties of freedom of thought, conscience, and association, this society (like any liberal society) is marked by a toleration of diverse comprehensive doctrines and ways of life, each of which is compatible with Rawls's liberal principles of justice. Moreover, according to Rawls a well-ordered society is a society in which, in spite of their differences in religious, philosophical, and moral convictions, citizens generally agree upon, and publicly affirm and accept, the principles of justice as regulative of their society; and this society, as well-ordered, generally realizes these principles.

A well-ordered society is, from the point of view of justice, an ideal social scheme. But consider the following problem. There might be many religious, metaphysical, or ethical views which accept and endorse, as part of their doctrines, justice as fairness as the "correct concept" of justice. Yet suppose they affirm the principles of justice (including the argument for it from the original position), not (or not simply) because it matches their considered moral convictions in reflective equilibrium. Instead they endorse justice as fairness because it follows from their comprehensive religious and metaphysical views. So, we might imagine a liberal Catholic who sees the principles of justice as true as a matter

---

21. Kant, *Perpetual Peace*, 33.
22. For Rawls's explanation of the fact of reasonable pluralism in terms of certain limits of our reasoning powers which he calls the "burdens of judgment," see *PL*, 54–58.

of natural law.[23] As such, she sees them as God's commands (or at least derived from them), which are knowable by the natural light of reason, and enjoined by God as part of the act of creating the universe, so that reasoning creatures might ultimately realize their essence and obtain the final ultimate and intrinsic good in the universe, the Beatific Vision of God.[24] And this is the primary reason she affirms and complies with the requirements of justice.

It is a feature of Rawls's view that not just the account of justice but also the complete justification of justice as fairness is to be publicly available, a part of the public culture. Nothing is, nor need be, hidden from the public's view. This is the "full publicity condition" (*PL*, 66). If so, then, according to A *Theory of Justice*, the Kantian argument for stability from congruence would be publicly available, perhaps made a part of civic education and called upon to show citizens, when in doubt, why they have sufficient reason to comply with and support just laws and institutions. But the Kantian congruence argument, as we have seen, would motivate individuals by demonstrating that justice is in their interest, because by acting on and from principles of justice, they fully realize their own capacity for a sense of justice, and therewith the intrinsic good of moral autonomy. But this is just the problem from the liberal Catholics' (and many others') particular points of view. According to their comprehensive religious and moral views, God alone, not human reason, is the ultimate source of morality, justice, and value. Justice, natural law, and the human good are requirements of our created essence, not of unaided human reason.[25] Ethical autonomy is not an intrinsic good; indeed, this value conflicts with what the liberal Thomist takes to be the only ultimate intrinsic good—the contemplation and enjoyment of God.[26] These are the ultimate reasons she would accept for doing anything. If so, then the public conception of justice, whose principles she accepts and affirms as God's natural law, contains justifying features that contradict her religion.

This is one example of the kind of problem Rawls has in mind when he says "the account of stability in Part III of *Theory* is not consistent with the view as a whole" (*PL*, xvii–xviii). There will be individuals in the well-ordered society of justice as fairness who endorse the public conception of justice and the institutions it supports, but who, because of toleration and the free use of reason and reason's limitations ("the burdens of judgment" [*PL*, 54–58]) form religious, philosophical, and moral views that conflict with the beliefs and final ends citizens need entertain and accept for justice as fairness (on A *Theory of Justice*'s account) to be stable. There is then a kind of public intolerance of non-Kantian philosophical and moral views built into the full public justification of justice as fairness. This is not, of course, a legal intolerance that affects freedom of conscience, thought,

23. An example here would be the liberal Thomism of Jacques Maritain, as set forth in his *Man and the State* (Chicago: University of Chicago Press, 1951), and his *Scholasticism and Politics* (New York: Macmillan, 1940).

24. See Maritain, *Scholasticism*, 121–22, on the Beatific Vision; also *Man and State*, 84–101, on natural law.

25. See Maritain, *Man and State*, 94, 97.

26. Maritain, *Man and State*, 83–84 (rejecting Rousseau's and Kant's arguments that natural law is based in autonomy of the will).

and speech. But it is a cultural intolerance that, because the public conception of the good conflicts with many citizens' comprehensive views, could affect their sense of self-respect (one of the primary social goods), and even undermine their allegiance and support for just institutions. In this way, there is something self-undermining about Rawls's stability argument from congruence.

This is one way to understand the background for the revisions contained in *Political Liberalism*.[27] It enables us to understand the need for such ideas as public reason, and overlapping consensus. They are intended as additions and revisions to the original argument, designed to show the possibility of a just and stable democratic constitution. This becomes apparent in Rawls's response to his "fundamental question about political justice in a democratic society":

> Three conditions seem to be sufficient for a society to be a fair and stable system of cooperation between free and equal citizens who are deeply divided by the reasonable comprehensive doctrines they affirm. First, the basic structure of society is regulated by a political conception of justice; second, this political conception is the focus of an overlapping consensus of reasonable comprehensive doctrines; and third, public discussion, when constitutional essentials and questions of basic justice are at stake, is conducted in terms of the political conception of justice. (*PL*, 44)

The aim of the next two sections is to show how the two ideas Rawls mentions in the second and third components of his solution, overlapping consensus and public reason, play a role in the reformulation of justice as fairness as a "freestanding" political conception that is not tied to any comprehensive doctrine or general moral conception (*PL*, 10, 12).

II. Overlapping Consensus

Political Liberalism sets out to formulate an independent branch of ethics in response to the practical needs of a liberal and democratic society. It is the public ethics of the political domain of a democracy, "the domain of the political" (*PL*, 38, 125, 139). Rawls thinks that for democratic political philosophy to respond to the problems it is called upon to address, it must restrict its aspirations and come to occupy a discrete and insulated position. Democratic political philosophy should not seek to address controversial metaphysical or epistemological issues, or incorporate comprehensive moral theories and general theories of value. This is not to say there is no place for social and political criticism. It means, rather, that such criticism is to be conducted in terms of concepts and principles that

---

27. I am not saying that this is just the way that Rawls understands the problem he now finds in *A Theory of Justice*. His understanding of the problem is, I believe, a good deal more complicated than the way I present it. See, however, Rawls's "Reply to Habermas," included as lecture 9 in *Political Liberalism* (beginning with the 1996 paperback edition), 388n, wherein Rawls cites this current essay in reference to how part III of *TJ* assumed a comprehensive moral doctrine.

are accessible and endorsable from many different perspectives. For Rawls, part of being reasonable (as opposed to rational) is to be willing to reason from shared premises, and to justify one's conduct and its consequences according to principles that all can accept.[28]

Rawls conceives of the primary purpose of political philosophy in a democratic society as practical (as opposed to epistemological or metaphysical): to provide bases for public justification and political agreement about basic social institutions among free and equal democratic citizens (*PL*, 9–10, 100). These bases consist of a set of concepts and principles, and standards of evidence and judgment, in terms of which citizens can debate public issues, criticize each other's conduct, and justify their legitimate activities. But given free institutions that allow for such liberties as freedom of conscience, thought, speech, and inquiry, citizens inevitably will have diverse and conflicting religious, metaphysical, and moral views in any free democratic scheme. This is the "fact of reasonable pluralism" (*PL*, 36). This fact considerably restricts the terms of public justification and debate. The common considerations that can count as good reasons in public discussion must be acceptable to and compatible with a wide range of conflicting views. Otherwise these reasons cannot play a role in public justification, and democratic political philosophy cannot achieve its practical aim of providing a basis for public justification. Democratic political philosophy, if it is to be successful, must then be an expression of citizens' "shared and public political reason" (*PL*, 9). "But to attain such a shared reason, the conception of justice should be, as far as possible, independent of the opposing and conflicting philosophical and religious doctrines that citizens affirm. In formulating such a conception, *Political Liberalism* applies the principle of toleration to philosophy itself" (*PL*, 9–10). To do so, Rawls seeks to present and justify a conception of justice that is compatible with a wide range of epistemological, metaphysical, and even ethical views, including non-Kantian perfectionist, intuitionist, and even utilitarian views (cf. *PL*, chap. 3).

If political philosophy is to achieve such a degree of "toleration" and achieve its purpose of providing a basis for public justification and agreement, then it must be "freestanding," and "doctrinally autonomous" (*PL*, 10, 12).[29] As freestanding, it is to be publicly expoundable and justifiable in terms of "fundamental ideas" that are a part of democratic culture, along with the considered convictions of justice democratic citizens share in common. It is not then to rely, in its public justification, on controversial metaphysical and epistemological premises, nor on comprehensive moral or religious doctrine. At the same time, its public

28. See *PL*, 48–50. Reasonableness, as a virtue of individuals, implies that one has to also reason and act in good faith. Reasonableness also involves a genuine willingness to guide one's conduct according to principles which are commonly shared with others. Moreover, it involves taking into account the consequences of one's actions on others' well-being and a willingness to modify one's conduct when it adversely affects others and violates shared principles. For other components of reasonableness, see note 31.

29. Rawls says political philosophy is to be "autonomous." As autonomous, it is to be seen as a distinctly normative inquiry, not in need of reduction or explanation in terms of some natural science. See *PL*, 87–88. See also *PL*, 98–99, on "doctrinal autonomy."

justification as a freestanding view cannot rule out other kinds of arguments for these same principles. Rawls says it is desirable that democratic principles of justice have other nonpublic justifications provided for within the terms of different and even conflicting reasonable comprehensive views.[30] Indeed, it would seem to be a practical necessity, if political liberalism is to be possible, that there be such nonpublic justifications; otherwise, the political conception of justice could not stably endure, since it could not form the basis for what Rawls calls an "overlapping consensus" (cf. *PL*, 11, 15).

Rawls thus aspires to a conception of justice that satisfies two dimensions that might seem to pull in different directions. (Here he refers to a "dualism in *Political Liberalism*" [*PL*, xxiii].) First, as freestanding, the conception must be publicly justifiable on its own terms. Given the "fact of reasonable pluralism" this means the political conception cannot be argued for in terms peculiar to any comprehensive moral doctrine or conception of the good, but rather only on the basis of premises and ideas all reasonable persons[31] can accept and endorse in their capacity as democratic citizens.[32] This first dimension is satisfied in "the first three lectures of *Political Liberalism* which set out the first stage of the exposition of justice as fairness as a freestanding view" (*PL*, 133). "The second stage of the exposition" is the argument for stability. For purposes of stability, Rawls now contends, the conception of justice must also be nonpublicly justifiable, in terms of the various reasonable comprehensive doctrines that gain adherents in a well-ordered society (*PL*, xxi). To convey this second dimension, Rawls speaks of the political conception of justice as a "module, an essential constituent part that fits into and can be supported by various reasonable comprehensive doctrines that endure in the society regulated by it" (*PL*, 12). It is a "theorem" that has the support of several different reasonable comprehensive views, each of which works from different premises (*PL*, 242). And so we are to imagine that there might well be several nonpublic justifications of a political conception in religious terms, as well as in terms of Kantian, natural law, perfectionist, and even utilitarian views.[33]

---

30. "While we want a political conception to have a justification by reference to one or more comprehensive doctrines, it is neither presented as, nor as derived from, such a doctrine" (*PL*, 12).

31. Rawls elaborates the complicated idea of reasonableness by specifying four of its aspects as virtues and characteristics of persons. See *PL*, chap. 2. Reasonable persons are those who (1) are willing to propose, govern, and justify their conduct according to public principles which they and others can accept, and who (2) accept the inevitable limitations of reasoning that come under what Rawls calls the "burdens of judgment," and therefore accept the limits on what can be reasonably justified to others (*PL*, 54–58). In particular, they recognize that no comprehensive ethical view can be the subject of reasonable agreement. Moreover, reasonable persons (3) not only are cooperative but want to be recognized as such. Finally, they (4) have a "reasonable moral psychology," including an effective sense of justice, a desire to do what justice requires of them and to be just persons.

32. This requirement follows from the practical aim of political liberalism, which Rawls incorporates into his account via "the liberal principle of legitimacy": our exercise of political power is fully proper only when it is exercised in accordance with a constitution the essentials of which all citizens as free and equal may reasonably be expected to endorse in the light of principles and ideals acceptable to their common human reason (*PL*, 137).

33. These two dimensions parallel Rawls's claim: "I assume, then, that citizens' overall views have two parts: one part can be seen to be, or to coincide with, the publicly recognized political con-

Recall that a political conception is just if it is reasonable and matches our considered convictions of justice in reflective equilibrium. It is stable if the political conception is rational and so motivates citizens, as part of their diverse conceptions of their rational good. The first dimension of argument restates Rawls's original aspirations and argument for the principles of justice and democratic institutions in parts I and II of A *Theory of Justice*. So far as *Political Liberalism* goes, that argument, while developed and clarified, remains substantially unchanged. It is still grounded in our shared considered convictions of justice, now elaborated in terms of certain fundamental intuitive ideas that are implicit in democratic culture (the conception of free and equal moral persons, etc). It is only when we consider "the second stage of the exposition," the stability argument, that *Political Liberalism* marks a substantial change from A *Theory of Justice*. If we are to see justice as fairness as justifiable from within different comprehensive points of view, then Rawls must limit, if not abandon, appeals to Kantian moral doctrine and the Kantian congruence argument that undergirds his case in part III of A *Theory of Justice* for stability. Rather than invoking such a general ethical theory as part of the public conception of justice (as in A *Theory of Justice*), there is now no public argument based in a comprehensive Kantian moral theory which shows why justice is an intrinsic good, the same good for every citizen. Instead, "citizens [are to] *individually* decide for themselves in what way the public political conception all affirm is related to their own more comprehensive views" (*PL*, 38; emphasis added).[34] This is, Rawls says, "part of the liberty of conscience" (*PL*, 140).

Here we have a major change from the argument presented in A *Theory of Justice*. That argument was not "freestanding" with respect to stability. Nor was it, given its Kantian premises, justifiable from within diverse reasonable comprehensive views (liberal Catholicism, or a reasonable utilitarianism, to take two examples). If justice as fairness is to be publicly justifiable, then it can no longer rely on Kant's general moral doctrine. Rawls can no longer argue that justice as fairness is part of a more general contractarian moral doctrine, rightness as fairness, nor contend on this basis that justice and moral autonomy are intrinsic goods of citizens in a well-ordered society. As an argument made from within a general and comprehensive moral doctrine, the Kantian congruence argument must be consigned to a position outside public justification and the political conception of justice.[35]

The removal of Kantian moral doctrine creates a gap in the stability argument, which carries over into the public justification of the theory. Recall the two stages of the stability argument. First, it is to be shown how citizens can acquire a sense of justice, including a willingness to act on and from princi-

ception of justice; the other part is a (fully or partially) comprehensive doctrine to which the political conception is in some manner related" (*PL*, 38).

34. See also *PL*, 140.

35. This does not mean Rawls must abandon the Kantian congruence argument altogether. As an argument made from within Kantian moral theory, it may still demonstrate, at least to Kantians, how justice as a virtue is intrinsic to the human good. But compare the reservations mentioned at the end of the preceding chapter of this volume.

ples of justice. In *Political Liberalism*, Rawls retains and further develops the moral psychology originally expounded in chapter 8 of A *Theory of Justice* that answers the first stability question (*PL*, lecture II, sec. 7). Second, it is to be shown how justice and the exercise of the sense of justice can be assigned sufficient importance within citizens' conceptions of the good, so that, when justice puts demands on their other ends and commitments, these demands are assigned a degree of priority normally sufficient to move agents to modify their nonconforming activities. The Kantian congruence argument was designed to resolve this second stage of the stability argument. It is, then, the second stage that requires revision. The idea of overlapping consensus is designed in part to fill the gap left by the omission of congruence.[36] What is the argument for stability from overlapping consensus?

Overlapping consensus is more a speculative hypothesis than a philosophical argument, for it is grounded in an "educated conjecture" (*PL*, 15) regarding the moral psychology and social interaction of individuals in a well-ordered society of justice as fairness.[37] Rawls's hypothesis is: (1) in the well-ordered society where justice as fairness is realized, the comprehensive doctrines that are reasonable will each affirm the freestanding public conception of justice, each for its own reasons; and (2) unreasonable comprehensive doctrines—"irrational, mad, and aggressive" views—will not gain enough adherents to undermine the stability of a just scheme (*PL*, 39, 170–71). So (to expand on Rawls's examples), a Kantian view, a classical utilitarian view, a pluralist view, and a religious doctrine with an account of free faith such as a liberal Catholic view, are all "reasonable comprehensive doctrines" that would gain adherents under the free institutions of a well-ordered society.[38] By hypothesis, we assume a state of affairs where jus-

36. See Rawls, *PL*, 141, where he discusses the two aspects of the stability argument, and indicates the role of overlapping consensus in the second part of the stability argument. Rawls says: "Stability involves two questions: the first is whether people who grow up under just institutions (as the political conception defines them) acquire a normally sufficient sense of justice so that they generally comply with those institutions. The second question is whether in view of the general facts that characterize a democracy's public political culture, and in particular the fact of reasonable pluralism, the political conception can be the focus of an overlapping consensus."

37. The dependence of the argument on conjectured facts is apparent when Rawls leaves open the possibility that an overlapping consensus among reasonable comprehensive views may never develop (*PL*, 36, 65–66, 168). In that case, justice as fairness would be "in difficulty" (*PL*, 66), perhaps utopian; it would not sufficiently instill in individuals, even under the best of circumstances, a settled disposition to maintain and support just institutions as that political conception defines them. To show that justice as fairness is not utopian, Rawls traces the social development of acceptance of the principles of a political democracy from a *modus vivendi*, to a constitutional consensus. From there, he contends this consensus should develop in its depth, breadth, and specificity, and evolve into an overlapping consensus on justice as fairness, or at least on a set of liberal conceptions with justice as fairness as its "focal point." This argument showing how an overlapping consensus is possible is found in *PL*, 158–68.

38. Rawls says that "reasonable comprehensive doctrines are in part the work of free practical reason within the framework of free institutions" (*PL*, 37). He defines them as doctrines that cover the major religious, philosophical, and moral aspects of human life in a coherent manner, and that call upon the exercise of both theoretical reason and practical reason, and the evolution of its doctrine in response to some notion of "good and sufficient reasons" (*PL*, 59). For Rawls to call such doctrines

tice as fairness is publicly recognized, and is generally adhered to and enforced. Rawls's "educated conjecture" is that each of these comprehensive views could and likely would affirm justice as fairness as reasonable and/or true based on its own reasons and resources, according to the values and principles affirmed within each respective view (*PL*, 170–71). So, Kantians can accept the political conception for reasons of ethical autonomy (as set forth, for example, in the congruence argument); utilitarians, because they might well believe (truly or falsely) that justice as fairness is the best workable approximation to the requirements of social utility in a democracy; a liberal Catholic, because she sees justice as fairness as compatible with natural law; and pluralists, because they accept the public justification of justice as fairness as sufficient moral argument, not in further need of justification in more comprehensive terms. In each case, the political conception is affirmed for reasons distinctive to each doctrine. If so, then none of the comprehensive views accepts the political conception as a matter of concession or compromise (*PL*, 169–71), and all of them accept it for the moral reasons specified by each respective view. (Here again, contrast Hobbesian views, for whom justice is always a compromise or concession.) Instead, in an overlapping consensus, the public conception of justice resembles, if it is not identical with, the requirements of justice affirmed by each respective view. Moreover, it is compatible with and may even affirm each doctrine's nonpolitical values.

To recognize classical and average utilitarianism (or, for that matter, a Thomistic Catholic view) as compatible with justice as fairness marks a major departure from *A Theory of Justice*.[39] Rawls there entertained the idea of a form of indirect utilitarianism which held that overall utility is best maximized by the public recognition and general acceptance of justice as fairness. But such a view, he claimed, was not genuinely utilitarian since it did not appeal to the principle of utility for regulative or even justificatory purposes. For the most part, *A Theory of Justice* was a sustained argument against the reasonableness of any utilitarian view. His criticism of the classical utilitarianism of Bentham and Sidgwick culminates with the claim that, like other "dominant end" conceptions of the good, it is "irrational, or more likely . . . mad. The self is disfigured and put in the service of one of its ends for the sake of system" (*TJ*, 554/486 rev.). In *Political Liberalism*, Rawls dispenses with any such attempt to so disqualify teleological views on grounds of such defects in their conception of the good. He even depicts them as compatible with, and capable of accepting, justice as fairness. This is indicative of the degree to which *Political Liberalism* departs from *A Theory of Justice*.[40]

"reasonable" is potentially confusing, given the other uses of this term within his view. The looseness of the notion of "reasonable comprehensive doctrines" is indicated by Rawls's claim that it potentially applies to all the main historical religions, except for certain kinds of fundamentalism (*PL*, 170).

39. See Rawls's subsequent argument which shows how a utilitarian might be led to affirm justice as fairness on average utilitarian grounds. *Justice as Fairness: A Restatement* (Cambridge MA: Harvard University Press, 2001), 107–9 (cited in text as *Restatement*).

40. It does not, however, mean that Rawls, from within his own comprehensive view does not still harbor the same judgments about utilitarianism.

We have then, in the idea of an overlapping consensus, what might be seen as a different kind of congruence argument. It is the congruence of public and nonpublic reasons and points of view. The freestanding democratic conception of justice that is found commonly and publicly justifiable, on the basis of shared democratic ideas, as reasonable from the public point of view, is at the same time held to be nonpublicly justifiable as reasonable or true from various comprehensive points of view. It is because the public conception of justice can be seen as reasonable and/or true from all the reasonable comprehensive perspectives, and requires none of them to compromise their nonpolitical values, that there can be an overlapping consensus on the publicly justifiable conception of justice. This is no longer the congruence of the right with a shared intrinsic good within a single comprehensive doctrine, as in A *Theory of Justice*. It is, rather, the congruence of the publicly justifiable conception of justice with different and competing comprehensive ethical views, each of which affirms justice as a good (intrinsic, or instrumental, as the case may be) for its own reasons.

Assume now that Rawls's "educated conjecture" is right. It is still not clear how overlapping consensus deals with the problem formulated in A *Theory of Justice*. For, even supposing that all in a well-ordered society have an effective sense of justice and a desire to act on just laws and institutions as defined by justice as fairness, what is to insure that justice will not give way when it conflicts with other values which people affirm within their comprehensive views? To resolve this problem of the priority of justice, Rawls can no longer appeal to the intrinsic moral good of justice, and especially not to its normative supremacy. For, the idea that justice can be an intrinsic moral good for each person in a well-ordered society has been given up along with the Kantian congruence argument. Rawls now recognizes that for many people nonpolitical values are likely to be seen as more significant than justice within many comprehensive views. It may then be that, on many views, justice is simply an essential good (essential to social cooperation), important but nonetheless instrumental to their realizing the independent nonpolitical values that form their intrinsic good. If justice is merely instrumental within the terms of some reasonable comprehensive doctrines, then how can people be expected to comply with justice when it conflicts with other more fundamental values?

It may be that many people cannot be expected to subordinate their nonpolitical ends to justice. But Rawls can say several things here (as he seems to). First, given the content of the principles of justice, the occasions on which people will be called upon to make such decisions are rare, rare enough so as not to undermine stability. For, with liberty of conscience and other basic liberties in place, each person is free to affirm and act on the normal requirements of a wide variety of reasonable conceptions of the good. A liberal conception of justice, like justice as fairness, puts minimal restrictions on the free pursuit of reasonable comprehensive views (*PL*, 157).

Second, we have to take into account that people brought up within a democratic culture are educated to its public conception of justice. They are made aware of the benefits of justice and toleration in enabling them to successfully pursue their own comprehensive views. Also, they are encouraged by the public culture to respect others' basic rights and adhere to justice; and they are educated to the duty of civility, to give publicly acceptable reasons to justify their actions when they adversely affect others' interests (cf. *PL*, 217). There are then forces within democratic culture itself which mitigate the likelihood that individuals will depart from justice in the event of conflicts.

Third, there are forces within their own comprehensive views which have similar effects. In a well-ordered society, the requirements of justice are themselves seen as normally compatible with the basic religious, philosophical, and moral values affirmed within reasonable comprehensive views. And there are few conceptions of the good that will admit that it is generally permissible to breach justice for the sake of other values. For example, hardly any of the major religions (again excluding fundamentalist sects) would admit, doctrinally, that justice is a value that can be dispensed with. Instead, they expound their doctrine to teach that conflicts between justice and more fundamental religious values, which require sacrificing justice for the sake of the greater good, are situations that hardly, if ever, arise. (For example, in Thomist doctrine, natural law is a necessary means to the Vision of God, not ever an impediment to it.)[41]

Fourth, as Rawls argues, the values of democratic justice, and the virtues of political cooperation (tolerance, reasonableness, the sense of fairness, and a willingness to meet others halfway), are themselves "very great virtues" and values (*PL*, 157). There will be many reasonable comprehensive views in a well-ordered society which assign to the values of justice a significant or even preeminent position, so that when other values conflict with them, they will be outweighed by political values. This is true of the comprehensive liberal views that develop from Kant and Mill; it is also true of the pluralist comprehensive view Rawls mentions (*PL*, 145, 155–56).

Finally, perhaps most importantly, Rawls emphasizes that most people adhere not to fully comprehensive doctrines but to partial ones instead; moreover, there is "a certain looseness in [their] comprehensive views" (*PL*, 159). This allows many ways for liberal principles of justice to cohere with comprehensive doctrines. Most people come to affirm principles of justice incorporated into the constitution without seeing any particular connection between justice and their other views. Because they come to appreciate the good justice realizes for them and those they care for, when an incompatibility later arises, they are more likely to adjust or revise their comprehensive views to cohere with justice, than they are to reject justice (*PL*, 160).

What now of the second strand of overlapping consensus, the contention that *unreasonable* comprehensive views in a well-ordered liberal society will not gain sufficient adherents to undermine stability? To begin with, why exclude these views from an overlapping consensus anyway? We saw in section I that Rawls's project is not the Hobbesian one of devising and justifying a conception of justice that would accommodate peoples' preferences and ends, whatever they

---

41. See Maritain, *Man and State*, 86. "This means that there is, by the very virtue of human nature, an order or a disposition which human reason can discover and according to which human will must act in order to attune itself to the essential and necessary ends of the human being. The unwritten law, or natural law, is nothing more than that."

might be. Unreasonable conceptions of the good are not to be accommodated by justice; they are rather to be contained by it. This reiterates the important point that democratic justice is not to be viewed as a compromise among given and essentially conflicting desires and interests. It is not a modus vivendi (as Rawls says of an overlapping consensus). Rather, a political conception is from the beginning worked up independently of particular desires and interests, from democratic self-awareness and convictions, and is displayed as an articulation of a free and equal moral person's self-conception and the ideal of a well-ordered society.[42] Only then is it to be shown how justice is compatible with people's good. Given the structure of Rawls's argument, clearly unreasonable conceptions of the good—intolerant, bigoted, imperialistic, or belligerent views—will be excluded from an overlapping consensus because their conceptions of the good are incompatible with liberal requirements of justice. This does not mean that Rawls simply dismisses the problem unreasonable views pose for stability. Intolerance, bigotry, and belligerence will likely be present even under the best of circumstances. A well-ordered society is not a utopia where irrationality and unreasonableness are absent. Still, Rawls speculates that, given the circumstances of a well-ordered society, conceptions of the good which require these anti-liberal vices will not gain sufficient adherents to destabilize that ideal scheme. His thought seems to be that anti-liberal vices are largely sustained by social and political conditions that encourage them (lack of toleration in the public culture, poverty and unemployment, lack of fair opportunities, etc.). These are not the conditions of a well-ordered liberal society.

These arguments for stability may not satisfy many, since they depend on hypothetical conjectures.[43] In one respect, they are not as strong as the original congruence argument, which argued for the strict priority of the intrinsic good of justice over other values. Still, in another respect, Rawls's revisions make the modified case for stability more realistic. With the idea of an overlapping consensus, Rawls no longer has to rely on a contestable general and partially comprehensive Kantian ethical view to prove stability. Public political toleration of other

42. See *PL*, lecture 3, where Rawls discusses political constructivism.

43. Joseph Raz contests Rawls's entire approach to stability in "Facing Diversity: The Case of Epistemic Abstinence," *Philosophy and Public Affairs* 3 (Winter 1990): 3–46. He contends that the stability of a political system depends not so much on common acceptance of a public justification of a conception of justice; rather, "affective and symbolic elements may well be the crucial cement of society" (30). Such factors as "identification of individuals with their society" and its culture ("language, literature, foods, flag, and anthem," etc.), its "history of past conflicts, the depth of feeling concerning current rivalries," and so on, are more important forces of stability. People are "only partially sensitive to the existence of anything remotely like Rawls's overlapping consensus" (30–31). Rawls need not deny that these forces often cause societies to remain stable. He may doubt their continuing efficacy in a liberal society, where people confirm many different values and comprehensive religious and philosophical views. In any case, Rawls is concerned to show that a well-ordered liberal society can be "stable for the right reasons" (*PL*, xlii), that is, because it is anchored in citizens' sense of justice. The question of stability he raises is whether justice and the willingness to do justice for its own sake are compatible with human nature and affirm a person's good. Anchoring stability in a sense of justice is not the only possible basis for the stability of a liberal society, but Rawls seems to think it is the only reliable one.

equally comprehensive views is considerably increased. This fact itself should increase the forces of stability.

Moreover, there is one further complication I will only allude to, which strengthens the stability argument even further. Recall that Rawls says that in the absence of public acceptance of a comprehensive doctrine, citizens must each in their own way decide how justice is part of their good on the basis of their own comprehensive views (*PL*, 38, 140). But there is more to it than this. For the public conception of justice itself contains an account of political goods. By "political goods," Rawls means not just goods that are desirable or necessary in political contexts but goods that are part of the freestanding public justification of the conception of justice. In chapter 5 of *Political Liberalism*, "The Priority of Right and Ideas of the Good," Rawls sets out five ideas of the good that are part of the public justification of justice as fairness: (1) a thin account of (goodness as) rationality, which is (he claims) appropriate for a political conception of justice; (2) the account of primary social goods as needs of free and equal citizens; (3) the idea of permissible comprehensive conceptions of the good; (4) an account of the political virtues; and (5) the idea of the good of a well-ordered (political) society (*PL*, 176). Among these ideas of the good that are part of the public conception of justice are not just instrumental goods like the primary goods; Rawls suggests that justice and "political society itself can be an intrinsic good," within the terms of the public political conception (*PL*, 207).

It appears, then, that what Rawls has taken away with one hand (the congruence argument in *Theory*), he remolds and now gives back with the other. It seems peculiar to say that justice is an intrinsic good, not for purposes of a comprehensive doctrine but in the limited terms of the political conception itself. Either an activity is intrinsically good or it is not, one might think. What can Rawls mean here? Perhaps one balks at Rawls's claim because of the philosophical obscurity of the concept of the good. For Rawls, the concept of goodness means, when used in a political context, that which is rational to want (from a standpoint of deliberative rationality) compatible with certain principles of rational choice. (This is the basis of the "thin theory of the good.") A political good is that which is rational to want in one's capacity as a citizen, if one is to fulfill the demands and expectations of that position, and take advantage of the opportunities and benefits of social cooperation in a democratic society. The primary social goods are instrumental political goods in that they are needed to exercise the moral powers and realize permissible conceptions of the good. These powers in turn are goods, since their exercise is necessary to one's taking part in and gaining the benefits of social cooperation. Rawls claims political goods need not be merely instrumental for citizens. To say that justice is an intrinsic good within the terms of the public conception of justice then seems to mean, for Rawls, that in our capacity as citizens, it can be rational to want something for its own sake, and not simply for the sake of other ends we have. Bracketing the question of what is a person's complete good, it can be rational as a citizen to want (1) to realize the moral powers by doing justice, thereby becoming politically autonomous; (2) to be publicly recognized as having the status of an equal citizen, a primary basis of self-respect in a democratic society; and (3) to be a participating member of a well-ordered society, working cooperatively to establish and sustain its institutions over time. These are (along with the political good of social union) among the intrinsic political goods Rawls mentions as part of the public justification of justice as fairness (*PL*, 201–7).

I will not go any further into the complications this argument raises, except to note that Rawls's contention is that a just political society can be an intrinsic good, within the terms of the political conception. His qualification implies his claim is defeasible: once a person's complete good is taken into account, justice may not be an intrinsic good, from within one's comprehensive perspective. But the important point is that (assuming Rawls's contentions make sense) the public justification of the conception of justice does not depend on a purely instrumental account of the good of justice. In the end, and even though Rawls has given up the Kantian congruence argument, there remains a place, within the public conception, for the intrinsic political good of justice, desirable for its own sake in one's capacity as citizen. As Rawls says, this further strengthens the argument for stability.[44]

III. Public Reason

Recall, now, Rawls's fundamental question: How is a just and stable constitution possible among free and equal persons with conflicting conceptions of the good and who affirm different reasonable comprehensive doctrines?[45] I focus now on the third component of his answer, the idea of public reason. Overlapping consensus is a substantial revision to Rawls's argument in *A Theory of Justice*. By contrast, the idea of public reason is more of a natural extension, though one that becomes all the more necessary because of Rawls's reliance on overlapping consensus for stability. The idea of public reason is an elaboration and development of the social contract idea and publicity requirement that occupy such an important place in the original argument for justice as fairness. That political principles be publicly known and accepted is a natural feature of any social contract view. Rawls develops the idea of publicity in *Political Liberalism* so that it

---

44. Rawls, *PL*, 209. Rawls says it needs to be shown how justice is a good, so the political conception can be "complete." Recall that a political conception of justice admits of two justifications, a public one that is the same for everyone, and a nonpublic one, in terms of one's reasonable comprehensive view. As political liberalism is reasonable from both perspectives, public and nonpublic, so it needs be shown how it can be rational from public and nonpublic points of view. Overlapping consensus is the conjecture that the political conception is rational from the point of view of each reasonable comprehensive view. For purposes of "completeness," Rawls says, it must be shown how justice, as a political good, can be rational within the terms of the public political conception itself. I assume that this is the purpose of Rawls's discussion of the various ways justice can be an intrinsic good within the terms of the political conception.

45. Again, Rawls summarizes his answer as follows: (1) The basic structure of such a society is effectively regulated by a political conception of justice. (2) This conception is the focus of an overlapping consensus of at least the reasonable comprehensive doctrines affirmed by its citizens. (3) The consensus enables that shared political conception to serve as the basis of public reason in debates about political questions when constitutional essentials and matters of basic justice are at stake (*PL*, 48).

comes to play a central role in many of his key notions. It is, to begin with, part of the idea of reasonableness. On Rawls's account, to be reasonable (as opposed to rational) is, in part, to be willing to guide one's (rational) conduct and ends, and justify one's actions, according to public standards. By acting reasonably, "we enter as equals the public world of others" (*PL*, 53) in governing our conduct by standards from which we can reason in common, and by taking into account the effect of our rational plans on their well-being (*PL*, 49 n. 1). Publicity is also implicit in the practical aim Rawls sets for democratic political philosophy, that is, to discover the appropriate bases for public justification among free and equal persons (*PL*, 9). As such, the (full) publicity of principles of justice is incorporated as one of the reasonable conditions on agreement in the original position. A publicly recognized conception of justice, then, comes to be part of a well-ordered society, where everyone accepts, and knows everyone else accepts, the same principles of justice (*PL*, 35).

Why is publicity such a pervasive component of Rawls's view?[46] Here I can only mention that, aside from its connection with the idea of reasonableness (noted above), the idea that reasons be publicly acceptable among free and equal persons generally is connected with the democratic values of freedom and equality that Rawls seeks to elucidate. Henry Sidgwick said that the principle of utility may require that utilitarianism be nonpublic, an "esoteric morality . . . which it is expedient to confine to an enlightened few," that is used to structure social relations, but which is not known or acknowledged by people.[47] The consequence of such a doctrine is that agents must have false beliefs about the basis of their relations in order for the ends of utilitarianism to be achieved. Who is to enforce such an "esoteric morality" politically? Its undemocratic consequences seem unavoidable. From Rawls's perspective, this view undermines democratic freedom and makes political autonomy impossible. "Freedom at the deepest level calls upon the freedom of reason, both theoretical and practical" (*PL*, 223 n. 9). That we be in a position to know why our political relations are as they are, and not forced to suffer mistaken impressions about this, is a condition of democratic freedom. Otherwise, we are subject to controllable forces that have been placed beyond our control, either by circumstances we create or by others' conscious manipulation. Publicity is then a condition of our realizing our status as free, equal, reasonable, and rational democratic citizens.[48]

46. For a criticism of the idea of publicity in Rawls's and others' views, see Bruce W. Brower, "The Limits of Public Reason," *Journal of Philosophy* 91 (January 1994). My remarks here only partly respond to his concerns.

47. Henry Sidgwick, *The Methods of Ethics* (1874), 7th ed. (Indianapolis: Hackett, 1981), 489–90 (cited in text as *Methods*).

48. This explains why Rawls's "Kantian form of the contract doctrine" (*PL*, 271) demands "full publicity." What is this requirement? That laws and social norms be publicly available, so that people have "notice" of them, is implicit in the idea of the rule of law. This is not so much a requirement of publicity (conceived as an independent moral or political requirement), as it is of fairness (due process) and the effectiveness of law. Cf. *PL*, 71. Publicity, as a separate requirement of justice, requires, at a minimum, (1) that people know the principles that underlie laws and social and economic norms. This is a standard feature of any social contract view (including Hobbes's), and contrasts with Sidg-

Now, what is the role of the idea of public reason? One way to approach this idea is by synthesizing it with the other two components of Rawls's answer to his problem of the possibility of a just constitution. Assume a well-ordered society in which there is public recognition of a common conception of justice, and there is available a public justification of this conception as a freestanding view in terms implicit in democratic culture. In this society there exists a reasonable pluralism of comprehensive doctrines, each of which affirms the public conception for its own moral reasons, and so there is an overlapping consensus. Now, how is the conception of justice to be interpreted and applied to specify a constitution, and make laws and social policies? What role does it have in citizens' and officials' deliberations and arguments about public issues? It is assumed that the conception of justice is compatible with all the reasonable conceptions of the good that gain adherents in this society. But what is to prevent citizens, or for that matter legislators and judges, from appealing to nonpublic values and principles implicit in their comprehensive views to interpret and apply the conception of justice in setting up and interpreting the constitution? Suppose citizens, or legislators, interpret freedom of thought by appealing to their religious or moral views so as to narrowly define freedom of speech. Or they interpret liberty of conscience according to their religious views (as John Locke, and perhaps Justices Rehnquist, Scalia, and Thomas, too), so that while it allows freedom of all (reasonable) religions, it does not rule out special government support to encourage religious over nonreligious belief, or even special support for a particular religion. Or they interpret freedom of the person (another vaguely defined basic liberty) according to their religious views about what is appropriate sexual conduct (deciding then that homosexuality, or any sex outside of legal marriage, should be legally prohibited). Nothing on the face of these abstract basic liberties would prevent such interpretations.

To provide a basis for public justification that will enable citizens to accept the laws and institutions of a democratic society, it is not enough that everyone be able to accept, individually, principles of justice and a constitution on the basis of their own reasons, stemming from their particular conceptions of the good. It is not even enough that there exist, too, a public justification of the political conception of justice, as a freestanding view. For the common conception of justice still must be interpreted and applied to specify the constitution, make laws, and shape policies and institutions. If each relied on his own con-

---

wick's idea of utilitarianism as an "esoteric morality." On Rawls's Kantian account, however, publicity must be "fuller" than this. In addition, the grounds of laws and political institutions must be such as to "stand up to public scrutiny" (*PL*, 68). People should then have available the ultimate reasons for political requirements on what they must do. This requires (2) that there be publicly shared methods of inquiry and forms of reasoning by which these principles are applied, which is part of what is meant by "public reason," and (3) the public availability of the full justification of the conception of justice of which these principles are a part. Anything short of this means that the bases of our political relations are hidden from view, perhaps based in illusions that would undermine the freedom of politically autonomous democratic citizens. Full publicity is appropriate because it enables democratic citizens to realize their moral powers (in particular their capacity for justice), the development and exercise of which are essential to their realizing their good as democratic citizens. For further discussion on full publicity, see *PL*, 66–71.

ception of the good to interpret and apply these abstract principles, there would be widespread disagreement as to what justice requires. (Consider a parallel situation now in our applying the U.S. Constitution. Though we may agree on many of its most essential provisions—free speech, due process, equal protection, no cruel and unusual punishment, and so forth—people interpret these provisions differently, often because they primarily rely on their comprehensive religious and moral views.) For this reason, there is a need for a shared set of reasons and methods of inquiry and reasoning, upon which to ground our interpretations.

> It is essential that a liberal political conception include, besides its principles of justice, guidelines of inquiry that specify ways of reasoning and criteria for the kinds of information relevant for political questions. Without such guidelines substantive principles cannot be applied and this leaves the political conception incomplete and fragmentary. (*PL*, 223–24)

To achieve this, we must be able to reason from the same standards of interpretation of the public conception of justice, endorsing and applying its principles to the constitution and laws for the same reasons.

The idea of public reason is then introduced by Rawls in part to deal with the problem of the interpretation and application of the public conception of justice in a liberal society in which citizens endorse the conception from several different nonpublic points of view. This problem of application of the public conception of justice to specify the constitution and laws arises because Rawls now admits the legitimacy of alternative justifications for the conception of justice, within the nonpublic terms of diverse reasonable conceptions of the good. The problem did not exist (not to this extent) in *A Theory of Justice*, for there the assumption was that most everyone accepted the same partially comprehensive moral doctrine, a general Kantian moral theory. Once that doctrine has been given up as part of the public understanding of justice, and replaced by reasonable pluralism and an overlapping consensus of diverse doctrines, a problem arises of sustaining agreement on the interpretation and application of the political conception of justice. Because they have different religious, metaphysical, and ethical doctrines, people have different standards for assessing evidence and different criteria of truth, and they will interpret shared principles of justice differently. It is in this context that the special need for an idea of public reason arises: it is needed to forestall undue reliance on the reasons and ways of reasoning implicit in conflicting conceptions of the good in settling matters of basic justice and essentials of the constitution, so as to be able to carry through the practical aim of discovering a basis for public justification in a democratic society.

Rawls responds to this problem by proposing a "liberal principle of legitimacy" along with the idea of public reason. Because of the freedom and equality of democratic citizens,

> our exercise of political power is fully proper only when it is exercised in accordance with a constitution the essentials of which all citizens as free and equal may reasonably be expected to endorse in the light of principles and ideals

acceptable to their common human reason. This is the liberal principle of legitimacy. (*PL*, 137)

Rawls concludes that only a constitution that all citizens can reasonably be
expected to endorse on the basis of common reasons can serve as a basis for
public justification (*PL*, 137). This immediately gives rise to a natural duty
of democratic citizens, to appeal to public reason: "The ideal of citizenship
imposes a moral, not a legal, duty—the duty of civility—to be able to explain
to one another on those fundamental questions how the principles and policies they advocate and vote for can be supported by the political values of *public reason*" (*PL*, 217; emphasis added).[49] Both principles, Rawls says, would be
endorsed from the original position (*PL*, 137 n. 5), along with guidelines for
public inquiry and standards of interpretation (familiar to common sense and
not dependent on any particular comprehensive view) needed to apply norms
of justice (*PL*, 225).

Rawls characterizes public reason as the reason of democratic citizens. Its
subject is the good of the public in matters of fundamental justice. And its content is given by the ideals and principles expressed by a democratic society's conception of political justice (*PL*, 213). By contrast, nonpublic reason, while social,
too, consists of the reasons and methods of inquiry that are peculiar to the many
associations, conceptions of the good, and reasonable comprehensive doctrines
that coexist in a democratic society (*PL*, 220).

Rawls speaks of public reason as both an idea and an ideal. Roughly, the ideal
of public reason seems to be that citizens, in the course of public argument and
debate, and even in their private deliberations before voting on candidates, laws
and social policies, will appeal to considerations that are acceptable to everyone
in their capacity as citizens and consistent with the freedom and equality of citizens. They will apply public, not nonpublic, reasons and standards of justification in coming to decisions about political issues of basic justice. To fully realize
this ideal, public reason has to have a certain content. First, the reasons citizens
appeal to must be stated in terms compatible with a liberal conception of justice,
which forms the basic content of public reason. Second, there must be guidelines for public inquiry and reasoning, based in common sense and amenable to

---

49. Rawls continues: "This duty also involves a willingness to listen to others and a fairminded-
ness in deciding when accommodations to their views should reasonably be made" (*PL*, 217). The
duty of civility is present in nascent form in *A Theory of Justice*, as part of the natural duty of mutual
respect (one of the natural duties the parties would agree to in the original position). Rawls says this
duty involves, among other things, "our willingness to see the situation of others from their point of
view, from the perspective of their conception of their good; and in our being prepared to give reasons
for our actions whenever the interests of others are materially affected" (*TJ*, 337/297 rev.). In matters of justice, this means "offer[ing] reasons in good faith, in the belief that they are sound reasons
as defined by a mutually acceptable conception of justice which takes the good of everyone into
account. Thus to respect another as a moral person is to try to understand his aims and interests from
his standpoint and to present him with considerations that enable him to accept the constraints on his
conduct. . . . in terms of principles to which all could agree" (*TJ*, 338/297 rev.).

the wide range of reasonable conceptions of the good, which specify how these principles are to be applied. The third component of the ideal of public reason is the full public justification of the liberal conception of justice and its guidelines for inquiry independent of any comprehensive doctrine, in terms of fundamental political ideas implicit in the public political culture of a democracy.

As an ideal with this content, public reason is realized only in a well-ordered society governed by a liberal public conception of justice (such as justice as fairness). The ideal of public reason is not something realized in our constitutional system since we are not well ordered (in Rawls's sense); we only faintly approximate this ideal. We have a written Constitution, a public charter, which serves as a sort of basis for public reasoning on constitutional essentials, but we have no agreement on the conception of justice which our Constitution incorporates. (This is one deficiency in our political culture which Rawls seeks to remedy by proposing justice as fairness as the most appropriate political conception for a democratic society.) Still, though we do not satisfy the ideal of public reason, the idea applies to us, for the principle of legitimacy and duty of civility are requirements on any democratic scheme, whether or not they are effectively regulated by a public conception of justice. In any democracy, these principles require that laws and policies be justified (so far as they affect what Rawls calls "constitutional essentials and questions of basic justice" [*PL*, 227–30]) according to common reasons all can accept as democratic citizens. And indeed, public reason is to a large degree implicitly recognized as part of our Constitution, for there is a sense in our political culture of the kinds of reasons that are and are not appropriate to invoke in support of laws and in interpreting the Constitution. Most everyone accepts that to argue for laws purely on grounds of their own religion, or on religious grounds in general, is not sufficient justification for political measures, and that often it is not even appropriate to appeal to religious reasons in democratic debate. Some may still claim we are a "Christian nation," but claims of this kind are not taken seriously in wider public debate, where non-Christians and many liberal Christians, too, are addressed. Appeals to Christian doctrine simply do not count as good public reasons in our political culture. This raises the question of the appropriateness of appeals to religion and comprehensive ethical considerations in a democracy. To clarify how the idea of public reason addresses this issue, I will, momentarily, compare Rawls's view with Kent Greenawalt's view.

But first, it is important to keep in mind the distinction between the ideal of public reason, which we do not realize, and the idea itself, which is applicable to us in any case. This will help forestall misreadings of certain claims Rawls makes (in *PL*, chap. 6) that might otherwise appear to be a retraction of his earlier views. For example, Rawls says: "Public reason does not ask us to accept the very same principles of justice" (*PL*, 41). Furthermore,

> It is inevitable and often desirable that citizens have different views as to the most appropriate political conception; for the public political culture is bound to contain different fundamental ideas that can be developed in different ways. An orderly contest between them over time is a reliable way to find which one, if any, is most reasonable. (*PL*, 227)

Soon following this passage, Rawls says of the difference principle: "Though a social minimum providing for the basic needs of all citizens is also a constitutional essential, what I have called the 'difference principle' is more demanding and is not" (*PL*, 228–29). The same holds true for fair equality of opportunity; while some conception of equal opportunity is a constitutional essential in a democracy, Rawls says his particular interpretation of that value is not (*PL*, 230). Following this, "about many economic and social issues that legislative bodies must regularly consider," Rawls says: "To resolve these more particular and detailed issues it is often more reasonable to go beyond the political conception and the values its principles express, and to invoke nonpolitical values that such a view does not include" (*PL*, 230).

These passages, taken together, invite a misreading. They might suggest to some that Rawls is giving up his commitment to the second principle of justice as the ideal standard for structuring access to social positions, economic systems, and property schemes, and is conceding to other proposals. This is not, however, what he means. Justice as fairness is the public reason of a well-ordered democratic society. (Or at least, so Rawls believes.) This is the ideal social scheme. This ideal and its regulative principles of justice are implicit, Rawls contends, in the considered convictions of justice and certain fundamental intuitive ideas of our democratic culture (cf. Rawls, *PL*, 26). It is part of Rawls's task to bring to public awareness the principles of justice we are committed to, to provide an agreed basis for public reasoning about justice. Our public reason now is confused and in need of clarification. Especially on questions of economic justice, there is widespread disagreement even about the constitutional necessity for a social minimum. Indeed, there is still disagreement about some of the basic constitutional liberties (e.g., freedom of association and the right of privacy, for example, or equal rights for women). It would be a mistake, then, to incorporate this sophisticated philosophical conception of justice into the constitution of our less than ideal liberal scheme, because it is not yet part of public reason of this society. Presently it might even be self-defeating, given our political culture, for the Supreme Court, or even the legislature, to attempt to restructure property arrangements so as to realize the difference principle. Moreover, Rawls does not see it as the appropriate role of the Courts, even in a well-ordered society, to review legislation bearing on the economy and property in terms of the difference principle.[50] It is the Court's role to enforce a social minimum, even now, since that is a "constitutional essential" in a democracy. But it would be a mistake for the Court, both now and any time in the future, to second guess legislative decisions regarding whether this social minimum has been accurately decided according to the difference principle. As he held in *A Theory of Justice*, for strategic and other reasons the difference principle should not be part of the (written) constitution of a well-ordered society (*TJ*, 199/174 rev.).

Rawls's principles of justice are not presently part of our public reason. He hopes that some day they will be. Before that point can be reached, there will need be widespread revisions in people's judgments about justice, especially eco-

---

50. See *PL*, 230, where Rawls summarizes reasons for this view.

nomic justice. It is in this context that Rawls (as quoted above) says it is a good thing that citizens have and debate their "different views as to the most appropriate political conception" (*PL*, 227). An "orderly contest between them over time" is necessary to bring to public awareness and public reason the principles of justice implicit in our democratic culture. When the debate is all over and done with (if it ever will be), Rawls hopes that his conception of justice will be accepted as the bases for our public reasoning, since he is as confident as ever that it is the most reasonable conception of justice for a democratic society.

Now to address the bearing of the idea of public reason on the role of religion, or any comprehensive doctrine, in citizens' political conduct. Rawls's liberal principle of legitimacy and duty of civility primarily address the reasons it is permissible for citizens and officials to publicly cite to one another, in political discussion and debate in the public forum, to justify or criticize laws and proposals that bear on constitutional essentials. As Rawls says, the duty of civility is a "duty to adopt a certain form of public discourse" (*PL*, 242). These principles do not mean that citizens cannot appeal to nonpublic religious or ethical reasons in their private or associational deliberations on laws and policies. Indeed, Rawls says that it would be contrary to the idea of overlapping consensus for public reason to prohibit people from relying politically on their religious or other comprehensive views (*PL*, 244 n. 33). But these political principles do require that citizens be prepared to justify, publicly, their decisions in terms of political values amenable to democratic reason.

Compare an ostensibly similar view by Kent Greenawalt.[51] He argues that liberal democracy does not require the wholesale exclusion of religion as a basis for political decisions by citizens (*RC*, 191–92). Many religious persons cannot reason about moral issues independent of their religious views, so their political reliance on religious reasons is necessary for them to come to political decisions (*RC*, 155). It would be unfair to require religious believers to abandon their faith in politics (*RC*, 87). The most that liberal doctrine can require, Greenawalt seems to say, is that religious persons address others in "publicly accessible terms" (*RC*, 155–56; see also chap. 12). With certain qualifications, "public discourse about political issues with those who do not share religious premises should be cast in other than religious terms" (*RC*, 217)

These claims, as far as they go, are compatible with Rawls's account of public reason, and Rawls seems to agree with them (*PL*, 244 n. 33). On the other hand, for Rawls, voting is not "a private or even personal matter" (*PL*, 219). To vote one's private prejudices, unconstrained preferences, or economic interests, or even one's comprehensive religious or metaphysical views, and to do this without regard to the requirements of public reason, is to refuse to recognize the "duty of civility." Again, this duty requires that the policies and principles we politically advocate be supportable "by the political values of public reason" (*PL*, 217). This requires that we vote our sincere judgments regarding the common good, as informed by considerations of justice (cf. *PL*, 219–20). It cannot then be

---

51. Kent Greenawalt, *Religious Convictions and Political Choice* (New York: Oxford University Press, 1988) (cited in text as *RC*).

that democratic liberalism merely requires that public discourse be conducted in terms of public reasons. To require only that, but then to allow people to vote their personal preferences and comprehensive views with impunity, is a kind of hypocrisy that public reason could not survive.[52] Even if Greenawalt's claim is true, that people cannot reason about political matters independent of their religion (or other comprehensive views), still, when their decisions are not amenable to the public political values of a democracy, they violate the liberal principle of legitimacy. For, they are proposing that state power be exercised in ways that cannot be justified on the basis of reasons all democratic citizens can endorse. State power then becomes an "unreasonable force," and violates the freedom and equality of citizens (PL, 247).

But, is it true that religious persons, or for that matter anyone who affirms a metaphysical or ethical doctrine, can only conduct their political deliberations by appealing to their comprehensive views? Or, is democratic culture sufficiently robust that it contains implicit in itself an independent, or "freestanding," political morality that citizens can also appeal to? If it is true that we can only reason in terms of our particular views, this suggests that shared public reasons are not very extensive, and insofar as they exist, are an accidental confluence of different comprehensive views. Moreover, it would seem to deny the possibility of Rawls's project in *Political Liberalism*, to discover a freestanding basis for public justification, one that can be the focus of an overlapping consensus, and which can serve as a basis for public reasoning among citizens with different reasonable conceptions of the good and comprehensive doctrines. Greenawalt appears to be skeptical about both the depth of public reason and the success of Rawls's project.[53] "Shared grounds are radically inconclusive about major social issues" (RC, 222; see also 146–47), including not just issues of the environment and treatment of animals, but also many political issues of justice (RC, 224). He suggests the possibility of no more than a shallow consensus on principles of liberal democratic justice. The domain of shared, reasonable, public political ideas and principles is narrow, so it is very unlikely that public political justification of any measure can be complete.

Greenawalt's lack of confidence in the depth or completeness of public reason is paralleled by the reduced significance he assigns to it where it exists. He contends that publicly accessible reasons and arguments do not always take priority over nonpublic ones, especially when majority will sufficiently outweighs a

---

52. Greenawalt, interestingly, must contemplate just the opposite position, for he strongly advocates the legitimacy of coming to political decisions from within one's own nonpublic conception of the good. He asks, if people come to their political positions on the grounds of personal beliefs that stem from their religious and other comprehensive views (or for that matter, out of pure self-interest), is it not likewise a kind of "concealment that is immoral and unwise" (RC, 220) for them not to publicly make known their religious reasons? The problem with this is that to encourage people to publicly argue for their positions on sectarian grounds is socially divisive. Greenawalt seems to realize this, and does not endorse full religious disclosure. See RC, 222.

53. For his criticisms of Rawls, see RC, 183–87. His arguments against Rawls largely depend upon denying that public reason and shared political intuitions are strong or deep enough to do with them all that Rawls needs.

minority.[54] This amounts to an implicit rejection of Rawls's liberal principle of legitimacy and the duty of civility. It suggests that an overlapping consensus on a conception of justice that provides an independent basis for public justification to all citizens not only is not possible but is not even desirable.

One should not misread Rawls's claim that "the idea of public reason . . . is consistent with the view of Greenawalt" (*PL*, 244 n. 33), since it appears that Greenawalt commits himself to a very different conception of democracy and the possibilities of liberalism than that for which Rawls argues. For Greenawalt to support his claim that nonpublic religious or other doctrinal reasons should take precedence over publicly available reasons on certain issues of justice, and to say this is true because of the weight of majority will and/or "deep-seated feeling" (*RC*, 167), makes it seem, on the face of it, that he is relying on considerations more amenable to a utilitarian conception of democracy (democracy as a means of discovering the greater weight of preferences).[55] If so, then Greenawalt needs to address Rawls's claim:

> Strong feelings and zealous aspirations for certain goals do not, as such, give people . . . a claim to design public institutions to achieve these goals. Desires and wants, however intense, are not by themselves reasons in matters of constitutional essentials and basic justice. The fact that we have a compelling desire in such cases does not argue for the propriety of its satisfaction any more than the strength of a conviction argues for its truth. (*PL*, 190)[56]

Not only can we not take such a conception of democracy as Greenawalt suggests for granted, his conception seems to require undemocratic reliance on the sectarian claims of religion and a comprehensive moral view.

IV. Public Reason and Judicial Review

To clarify the idea of public reason, I conclude with some remarks on Rawls's account of the Supreme Court as the "exemplar of public reason," and the role of the Court in judicial review (*PL*, 231–40).

Rawls had little to say in *A Theory of Justice* about the American institution of judicial review, but from what he does say about democracy, it is clear

---

54. According to Greenawalt: "In a liberal society in which 90 percent of the people regarded an early fetus as having the same moral status as a newborn, legal implementation of that judgment by a restrictive law would be apt even if people recognized that a woman's claim to abort could be grounded on rational arguments alone, whereas belief in the moral status of the fetus required a critical judgment beyond reason. Whether the claim based on ordinary reasons should take priority if it is roughly equal in power and if opinion is closely divided is much more troublesome. I am inclined to reject even that notion, believing that it assigns too high a place for the products of rational analysis as opposed to deep-seated feeling" (*RC*, 167).

55. I do not mean to suggest that Greenawalt is a utilitarian—he is not—but to suggest that he relies on seemingly utilitarian reasons to argue why majority will can outweigh public reasons.

56. Also relevant here is Rawls's claim: "Government can no more act to maximize the fulfillment of citizens' rational preferences, or wants (as in utilitarianism) . . . than it can act to advance Catholicism or Protestantism, or any other religion" (*PL*, 180).

that he sees judicial review as a legitimate democratic institution under certain circumstances. To the standard criticism that judicial review is antidemocratic, Rawls would respond that it is a mistake to see democracy as simply a voting procedure, or a form of government where laws are decided by majority rule. Rather, at a more fundamental level, democracy is a kind of constitution which specifies the equal status of free citizens, who themselves join together as equals to make the constitution. While democracy, as a kind of constitution, provides for equal political rights and majority legislative rule, it also affords other equal basic liberties to all citizens, provides for equality of opportunity of some form, and insures each person a social minimum. It is the proper role of a democratic government to promote these ends of justice as specified in a democratic constitution. And majoritarian legislative procedures, insuring equal political rights of participation, are the primary means for doing this. But when ordinary democratic procedures, for whatever reason, consistently fail to promote the requirements of a just democratic constitution, it is democratically legitimate to impose limitations on these procedures (so long as they effectively remedy the injustice.) This justifies, Rawls claims in A *Theory of Justice*, many of the constraints on majority rule that presently exist in representative democracies, for example, bicameralism, various checks and balances, separation of powers, a bill of rights. Judicial review, Rawls contends, is among the legitimate institutions that may be needed in certain constitutions to constrain potential abuses of majority legislative rule in the interests of maintaining the requirements of a democratic constitution.[57] Whether judicial review is appropriate for a democracy is then, according to the account in A *Theory of Justice*, a strategic issue, which can only be decided by looking at the historical circumstances of a particular democracy, and asking whether judicial review is needed to maintain the basic justice of a democratic constitution.[58]

The general point, then, is that democracy is more than a form of government; we cannot adequately specify the requirements of a democratic constitution and more generally a democratic society by reference to the mechanisms of democratic voting procedures, equal political rights, and majority rule. So, to the standard critique that judicial review is antidemocratic, the Rawlsian response is that when this is true, it cannot be simply because judicial review contravenes majority will. Sometimes majority will itself contravenes the basic demands of a constitutional democracy (for example, where majorities unduly limit the exercise, or allow for the unequal application, of the basic liberties, such as the right to vote, or freedom of religion). Judicial review is antidemocratic only when it is unnecessary to maintain constitutional essentials and basic justice, or when courts exercise this power to overturn legitimately enacted laws that are designed to promote democratic justice and the effective exercise of the basic liberties of citizens. An example of the antidemocratic exercise of judicial review on a

---

57. See *TJ*, 224/196 rev., 228–34/200–206 rev., where Rawls discusses limitations on the principle of participation.

58. For an account of the democratic legitimacy of judicial review worked out along similar lines, see Samuel Freeman, "Constitutional Democracy and the Legitimacy of Judicial Review," *Law and Philosophy* (1990–91): 327–70.

Rawlsian view would be the Court's holdings, after Reconstruction and during the Lochner era,[59] that the Fourteenth Amendment, designed to eradicate the evils of slavery and servitude and provide for the equality of citizens, was really a protection for laissez-faire capitalist liberties (*PL*, 233 n. 18).[60] The Court abused judicial review in that it forbade democratic legislatures from exercising their legitimate powers to enact measures regulating the legal institution of property and the economy, which measures were designed to alleviate abuse in the workplace, provide a social minimum, and enable citizens to effectively exercise the basic rights of democratic citizens.

The account of judicial review Rawls gives in *Political Liberalism* is more explicit and allows for a more robust role for the Supreme Court. Rawls maintains that judicial review is not necessary for a constitutional democracy but that it is defensible "given certain historical circumstances and conditions of political culture" (*PL*, 240). As such, judicial review serves two roles. First, there is the "defensive" role, alluded to in *A Theory of Justice*, of maintaining the constitutional essentials of a democracy, in particular the basic liberties. Rawls develops the defensive role of judicial review, now in terms of the idea of public reason. Borrowing from Locke a distinction between the constituent power of the people to establish the "higher law" of the constitution as opposed to the ordinary powers of government, to make and apply ordinary laws, Rawls says the "aim of public reason is to articulate this ideal" expressed in higher law by the people in the exercise of their constituent power (*PL*, 232). So we have (in Bruce Ackerman's terms) the idea of a "dualist constitutional democracy" (*PL*, 233), where democratic government, acting as agents of the people, make ordinary law so as to realize the principles and ends of justice set forth in the higher law that is the product of the people's will. A supreme court could be one of the institutions set up by the people in the exercise of their constituent power "to protect the higher law." Where it is adopted, "the political values of public reason provide the Court's basis for interpretation" (*PL*, 234). By applying public reason one of the court's roles is to prevent higher law from being eroded by "the legislation of transient majorities" and well-organized narrow interests (*PL*, 233). When the court effectively maintains the higher law enacted by the people, it cannot be said to be antidemocratic, for it executes the people's will in matters of basic justice (*PL*, 233–34).

The second role of judicial review in a democracy is that the Supreme Court serves as "the exemplar of public reason." It does this in three ways. First, unlike other branches of government, the political values of public reason are the only reasons appropriate for the court in judicial review. Second, Rawls contends that in applying the political values of public reason as the basis for constitutional interpretation, the supreme court serves the "educative role of public reason," bringing to public awareness the principles of justice underlying the constitution, while developing and refining constitutional essentials in publicly acceptable

---

59. *Lochner v. New York*, 198 U.S. 45 (1905); overruling recognized by *Planned Parenthood of Southeastern Pennsylvania v. Casey*, 112 S. Ct. 2791 (1992).

60. Alluding to *Lochner v. New York* (1905) and other judicial failures to realize democratic justice.

terms (*PL*, 236).[61] A third aspect of the court's role as institutional exemplar is that, through its authoritative judgments, the court gives public reason "vividness and vitality in the public forum" (*PL*, 237). By this Rawls seems to mean that the court's judgments focus public attention upon the political values of public reason that are at stake in constitutional debate, and provide the locus for further public discussion and reasoned controversy.

Rawls contends (against Greenawalt) that public reason is "complete"; that is, that shared democratic political values are sufficient to address controversial issues of basic justice without needing to appeal to particular conceptions of the good (*PL*, 240–41, 244–46). To illustrate the completeness of public reason, Rawls alludes to the question of abortion and the political values that are sufficient to resolve this issue for constitutional purposes (*PL*, 243 n. 32). But his most extended illustration of the applicability of the political values of public reason to constitutional issues comes at the end of the book, in his extended discussion of political liberties and freedom of speech (*PL*, 340–68). There is here a very significant assessment of the history of freedom of speech doctrine, ending with an argument about what is democratically wrong with the Court's holding in *Buckley v. Valeo*, striking down congressional limits on campaign expenditures in the name of freedom of speech.[62]

Rather than pursuing further either of these constitutional discussions, I want to conclude with some remarks on an even more controversial claim of Rawls's. In discussing the Supreme Court's role as the exemplar of public reason, Rawls endorses Bruce Ackerman's view that Article V of the U.S. Constitution is not the sole legitimate means of amendment for our constitution (conceived not as a document but as the set of democratic institutions of which that document is a part). But he goes beyond Ackerman in embracing the radical idea that not everything enacted according to Article V procedures constitutes a valid amendment to the constitution. This implies that the Court could legitimately find constitutionally invalid enactments that, on the face of it, procedurally satisfy Article V's terms (*PL*, 238). On what grounds could an amendment by the people of higher law in accordance with Article V be considered invalid? Rawls's answer would have to be that not only is democracy not simply majoritarianism in the making of ordinary laws; it is also not even supermajoritarianism in the making of higher law. Not everything that the people actually will in the exercise of their constituent power can count as a valid amendment. Rawls implies this position when he claims that an amendment, under Article V, is not simply a change (*PL*, 238). To be a valid amendment, constituent power must be exercised in a way that (1) adapts basic institutions to remove weaknesses revealed by constitutional practice (as in the case of the many amendments that concern

61. Alexander Bickel, among others, discussed the somewhat similar idea of the "educative role" of judicial review. See *The Least Dangerous Branch: The Supreme Court at the Bar of Politics* (Indianapolis: Bobbs-Merrill, 1962).

62. See *PL*, 359–63. See also *Buckley v. Valeo*, 424 U.S. 1 (1976); *First National Bank v. Belloti*, 435 U.S. 765 (1978). Rawls argues why Buckley offends the "one-person, one-vote" principle set forth in *Wesberry v. Sanders*, 376 U.S. 1 (1964), and *Reynolds v. Sims*, 377 U.S. 533 (1964).

the institutional design of government, such as the Twenty-second Amendment limiting the president to two terms); or (2) adjusts basic constitutional values to changing circumstances; or (3) incorporates into the constitution a more inclusive understanding of those values (as in the case of the Thirteenth–Fifteenth Amendments, the Nineteenth, and the failed equal rights amendment, all of which sought to extend the ideal of equality to oppressed or exploited classes of people.) But, taking Ackerman's example, an amendment to repeal the Religion Clause, or, more generally, the First Amendment, and replace it with its opposite would be invalid, Rawls says, since it is not a true amendment, but a breakdown of the Constitution (*PL*, 239).

One way to understand Rawls's position here is that the First Amendment, in its protection of freedom of religion and of speech and assembly, specifies the most fundamental democratic liberties—liberty of conscience and freedom of thought. These basic liberties are the most fundamental democratic freedoms, in part because they provide the basis for public reason. Without freedom of thought, inquiry, and discussion, public reasoning about the constitution and democracy itself would not be possible. For the sovereign people to attempt to give up these liberties for the sake of other values is not a legitimate amendment to the constitution. It is constitutional suicide, the destruction of the most fundamental features of a democratic society. These basic liberties are then "inalienable," to use the eighteenth-century term; they cannot be bartered away. As such they are constitutionally entrenched. If so, then, it would seem that the U.S. Supreme Court should have the power to overturn any such invalid amendment, to save the basic political values on which our constitution is based.

Insofar as these claims appear peculiar, or even false, to lawyers (and to many they surely will), this reveals the extent to which the legal community envisions a particular conception of democracy as part of our constitution. We might call this a "procedural conception" of democracy, one which holds that democracy essentially consists in bare majoritarian or, at most, supermajoritarian procedures that place no substantive restrictions on what majorities can will, at least not at the constitutional level. I am not sure what the constitutional argument would be that would support this conception of our constitution. It cannot be found in the written Constitution. Nor am I aware of Supreme Court opinions that commit us to view the constitution (considered as either the document or the practices of which that document is a part) in such a way. And even if such opinions existed, there would be an especially good reason for ignoring them as establishing any kind of precedent in this instance. As Rawls contends, the constitution is not what the Court says it is (*PL*, 237). It is a mistaken conception of both constitutional practice and the authority of judicial review to make the Supreme Court the supreme arbiter in a constitutional democracy. Rather, the people are supreme, and the Constitution is "what the people acting constitutionally through the other branches . . . allow the Court to say it is" (*PL*, 237). Rawls's view here resembles Abraham Lincoln's view of the Court, expressed in connection with *Dred Scott*,[63] that the decisions of the Supreme Court, while

---

63. *Dred Scott v. Sanford*, 60 U.S. (19 How.) 393 (1851).

binding in a particular case, are not by themselves binding on Congress or the president in making or enforcing future laws until they have been, as Lincoln said, "acquiesced in by the people."[64]

But according to Rawls, even the people can conceivably make mistakes, as in his example of an effort to repeal the First Amendment (PL, 238). These passages seem to imply that, for Rawls, "the people" cannot be identified even with the actual will of transient supermajorities. It is no more legitimate for the supermajorities of one period to perpetually bind some or all their descendants (or even themselves) to the deprivation of basic democratic freedoms, as it is for a deranged court to deprive the people (or even some of them, as in Dred Scott) of those same freedoms. Not only is a democratic constitution not what the Court says it is, it is not what our ancestors say it is, nor even simply what actual current supermajorities say it is. In the end, Rawls seems to commit himself to the view that the "people" is an ideal implicit in democratic political culture: that of free and equal persons, united together as one legal body, the body politic, which exercises constituent power to make the higher law in such a way that it expresses the political values of public reason, thereby enabling them to realize the (moral) powers that make them free and equal democratic citizens. This conception of the person and the people seems to be the basis for the substantive conception of democracy that Rawls sees as implicit, if not in our constitution as historically interpreted by the Supreme Court, then in the public political culture of which that constitution is an integral part. His view in the end seems to be that we (at least as citizens, if not also the Court) cannot fully legitimately interpret our constitution without appealing to the political values of public reason and the ideal of democratic citizens and society that are a part of our democratic culture.

This is not to say that Rawls sees justice as fairness as implicit in our Constitution. He does say (later in chap. 8 of Political Liberalism): "These principles of justice enable us to account for many if not most of our fundamental constitutional rights and liberties, and they provide a way to decide the remaining questions of justice at the legislative stage" (PL, 339). But this is simply a proposal; it does not commit him to the claim (made by David Richards) that justice as fairness is already implicit in our constitution.[65] Rawls is not trying to justify the American, or any other, actual historical constitution. Nor does he seek to offer a method of constitutional interpretation that would enable jurists to apply justice as fairness to our constitution. At most, he says, justice as fairness can be used by jurists to "orient their reflections, complement their knowledge, and assist their

64. See Abraham Lincoln, Speeches and Writings, ed. Don Fehrenbacher (New York: Viking Press, 1989), 140–41, 150–53, 163, 182, 185. Rawls refers to Lincoln's view in claiming that ultimate political power is not held by either the legislature or the supreme court in a democracy, but "by the three branches in a duly specified relation with one another with each responsible to the people" (PL, 232). Bruce Ackerman and Robert Burt also rely on Lincoln's views of judicial review in developing their recent accounts. See Bruce Ackerman, We the People (Cambridge, MA: Harvard University Press, 1991); Robert A. Burt, The Constitution in Conflict (Cambridge, MA: Harvard University Press, 1992), 77–102.

65. See David A. J. Richards, Foundations of American Constitutionalism (New York: Oxford University Press, 1989).

judgment" (*PL*, 368). In the first instance, justice as fairness is designed to overcome "the impasse concerning the understanding of freedom and equality" that now exists in the public reason of our democratic culture. It is then "addressed not so much to constitutional jurists as to citizens in a constitutional regime" (*PL*, 369). For justice as fairness (or any other liberal conception of justice) to be found implicit in our constitution, it would first have to be endorsed by citizens, taken up by them as the basic content of public reason.

Of course, given the educative role of the Supreme Court as "exemplar of public reason," jurists play a significant role in shaping and guiding citizens' views about which liberal conception of justice is articulated by the constitution. But this does not give the Court license to impress a particular conception on the constitution. The Court has no authority to do this. It is the agent of the people's will and of public reason. Its duty is to interpret the constitution in the course of carrying out its normal functions, according to the political values of public reason, so as to protect constitutional essentials and basic justice. It must then formulate and apply some view of the basic liberties implicit in our constitution, as well as equal opportunity and a social minimum (the three constitutional essentials, Rawls says). In performing this role, the Court may over time itself come to discover the ideal of the person and of social cooperation most congenial to democratic culture, and from there assist the public reason of citizens to accept a particular conception of justice, like justice as fairness, as the basis for our public reason. If and when that occurs, it would be a major step towards realizing Rawls's ideal of a well-ordered society of justice as fairness. But to enforce that conception now, under our less than ideal circumstances, where our public reason regarding the requirements of freedom and equality is divided and confused (as is that of the Court itself—justices are after all citizens first, like the rest of us) would undermine the Court's effectiveness and its role as defender and exemplar of the political values of public reason.

Finally, it warrants emphasizing that one of the main contributions of Rawls's work to liberal and constitutional theory is the idea that the liberties and procedures historically associated with constitutional democracy, and with different versions of liberalism, depend upon a conception of the person as free and equal citizen.[66] As applied to constitutional interpretation and judicial review, this means that essential to interpretation in a democracy, to the clarification and specification of constitutional rights and procedures, is a conception of the person, and of those features of persons that are most central to their being free and equal citizens. As he says, regarding the basis of a democratic constitution: "This conception of the constitution does not found it, in the first instance, on principles of justice, or on basic (or natural) rights. Rather, its foundation is in the conceptions of the person and of social cooperation most likely to be congenial

---

66. See *PL*, 303–4. Rawls says his aim is to carry liberal theory one step further than the nineteenth-century views of Mill, Toqueville, and Constant, by showing how the liberties of democratic citizens and the inevitable plurality of conceptions of the good that is a fact of modern life under free institutions, must be accounted for in terms of ideas of the person as free and equal and their capacities for social cooperation.

to the public culture of a modern democratic society" (*PL*, 339). Rawls presents us with a political conception of persons that serves such a role in constitutional interpretation. It is based in his (Kantian) account of the centrality of the moral powers of practical reasoning as applied to justice, as the powers of citizens that enable them to be free, equal, and fully cooperative members of a democratic society. There are alternative conceptions of the person that some have found implicit in democratic culture and our constitution. Clearly, jurists such as Robert Bork and Richard Posner rely on very different conceptions of persons than Rawls to make their arguments. Bork, Posner, and others see us as rational utility-maximizers, willing to make trade-offs between all desires and interests (perhaps even trade-offs that would jeopardize basic liberties and the powers that enable us to be democratic citizens if the stakes are high enough). Moreover, constitutional proponents of Fourteenth Amendment absolute property rights and the Contract Clause's protection of capitalist freedoms (such as Richard Epstein, Bernard Siegan, and Randy Barnett) must rely upon an equally different conception of personhood than Rawls. The important point is that jurists should be aware that the conception of the person as democratic citizen is ultimately what is at issue in constitutional interpretation. In interpreting constitutional provisions, not only do we implicitly rely upon some such conception, but we also shape the kinds of persons that we and others will come to be. Given the importance of a conception of the person as free and equal citizen to specifying and interpreting constitutional rights and procedures, it is best that we, jurists and citizens, seek to clarify, publicly, the conception of citizens and their powers that underlie proposed interpretations. This would seem not only to be required by the liberal principle of legitimacy, the duty of civility, and public reason but also to be essential to our good as individuals, a matter of our self-knowledge as democratic citizens.

Conclusion

In the Introduction to *Political Liberalism*, Rawls says: "The account of the stability of a well-ordered society in Part III of *A Theory of Justice* is . . . unrealistic and must be recast. . . . Surprisingly, this change in turn forces many other changes and calls for a family of ideas not needed before" (*PL*, xix). I have indicated one way to perceive the problem with Rawls's original stability argument, and have shown how the ideas of overlapping consensus and public reason respond to this difficulty.

To summarize, in *Political Liberalism* Rawls seeks to carry the liberal idea of toleration down through the justification of liberalism itself (cf. *PL*, 10, 154). The "inherent stability" of a liberal society requires not simply the free acceptance of its institutions, but also the willing support of its members. Externally coercive measures of the kind envisioned by Hobbes, while they may make for stability in a nonliberal regime, are incompatible with the basic institutions of a liberal and democratic society. But if such fundamental liberal institutions as liberty of conscience, freedom of thought, and toleration of diverse ways of life are to be taken seriously and securely established within a stable liberal scheme, society must allow for the full development of different and conflicting reasonable comprehensive doctrines, and, consequently, different justifications of liberal institutions. The acceptance and support of liberal institutions requires, then, (1) an overlapping consensus for inherent stability. But the different comprehensive views forming this consensus themselves give rise to the need for common standards, independent of any comprehensive view, for interpreting and applying basic liberal values and institutions. Here arises the need for (2) a shared public reason, one that is responsive to reasons that we can endorse in common in our capacity as democratic citizens. If public reason is to be of sufficient depth, breadth, and completeness, it must have a certain content, which is provided by (3) a political conception of justice. The political conception provides a public justification of liberal institutions that is "freestanding," hence based in fundamental ideals democratic citizens share in common, and independent of the comprehensive views that form an overlapping consensus. A society which is effectively regulated by such a political conception of justice that is both the focus of an overlapping consensus and the basis of its public reason is a just and stable liberal scheme.

7

Public Reason and Political Justification

In a constitutional democracy, citizens normally have a sense of the kinds of reasons that are fittingly appealed to, as well as those that are not, in legislative and judicial forums and when arguing about laws and the constitution with people who hold different religious or philosophical views. We see this all the time in arguments in news editorials, for example. But it is very hard to characterize these reasons in any straightforward way. It is not enough to say that, because people have different faiths and their differences are irresolvable, religious considerations ought to be kept out of politics. For, people have irresolvably conflicting philosophical and ethical beliefs, too. Moreover, sometimes it may be wholly fitting within public political life for members of a faith to declare the religious beliefs that lead them to support or oppose measures involving fundamental questions of justice (Martin Luther King's religious declarations in support of civil rights is one example). How, then, are we to make sense of this idea of "public reasons"?

John Rawls takes the rather inchoate idea of public reason and explicates it, characteristically, in a complicated way. For example:

- Public reason is characteristic of a democratic people; it is the reason of equal citizens.
- Public reason's subject is the good of the public; its content is a political conception of justice.
- Public reason's constraints apply in the "public political forum," not in the "background culture."
- Public reason is "complete": It is capable of providing reasonable answers to questions involving constitutional essentials and matters of basic justice.
- Public reason aims for public justification and is reasoning addressed to others in their capacity as reasonable democratic citizens.
- Public reason and public justification meet the "criterion of reciprocity"; they proceed from reasons or premises we reasonably think others could reasonably accept to conclusions they also could reasonably accept.

- When government officials act from public reason, legal enactments by a majority are politically legitimate, even when they are not fully just.

Given the complexity of Rawls's account, the idea of public reason and the related ideas of political legitimacy and public and political justification are easily, and often, misunderstood. I hope to shed some light on what Rawls means by these key ideas in political liberalism. In the first three sections (I–III) of the paper, I discuss the background to Rawls's idea of public reason and how public reason is closely bound up with conceptions of democratic citizens and democratic institutions. Then in sections IV and V, I discuss how public reason is integrally related to other central ideas, including political reasonableness and political legitimacy, and public and political justifications. Here, to help clarify these ideas, I address some powerful criticisms of them by Joseph Raz. In Section VI, I discuss the completeness of public reason and address the opposing argument that appeals to comprehensive moral reasons are unavoidable to resolve many constitutional disputes. I discuss versions of this objection by Ronald Dworkin and by Amy Gutmann and Dennis Thompson. Since the right of abortions is often said to be the kind of problem that cannot be politically resolved without appealing to comprehensive reasons, I outline a defense of abortion rights that relies entirely upon public reason. In section VII, I discuss Rawls's claim that the Supreme Court is the exemplar of public reason. The paper concludes with some reflections on the evolution of Rawls's idea of a well-ordered society.

I. The Need for the Idea of Public Reason

Few moral philosophers have devoted as much effort and painstaking detail as Rawls to the nature of moral justification. Rawls began his career writing, not on justice, but on justification in moral philosophy. His first article, "Outline of a Decision Procedure for Ethics," deriving from his doctoral dissertation, provided the basis for his later account of reflective equilibrium.[1] In that work, Rawls sets forth a four-part test for "the reasonableness of moral principles." The first part says that moral principles are to be a "comprehensive explication of the considered judgments of competent judges" (CP, 10). In the second and third parts of Rawls's test, his contractarianism becomes evident, though not yet explicitly referred to in those terms. The second test says reasonable principles are those that "show a capacity to become accepted by competent moral judges" after criticism and open discussion, and which "exhibit a capacity to win free and willing allegiance and be able to implement a gradual convergence of uncoerced opinion" (CP, 10–11). "Thirdly," Rawls says,

1. John Rawls, "Outline of a Decision Procedure for Ethics" (1951), in Collected Papers, ed. Samuel Freeman (Cambridge, MA: Harvard University Press, 1999), 1–19 (cited in text as CP). "The aim of the present inquiry [is], namely, to describe a decision procedure whereby principles, by means of which we may justify specific moral decisions, may themselves be shown to be justifiable. Now part of this procedure will consist in showing that these principles are implicit in the considered judgments of competent judges" (6).

the reasonableness of a principle is tested by seeing whether it can function in existing instances of conflicting opinion, and in new cases causing difficulty, to yield a result which, after criticism and discussion, seems to be acceptable to all, or nearly all, competent judges, and to conform to their intuitive notion of a reasonable decision. (CP, 11)

Here it is evident that Rawls from the beginning conceived of justification in moral philosophy as establishing the reasonableness of moral principles. For Rawls, reasonableness stands in for the notion of truth in moral philosophy. The idea that reasonable moral principles are those that are generally acceptable to conscientious, informed, and morally motivated moral agents resurfaces in *A Theory of Justice*.[2] It is found, not directly in the agreement in the original position, but in Rawls's account of moral persons and a well-ordered society. A condition upon rational parties' agreement in the original position is that the principles of justice be publicly knowable and generally acceptable among free and equal moral persons with a sense of justice in a well-ordered society regulated by those principles.

The publicity condition implicit in Rawls's account of a well-ordered society suggests that he was concerned with an idea of public justification prior to explicitly appealing to that idea.[3] The publicity condition in *A Theory of Justice* implies that principles of justice are reasonable only if they are generally acceptable to the members of a well-ordered society and could serve as a basis for public justification for them in resolving issues and disputes about justice. One of Rawls's primary arguments against utilitarianism is that the principle of utility could not serve as a basis for public justification in a well-ordered society that remains stable, whereas the principles of justice are ideally suited to play this role because of their emphasis on reciprocity (see *TJ*, sec. 29). Still, however much the idea of publicity and even public agreement and justification might have guided Rawls's arguments for the principles of justice up to and including *A Theory of Justice*, and afterwards in the 1980 Dewey Lectures, it is not until *Political Liberalism* that we find a need for the distinct idea of public reason.[4]

The idea of public reason initially was designed to deal with a gap in Rawls's theory of justice, which arose after he discerned problems with the account of the stability of a well-ordered society, as depicted in *A Theory of Justice*. That account relied on the assumption that everyone in a well-ordered society of justice as fairness would find it rational to develop and exercise their capacities for justice in order to achieve the good of social union and realize their nature as free and equal autonomous moral beings. What made this argument for the "congruence of the right and the good" (*TJ*, sec. 86) succeed (insofar as it did) was an assumption that the great majority of people in a well-ordered society

---

2. Rawls, *A Theory of Justice* (Cambridge, MA: Harvard University Press, 1971; rev. ed., 1999) (cited in text as *TJ*: sometimes referred to as *Theory*). For a discussion, see chapter 5 of this volume.

3. The first explicit appeal to the role of principles in public justification comes in the 1980 Dewey Lectures, "Kantian Constructivism in Moral Philosophy," in *CP*, 303–58, at 327–56.

4. Rawls, *Political Liberalism* (New York: Columbia University Press, 1993; paperback edition, 1996, 2004) (cited in text as *PL*; references are to paperback edition).

would find it rational to affirm their (purported) nature as free rational beings by endorsing the Kantian ideal of moral autonomy as an intrinsic good. In order to achieve the good of autonomy, agents must incorporate into their life-plans a highest-order virtue to act for the sake of justice, which enables them to realize their moral capacities for justice and thereby achieve moral autonomy (see *TJ*, sec. 86). For our purposes, the important point in Rawls's complicated argument for the congruence of the right and the good is that, if it were true that the stability of a well-ordered society depended on such a congruence, then reasons of moral autonomy, self-realization of moral and rational capacities, and related Kantian ideas would serve as fundamental justifying reasons in making and interpreting laws, and more generally in public justification in a well-ordered society.

To see why, consider what is needed to apply abstract principles of justice to decide on laws and to interpret and enforce their implications in particular cases. For example, what kinds of considerations are relevant to deciding the scope and limits of the basic liberties in Rawls's first principle, such as freedom of the person and freedom of association? What kinds of constitutional rights do these abstract liberties require? Do they imply a general right of privacy that protects a right of abortion and a right to same-sex relations? People with different religious and philosophical views disagree about this. But in *A Theory of Justice* Rawls envisioned political recourse to the values of moral and rational autonomy to decide such questions. In Rawls's first principle of justice, as stated in *A Theory of Justice*, basic liberties can only be limited for the sake of a more extensive system of basic liberties. One reason for the priority given to maximal basic liberty is that the most extensive scheme of basic liberties is needed to realize the moral and rational autonomy of free and equal moral persons (see *TJ*, sec. 82). Following *A Theory of Justice*, public recourse to these kinds of reasons is perfectly appropriate, if not necessary, to interpret the constitution in a society governed by Rawls's principles of justice.

The problem Rawls subsequently discovered with official political appeals to autonomy are familiar. The value of autonomy is part of one or more "comprehensive doctrines" which (because of certain "burdens of judgment" (*PL*, xviii, 54-58) could not be generally endorsed by conscientious moral agents, even in a well-ordered society where Rawls's own principles of justice are generally accepted. To justify application of the principles of justice by appealing to this and other Kantian or Millian values is to appeal to moral values which some conscientious citizens (liberal Catholics for example) explicitly reject. Now for many political and legal theorists, there is no genuine problem here. They will say that liberalism, if it did not originate with the idea of autonomy, receives its most robust and securest defense when grounded in the value of moral and rational autonomy (as in Kant, Mill, or Rawls himself). If so, then these values should be made part of public political culture and education if liberalism is to be best secured against its adversaries.

Rawls gradually came to think that this position—namely, enforcing a generally accepted public conception of justice under the auspices of a philosophical doctrine that many reasonable citizens reject—borders on a violation of liberty of conscience. For, even if that philosophical doctrine were true, still to enforce it politically differs little from the political enforcement of a religious faith from the point of view of reasonable and rational citizens rejecting that doctrine. From their perspective, they are required as citizens to rely upon a comprehensive doctrine whose reasons and values run contrary to their most fundamental convictions. These comprehensive reasons are politically endorsed since they are officially consulted by legislatures and the courts to determine the application of principles of justice to the constitution. For Rawls, any conception of justice (including justice as fairness) endorsed under these conditions no longer provides a public basis for justification, even though all reasonable people accept the principles embodied in that very conception and it is politically embodied in laws.

Rawls developed political liberalism to alleviate these problems. Its main ideas include (1) the ideas of the domain of the political and a political conception of justice, (2) the idea of an overlapping consensus, and (3) the idea of public reason. As Rawls describes it, a *political conception of justice* differs from a moral conception of justice (such as that offered in A *Theory of Justice*) in that it is "freestanding" from comprehensive views and is worked up from fundamental ideas implicit in democratic culture and shared by reasonable citizens.[5] Because it is freestanding and its fundamental ideas are widely shared, Rawls conjectures that a political conception should be able to generate (in a well-ordered society) an *overlapping consensus* on its principles and basic ideas among different reasonable comprehensive doctrines, each of which then endorse it for their own particular reasons. Finally, a political conception that is widely affirmed in an overlapping consensus of reasonable views provides needed content to *public reason*; it thereby legitimates the laws and serves as a basis for public justification among people with differing moral and religious views. This litany roughly describes the relationships among Rawls's key ideas in political liberalism. Here I'll try to clarify the idea of public reason.

Rawls contrasts public reasons with both non-public and comprehensive reasons. Public reason (as Rawls understands the idea) involves a set of shared considerations which count as good reasons in public deliberation and argument about laws and their interpretation, among reasonable and rational democratic citizens who endorse different fundamental values. Because of liberty of conscience and other basic liberties, citizens in a democratic society are inevitably going to have, not just different values or conceptions of their good, but also different religious, philosophical and ethical views. (This is the *fact of reasonable pluralism*.) It is because reasonable doctrines disagree about basic values and reasons that there is (for Rawls) a need for the idea of public reason—public reason presupposes reasonable pluralism.[6] In A *Theory of Justice*, there was no need for an account of (public) reasons that was any different from

---

5. On the features of political conceptions, see *PL*, 11–15.
6. See Rawls, "The Idea of Public Reason Revisited" (1997), in *CP*, 573–74.

the reasons that accompanied the Kantian interpretation of justice as fairness. For, everybody in a well-ordered society already accepted the comprehensive reasons provided by a Kantian view. But given reasonable pluralism, there is no longer a shared set of comprehensive reasons and guidelines for reasoning that all can appeal to in applying principles of justice. Public reason aims to delineate such a shared set of considerations that are not peculiar to any comprehensive view, but which can be accepted by all reasonable views in so far as they accommodate democratic ideals. For Rawls, public reasons are part of the "domain of the political." The moral ideal of free and equal autonomous moral persons cannot provide a basis for public justification in a well-ordered democracy (as Rawls had hoped in A *Theory of Justice*); however, the *political* ideal of free and equal democratic citizens can serve this public role because this political ideal can be endorsed by different reasonable comprehensive views (so Rawls contends) (*CP*, 586).

Rawls says "public reason is characteristic of a democratic people: it is the reason of its citizens [as such], of those sharing the status of equal citizenship" (*PL*, 213).[7] This suggests that the mere fact that people in a society commonly accept and reason in terms of some common religion or other comprehensive doctrine does not make that doctrine part of public reason. Even assuming that all the members of an Islamic state, such as Saudi Arabia, accept the Muslim religion and appeal to religious reasons in deliberating and discussing laws, this does not make Islam part of public reason. Saudi Arabia has no public reason in Rawls's sense, only shared comprehensive reasons which rule out the possibility of a public reason.

In his earlier presentation of the idea of public reason, Rawls introduces public reason as part of justice as fairness. He distinguishes two kinds of liberal political values: first, "the values of political justice [that] fall under the principles of justice for the basic structure"; and second, "the values of public reason [that] fall under the guidelines for public inquiry, which make that inquiry free and public" (*PL*, 224). The values of public reason are among the guidelines for applying the principles of justice that presumably all reasonable persons accept in a well-ordered society. If we assume different comprehensive conceptions in a well-ordered society, then even though everyone accepts the same principles of justice, they will apply the principles of justice differently because they have different comprehensive views. For, standards of evidence, inference, good reasons, and judgment differ among comprehensive views. As a result there is a need in a well-ordered society for standards of inquiry and reasoning that will allow people holding different comprehensive views to come to the same conclusions in applying the public conception of justice. So Rawls depicts the parties in the original position as agreeing, in addition to principles of justice, to "guidelines of public reason" for applying these principles (*PL*, 225).

---

7. See also *CP*, 577. "The idea of public reason arises from a conception of democratic citizenship in a constitutional democracy."

But Rawls has another route to the idea of public reason, one that is not tied specifically to justice as fairness. Here Rawls introduces the idea of public reason by way of a principle of *liberal legitimacy*.[8]

> Our exercise of political power is proper and hence justifiable only when it is exercised in accordance with a constitution the essentials of which all citizens may reasonably be expected to endorse in the light of principles and ideals acceptable to them as reasonable and rational. (*PL*, 217)

Liberal legitimacy imposes a moral *duty of civility* on citizens: a duty "to be able to explain to one another on those fundamental questions [regarding constitutional essentials and matters of basic justice] how the principles and policies they advocate and vote for can be supported by the political values of public reason" (*PL*, 217).[9] Legitimacy is not an idea that plays any explicit role in *A Theory of Justice*. Again, like public reason, the need for it arose largely as a result of the same problems implicit in *A Theory of Justice*'s argument for stability. Even if everyone endorses the same conception of justice, and this conception (justice as fairness, let us assume) were the most reasonable, still it would not be legitimate to make and enforce laws under it for reasons (such as autonomy) that cannot be reasonably endorsed by other reasonable comprehensive views. Rawls indicates that this conception of legitimacy, like public reason, is necessary "if each citizen [is to have] an equal share in political power" (*Restatement*, 90). Moreover, as suggested, liberty of conscience is at issue, since for Rawls there is no genuine difference between government officials deciding on and enforcing a law or decree that is purely for reasons of autonomy and their deciding on and enforcing the same law or decree purely for religious reasons (because it is compatible with God's commands as expressed in Natural Law). Both cases are not legitimate exercises of political authority, even though the laws concerned may be substantively just.

Another use Rawls makes of the idea of legitimacy is to deal with the problem of the status of duly enacted laws that are not wholly just or reasonable. Even the most conscientious legislators who apply a just constitution and follow just democratic procedures can make laws with unjust results. Rawls contends that these laws are still legitimate, even if not wholly just or reasonable, insofar as

---

8. For Rawls's initial statement of the principle, see *PL*, 137; a later statement is in "Reply to Habermas," in *PL*, 393; and Rawls's final statement of the principle is in "Public Reason Revisited" (in *CP*, 578). See also the earlier statement of the principle in Rawls's Harvard lecture notes, *Justice as Fairness: A Restatement*, ed. Erin Kelly (Cambridge, MA: Belknap Press, 2001), 41, 84, 90–91 (cited in text as *Restatement*). For a discussion of how political legitimacy is related to but differs from justice, see *PL*, 427–29.

9. A duty of civility is in *TJ*, but is stated differently: it "imposes a due acceptance of the defects of [just] institutions and a certain restraint in taking advantage of them" (312). Rawls appeals to this duty to argue for a duty to normally comply with unjust laws provided that they do not exceed certain bounds of injustice.

they meet the liberal principle of legitimacy. Provided duly enacted laws do not exceed certain limits of injustice and meet the legitimacy principle, democratic citizens normally have a duty to obey them.[10]

II. The Content of Public Reason

The idea of public reason presupposes a diversity of conflicting reasonable comprehensive views, and it excludes reasons that are peculiar to one or another view (autonomy, aggregate utility, the will of God and natural law, etc.). But public reason is something more than simply the reasons and standards of judgment that reasonable comprehensive views all hold in common (an important point returned to later). What, then, is the nature and content of public reason? First, for Rawls, public reason is the *"reason of [democratic] citizens as such"* (*PL*, 213; emphasis added). By "as such," he means that it is the reason of democratic citizens in their capacity as citizens, and not in any other status or position they occupy (as parent, or a member of a particular profession or religion, for example). Public reasoning implies the adoption of a general standpoint, one where people abstract from their ordinary perspectives guided by their particular interests and comprehensive views and take up the point of view of a democratic citizen. From this point of view, one is to focus on the reasons and interests of free and equal democratic citizens and what they require in order to function in their role as citizens and to freely pursue a conception of their good.

This leads to the second aspect of public reason, namely its proper subject. The *subject* of public reason is the good of the public and matters of fundamental justice. The good of the public and matters of fundamental justice are what democratic citizens are to reason about when engaged in public reasoning—not their own particular good, or that of some group they identify with, or even justice or the good as determined by a comprehensive doctrine. How do we know the good of the public? For Rawls, it appears to be defined in terms of the political values needed to realize the common interests that democratic citizens share—again, in their capacity as citizens. Democratic citizens have certain fundamental interests, which provide them with reasons as citizens and, in turn, supply a basis for public reason. On Rawls's political conception of free and equal moral persons, democratic citizens have "higher-order interests" in the exercise and development of the "moral powers" (*PL*, 74, 19) that enable them to cooperate and take part in social life and rationally pursue a conception of their good, as well as interests in establishing conditions needed to secure and maintain their freedom and

---

10. See *PL*, 393, 427–29. "It is unreasonable to expect in general that human statutes and laws should be strictly just by our lights" (*PL*, 393 n. 30); see also *TJ*, sec. 53; Rawls, "Public Reason Revisited," in *CP*, 578. Another clear need for an idea of legitimacy is in the case of just laws that are not duly enacted, but which are enforced by fiat. Universal health care is for Rawls a requirement of justice, but it would not be legitimate for an executive body to put such a system into effect by decree if it had been democratically rejected. As Rawls says, "Being legitimate says something about [laws' or governments'] pedigree" (*PL*, 427).

equality. They also have a higher-order interest in social and political conditions that enable them to freely pursue reasonable conceptions of the good. These fundamental interests of democratic citizens provide the ultimate basis for public reasoning about fundamental justice and the common good. What are the political values and the measures needed to enable democratic citizens to realize their capacities for justice and rationality? What measures enable citizens to freely and fairly pursue their conceptions of the good? What duties and obligations to one another and to the public should citizens have if they are to achieve the common good? These are the kinds of questions that ultimately regulate public reason.[11]

Third, public reason is guided by a *criterion of reciprocity*. "The criterion of reciprocity is an essential ingredient specifying public reason and its content" (*CP*, 609). To give public reasons is to give reasons that we can reasonably expect that others can reasonably accept as democratic citizens, in view of their fundamental interests in maintaining the conditions of their freedom and equality (cf. *CP*, 578). I discuss the idea of reasonableness further below, in Section IV. Here the main point is that this idea is to be interpreted in this context in terms of an ideal of free and equal citizens. For this reason, Rawls frequently refers to the "politically reasonable."

Fourth, the *content* of public reason, Rawls says, is "given by the ideals and principles expressed by society's conception of political justice" (*PL*, 213). Or, as Rawls says in later discussions, "The content of public reason is given by a family of political conceptions of justice, and not by a single one" (*CP*, 581). To engage fully in public reason is to deliberate within the framework of a political conception when debating fundamental political questions, each of which satisfy the criterion

---

11. Regarding the political values, Rawls says, "These values provide public reasons for all citizens" (*CP*, 601). Among the liberal political values Rawls mentions are such values of justice as equal political and civil liberty, equality of opportunity, social equality and economic reciprocity, the common good, the social bases of self-respect, and the necessary conditions for these values. There are also the political values of public reason, including guidelines for free and public inquiry, the appropriate use of concepts of judgment, inference and evidence, and such political virtues as reasonableness, fair-mindedness, and a readiness to honor the duty of civility, all of which make reasoned public discussion possible. (See *PL*, 139, 224.) Later, Rawls says that the values mentioned in the Preamble to the U.S. Constitution are examples of political values: a more perfect union, justice, domestic tranquility, the common defense, the general welfare, and the blessings of liberty for ourselves and our posterity, all of which include more specific values under them, such as the fair distribution of income and wealth (*CP*, 584). Efficiency and effectiveness are political values, which would include controlling economic, environmental and other kinds of social loss or waste (ibid.). Political values that relate to human health, the environment, and so on that Rawls mentions are: preserving the natural order to further the good of ourselves and future generations; promoting biological and medical knowledge by fostering species of animals and plants; and protecting the beauties of nature for purposes of public recreation and "the pleasures of a deeper understanding of the world" (*PL*, 245). From his brief discussions of abortion we learn that among the political values are: appropriate respect for human life, the reproduction of liberal society over time, full equality of women, and respecting the requirements of public reason itself in political discussion of controversial issues (such as abortion) (see *Restatement*, 117). Political values that relate to the family are: the freedom and equality of women, the equality of children as future citizens, the freedom of religion, and the value of the family in securing the orderly production and reproduction of society and its culture from one generation to the next (*CP*, 601).

of reciprocity.[12] Here Rawls clearly indicates that public reasoning involves more than simply appealing to political values that democratic citizens hold in common. It also requires interpreting democratic political values according to the principles and ideas of a political conception of justice, and not according to anyone's comprehensive view. The need for political conceptions to give content to public reason arises because, in the absence of a political conception of justice, public reason is incomplete — it is without sufficient content to resolve many of the political questions of justice encountered in democratic political life. The incompleteness of public reason means citizens and officials have to rely upon some comprehensive doctrine to make or interpret laws. For Rawls, this deprives laws of their legitimacy, since they no longer have a political justification. Why a lack of public justification should matter will be discussed further, in section VI (cf. *PL*, 247).

Fifth, because public reason limits itself to considerations that reasonable citizens can reasonably accept in their capacity as democratic citizens, public reason does not aim to state the "whole truth" about metaphysics, morality, or ultimate values. There are many good and true reasons that are not a part of public reason, but which belong to comprehensive views. Rawls first used the term "public reason" just to make the point that the aim of public justification as reasonable agreement on a political conception cannot be achieved in a democracy if a conception is based in the whole "truth about an independent metaphysical and moral order" (*CP*, 395). For most, if not all, reasonable comprehensive doctrines endorsed by reasonable citizens contain at least some false judgments about metaphysical and moral issues. As a result, reasonable agreement among persons endorsing different doctrines can never be achieved on the basis of the whole truth. Rather than the whole truth, public justification is "founded on public agreement in judgment on due reflection. The aim is free agreement, reconciliation through public reason" (ibid.). Rawls's position gives rise to the objection (by Joseph Raz) that, in eschewing the whole truth, a public justification of a political conception might end up "publicly justifying" false principles on the basis of false beliefs. This objection is to be considered in section V below. As we will see, in response Rawls argues that, in eschewing the whole truth, public reason does not eschew objectivity of judgment, and indeed that reasonable judgments in political conceptions do not conflict with true judgments in reasonable comprehensive doctrines that endorse these political conceptions (see *CP*, 609).

III. The Institutions of Public Reason

Like many of his key ideas, the idea of public reason takes on increasing complexity each time Rawls discusses it. In his later works, Rawls comes to envision a background of institutions required by public reason if its ideal is to be realized.

---

12. "A citizen engages in public reason, then, when he or she deliberates within a framework of what he or she sincerely regards as the most reasonable political conception of justice, a conception that expresses political values that others, as free and equal citizens might also reasonably be expected reasonably to endorse" (*CP*, 581).

In the 1996 introduction to the paperback edition of *Political Liberalism* (xxx-vii–lxii), then again in the *Law of Peoples*,[13] Rawls discusses what is held in common by the political conceptions that provide content to public reason. They are all *liberal conceptions* insofar as first, they guarantee certain familiar basic rights, liberties and opportunities; second, they assign priority to these basic rights, liberties and opportunities over other social and political values; and third, they insure measures providing all citizens, whatever their social position, adequate all-purpose means to make effective use of their basic liberties and opportunities.[14] From prior discussions, one might infer that by this third condition, what Rawls intended was simply a social minimum, namely, income supports for the less advantaged, which might be decided in a number of ways in addition to Rawls's difference principle. But Rawls, here, goes on to say that, in order for a liberal political conception to satisfy the third condition, it must (as a matter of "common sense political sociology") allow for five kinds of institutions: (1) public financing of political campaigns and ways of assuring the availability of information on matters of public policy, to prevent the distortion or manipulation of public reasoning; (2) "a certain fair equality of opportunity" especially in education and training; (3) a decent distribution of income and wealth; (4) society as an employer of last resort, needed in order to provide security and meaningful work, so citizens can maintain their self-respect; and (5) "basic health care assured all citizens" (*PL*, lviii–lix).

Any political conception, unless it meets these conditions, is unreasonable for Rawls. It is unreasonable since, in the absence of these conditions, a political conception cannot meet the criterion of reciprocity. It cannot reasonably or sincerely be thought that other democratic citizens could reasonably accept the absence of effective means to exercise the basic liberties as a basis for cooperation. Thus Rawls says, libertarianism is unreasonable since it does not try to meet these conditions, but indeed explicitly rejects them (*LP*, 49).

Now, it comes as some surprise when Rawls goes on to suggest that these same institutions are required by, or are a precondition for, public reason. These institutions are, he says,

> essential prerequisites for a basic structure within which the ideal of public reason, when conscientiously followed by citizens, may protect the basic liberties and prevent social and economic inequalities from being excessive. *Since the ideal of public reason contains a form of public political deliberation, these insti-*

13. Rawls, *The Law of Peoples* (Cambridge, MA: Harvard University Press, 1999) (cited in text as *LP*).

14. Cf. *PL*, xlviii; *LP*, 49. From "The Idea of an Overlapping Consensus" and *Political Liberalism*, it is apparent that Rawls sees all liberal political conceptions as protecting basically the same set of abstract basic liberties that he says are protected by his first principle of justice: namely, liberty of conscience and freedom of thought, freedom of association and equal political liberties, the freedom specified by the liberty and integrity of the person, and the rights and liberties covered by the ideal of the rule of law. See Rawls, "The Idea of an Overlapping Consensus" (1987), in *CP*, 421, 440 n. 27; also *PL*, 6, 291–94. Since these liberties, along with equal opportunities and adequate all-purpose means, can be understood in different ways, Rawls says there are many liberalisms (*PL*, 6).

tutions, most clearly the first three, are necessary for this deliberation to be possible and fruitful. A belief in the importance of public deliberation is essential for a reasonable constitutional regime, and specific institutions and arrangements need to be laid down to support and encourage it. The idea of public reason proposes how to characterize the structure and content of society's fundamental bases for political deliberations. (*PL*, lix–lx; emphasis added)[15]

Here Rawls suggests that the ideal, if not the idea, of public reason requires as background conditions not only a decent social minimum, but also the institutions of a deliberative democracy if that ideal is to be realized in political life. The distinction between the idea and the ideal of public reason may be important here. Rawls is not saying that a democracy cannot be governed by public reasons to any degree unless it guarantees all these background institutions. But it is clear that he thinks something essential to public reasoning is missing in the absence of a deliberative democracy and its background conditions. Public reason is the mode of discourse in a deliberative democracy and one of its most essential features (*CP*, 580). Moreover, deliberative democracy is the primary forum within which public reasoning takes place. Citizens in a democracy cannot effectively engage in public reasoning (1) if they or some of their members' basic needs are not adequately provided for, to the degree that they can take effective and intelligent advantage of their basic freedoms; (2) if the political forum and the free flow of public information is corrupted by monied interests or by other concentrations of power; and (3) if there are not widespread fair opportunities for education, job training, and participation in public life. "Otherwise all parts of society cannot take part in the debates of public reason or contribute to social and economic policies" (*LP*, 50).[16]

IV. Public Reason and Political Reasonableness

What kinds of considerations are to be expressed in public reason and count as public reasons?[17] The public reasons that are to be expressed in public reason are considerations regarding political values that satisfy the criterion of reciprocity. In public reasoning, we are to present, as justifications for laws and policies, "rea-

---

15. See also *LP*, 50–51.

16. For the relationship between public reason and deliberative democracy, see Joshua Cohen, "Deliberation and Democratic Legitimacy," in *The Good Polity: Normative Analysis of the State*, ed. Alan Hamlin and Philip Petit (New York: Blackwell, 1989), 17, 21, 24; Joshua Cohen, "Democracy and Liberty," in *Deliberative Democracy*, ed. Jon Elster (New York: Cambridge University Press, 1998), 185–231; Joshua Cohen, "For a Democratic Society," in *The Cambridge Companion to Rawls*, ed. Samuel Freeman (New York: Cambridge University Press, 2003), 86.

17. While Rawls normally discusses "public reason," he occasionally refers to the plural, "public reasons." On at least two occasions, he uses the singular and the plural in the same sentence: (1) "Reasonable [comprehensive] doctrines may be introduced in public reason at any time, given that in due course public reasons, provided by a reasonable political conception, are presented sufficient to support whatever the comprehensive doctrines are introduced to support" (*PL*, li–lii). (2) "However,

sons we might reasonably expect that [citizens] as free and equal might reasonably also accept" (*PL*, li; cf. *CP*, 578).

The idea of *reasonableness* plays a major role in this criterion, and in understanding the idea of public reason. What does it mean? Throughout his career Rawls used the idea of reasonable—or "the Reasonable"—in a number of ways. At some point or another, he refers to "reasonable acceptance," "reasonable political conceptions," "reasonable principles," "reasonable claims," "reasonable persons," "reasonable conceptions of the good," "reasonable comprehensive doctrines," "reasonable conditions on agreement," and "politically reasonable." In all instances, he refuses to offer a definition of "reasonable" in terms of necessary and sufficient conditions. Many express frustration at this, and say the idea of reasonableness only masks appeals to inchoate intuition.[18] But any attempt to provide a definition of "reasonable" would be incapable of capturing all that is involved in the many uses of this rich concept.[19] What can be provided are clarifications, by focusing on important features of the idea of reasonableness as it is used in different contexts, and developing these ideas within the context of a theory in hopes that this will help explicate the concept. In many regards, Rawls's moral and political philosophy is such an attempt to explicate the meaning and import of moral reasonableness—what reasonable principles of justice are, what it is to be a reasonable person, what is a reasonable conception of the good, and so on. Rawls provisionally characterizes a reasonable person as one who has a willingness to cooperate on fair terms, recognizes and appreciates the consequences of the "burdens of judgment," and has a sense of justice. He aims to show that a reasonable person with these and other relevant features affirms his principles of justice. Principles of justice that are (most) reasonable for free and equal citizens are those which would be agreed to by representatives of reasonable persons in the original position, and which fit with our fixed and considered moral convictions in reflective equilibrium. Of course, these are not definitions (which, for Rawls, are always provisional) but substantive claims about reasonable principles and persons (*TJ*, 51/44 rev.).

Rawls, then, explicates the idea of reasonable principles by way of the related idea of reasonable persons:[20] reasonable principles of justice are those that rea-

---

it [public reason] does not, as such, determine or settle particular questions of law or policy. Rather, it specifies the public reasons in terms of which such questions are to be politically decided" (*PL*, liii).

18. See, for example, Jean Hampton, "Feminist Contractarianism," in *A Mind of One's Own: Feminist Essays on Reason and Objectivity*, ed. Louise M. Antony and Charlotte Witt (Boulder: Westview Press, 1993), 227, 249.

19. Rawls said the same thing about "rationality" as well (*LP*, 87–88). A parallel case: Burton Dreben said in his seminar on Quine at Harvard that, if pressed to define "rational beliefs," Quine would say that rational beliefs are the beliefs that Einstein has. Like Quine and Wittgenstein, Rawls thought philosophical efforts to provide necessary and sufficient conditions on the use of most significant terms or concepts to be futile endeavors. "Definitions and analyses of meanings do not have a special place: definition is but one device used in setting up the general structure of theory. Once the whole framework is worked out, definitions have no distinct status and stand or fall with the theory itself" (*TJ*, 51/44 rev.).

20. Cf. *PL*, 94. Reasonable persons have the following four features: They want to cooperate with others on terms that are fair and they are willing to propose and honor such terms; they recog-

sonable persons or their representatives would endorse from a perspective that is fair between them (the original position on Rawls's account). Here it is important that the idea of reasonableness and reasonable persons suggests being responsive not just to the reasons others have but also to the reasons they think they have. The idea of reasonableness assumes that people often will act for reasons that are not valid or true (as determined by science or by the true comprehensive doctrine, if there is one). Many reasonable people have religious convictions that they believe provide them with reasons for acting and ordering their lives. Since conflicting religions (and more generally, conflicting reasonable comprehensive doctrines) cannot all be true, most, if not all, contain reasons that are false or which are based on false beliefs about the world. Still, Rawls claims it would be unreasonable to ignore or not be sensitive to these reasons, or not normally accept or tolerate people's affirming and acting on the particular beliefs that provide them with reasons. Persons and principles of justice are unreasonable insofar as they do not tolerate or accept that false beliefs can provide others with good reasons for acting—good reasons insofar as these reasons fit with their rational plan of life and reasonable comprehensive views. It would be unreasonable for a professor to give an exam on Yom Kippur or Good Friday and refuse to allow practicing Jewish or Christian students a makeup date because their beliefs (assumedly) are false. Their religious holy days provide practicing Jews and Christians with good reasons for not attending an examination on those days, and for a person in authority to be insensitive and unresponsive to these particular reasons ("personal reasons" as Scanlon would call them) is to be unreasonable.[21] To insist that others cooperate with you only on grounds and for reasons which you believe are true is the paradigm case of an unreasonable person. All the religious, moral, and ethnic fanatics in history meet this description. Even if the doctrine of "intelligent design" were true, it would be unreasonable to expect everyone else to endorse it; it could not serve as a source of public reasons, for there is no empirical evidence for it. It does not fit with the ways of reasoning and kinds of evidence that are part of public reason.

"Fair enough," one might say. "Of course we should tolerate false comprehensive views so long as their practice does not undermine the requirements of justice and legitimacy. But what is objectionable is that (A) Rawls sees people with such false beliefs, and even their false beliefs, too, as nonetheless reasonable (in a moral, even if not necessarily epistemic, sense of 'reasonable'); moreover, (B) a reasonable political conception providing content to public reason cannot

---

nize and accept the consequences of the burdens of judgment; they both want to be, and want to be recognized as, fully cooperative and fairminded; and they have a "reasonable moral psychology," including a sense of justice, and thus want to do what is right and just for its own sake (*PL*, 81–82). Each of these features of reasonable persons can be further clarified: for example, we can assume that reasonable persons respect others and are sensitive to the reasons they have. They "take into account the consequences of their actions on others' well-being" (*PL*, 49 n. 1). They don't exploit others or take advantage of them whenever the opportunity arises, and so on.

21. See T. M. Scanlon, *What We Owe to Each Other* (Cambridge, MA: Belknap Press, 1998), 219.

even question the alleged truth of these false comprehensive beliefs, but must accommodate or work around them; as a result (C) these false beliefs influence the range of considerations and of political conceptions which are themselves reasonable and which provide content to public reason. But this means that (D) public reason ultimately deflects public acknowledgment of the truth about justice and the legitimate use of political power and can inculcate or propagate public affirmation of false principles. How can false principles and beliefs provide a basis for legitimacy? Moreover, how do governments show respect for persons as rational self-directing agents by inculcating in them false beliefs regarding justice and legitimate political power?"[22]

It is true that for Rawls reasonableness is largely a moral, not an epistemic category. One can be fully reasonable, politically speaking, and have reasonable views, and yet still have false metaphysical, ethical, or religious beliefs.[23] Here it is important to recognize that, even if Rawls were to allow people with false beliefs to influence the range of political conceptions that are seen as reasonable and politically effective (not that I believe he does—see below), still, he is not advocating that justice and the conception of justice that is *most reasonable* in any way assumes or is substantively influenced by these or other false beliefs. For Rawls, the most reasonable conception of justice is justice as fairness, and it (presumably) assumes no false beliefs. (For example, the parties in the original position have only true beliefs regarding the general information relevant to their decision on principles of justice [see *TJ*, 517/454 rev.].) The problem that Rawls confronts in *Political Liberalism* is not the same problem as in A *Theory of Justice* (*PL*, xxxix). In setting forth the conditions for reasonable conceptions of justice that may provide content to public reason, he is not directly addressing the question of the true or (as he says) most reasonable conception of justice that he addressed in A *Theory of Justice*. Instead, he speaks to the questions of the conditions of the *stability* of a liberal constitution and its *political legitimacy*—its authority to make and enforce coercive laws and legitimately use political power among citizens who conceive of themselves as free and equal.

Given this understanding of the issues at stake in political liberalism, for Rawls, it is enough for the legitimate exercise of political power that those who exercise it be able to justify their actions by a reasonable political conception that meets the reciprocity criterion. It is not necessary for political legitimacy that all political power be exercised only on terms allowed by the true comprehensive doctrine and its account of justice. To hold that is to collapse the

---

22. This objection is based on Joseph Raz's remarks in his paper, "Disagreement in Politics," *American Journal of Jurisprudence* 43 (1998): 25–52, 42 (cited in text as DP). With regard to the final question above, it would be ironic if Rawls's account were subject to the criticism that it allows for government's *knowing* inculcation of false beliefs among citizens. (Later I contend it is not.) For, one of Rawls's primary arguments against utilitarianism and other teleological conceptions is that they do allow for, if not require, the inculcation of false beliefs regarding the bases of social cooperation when needed to achieve stability. Justice as fairness rules out this potentiality by way of its publicity condition on principles of justice. See *TJ*, 177–82/154–58 rev.

23. For Rawls's definition of "reasonable person'" and "reasonable comprehensive doctrine" see *PL*, 49–50 and 59 respectively.

idea of legitimacy into the idea of justice. Rawls always believed that justice as fairness is the most reasonable (or true, if you will) political conception and that it is in the best position to meet the criterion of reciprocity and provide a basis for public justification required by the liberal principle of legitimacy. But Rawls eventually came to recognize that reasonable people can disagree, not only about reasonable comprehensive doctrines but even about which liberal conception is the most reasonable conception of justice. For this and other reasons, Rawls did not maintain that only laws conforming to justice as fairness are legitimate and therefore worthy of respect. The legitimate exercise of political power must meet certain conditions of justice, namely respect the broad outlines of a liberal constitution and requirements of "basic justice," but within these parameters political power can be legitimately exercised without being wholly just.

If these are the sorts of issues Rawls is addressing in formulating the idea of public reason, then perhaps the objections mentioned above are not as serious as they might seem. To begin with (and answering the objections above in the order presented):

(A) If being reasonable means having no false fundamental or significant beliefs, then there are few if any reasonable people. Also, if beliefs cannot be reasonable without being true, then no one's important beliefs are all reasonable. This is not what Rawls means by reasonableness.

Moreover, (B) what difference does it make that a political conception of justice does not draw into question the false comprehensive convictions of those to whom it is addressed, when it is required that any reasonable political conception be *freestanding* of the false (as well as true) values and metaphysical ideas that are peculiar to people's comprehensive views? Is it really a liberal constitution's role to insist of reasonable people who already accept and observe liberal principles of justice that they must accept them for the right comprehensive reasons, thereby imposing on reasonable people against their conscientious convictions the true comprehensive moral view?

More importantly, (C) since a reasonable political conception and public reason itself are freestanding of false comprehensive views and are based on ideas implicit in democratic culture, the content of public reason and the legitimacy of political power are *not* jeopardized by the false comprehensive values or beliefs that reasonable citizens hold. If, then, a reasonable political conception does contain false principles, it is not due to inference from false judgments in comprehensive views but to misinterpretation within public reason itself of the implications of democratic ideas. Here it is relevant that Rawls does not see public reason as consisting of false judgments or under the influence of false comprehensive views. He says it involves "knowledge and ways of reasoning—the plain truths now common and available to citizens generally" (*Restatement*, 90). Public reason is part of the truth and not the "whole truth as we see it" (*PL*, 218, 225). In bracketing true (and false) comprehensive reasons, public reason clearly limits the range of judgments that may be appealed to and justified since "politics in a democratic society can never be guided by what we see as the whole truth" (*PL*, 243). But there is no reason to think that bracketing what we see as the "whole truth" renders "part of the truth" somehow false (ibid.).

Finally, (D) regarding the potential falsity of the political conceptions of justice that inform public reason and their role as a basis for legitimacy: It is true that if all liberal conceptions of justice (as defined by Rawls) are false, and, instead, some other non-liberal conception is true (libertarianism, for example, or Straussian perfectionism), then public reason involves inculcating false beliefs. Then the entire project underlying political liberalism is misguided, not just its account of public reason. But it is misguided because liberalism itself is false, not simply because of some defect in Rawls's account of public reason and public justification. For, public reason can accommodate the principles of justice of most any comprehensive liberal doctrine (including Raz's, I believe), so long as it does not insist on a perfectionist requirement that liberal justice requires of its citizens not just that they accept and conform to liberal principles, but also that citizens accept liberal principles for the right reasons according to the true comprehensive doctrine (and thus according to Kantian autonomy or utilitarianism or liberal perfectionism or ideal discourse theory or natural law doctrine or whichever comprehensive doctrine that is true). Short of this, for this to be a real objection, it first has to be shown that liberalism is a false view (which is not argued by those raising the objections above).

To sum up, three aspects of public reason can be distinguished: (1) standards of judgment, evidence, inference, and reasoning; (2) empirical judgments, that is the facts, reliable statistical regularities, and uncontested scientific laws or generalizations; and (3) the political values of democratic justice and the public conception of justice that give content to public reason. Clearly, Rawls did not see the standards of inference, evidence, and justification that are to govern public reasoning to be false or jeopardized by the falsity of reasonable comprehensive doctrines. Nor did he intend to allow false empirical judgments into public reasoning.[24] So if public reason leads to false judgments that are not the result of misapplying 1 or 2, then it must be because of the falsity of 3, the values and principles of liberal and democratic justice relied upon. But what reason do we have to believe that these values and principles are false? This question cannot be settled within public reason, for it takes these values as given. The question would have to be settled on the basis of argument among comprehensive views — those endorsing liberal and democratic values versus those advocating non-liberal and non-democratic values. Rawls believed justice as fairness, presented as a comprehensive Kantian doctrine as in A *Theory of Justice*, is closer to moral truth, or what is most reasonable, than any other comprehensive doctrine of justice. Raz, Dworkin, and other liberals endorsing different comprehensive liberal views think otherwise. But according to Rawls, there is nothing about liberal comprehensive views that would prevent their agreeing upon a liberal political conception that provides content to public reason, and this political conception will be true, assuming that *any* true comprehensive doctrine (whether Rawls's, Raz's, Dworkin's, or anyone else's) endorses the same principles.

---

24. Compare Rawls's claim regarding the original position: "Since principles are consented to in the light of true general beliefs about men and their place in society, the conception of justice adopted is acceptable on the basis of these facts" (*TJ*, 454/398 rev.).

These remarks go some way towards responding to certain criticisms of Rawls and others who rely upon a moral idea of reasonableness and reciprocity in justification. Joseph Raz particularly objects to (1) the idea of justification *to* a person (which I address in the next section), and (2) the claim that we can have any basic obligation to justify the exercise of political power to people with false beliefs about values and the origins of justice and political authority (which would include many if not all people with religious beliefs, for example). Raz contends that the mere fact that people conscientiously believe something does not provide them with reasons for anything. "Our reason is that, as we see it, things are so and so. Naturally, we may be wrong" (DP, 28). But if our beliefs are false, then we cannot have reason to act upon them, even though we believe we do. But if this is so, then the fact that others conscientiously believe something does not provide them with reasons, nor should they expect it to provide us with reasons either.[25] If so, Raz contends, it is far from obvious to what degree we should defer to others' judgments and aim for consensus. It may be important to justify political authority to people with false moral and metaphysical convictions, to bring them to understand its bases and get them to agree, but deferring to consensus should not be allowed to structure the idea of political justification or provide a basis for political legitimacy. For Raz (and many others), political justification is like justification of any other kind in that it involves, not reasonable agreement but showing propositions and principles to be true. To justify moral principles to people with false values is to show them the truth of those principles and the falsity of their values. Moreover, public reason consists only of true reasons. No principle or value that is false can provide anyone with a reason for doing anything.

It is arguable whether or not false beliefs can provide reasons for people with those beliefs. J. S. Mill's account of individuality suggests that if our values and beliefs are the product of a freely chosen plan of life that fits our "character" and is arrived at after critical reflection, then we may have more reason to act on them than we do the true values imposed on us by the dead hand of custom. Knowing and acting on true judgments is not an absolute value or reason that trumps all others. Second, while the false beliefs of others clearly do not provide us with reasons to follow them in doing what those false beliefs dictate, still, we can be under a stringent duty and have sufficient reasons to respect others following the dictates of their false convictions, particularly if they involve freely chosen values of great importance to a person. Respecting others as persons and as citizens involves allowing them to non-coercively decide their values and (within limits of justice) act on their chosen ways of life. This moral requirement implies a duty to allow others to make their own mistakes of judgment and action, and, within limits of justice, act on their false beliefs as well. We do not respect others as persons by insisting that they only act according to the true view about the comprehensive good, and we surely do not respect them if they are coercively required to observe only what we or the government *believes* are true comprehensive values.

25. Raz says: "If I do not think that the fact that I hold a view is a reason for me to follow it, why should I think that it is a reason for others?" (DP, 28).

But from the perspective of citizens with different comprehensive views, this is how the public political enforcement of any comprehensive doctrines appears, whether it be the purported truths of religion, or the purported truths of autonomy and individuality. It may be true that respect for persons does not require respect for their false views (DP, 43). Still, respect for persons as citizens does require allowing them to form and act on their false views so long as they are within limits of justice. Where someone is coercively forced to act according to the requirements of a comprehensive conception of values that person rejects, freedom of conscience and equal political liberty has been violated. It is "unreasonable force" to insist that one's comprehensive view prevail when constitutional essentials and basic justice is at stake (see *PL*, 247).

Raz and others who endorse liberal comprehensive doctrines would surely reply that their doctrine does allow people to act upon their false beliefs. What is rejected is the political liberal idea that controversies over values, and therewith false comprehensive doctrines, should in *any* way be allowed to affect the standards for the legitimacy of constitutions. The correct standard for legitimacy is not whether purportedly reasonable people with conflicting reasonable comprehensive views endorse or reasonably can endorse the constitution but whether the constitution itself meets independent standards that are true. Disagreement in politics is of no substantive importance in determining standards of justification and legitimacy. Only truth can justify and only truth can bestow legitimacy (see DP, 40–43).

I have already discussed above why it is mistaken to understand Rawls's account of public reason as if it allowed false comprehensive doctrines and values to determine or even influence standards of public reason, political justification, and political legitimacy: public reason derives its content from a liberal political conception that is freestanding of all comprehensive doctrines. Moreover, this is not the place to discuss and compare Raz's own complicated account of reasons and justification in ethics.[26] Still, it should be noted that Raz's disputes with Rawls evidence deep differences regarding the nature of reasons and of justification, and their relationship to the requirements of liberalism. For Rawls, political justifications in terms of public reasons (as opposed to justifications in terms of comprehensive liberal doctrines) are required to respect liberty of conscience and the political autonomy and independence of democratic citizens. In the context of political liberalism, to knowingly act on the truth (even if we could know the whole truth) of the correct comprehensive (liberal) doctrine (as opposed to what one believes is the true doctrine) is still not such a fundamental value that it trumps all others, particularly the values of political reasonableness and the freedom and equality of citizens. What is really distinctive about Rawls's political liberalism is that certain moral values are conceived as determining not just the kinds of reasons political officials can appeal to in political justification but also independent standards of justification, objectivity, and validity that apply within the domain of the political. Political liberalism extends Rawls's earlier idea of the "independence of moral theory" from epistemology and metaphysics

26. See Joseph Raz, *Engaging Reason* (New York: Oxford University Press, 1999).

(which includes for Rawls any account of truth).[27] Standards of moral justification, moral objectivity, and correctness of moral judgments are regarded as different from standards appropriate for the sciences and other theoretical disciplines. What is behind this?

For Kant, the values of moral and rational autonomy imply that reason can be the source of its own principles of action (reason "legislating" principles for itself), and that these principles are not therefore imposed upon reason and the will by an independent metaphysical or moral order. In order that moral agents may realize their autonomy, standards for moral justification, objectivity, and correctness ("universal validity") of moral judgments must conform to the moral (not just theoretical) requirements of practical reason. Rawls "demythologizes" Kant's account of pure reason and the a priori and then extends Kant's basic idea. "The independence of moral theory" (CP, 286) means that moral philosophy is independent from the problems of metaphysics and epistemology: a moral concept's soundness does not depend upon metaphysical accounts of free will or personal identity, or the conditions of theoretical truth, for example. Political liberalism goes one step further than this: it means that a significant part of morality—"the domain of the political" (PL, 38)—is independent, not just of epistemology and metaphysics, but of comprehensive moral conceptions as well (including Kantian morality and the value of moral autonomy). For Rawls, *political autonomy* requires that democratic citizens "legislate" principles for themselves, meaning that they should be able, as reasonable citizens, to understand liberal principles of justice as given to themselves by themselves in their capacity as free and equal citizens, and endorse and act from these principles out of a sense of justice.[28] This is a moral ideal of citizens in a democratic society shared by reasonable and rational citizens. But for this moral ideal to be possible, the standards for political justification and legitimacy must differ from those required by other domains of inquiry, including moral philosophy itself. For Rawls, prior to political liberalism, a conception of moral objectivity and valid moral judgment—judgment from an impartial perspective (the original position) that embodies "all the requirements of practical reason"—provides the standard for valid and correct moral judgments (or, if you will, moral truth). *Kantian constructivism* is Rawls's attempt to incorporate an ideal of the autonomy of reasonable and rational agents into the procedures for moral justification that issue in standards of moral truth (moral principles). In Rawls's political liberalism, an account of objectivity and objective reasons "politically speaking," and of reasonable political judgment provide the standard for correct (most reasonable) judgments of democratic justice (see PL, 110-116, 119-125). This account is cast in terms of agreement in judgments from an impartial perspective that embodies, not any longer "all the relevant

---

27. See Rawls, "The Independence of Moral Theory" (1975), in CP, 286–302.

28. See PL, 402. "Citizens gain full political autonomy when they live under a reasonably just constitution securing their liberty and equality, with all the appropriate subordinate laws . . . and when they also fully comprehend and endorse this constitution and its laws, as well as adjust and revise them as changing social circumstances require, always suitably moved by their sense of justice and the other political virtues" (ibid.).

requirements" of a philosophical conception of practical reason (as in Kantian constructivism), but the basic ideals and requirements of public democratic reason that all reasonable and rational citizens presumably share (*PL* 90, *LP*, 86–87, 86 n33). *Political constructivism* seeks to represent an ideal of the political autonomy of free and equal citizens in the objective procedures for political justification that issue in the standards for "political truth," or what is most (politically) reasonable. It is in order to fully realize the ideal of the political autonomy of free and equal democratic citizens that Rawls sees it as necessary to establish an account of political justification and public reasons, as well as the political legitimacy of democratic constitutions and laws, independent of conceptions of the truth of comprehensive doctrines (including even comprehensive moral doctrines, or comprehensive liberal doctrines of justice).

V. Reasonable Persons, Liberal Legitimacy, and Political Justification

I've argued, in response to Joseph Raz's objection, that public reason and the liberal political conceptions that provide it with content are not influenced by false comprehensive doctrines, even when political conceptions are endorsed by religious and philosophical doctrines with false views. Rather, public reason and its political conceptions gain their content from ideas and values implicit in democratic culture. In this section and the next, I emphasize how reasonableness for Rawls is primarily a moral-political category, and that what is politically reasonable is to be determined from the "public point of view" of reasonable and rational free and equal citizens, and not from the point of view of any (nonpublic) reasonable comprehensive doctrine (*PL*, 384 n. 16). This means that one has to be very careful not to import a particular philosophical account of "reasonableness" into political liberalism that is at odds with public reason itself. To illuminate this aspect of Rawls's view, I address here some further arguments Joseph Raz makes against Rawls.

A. *The Liberal Principle of Legitimacy*. Raz criticizes the following principle which he seems to attribute to Rawls: "A political authority is legitimate only if its authority is established by a principle which all people are committed to accepting by their current views, whatever they are, provided only that they are reasonable" (DP, 33). Legitimate political authority is, then, to be based on the agreement of reasonable comprehensive views of people, or at least agreement among people holding reasonable views.[29]

Here Raz objects that the agreement of those who hold unreasonable views should count too in determining the legitimacy of authority, since "their life and well-being are of moral consequence" (DP, 33). Contractualists will reply, he

---

29. This implies, Raz says, that "the legitimacy of a political authority comes to an end when the principles on which it is based no longer enjoy the agreement of all the reasonable. This makes the principle very demanding" (DP, 33n). Here it is clear from the context that Raz means "reasonable views" rather than "reasonable person."

continues, that the liberal criterion of legitimacy is based in respect for rational self-directing agents as such. Agents who hold unreasonable beliefs are unreasonable, and thus do not respond to reason as they should. Hence (the contractualist concludes), "The reason for treating people as rational self-directing agents does not apply to them." (DP, 34). But this reply, Raz says, does not respond to his objection, for it refers to the reasonableness/unreasonableness of people, whereas the contractualist criterion for legitimacy refers to the reasonableness of belief. It is not true that people with unreasonable beliefs are all unreasonable people. Unreasonable people are "unyielding," or unresponsive to reason and evidence. Beliefs, however, are unreasonable "if they are, in relation to all the evidence available to the experts, patently false" (ibid.). Reasonable people can have unreasonable beliefs if that is all they have been exposed to (e.g., those creationists who have only been exposed to creationism might be reasonable people). Likewise unreasonable people can have reasonable beliefs for the same reason.[30] This shows that "one cannot take the rejection of any proposition as in itself strong evidence that the agent is unreasonable (in the sense that this is a cognitive vice)." Raz concludes that the contractualist criterion for political legitimacy "has no political teeth" (DP, 36). For, "there is no proposition which has currency in Western societies and which some people in them could not reasonably accept" (DP, 37). As Raz suggests later, "Any convinced anarchist, or indeed anyone else who has a principled objection to the current government, [has] a veto on its legitimacy" (DP, 40).

This argument has two major shortcomings: it misreads Rawls's principle of legitimacy, and it relies on Raz's (not Rawls's) definition of "reasonable." First (the question of how to understand "reasonable" aside), Rawls's principle does not say that political legitimacy is based on the agreement on principles by all reasonable views or doctrines, or agreement by all reasonable persons, or even agreement by all persons (even reasonable persons) holding reasonable views or doctrines. It says: "The exercise of political power is legitimate only when it is exercised in fundamental cases in accordance with a constitution, the essentials of which *all reasonable citizens as free and equal might reasonably be expected to endorse*" (PL, 393; emphases added). This indicates that political legitimacy depends upon acceptance *from a particular standpoint*, that of reasonable and rational free and equal citizens (guided by certain fundamental interests). The principle's focus, then, is on (politically) reasonable persons who are defined in a certain way—not (as Raz says) on any person who holds reasonable views. Which principles are acceptable to people who have reasonable views or subscribe to reasonable doctrines is simply not Rawls's criterion of legitimacy. Nor is political legitimacy determined by the consensus of reasonable views or doctrines

---

30. Raz says that Rawls's moral definition of a reasonable person—as one who has the belief and disposition of valuing willing cooperation above all other virtues or values—does not help here either; for, as a belief or character trait, it "is not one which has any bearing on the intellectual virtues." It may turn out that a person who is reasonable in Rawls's sense is unreasonable, cognitively speaking, and vice versa (DP, 36). This shows, Raz says, that Rawls misapplies his own test of legitimacy.

themselves, or even of reasonable persons judging from the standpoint of their reasonable views; (politically) reasonable persons holding reasonable views may in fact reject laws that are politically reasonable and legitimate. Conscientious liberal Quakers, for example, may reject all war, even if in self-defense or to protect human rights. But this does not deprive a just war of its legitimacy for Rawls (PL, 393–94). The important point is that political legitimacy, like political reasonableness, both are to be decided from the public point of view of reasonable democratic citizens.

In regarding political legitimacy as agreement on principles by all reasonable views or persons holding reasonable views, Raz appears to confuse political legitimacy with the idea of an overlapping consensus. But overlapping consensus is a standard for stability, which is different from political legitimacy. The political legitimacy of a constitution is a precondition of its stability "for the right reasons" (PL, xlii). In effect, Rawls's idea of an overlapping consensus is a conjecture that all reasonable doctrines in a well-ordered constitutional democracy can endorse, each for their own particular reasons, only those constitutions based on political conceptions that meet the liberal principle of legitimacy. If they can, then a legitimate constitution is stable, not as a compromise or modus vivendi but "for the right reasons," namely, for the moral reasons endorsed by each reasonable view. On the other hand, if too many reasonable views cannot endorse a legitimate constitution, then legitimate liberal authority may be unstable. Then the question becomes whether it is possible for a just constitution to endure. But whether or not a reasonable doctrine departs, in whole or part, from acceptance of the liberal political conception and is no longer in an overlapping consensus, this does not deprive the constitution or laws of their legitimacy. It is simply not true that Raz's argument has shown that "any of the views, ideologies, philosophies, religions, or what not which have currency in that society should vindicate the principles of the constitution, or else they lack legitimacy" (DP, 37).[31]

B. *The Idea of a Reasonable Person.* To make the argument that Rawls's principle of legitimacy allows most any ideology or misfit in society to defeat government's legitimacy, Raz imports his own definition of "reasonable person" and "reasonable belief" into his argument; these underlie his contention that reasonable people (those responsive to reason and evidence) can have most any unreasonable ("patently false" [DP, 34]) belief, and unreasonable people can have any reasonable belief. Perhaps they can on Raz's purely cognitive account of "reasonable," but this is not Rawls's specification of the concept of a reasonable person. While cognitive reasonableness to some degree (responding to evidence, making logical inferences, etc.) must be presupposed

---

31. This misreading of Rawls's principle of legitimacy underlies Raz's extraordinary claim that under this principle, the anarchist can deprive any government of legitimacy, and even "the state has no authority over the fanatical murderer. It does not even have authority to defend people against him" (DP, 40). Clearly, anarchists and fanatical murderers are unreasonable people with unreasonable views in Rawls's sense. Their actual or hypothetical consent is not required or relevant for any of Rawls's purposes.

in Rawls's account (otherwise people could not think clearly),[32] the characteristics of *politically* reasonable persons Rawls designates are mainly moral
characteristics: a willingness to cooperate on fair terms; having a reasonable
moral psychology, including a sense of justice; appreciating and accepting the
implications of the burdens of judgment for social life, and so on. Given these
characteristics, it is simply not true that a reasonable person can accept most
any proposition, or that the rejection of any proposition is not evidence that a
person is unreasonable (DP, 36). Because of their moral-political convictions
and dispositions, reasonable persons in Rawls's sense are responsive to *public
reason* and not just to reason in a cognitive sense. There are all kinds of unreasonable propositions (in Raz's sense, and in Rawls's) which conflict with public
reason and which for this reason are not acceptable to politically reasonable
persons.[33] Raz's claim that the principle of legitimacy "has no . . . teeth" (DP,
36) does not apply to Rawls.

The same problem besets Raz's argument that being unreasonable and having unreasonable beliefs is not a moral defect that should exclude a person from
influencing what principles are legitimate. An absence of the characteristics and
beliefs of politically reasonable persons is decidedly a moral defect. Politically
unreasonable people are not willing to cooperate with others on fair terms; or,
they insist on politically enforcing what they believe to be "whole truth" even
though they know that others reasonably disagree; or, even worse, they do not
have a sense of justice or other moral dispositions. Anyone who has all these
characteristics and all they entail is deeply flawed morally: he or she has no
respect for others with different values or for their rights, and thus is hardly fit
for social life, at least not among people who do not think as he or she does. Of
course, the lives of politically unreasonable people, so described, should count
as much as anyone else's insofar as they have the same rights and liberties (so
long as they do not violate others' basic rights). But this does not imply that their
unreasonable views should be taken into account and accommodated within
public reason.

C. *The Bases of Legitimacy.* Is Rawls's principle of legitimacy designed
so as to achieve respect for rational self-directed agents as such (as Raz suggests)? Here it is more accurate to say that it is (in part) directed to achieving the political autonomy of free and equal democratic citizens, when seen
as politically reasonable and rational. Political liberalism aspires to discover a
basis for social cooperation and the exercise of political authority that is freely
acceptable to reasonable democratic citizens. If we see the principle of legiti-

---

32. Here it is relevant that Rawls says that standards for what are to count as politically reasonable judgments within public reason are informed by the guidelines for inference, evidence and judgment that are part of public reason, as well as "criteria and procedures of commonsense knowledge
and . . . the methods and conclusions of science when not controversial" (*Restatement*, 91–92).

33. Indeed there are many reasonable propositions in Raz's sense, and reasonable doctrines in
Rawls's sense, which are not acceptable to public reason, and which (Rawls's) reasonable citizens will
not insist on as a basis for their political relations, even though they may believe them true.

macy in this way, then Rawls's principle—unlike the principle Raz attributes to him—quite readily converges with the argument (summarized above) Raz attributes to contractualists for excluding unreasonable persons from the test for political legitimacy. The reason the agreement of politically unreasonable persons is not necessary, or even desirable, for political legitimacy of principles is that, as unreasonable, they are not simply unyielding in their judgments but are also intolerant of other reasonable comprehensive views and the reasonable persons who endorse them. So most anything politically unreasonable people might agree to regarding constitutional essentials and basic justice could not be justified to reasonable and rational citizens endorsing reasonable views or comprehensive doctrines.

D. *Political and Public Justification*. Rawls says, "Public justification is not simply valid reasoning, but argument addressed to others" (*CP*, 594). Raz questions the idea of justification to a person. "The claim is that a condition of legitimacy is that the principles on which the constitution is founded can be justified to the people who are supposed to be subject to them. Does that mean more than that the principles of the constitution are justified?" (DP, 37) He argues that it cannot, citing a number of reasons: (1) justifications are not "inherently private" or addressed to specific people, as the contractarian position implies, but "are in principle publicly available" (ibid.). (2) Some people are not capable of understanding justifications of authority, due to limited mental capacities, or mistaken ideologies, or misguided religious beliefs (DP, 38); and (3) justifications do not have to be articulated to be known and understood, and, in any case, "full articulation of the justification of authority is impossible in practice" (DP, 39).

To adequately respond to this objection would require a discussion of Raz's more general argument against contractarianism, put forth elsewhere, as well as his alternative conception of reasons and justification, which are themselves quite complicated. But at least it should be emphasized that Rawls's idea of justification does not imply addressing arguments designed to convince people whatever their circumstances, capacities, beliefs, and desires. What Rawls calls "political justification" (which is part of "public justification") does not even require justification to reasonable people in the terms of standards set by their reasonable comprehensive views. Rather, political justification is addressed to persons seen as reasonable and rational and in their capacity as free and equal citizens. Moreover, it is framed in terms of the political values of justice and of public reason. On this understanding of political justification, some (if not all) of the criticisms Raz directs at Rawls are wide of their mark. For example (in response to 1 above), on Rawls's account political justifications *are* inherently public, for they are addressed to persons who occupy the "public point of view" of reasonable democratic citizens. Moreover (in response to 2), they are not tailored to meet the limited capacities, mistaken ideologies, or particular interests people have, but address them *as* reasonable and rational democratic citizens with an interest in developing and exercising the moral powers needed to engage in social cooperation, and an interest in pursuing some politically permissible conception of the good.

To appreciate better what Rawls means by "justification to persons," it may help here to look to his late article "Reply to Habermas" (*PL*, 393). Here Rawls distinguishes three kinds of justification at work in political liberalism: (1) *Political justification* is justification *to* persons in their capacity as reasonable democratic citizens with interests in developing and exercising their moral powers; it is justification in terms of public reasons and hence relies on political values and their ordering in terms specified by a freestanding political conception of justice. Political justification is, in this manner, *pro tanto*, Rawls says; it does not take into account all moral and other values, as they might be ordered by a reasonable comprehensive doctrine. (2) *Full justification*, Rawls says, "is carried out by an individual citizen as a member of civil society" (*PL*, 386). Full justification is justification *to* a person in terms of his or her reasonable comprehensive doctrine. In full justification a reasonable person incorporates the political conception of justice that is *politically* justified into, and justifies it according to the terms of, his or her own reasonable comprehensive doctrine by bringing his or her judgments into reflective equilibrium. This is a task left to citizens themselves, together with others who affirm the same reasonable comprehensive doctrine. "The political conception gives no guidance in such questions, since it does not say how non-political values are to be counted. This guidance belongs to citizens' comprehensive doctrines" (*PL*, 386–87). Notice that while there are as many full justifications as there are reasonable comprehensive doctrines, full justification is not justification to persons whatever their subjective dispositions and whatever values they may affirm. Rawls's philosophy does not envisage "justification to a person," regardless of his or her aims or intelligence or subjective point of view. Justification, for Rawls, is always in terms of certain objective interests individuals have and for reasons that stem from one or another conception of the person or comprehensive doctrine. A full justification addresses reasonable and rational persons who occupy the standpoint, and affirm the values and ideals, of one or another reasonable comprehensive view. Moreover, while full justifications involve justifications of the political conception according to the terms of reasonable comprehensive doctrines that are not wholly true—"mistaken view(s)" as Raz says (DP, 32)—the falsities affirmed by doctrines do not influence or affect the truth or reasonableness of the freestanding political conception itself (as discussed in the previous section).

Finally, there is (3) *public justification*, a condition of public justification of the political conception of justice is that it stands in full justification (or reflective equilibrium) within all reasonable comprehensive doctrines endorsed in society. There is, then, a reasonable overlapping consensus among reasonable comprehensive doctrines (*PL*, 388). Given an overlapping consensus, each citizen can aver to others that the reasonable comprehensive doctrine he or she endorses both incorporates and justifies (in terms characteristic of each reasonable doctrine) the liberal political conception that is recognized to be politically justified. "This mutual accounting shapes the moral quality of the public culture of political society" (*PL*, 387). It is the public knowledge of a reasonable overlapping consensus—citizens' awareness of the fact that each reasonable citizen has fully justified and embedded the political conception into his or her reasonable comprehensive view—that constitutes (for the most part) the public justification of the political conception (*PL*, 392).[34]

E. *Legitimacy and False Beliefs Revisited.* Finally, Rawls is clearer in his late works that there is a "family of reasonable political conceptions of justice" (*CP*, 581) that provide content to public reason, and which therefore play a role in political and public justification. These political conceptions are reasonable in that they all affirm the essential features of liberalism (that is, the basic liberties and their priority, and all purpose means for effective exercise of the basic liberties). But liberal political conceptions differ in several ways: how they specify the social minimum and equality of opportunity, determine the fair value of the political liberties, and assign significance to other political values of public reason.[35] "Reasonable political conceptions . . . do not always lead to the same conclusion; nor do citizens holding the same conception always agree on particular issues" (*CP*, 606). If so, then at most only one of these political conceptions can be completely true. But the fact that the other liberal political conceptions contain false beliefs to some degree (regarding how to set the social minimum, for example) does not imply that government officials, when they rely on them, are, as Raz contends, "inculcating" or "propagating" false beliefs among its citizens, certainly not knowingly, and even if unknowingly, then not any more so than any government or society inculcates false beliefs in its members when it allows for freedom of speech and discussion. Democratic citizens and government officials (legislators and often judges too) can always argue about and contest the laws and the correct understanding of constitutional provisions, and even the alternative liberal conceptions of justice that are appealed to in public reason to justify laws. What they cannot do, if they are to satisfy the moral (not legal) duty of civility, is contest liberalism itself, or provide reasons incompatible with a liberal constitution. It is true that public reason inculcates the values of a liberal and democratic constitution. But this is a problem only if liberal and democratic constitutions all embody false conceptions of justice. Only then would government officials in a constitutional democracy propagate and inculcate false beliefs in a way that

---

34. Two other aspects of public justification are stability for the right reasons and political legitimacy. Political legitimacy has been discussed. As for stability, when there is an overlapping consensus on the most reasonable political conception, society is effectively regulated by this conception, and public political discussions on constitutional essentials are reasonably decidable in terms of public reason as informed by the family of political conceptions, society is then "[stable] for the right reasons" (*PL*, 391). For, each citizen now endorses the governing political conception not as a compromise but because it expresses the conception of justice that is best justified according to his or her own reasonable comprehensive doctrine (ibid.). In the terms used in *A Theory of Justice*, the right is then *congruent* with each citizen's good, as determined by her rational plan of life and the reasonable comprehensive doctrine she endorses. See generally, *TJ*, sec. 86.

35. Rawls seems to hold that liberal political conceptions endorse roughly the same basic liberties, those "familiar from constitutional democratic regimes" ("Overlapping Consensus," in *CP*, 440, 440n.). See also *PL*, xlviii–xlix, 6; *CP*, 581. Rawls also says that liberal political conceptions all endorse ideas of citizens as free and equal persons, and of society as a fair system of social cooperation over time, yet interpret these ideas in different ways (*CP*, 582).

should cause serious concern from the perspective of the true comprehensive view. But since Raz endorses liberalism and democracy, this is not a problem that he is concerned about.

VI. The Completeness of Public Reason

Is the idea of public reason feasible? That is, is public reason up to the task of providing a basis for public justification in all, or nearly all, issues regarding constitutional essentials and basic justice? One common objection to the idea of public reason is that it is not very deep, insufficient to deal with all the political issues it must to serve as a basis for constitutional argument.[36] It is said that, because people have such different comprehensive views in a liberal democracy, there is little hope of their agreeing on values and principles to the degree needed to resolve many highly disputed constitutional issues. The problem of abortion is often brought up in this connection. Many say that to resolve this problem, officials and citizens have to appeal to comprehensive views to interpret the scope of basic constitutional liberties and other abstract liberal principles they all agree on.

Here it should be emphasized that public reason gains its "content" from a political conception of justice. One of the main roles of political conceptions of justice is that they enable public reason to be complete. In the absence of a political conception, public justification cannot be carried through and the duty of civility remains unfulfilled—we could not then provide justifications that others could reasonably accept in their capacity as free and equal citizens.

But the fact that political conceptions provide content to public reason may not adequately respond to the objection; it only states, but does not show, that public reason actually is capable of providing satisfactory arguments for all constitutional essentials and questions of basic justice. It is hard to see how one could satisfactorily answer this broadside objection without first trying to work out in some detail resolutions to constitutional disputes by relying solely on public reason (cf. PL, 395). One question the objection raises, however, is, What *is* a complete resolution of a constitutional dispute (for example, regarding abortion rights) which can be addressed solely in terms of public reason? Clearly, a complete resolution cannot be a general consensus, for that is hardly if ever to be had for any significant constitutional dispute. For Rawls, a complete resolution is not even one that every reasonable person accepts on the basis of his or her reasonable comprehensive doctrine. Again, such a resolution may not be possible for many issues under any circumstances. Instead, for Rawls, a resolution regarding a constitutional essential is always a political resolution: it is one that is framed in terms of political values of public reason and is an argument to a conclusion

---

36. See, for example, Kent Greenawalt, *Private Consciences and Public Reasons* (New York: Oxford, 1995), 106–20, 160; *Religious Convictions and Political Choice* (New York: Oxford, 1988), 183–87 (cited in text as RC).

which reasonable persons in their capacity *as* democratic citizens can reasonably expect other citizens in the *same* capacity reasonably to accept.

Two questions need to be kept separate here. First, there is the question of whether public reason is capable of *politically* resolving a constitutional essential such as the abortion issue, in terms of the political values of public reason and without appealing to comprehensive reasons and doctrines. Second, there is the question whether all reasonable citizens affirming reasonable comprehensive doctrines can accept the political resolution provided by public reason on the basis of their comprehensive doctrines. We have seen that the first question is to be addressed in terms of public reasons and political values that address the circumstances and interests of free and equal citizens. In response to the first question, Rawls gives an example of the kinds of public reasons that need to be taken into account in politically resolving the abortion dispute (suggesting that other political values may also be relevant) (*PL*, 243 n. 32). Among the political values relevant to abortion are due respect for human life, women's freedom and equality, and society's interests in the family and the ordered reproduction of liberal society over time. He says that a reasonable balance of these and other relevant political values does provide a politically reasonable answer—one satisfactory to reasonable persons in their capacity as free and equal citizens—to the question whether women should have a right to abortion at some stage of pregnancy. The answer, he believes, justified on the basis of these political values, is that women should have such a right during the first trimester. It may be that he would be open to the suggestion that a longer term, perhaps even a somewhat shorter term, is also politically reasonable. But Rawls says that to afford women no right whatsoever to abortion is unreasonable. Presumably, he says this because to refuse to recognize a right to abort under any circumstance is to give absolute weight to one political value (respect for human life) at the expense of all others—and this is politically unreasonable. It is unreasonable since the reasonable balance of public reasons is to be determined by taking into account such considerations as the interests of citizens in maintaining the conditions of their freedom and equality, their higher-order interests in the moral powers, and other political values regarding the good of citizens. A reasonable balance of public reasons is not determined by taking into account the religious, philosophical, or moral values of people occupying one or another comprehensive view. And it is only by making that illicit move that one could assign absolute weight to respect for human life over all other relevant political values.

The important point here is that the question of the completeness of public reason regarding abortion depends upon whether there is a balance of political values that is satisfactory to reasonable persons in their capacity as free and equal citizens, in light of the political conception of justice they affirm. My own view is that, because Rawls recognizes a family of political conceptions providing content to public reason, there has to be more than one politically reasonable answer to this issue. "Reasonable political conceptions of justice do not always lead to the same conclusion; nor do citizens holding the same conception always agree on particular issues" (see *CP*, 606; see also *PL*, lvi). This means that, far from being incomplete (as Greenawalt contends), public reason is overdetermined insofar as it provides more than one politically reasonable answer to many constitutional issues.[37]

Now, the second question mentioned above is whether reasonable people, given the reasonable comprehensive doctrines they affirm, will in fact *accept* the politically reasonable resolution of the abortion problem as determined by a proper balance of public reasons. Perhaps some will not, even in a well-ordered society where all accept a liberal political conception. So it may be that there are some reasonable people who cannot accept the political resolution of the abortion issue in terms of public reason. They sincerely believe that the fetus is a (metaphysical and moral) person, at all or most stages of development; that to abort it is akin to murder; that since protecting the lives of persons is the most important human value, and murder the greatest wrong, it is morally and politically unjust for any government to permit abortions at any stage for any reason; and that they as individuals ought to politically reject (and perhaps even resist) abortion whatever the cost to themselves. In that case, a citizen is no longer able to fully affirm the politically reasonable resolution—one based in the political values of public reason—as a sufficient basis for resolving all constitutional essentials.

This may indeed happen, even in a well-ordered constitutional democracy governed by a liberal political conception endorsed by all reasonable doctrines. Rawls does not rule it out. The *main point*, however, is that the fact that some reasonable people or reasonable doctrines may not be able to accept the resolution of the abortion issue as determined by political values of public reason does not imply that public reason is incomplete or that it is incapable of resolving a constitutional essential or matter of basic justice. What it implies is that not all reasonable people or reasonable comprehensive doctrines are always capable of accepting the politically reasonable resolution to constitutional disputes provided by public reason.[38] Is this a problem for Rawls? It will be a problem only if, as a result of their inability to accept the political resolution by public reason for one or more constitutional issues (e.g., regarding abortion), they are led to reject public reason itself in all other cases. Then, those citizens and their comprehensive doctrine can no longer endorse a political conception of justice in an overlapping consensus with other reasonable comprehensive doctrines. Depending on how many citizens and how many reasonable comprehensive doctrines are in this position, it raises questions regarding the stability of the family of liberal political conceptions. But Rawls conjectures that, even though some reasonable comprehensive doctrines may not be able to accept the resolution to a disputed constitutional issue on the basis of public reason, still, in a just and well-ordered constitutional democracy, they will continue to endorse in the main the require-

---

37. Jon Mandle suggested this point to me with regard to abortion: there is more than one politically reasonable solution (which does not rule out there being a solution that is most reasonable).

38. In *Political Liberalism*, Rawls seems to say that for a citizen to reject the conclusions of public reason is to be politically unreasonable, but that "a comprehensive doctrine is not as such unreasonable because it leads to an unreasonable conclusion in one or even in several cases. It may still be reasonable most of the time" (*PL*, 244 n. 32).

ments of a liberal political conception and the deliberations of public reason. This mainly is all that is required for "stability for the right reasons," not that all reasonable doctrines and reasonable persons agree with all politically reasonable applications of the liberal political conception.

Rawls discusses just this kind of case. His example is Quakers, who are pacifists, and who, for religious reasons, reject all war, even when it is politically justified in a just society on the basis of public reason (see CP, 594 n. 57). On all other political issues but war, Quakers can endorse constitutional democracy and can abide by its legitimate laws decided on the basis of the political values of public reason. Rawls seems to say that, so long as they recognize it as legitimate law and accept the obligation not to violate the law, Quakers act properly when, through "witnessing," they express their dissent from public reason and laws allowing for just war, thereby letting other citizens "know the deep basis of their strong opposition" and "bear witness to their faith by doing so" (ibid.). In this connection, Rawls alludes to "the parallel case of Catholic opposition to abortion," and apparently sees religious witnessing against all abortions as appropriately expressed in the same way, even though it is not an expression of public reason but indeed opposes the conclusions of public reason. Both examples are appropriate exercises of freedom of speech, certainly in the "background culture," if not in the public political forum or by government officials executing their duties.

Amy Gutmann and Dennis Thompson's position, which in many respects resembles Rawls's,[39] disagrees with him on this point. "Politics cannot be purged of moral conflict" in their view (DD, 93). The "value of public reason" (DD, 67) is mainly expressed via a requirement of deliberative reciprocity, that "reasons must be mutually acceptable" (DD, 54) to equal citizens. But even given this principle of reciprocity, Thompson and Gutmann say that there are certain fundamental "deliberative disagreement[s]" — "conflicts in which moral reasons so deeply divide citizens that no resolution seems possible on any fair terms of cooperation" (DD, 73). Deliberative disagreements are "fundamental because citizens differ not only about the right resolution but also about the reasons on which the conflict should be resolved" (ibid.). The controversy over the legalizing of abortion is the paradigm case of a deliberative disagreement (DD, 74). In the case of deliberative disagreements like abortion, "government must take a stand on questions involving such disagreement, even if reciprocity . . . do[es] not determine the answer" (DD, 77). To resolve such disagreements, government officials and citizens must appeal to moral considerations that are not acceptable to one another. Here I assume they mean that officials as well as citizens are to decide in terms of their conscientious moral convictions, after considering all relevant reasons. But in so doing, they should practice an "economy of moral disagreement" (DD, 84), namely, "seek the rationale that minimizes rejection of the position they oppose" (DD, 84–85).

---

39. "When citizens make moral claims in a deliberative democracy, they [should] appeal to reasons or principles that can be shared by fellow citizens who are similarly motivated" to find fair terms of social cooperation. Amy Gutmann and Dennis Thompson, *Democracy and Disagreement* (Cambridge, MA: Harvard University Press, 1999), p. 55 (cited as DD in text).

Gutmann and Thompson's position differs from Rawls's in allowing appeals within the "public political forum" (Rawls's term) to moral values that he would see as belonging to comprehensive doctrines rather than the political values of public reason. In this regard, Gutmann and Thompson do not see public reason (in their sense of mutually acceptable reasons) as complete. I do not think that they would see public reason in Rawls's sense as complete or adequate to its task either. Why this is so, I am not sure. It may be that Thompson and Gutmann see the political values of public reason Rawls appeals to (respect for human life, equality of women, etc.) as insufficient to provide either or both (a) a constitutional solution to the abortion problem or (b) a satisfactory solution acceptable to all the parties in the abortion dispute. Some have argued that to provide either a constitutional solution or a mutually acceptable solution to the abortion dispute, the question of the metaphysical personhood of the fetus must be decided, or at least the fetus's moral status must be addressed politically, and decided one way or the other.[40]

This is just the sort of claim that Rawls hopes to avoid with the idea of public reason. While Rawls does not explicitly say so, I believe the best way to understand his position is as follows. Questions regarding the metaphysical personhood of the fetus, or its moral status as a being with interests, are not questions which are resolvable by public reason and about which free and equal citizens can reasonably agree. But it is not necessary to resolve them to address the constitutional issue of abortion and whether women have constitutional rights of choice at some stage of pregnancy. On political grounds of public reason, reasonable citizens can agree that no abortion rights at all are a severe restriction on women's freedom and their ability to function as equals in social and civic life. Moreover, there is no compelling case that the fetus is a person, constitutionally speaking. Applying standards of evidence consistent with public reason, the fetus, certainly in earlier stages, does not have the capacities of political personhood (the moral powers), even in an undeveloped state. This does not necessarily imply that, constitutionally speaking, the fetus is not a person; while having these capacities are clearly sufficient for constitutional personhood,[41] they may not be necessary. Still, there has to be *some* compelling case for the constitutional personality of the fetus if we are to limit altogether women's freedom to choose, and it has not

40. See Ronald Dworkin, *Life's Dominion: An Argument about Abortion, Euthanasia, and Individual Freedom* (New York: Knopf, 1993). Dworkin contends that the question of the personhood of the fetus should be avoided politically since it is so ambiguous (22–23). But he is clearly skeptical about the claim that the fetus is a person (112). He says the fetus prior to six months is incapable of having rights, since it is incapable of experiences, and therefore incapable of having interests (14–21). Moreover, he implies, the Supreme Court in *Roe v. Wade*, 410 U.S. 113 (1973), implicitly made such a decision in finding in favor of a right of abortion (chap. 4).

41. That possession of (a capacity for) the moral powers is sufficient for constitutional personhood takes care of the ridiculous argument which says: "For pro-choice advocates to question the personhood of the fetus is just like supporters of slavery questioning the personhood of slaves." The correct reply is that clearly slaves do possess the moral powers and deserve to be treated as persons under the Constitution, and it is not at all clear—indeed all the empirical evidence is to the contrary—whether fetuses do.

been—and it is not clear how it could be—established in terms satisfactory to public reason.

Hence, the reason that women should have rights of choice is that there are substantial political values and interests—regarding women's privacy, their social and civic equality, and their freedom—that would be greatly burdened by an absence of rights of choice. Moreover, there is no indication or agreement that any undisputed constitutional person would be burdened by women exercising rights of choice. Given these substantial political values, the burden of proof—to make the case that there are sufficiently compelling public political reasons that justify burdening those political values and women's interests—should reside on the side of opponents to choice. That there are such burdens on women's interests should not be a point of dispute between pro-choice and anti-choice views, for these are political values of public reason acceptable to reasonable citizens. The disagreement, rather, is (or should be) over whether there are sufficient public reasons for entirely overriding those political values. The pro-choice argument is that there is no acceptable case within public reason for the constitutional personhood of the fetus, and that the political value of due respect for a form of human life during its gestation is not sufficiently compelling, for public political reasons, to *completely* outweigh the political values regarding women's political interests; therefore, there is no acceptable case for burdening women's privacy, equality, and liberty so completely as to deny any right of choice whatsoever.[42]

This is, I believe, a better way to understand the position the Supreme Court adopted in *Roe v. Wade*[43] than the position which contends that the Court did not and could not avoid the (metaphysical) question of the personhood of the fetus and indeed must have found that it was not a person. Of course, as Ronald Dworkin points out,[44] Justice Blackmun's argument from precedent—that the fetus is not a person within the terms of the Constitution because it has never been treated as such in law or under the Constitution—is not a satisfactory argument. The Court might have said the same thing (and probably did) about slaves before the Civil War Amendments, but clearly this would not be a political justification for perpetuating the injustice of slavery. Yet Blackmun might have gone on to say that, whatever its metaphysical or moral status according to the most reasonable comprehensive doctrine, the fetus is not protected by equal protection or the

---

42. I am grateful to Joshua Cohen for providing this argument in correspondence, and for the idea that Rawls does not have to deny the constitutional personhood of the fetus to argue in favor of a constitutional right to choose. As Cohen said in the same correspondence, the general point is that the pro-choice and the anti-choice positions are not symmetrical. The uncontroversial burdens placed upon women by a ban on abortion, and the lack of any obvious constitutional person who is burdened by abortion, establish an asymmetry that imposes a special argumentative burden on the anti-choice position, which it cannot meet in terms of public reason.

43. 410 U.S. 113 (1973).

44. Dworkin made this point in discussion at the Fordham conference on Rawls (Rawls and the Law, Fordham University School of Law, November 7–8, 2003). In *Life's Dominion*, Dworkin seems to assign greater weight to precedent in establishing the claim that the fetus is not a constitutional person (see 109–12).

Due Process Clause protecting life, liberty, and property, since no acceptable justification has been provided within public reason for treating the fetus as a constitutional person.[45]

Now for the second question mentioned above—whether political values of public reason can provide a satisfactory solution, moral or political, to all reasonable persons. That, of course, will depend on the content of their reasonable comprehensive views and the priority they give to political values of justice. It may well be that many reasonable orthodox Catholics and Jews and theologically conservative Protestants in a well-ordered constitutional democracy will never be able to morally accept that the political right to abortion is justified on the basis of public reason. But this does not mean that they must reject public reason or even the political legitimacy of abortion rights.[46] Moreover, even if they *do* reject the moral and political legitimacy of abortion rights, it still does not mean they must reject the requirements of public reason in all other constitutional essentials and matters of basic justice. They are in the same position as Quakers who reject the politically liberal account of just war: even though they dissent from the conclusions of public reason on that particular issue, and see the law as itself unjust and not morally legitimate, this does not mean that they must reject the political legitimacy of the law or of the constitution. This, of course, will be decided by their reasonable comprehensive doctrine. But I conjecture that there are few reasonable opponents of abortion who are prepared to abandon democracy, or who, aware of the burdens of judgment, are prepared to abandon public reason and use whatever political means are available to legally enforce the demands of their comprehensive views.

45. I do not mean to claim here that my interpretation of *Roe v. Wade* provides a better "fit" along the lines of Dworkin's account of Law as Integrity than does his own reading, which sees the Court as appealing to comprehensive reasons. See Dworkin, *Life's Dominion* (New York: Vintage, 1994), chaps. 4–6. Law as Integrity would require that *Roe* be read in light of later abortion decisions, including *Planned Parenthood v. Casey*, 505 U.S. 833 (1992), and other constitutional privacy cases. In *Casey*, Justices O'Connor, Kennedy, and Souter appeal to the value of personal autonomy as a reason for upholding women's right to abortion (ibid., 851). This appeal to autonomy seems to be nothing more than an appeal to the liberty and equality of women to control their own lives unimpeded by legal restrictions on their reproductive decisions. As such, it is a legitimate public reason. But suppose O'Connor, Kennedy, and Souter meant autonomy in the full sense, as a kind of positive freedom that partially defines the human good, and that underlies the comprehensive liberalism of Kant, Mill, early Rawls, and perhaps Dworkin, too. On that reading of *Casey*, it may well be that the best way to understand the abortion decisions is that they do appeal to comprehensive values and perhaps even a metaphysical conception of personhood. But this would not undermine Rawls's view of a supreme court as an "exemplar of public reason" (*PL*, 231). Rather, it would mean that the U.S. Supreme Court, as it sometimes does, improperly (and perhaps unnecessarily) has gone beyond the strictures of public reason and appealed to comprehensive reasons, to justify a decision that is justifiable (or perhaps is not) purely on the basis of public reasons. Sometimes the best interpretation of constitutional law according to Law as Integrity may not accord with the political values of public reason. But I do not see how, by itself, this can be an objection to Rawls's account of public reason. Rather, it suggests that the Supreme Court has violated its role as the exemplar of public reason.

46. See "Public Reason Revisited," in *CP*, 607 n. 83. Here Rawls cites Governor Cuomo's lecture on abortion.

It is important to emphasize once again that Rawls's main concern in political liberalism is to show how a well-ordered constitutional democracy governed by a liberal political conception is politically legitimate and practicably possible, or "stable for the right reasons." He is not trying to argue, nor does he need to argue for his purposes, that all reasonable persons morally will agree on all the politically reasonable decisions reached by deliberations based on public reason. As we have seen, clearly some will not (Quakers and liberal orthodox Catholics). So the fact that public reason does not take into account all reasons that are relevant to deciding "the whole truth" regarding the moral permissibility of abortion should not raise serious problems for his account. Serious problems arise only if many reasonable comprehensive doctrines in a well-ordered constitutional democracy cannot endorse a liberal political conception in an overlapping consensus and accept as politically legitimate most (not necessarily all) of the deliberations and conclusions of public reason based on the family of liberal political conceptions.

Finally, Ronald Dworkin has raised an important question that I cannot fully address but that demands a brief reply. Dworkin says that the idea of public reason is not well-formed. His objection, as I understand it, is as follows.

Rawls says political officials and democratic citizens are under a duty of civility, to satisfy the criterion of reciprocity and give reasons for policies they support to others that they could reasonably accept. Suppose someone finds a comprehensive doctrine, such as Kant's or Mill's defense of liberty in terms of autonomy, not only reasonable but also persuasive. Or suppose, like Dworkin, one finds reasonable an argument for equality that begins with a view about the objective and equal importance of every human life going well—which is part of a comprehensive ethical position. What is there to prevent him from thinking that other reasonable people *could* reasonably accept the comprehensive position that he finds not only reasonable but persuasive? What prevents him from saying of such people: "Yes, if they are reasonable, they can accept this; maybe they won't, but they can"? Now, Rawls may reply that Dworkin is asking the wrong question; the question is not "Can they reasonably accept this as people, or from the point of view of their comprehensive view?" but "Can they reasonably accept it in their capacity as free and equal citizens?" But it is not clear if this limitation means anything. It may be that in his account of public reason, Rawls builds into the definition of free and equal persons that they are persons who demand and will offer only arguments of a certain kind. But that is not helpful. What is needed is an account of why the notion of justification to others as reasonable and rational and free and equal citizens prevents one from saying that citizens, if they are reasonable, could or should reasonably endorse this comprehensive position.[47]

To respond: it is important to recognize that for Rawls, the notion of reasonableness, like the notion of "reason," is itself constrained by political liberalism and the requirements of public political argument. The sense in which Dworkin

47. Here I rely on a transcription of Dworkin's remarks at the 2003 Fordham conference. See also Dworkin, "Keynote Address: Rawls and the Law," *Fordham Law Review* 72, no. 5 (2004):1387–1406.

and others contend that it is reasonable for other reasonable citizens to accept their comprehensive doctrines is not the sense of reasonableness used in political liberalism. To take a parallel case (suggested to me by Joshua Cohen): Pope John Paul II says in *Evangelium Vitae*[48] that we can know by reason that the fetus has the rights of a person from conception and that abortion is a crime. The empiricist and the Kantian deny this and also deny that we can know God's existence by reason. The empiricist, Kantian, and Catholic natural law theorist clearly have different views of reason, its operation, and its competence. But surely when the pope says that the pro-choice position is unreasonable—because reason tells us that life begins with conception—and that we can reasonably expect everyone, insofar as they are reasonable, to accept the anti-choice view, he is relying on a view about reason that cannot be part of a liberal *political* conception. The same is true of the empiricist's notion of reason and the Kantian idea of (pure) reason. Opponents of natural law (or of Hume's or Kant's views of reason and reasonableness) may be, in some comprehensive sense, "unreasonable," but they are not *politically unreasonable*.

The more general point here (and, again, I am indebted to Joshua Cohen) is that Rawls's idea of the domain of the political implies that we cannot generate the need for and requirements of a liberal political conception by starting "outside" political argument with a philosophical conception of reason and reasonableness. Reason and reasonableness themselves need to be given a moral-political interpretation in terms of what is appropriate to demand or expect of others in their capacity as democratic citizens. So Rawls specifies the ideas of *public* reason, and *political* reasonableness. When is someone being unreasonable, politically speaking? That is in part a matter of working out whether someone is offering and insisting on using considerations in political justification that are unsuited to the setting of justification addressed to free and equal persons with different reasonable comprehensive views. It is politically unreasonable for legislators, judges, and lawyers engaged in constitutional argument to rely on Catholic natural law doctrine in deciding whether women have a right to abortion. But the same is true of other comprehensive metaphysical and moral doctrines.

With this as background, let us consider now whether it is reasonable (as Dworkin contends) for those who accept one or another liberal comprehensive doctrine to expect that others endorse not only the same liberal political conception these doctrines support and their public political justification but also the comprehensive reasons (moral and rational autonomy, individuality, and so on) that Kant's, Mill's, Raz's, or Dworkin's liberal doctrines use to justify these liberal conceptions. It is perhaps *not un*reasonable to expect that they will. But this does not imply, and indeed it is wrong to say, that it is reasonable, *politically speaking*, to expect them to. For, to begin with, there are many other reasonable comprehensive doctrines justifying the same or similar liberal political conceptions that

---

48. John Paul II, *Evangelium Vitae*, Encyclical Letter on the Value and Inviolability of Human Life, 25 March 1995, secs. 2–3.

also would not be unreasonable for reasonable persons to accept.[49] But more to the point, to see why a reasonable democratic citizen could not reasonably expect other citizens to reasonably accept a doctrine of moral autonomy or Equality of Resources when framed as a comprehensive doctrine, we should look again to Rawls's definition of a reasonable person, and the aims and interests that guide reasonable persons' judgments from the public standpoint of free and equal citizens. First, reasonable persons want to cooperate with others on fair terms that other reasonable persons can willingly accept and abide by. (Among other things, reasonable persons do not want other reasonable people to feel unduly coerced in complying with the basic terms of their political system.) This implies living with others on terms that are justifiable to them (PL, 49). Moreover, reasonable persons appreciate and accept the consequences of the burdens of judgment—reasonable persons inevitably will differ in their reasonable comprehensive views. These features of reasonable persons suggest that reasonable persons will look for terms of cooperation that, so far as possible, do not rely on a particular comprehensive doctrine. For, if the terms of cooperation depend exclusively on comprehensive doctrines, then people with conflicting reasonable doctrines cannot *willingly* accept them (thereby contravening the first aspect of reasonable persons). Avoiding comprehensive doctrines is especially important given the further purpose for which liberal political conceptions are to be used. In addition to their role as terms of willing cooperation, a liberal conception also is to serve *as a basis of public and political justification* among reasonable citizens who endorse different and conflicting reasonable comprehensive views. Terms of cooperation that depend on a particular doctrine in order for their terms to be understood simply cannot serve this role.

This is where the idea of a political justification, as justification *to* persons in their capacity as free and equal citizens, becomes important. Reasonable citizens in a democratic society normally regard themselves and each other in this way in their political relations. They cannot agree on the "whole truth," or on the nature of truth or of reason. But the aim of a political justification is not showing-the-truth, as it is conceived by one or another comprehensive view. Rather, political justification addresses others in terms of their shared political self-conception, namely, as reasonable and rational democratic citizens. Democratic citizens have a rational interest in maintaining their status as free and as equals, and in developing and exercising the reasoning and other capacities (including the moral powers) which enable them to be cooperating members of a democratic society. They also have a fundamental interest in the social conditions within which they pursue their conception of the good. To justify terms of cooperation and provide reasons *to* people that they can reasonably accept *in their capacity as* reasonable and rational and free and equal citizens, is to provide them with

---

49. Rawls uses the concept of "not unreasonable" to denote a space between being reasonable and unreasonable. See, for example, *Restatement*, 184, 190; cf. *PL*, 74. Because of the burdens of judgment, it is not unreasonable for reasonable persons to endorse one or another reasonable comprehensive doctrine within a wide range.

reasons that are responsive to these fundamental interests they share. These public reasons express political values—the measures society and its citizens need to support, and social conditions that need obtain, if citizens are to realize these capacities and freely pursue their determinate conceptions of their good.[50]

This is how the idea of political justification, and reasonable acceptability to people in their capacity as reasonable and rational and free and equal citizens, differs from the idea of reasonable acceptability that Dworkin invokes in his criticism of Rawls above. Of course, it is still open to Dworkin to object that the constraints of public reason prevent him from making the best arguments for his position within the political forum (in democratic legislatures and the courts). The best arguments for a liberal political conception are provided, he will say, by his own liberal comprehensive doctrine and cannot be made solely in terms of public reason. But even if the comprehensive reasons Dworkin's account provides supply the best argument for liberal principles from the point of view of the "whole truth," still, from the perspective of other reasonable citizens who endorse different comprehensive doctrines (liberal Catholics, Kantians, utilitarians, and so on), these arguments do not appear to be the best, or even the most persuasive, arguments. They do not provide a justification *to* them, one that they can reasonably be expected to reasonably accept, either in their capacity as reasonable democratic citizens, or in terms of their reasonable comprehensive doctrines.

VII. Public Reason and the Courts

I conclude with some remarks on the relevance of Rawls's idea of public reason to the courts and legal reasoning. Rawls says that public reason is the reason of a supreme court and that a supreme court is the "exemplar of public reason" (*PL*, 231). He does not mean that the Supreme Court of the United States is an exemplar of public reason but rather that it belongs to the office of a supreme court, as such, to be the exemplar of public reason. Some might interpret this as undemocratic, since it seems to favor courts over democratically elected legislative bodies in interpreting the constitution. It is true that Rawls believes that a supreme court is "one of the institutional devices to protect the higher law" (*PL*, 233). But he does not say that a supreme court is necessary in all constitutional democracies. It is a contextual question to be decided for each society whether a supreme court is needed to protect constitutional essentials there (*PL*, 235). But where a supreme court is needed, it has final institutional authority to interpret the constitution. Then "the political values of public reason provide the Court's basis for interpretation" (*PL*, 234). "By applying public reason the court is to prevent that [higher] law from being eroded by the legislation of transient majorities" (*PL*, 233).

Does this protective role of a supreme court make the court antidemocratic? It makes it antimajoritarian with respect to ordinary law, but on the best under-

50. For a list of some of the liberal political values that serve as the basis for public reason, see note 11.

standing democracy is not simply majoritarian government. It is, most generally, a society of free and equal persons which is governed by a constitution that is the product of the constituent power of the people consisting of the body of free and equal citizens. This idealization of democracy incorporates not simply majoritarian legislative procedures but a substantive ideal of society and of a political constitution that is the product of the will of free and equal citizens. A supreme court, when it acts to uphold a democratic constitution, is not being antidemocratic. Though it may frustrate majority legislative will, "the court is not antimajoritarian with respect to higher law when its decisions reasonably accord with the constitution itself," as the expression of the constitutive power of a democratic People (PL, 234).

Rawls's account of a constitutional democracy will not satisfy proponents of majoritarianism and parliamentary democracy for whom judicial review is, by (their) definition, antidemocratic. But what about advocates of deliberative democracy, who also assign if not an exclusive role then the leading role for elected legislative representatives in interpreting the constitution? Cass Sunstein speaks for many when he says that it is not the role of the courts in a democracy to invoke abstract legal and political theories to justify their decisions. Judges lack "democratic pedigree," he says, and their political theories do not have democratic approval by the people. Democratic legislatures, not the courts, should be "the forum of principles."

> The American system is a deliberative democracy in which the system of electoral politics is combined with an aspiration to political reason-giving. The real forum of principle in American government has been democratic rather than adjudicative; consider the founding, the Civil War, the New Deal, and others–progressivism, the civil rights movement, the women's movement. . . . Fundamental principles are best developed politically rather than judicially.[51]

In saying a supreme court is the exemplar of public reason, Rawls is not saying that a democratic legislature cannot be relied upon to interpret the constitution and express public reason too. "A supreme court is not the only institution," he says, to give "due and continuing effect to public reason" (PL, 235 and n. 22). Public reason is to govern just as much the deliberations of legislative representatives as the reason of citizens when they vote on constitutional essentials and matters of basic justice. For Rawls, there is no inconsistency between deliberative democracy and a constitutional democracy with judicial review, even if a deliberative democracy may be required for public reason's appropriate expression, whereas a supreme court is not (see CP, 579). Still, what makes the Supreme Court the exemplar of public reason where it exists is that, while legislative representatives and citizens may vote their comprehensive views on non-essential questions, "public reason is the sole reason the court exercises. It is the only branch of government that is visibly on its face the creature of that reason and of

51. Cass Sunstein, *Legal Reasoning and Political Conflict* (Cambridge MA: Harvard University Press, 1996), 60.

that reason alone" (*PL*, 235). As such, a supreme court has a special educative role in a democracy. Judges, as judges, should have and express no other values than the political values of public reason as they are understood by a political conception of justice (cf. *PL*, 236–37).

We might agree with Sunstein's aspirations and still assign to the courts a significant role in expressing the democratic principles that the People have developed, legislatively and constitutionally. There is more to deliberative democracy, on any account, than simply legislative rule by officials elected subject to equal political rights and majority rule. Deliberative democracy has preconditions, including the institutions of public reason discussed earlier in section III. What makes a democracy deliberative for Rawls is that it is governed by public reason. This is the "ideal of public reason." But ideals are often not followed. Who is to attend to the preconditions of deliberative democracy and its public reason when elected representatives are corrupted by the influences of wealth and other particular interests? The courts can be an essential ingredient of deliberative democracy and interpreter of public reason in a nation like ours, with a federal system and diverse population that constantly generates democratic conflicts in understandings of the Constitution. Recognizing a supreme court as the exemplar of public reason does not displace elected representatives in their crucial role as interpreters of public reason. But legislators are not always prepared to give voice to public reason.

Of course, as Jeremy Waldron rightly argues, courts are not disinterested purveyors of public reason either. Sometimes they can be just as partisan as legislatures, with far more damaging consequences, since their decisions can be democratically overturned only by constitutional amendment.[52] The history of the Supreme Court of the United States often confirms Waldron's point, but it has not always acted in such a partisan manner, and for much of the past seventy years it frequently has acted compatibly with democratic justice and according to public reason. Whether this is sufficient to justify the institution in our history is a question better addressed by constitutional theorists and legal historians. But that there is a legitimate question at all belies Waldron's position, which is that judicial review is *never* justified in a democracy. If we see democratic lawmaking as justified when it serves democratic justice and do not identify the two as being one and the same, then I do not see how Waldron's argument that judicial review is never justified in a democracy can be sustained.

VIII. Conclusion: The Feasibility of a Well-Ordered Society of Justice as Fairness

It is often said that in *Political Liberalism*, Rawls increasingly departed from the two principles of justice and the egalitarian features of his view, that he came to doubt the difference principle, that he became more conservative. None of

52. See Jeremy Waldron, *Law and Disagreement* (New York: Oxford University Press, 1999), 255–81.

these claims is true. Rather than being a rejection of justice as fairness and its egalitarian aspects, political liberalism, and particularly "The Idea of Public Reason Revisited," is Rawls's final affirmation of justice as fairness. As Rawls states, political liberalism grew out of his concerns with the arguments for stability in A *Theory of Justice*. Because the congruence argument depended on everyone's adopting the same comprehensive doctrine in a well-ordered society of justice as fairness, the argument for stability of that conception relied upon an unrealistic assumption about people's philosophical, religious and ethical views.[53] Justice as fairness allows for the very conditions that encourage reasonable people to have different and conflicting comprehensive views, all of which are reasonable. The question then becomes: How can it realistically be assumed that justice as fairness might be generally accepted and endorsed and remain stable in a well-ordered society, where that conception of justice specifies the terms of social cooperation? Rawls's reply within political liberalism is: The conditions under which justice as fairness might specify a realistic conception of social cooperation that is generally endorsed by all reasonable people, who now have not only different and conflicting conceptions of their good but who also endorse different comprehensive doctrines, is a society in which justice as fairness (1) is conceived by citizens as a freestanding political conception of justice implicit in democratic values and culture; (2) is affirmed by all reasonable comprehensive doctrines in an overlapping consensus; and (3) allows the exercise of political power to be recognized by all as legitimate since this freestanding political conception is regularly appealed to in order to specify political values and provide the content of public reason.

Conceived this way—as a realistic account of the conditions under which justice as fairness might provide a stable basis for a well-ordered society—there is no dilution of the egalitarian elements of justice as fairness by political liberalism. Moreover, according to A *Theory of Justice*, justice as fairness is the most just liberal conception, and, according to *Political Liberalism*, it is also the most legitimate political conception, or, rather, it is the political conception that is most capable of providing legitimacy to the exercise of political power. What happens, however, once Rawls comes to accept (as he did in his last works) not only reasonable pluralism and reasonable disagreement in comprehensive doctrines but inevitable disagreements among reasonable democratic citizens and reasonable comprehensive doctrines about justice itself, even in a well-ordered liberal society? "These doctrines in turn support reasonable political conceptions—although not necessarily the most reasonable" (*CP*, 615). That there may be reasonable disagreement about justice in a well-ordered society is implicit in Rawls's claim that the forms of public reason are several and that a family of liberal political conceptions provide the content of public reason. The implication of this conclusion is far-reaching. For, it may mean that Rawls gave up on an idea which moved him from early on. This is the idea of a well-ordered society, defined as a society in which everyone publicly accepts the same conception

---

53. See *PL*, xix, 388 and n. 21; *CP*, 614. On the congruence argument and its problems, see chapters 5 and 6 of this volume.

of justice, and where this conception provides the basis for laws and political policies as well as public justification and agreement. The idea of a well-ordered society is significant for Rawls for several reasons. It is a society in which everyone can be seen as genuinely free and as legislators of the laws, since everyone freely accepts the constitution and endorses the public justification for laws and procedures which lead to them, compatibly with the conception of citizens as free and equal, reasonable, and rational. Because the constitution and the laws issue from a conception of justice that is constructed on the basis of citizens' conception of themselves as free and equal moral persons, a well-ordered society is, to this degree, a society in which all citizens can be said to be politically autonomous (and, if they endorse a liberal comprehensive doctrine, morally and rationally autonomous as well).

In suggesting that even under the best of conditions, where justice as fairness itself is in effect, there will be a pluralism not just of reasonable comprehensive doctrines but of liberal political conceptions of justice, Rawls appears to concede that a well-ordered society of justice as fairness is not feasible, at least not as originally conceived. For, a well-ordered society is defined as one where everyone publicly acknowledges and is motivated by the *same* conception of justice. But because of the burdens of judgment, this ideal is not practicable and is, by Rawls's own lights, unrealistic. The most that we can expect is a society where there is general acceptance by all reasonable people of *one or another* liberal and democratic political view (justice as fairness being among them) (cf. CP, 614–15). For Rawls, this must have been a difficult concession to have to make. It means that his original contractarian ideal of a society in which all reasonable and rational persons agree on the *most* reasonable principles of justice is beyond human capabilities. A just society in the fullest sense for Rawls—a well-ordered society conforming to justice as fairness that is stable for the right reasons—is not after all realistically possible. We can take consolation in the fact that something near-justice still is—a liberal society that satisfies the requirements of public reason and which "specifies the basic rights, liberties, and opportunities of citizens in society's basic structure" (CP, 615).

Part III

The Law of Peoples

8

The Law of Peoples, Social Cooperation, Human Rights, and Distributive Justice

I. Introduction

My aim in this essay is to discuss, and defend against some frequent objections, John Rawls's rejection of a global principle of distributive justice. As is well known, Rawls's *A Theory of Justice* argues for a principle of distributive justice, the difference principle, that is to be applied within different societies but not among them.[1] According to *A Theory of Justice*, each society has the duty to set up its economic and legal institutions in such a way that they make the least advantaged among its own members better off than the least advantaged would be if that society were structured according to any other distribution principle. But each society does not have a duty to structure its system so as to maximize the position of the least advantaged in the world at large. Though it is a universal principle that is to apply severally, or within every society, the difference principle is not global in reach, applying jointly to all societies simultaneously. To critics of many political persuasions, this seems a peculiar position. Why should principles of justice be domestically rather than globally applied?

Rawls's position in *A Theory of Justice* becomes even more complicated in *Political Liberalism* and *The Law of Peoples*, where he is guided by questions of political legitimacy and the feasibility (or "stability") of liberal regimes.[2] In *Political Liberalism* and later works,[3] Rawls appears to give up on the idea that a well-

1. John Rawls, *A Theory of Justice* (Cambridge, MA: Harvard University Press, 1971; rev. ed., 1999) (cited in text as *TJ*; sometimes referred to as *Theory*).

2. Rawls, *Political Liberalism* (New York: Columbia University Press, 1993; paperback edition, 1996, 2004) (cited in text as *PL*; references are to the paperback edition); Rawls, *The Law of Peoples* (Cambridge, MA: Harvard University Press, 1999) (cited in text as *LP*).

3. Here I have in mind particularly Rawls's last paper, "The Idea of Public Reason Revisited" (1997), in Rawls, *Collected Papers*, ed. Samuel Freeman (Cambridge, MA: Harvard University Press, 1999) (cited in text as *CP*).

ordered society of justice as fairness is feasible. (Such a well-ordered society is one where every rational and reasonable citizen affirms, for moral reasons, justice as fairness, including the difference principle.) The best we can expect of this world, he now seems to claim, are liberal and democratic societies in which all citizens recognize and accept the basic liberties and their priority, and the duty of society to provide a social minimum adequate to the exercise of the basic liberties. The social minimum need not be defined by the difference principle for liberal societies' economic systems to be politically legitimate and their laws worthy of respect.

It is this conception of the legitimacy of liberal regimes and of their economic distributions that underlies Rawls's account in *The Law of Peoples* of a "reasonably just Society of Peoples" (*LP*, 11). A just Society of Peoples is not (necessarily) a world in which all, or even any, of its member-nations structure their economies according to the difference principle. So long as a society provides for the basic needs of its citizens, respects their human rights, and is regulated by a common-good conception of justice, it is "decent" and has political legitimacy within the Society of Peoples and is to be tolerated and its independence respected by other peoples. There is no specific principle of distributive justice that must be met, either domestically or globally, within a just Society of Peoples. The difference principle simply drops out of the picture in Rawls's account of the Law of Peoples.

Oddly, perhaps, even within the Law of Nations that Rawls outlines in *A Theory of Justice* (*TJ*, sec. 58), Rawls held (or would have held) the same position. That is, even though, according to *A Theory of Justice*, each nation has a duty to realize the principles of justice in its basic institutions, the domestic justice of all member nations is not a condition of the justice of the well-ordered Society of Peoples. Moreover, Rawls still believed, when he wrote *Political Liberalism* and *The Law of Peoples*, that the difference principle defined the conditions of distributive justice for any and all societies; or at least it was for Rawls the ideal that societies should strive for. (This was part of his comprehensive liberal view.) However, being a just member of the Society of Peoples never meant for Rawls, even in *A Theory of Justice*, that a society must be fully just, especially not in its economic distributions of income and wealth among its members. For Rawls, it is simply not the role of peoples, individually or collectively, to enforce distributive justice anywhere except among their own peoples.

There are then two points of contention. First, Rawls, early and late, rejects the idea of a global principle of distributive justice, a principle of justice that is global in reach. The reference point for assessment of judgments of distributive justice is the "basic structure" of particular societies. This means we cannot know whether a person has his or her fair share of resources without knowing (at least) which society he or she is a member of and details about the basic institutions of that society. Second, Rawls holds that a society can be in good standing in a "reasonably just Society of Peoples" without complying with requirements of distributive justice, or for that matter, even respecting basic liberties, so long as it respects human rights.[4] How can the Society of Peoples be just if all its members are not just?

---

4. For Rawls, the human rights all persons have under the Law of Peoples are a subset of the basic liberties all societies should provide. "Among the human rights are the right to life (to the means

Many different kinds of objections have been raised against Rawls's position. Utilitarians (R. M. Hare, Peter Singer, et al.), libertarians (Robert Nozick et al.), communitarians, and others who reject the entire Rawlsian framework (Joseph Raz, John Finnis, et al.) claim that Rawls starts out by focusing on the wrong values and ideas. Then there are other critics who are more sympathetic to Rawls, insofar as they accept many of his ideas and the principles of justice. Their primary objection, in effect, is that Rawls goes astray by limiting the reach of the difference principle to the basic structure of society, thereby making membership within a particular society a condition for assessing claims of distributive justice. These critics contend that whatever reasons there are for applying a principle of distributive justice internally within a society must also justify its application to individuals all over the world. I want to limit my discussion here mainly to objections by these "Rawlsian cosmopolitans," as I call them. I cannot here defend the entire Rawlsian framework against its external critics. I do hope to argue, however, that the position is not guilty of some blatant or even subtle inconsistency, as Rawlsian cosmopolitans seem to suggest.

Finally, by way of introduction, many of the criticisms from all sides brought against Rawls assume current conditions, with all their injustices. For example, some critics claim that Rawls's Law of Peoples would allow for exploitation by private corporations of helpless people, or would permit conditions of peonage, apartheid, etc. Some also claim that it would allow for a government to impose egregiously unjust conditions on its people, such as ethnic cleansing, and anything short of slavery and forced servitude.[5] The problem with these sorts of objections is that they fail to recognize that the Law of Peoples is formulated to apply to ideal conditions (of a sort), among "well-ordered societies" all of whom are members of a "Society of well-ordered Peoples" (*PL*, 17–19). Well-ordered societies (both liberal and "decent") are societies where reasonable and rational members generally accept the governing principles of justice and terms of cooperation of their society, and rely upon these principles and terms in their public reasoning about justice. Moreover, these terms of cooperation comply with a conception of the common good according to which all members of society are benefited, and the members of society generally endorse this conception of the common good. (In a liberal society, the conception of the common good is largely defined by

---

of subsistence and security); to liberty (to freedom from slavery, serfdom, and forced occupation, and to a sufficient measure of liberty of conscience to insure freedom of religion and thought); to property (personal property); and to formal equality as expressed by the rules of natural justice (that is, that similar cases be treated similarly)" (*LP*, 65).

5. See Simon Caney, "Cosmopolitanism and the Law of Peoples," *The Journal of Political Philosophy* 10, no. 1 (March 2002): 95–123. He says: "Rawls's schema, thus, allows racial discrimination, the political exclusion of ethnic minorities, the forcible removal of members of some ethnic communities (that is, ethnic cleansing), the reduction of some to just above subsistence whilst other members of that society luxuriate in opulent splendor, and the perpetuation of grossly unequal opportunities and political power" (102). None of these accusations is correct, for these practices are unjust, according to Rawls's principles of justice, wherever they occur. Moreover, some of them violate human rights, and all are difficult, if not impossible, to reconcile with any reasonable common-good conception, which is a condition of decency of peoples.

a liberal conception of justice; in "decent hierarchical societies" [PL, 71], it is defined by some nonliberal moral conception.) These conditions virtually guarantee that apartheid, ethnic cleansing, and other egregious forms of discrimination will not be practiced in well-ordered decent societies. If Rawls's account of human rights does not prohibit such unjust practices (though I believe it does), then the implications of any common good conception of justice conjoined with the general acceptability of terms of cooperation within decent societies should prohibit them. (I assume here that those who suffer from apartheid and ethnic cleansing would not endorse the treatment they endure. Even if they did, however, it is practically impossible to conceive of a feasible conception of the common good that incorporates terms of apartheid and ethnic cleansing directed toward those who are supposed to benefit from these very same terms.)

One question I consider is whether these conditions and restrictions will be adequate to prevent the economic exploitation of poorer peoples by richer peoples or multinational corporations. I contend that just as liberal societies will not permit economic exploitation of their own citizens since it presumably makes them worse off than many alternative terms of cooperation, so a decent society that domestically enforces a common-good conception of justice will not allow foreign or multi-national corporations to take advantage of its members in exploitative ways. Moreover, there is plenty of room within Rawls's Law of Peoples for the Society of Peoples to limit exploitative economic dealings between private corporations and the political representatives of poorer peoples. Just because Rawls does not provide a principle of global distributive justice does not mean that unmitigated laissez-faire is the general rule of economic interaction within the Society of Peoples.

The Law of Peoples, then, is designed to apply in the first instance to hypothetical conditions among well-ordered liberal and decent societies, each of which has concern for the well-being of its own people and seeks their common good and respects others as free and equal peoples. Rawls did not envision the Law of Peoples as the sole element of the terms of cooperation that apply among peoples "in our world as it is with its extreme injustices, crippling poverty, and inequalities" (LP, 117). Under current conditions, we are in the realm of nonideal theory and partial compliance. Just as Rawls regarded preferential treatment as permissible as a means of transition to a just liberal society, but as inappropriate under conditions of a well-ordered liberal society that is just, so, too, nations in the contemporary world are in less than ideal conditions and may require special remedies as a means to establishing a well-ordered Society of Peoples. Similar considerations apply to Allen Buchanan's claim that Rawls's Law of Peoples suffers from a failure to address questions of secession. The Law of Peoples is not a general theory of global justice that is designed to address all the problems that arise in the contemporary world. Rather, it is set forth as part of political liberalism, to provide the principles of foreign policy for a well-ordered liberal society (LP, 9–10). Questions of secession simply do not arise within this setting; they are, again, problems that arise within nonideal theory. It is no more a problem with Rawls's Law of Peoples that it fails to address issues of secession than is its failure to address many other problems that arise within nonideal theory (for example, the problem of resolving boundary disputes, or a formula for deciding war reparations). Of course, it would have been wonderful had Rawls been able to tell us what he thought about rights of secession before he died, just as it would have been wonderful had he addressed many other political and moral issues. But Rawls's Law of Peoples cannot be dismissed or criticized for failing to address problems not within its intended purview.

II. Social Cooperation and Social Justice

The use of the term "distributive justice" to connote standards for assessing the distribution of income and wealth is relatively recent; it seems to have evolved out of the socialist critique of capitalism.[6] In *Anarchy, State, and Utopia*, Robert Nozick says that the term "distributive justice" is not neutral, since it suggests a central distribution mechanism that doles out a supply of resources to people and redistributes resources among people when their individual choices fail to match some principle.[7] Still, Nozick must have found the idea useful, since he entitles the central chapter in his book, covering eighty-three pages, "Distributive Justice." I will use the term "distributive justice" as neutrally as I can: namely, to designate moral standards for assessing ongoing methods of distribution of rights to income and wealth that are implicit in any economic system. It is the sense in which I believe that both Nozick and Rawls used the term. A principle or conception of distributive justice applies to all existing income and wealth within an ongoing system of production, exchange, and consumption. It specifies standards for deciding how and whether income and wealth are justly distributed among individuals—who should have rights to what and in exchange for what (if any) contributions. The difference principle, the principle of utility, and the equality principle are all distributive principles insofar as they cover all the economic resources that exist in any economic system. So, too, are Nozick's libertarian entitlement principles, according to which (very roughly) rights in things are fairly distributed only if they are transferred by market exchanges, gifts, bequests, gambling, or some other voluntary mode of transfer by the person who holds those rights. Such common-sense precepts as "To each according to effort," "To each according to contribution," and "To each according to need," when left unsupplemented, may not fit this definition of distributive principles. (For example, what if all needs are satisfied, or all efforts and contributions are rewarded, and there is still a remaining surplus?) Still, I presume these precepts can be made to fit the definition easily enough so long as we supplement each precept

---

6. The idea of "fair distribution" was current among nineteenth-century non-Marxian socialists. Marx himself disdained the French socialists' idea of fair distribution, along with the idea of "equal right," calling them "obsolete verbal rubbish." See Karl Marx, "Critique of the Gotha Program," in *Karl Marx: Selected Writings*, ed. David McLellan (Oxford: Oxford University Press, 1977 [originally published 1875]), 569. Aristotle distinguished distributive justice from commutative justice, but the term was not used in the contemporary sense. For a discussion, see Samuel Fleishacker, *Distributive Justice* (Cambridge, MA: Harvard University Press, 2005).

7. Robert Nozick, *Anarchy, State, and Utopia* (New York: Basic Books, 1974), 149.

with some other (for example, the surplus remaining after all needs, efforts, or contributions are met might then be equally distributed, or distributed to maximize utility, etc.).

On this understanding, a people's duty to assist its own and other peoples so that their basic needs are met is not (by itself) a principle of distributive justice. For, this duty, once satisfied, extends no further and establishes no further claim within the ongoing system of economic production and exchange. The same is true of duties to meet special needs of the handicapped; by themselves, these duties are not principles of distributive justice. In contrast, a principle of restricted utility which says "A society has a duty to provide a social minimum for all its citizens sufficient to meet their basic needs, and once basic needs are met, the economy is to be designed to distribute income and wealth so as to maximize utility" (or alternatively "to satisfy the principle of efficiency") is a distributive principle; for, it applies to and enables an assessment of the justice of the distribution of all wealth within the economic system.

Rather than providing a specific global distribution principle, Rawls provides an account of human rights, coupled with the claim that the basic needs of all individuals in the world are to be met, partly as a matter of their human rights. This provides the basis for a duty of peoples to assist "burdened peoples" who are unable to meet the basic needs of all their members. The "target" of the duty of assistance is the capacity of a people to be economically independent so that they may at least meet all citizens' basic needs, and become bona fide members of the Society of Peoples.[8] At a minimum, a person's basic needs are those that need to be met to enable him or her to effectively exercise human rights. The human rights that Rawls mentions (initially) are: "the right to life (to the means of subsistence and security); to liberty (to freedom from slavery, serfdom, and forced occupation, and to a sufficient measure of liberty of conscience to ensure freedom of religion and thought); to property (personal property); and to formal equality as expressed by the rules of natural justice (that is, that similar cases be treated similarly)" (LP, 65).[9]

Here it is important to note that by "basic needs," Rawls is not just talking about subsistence needs that are protected by human rights—or what is needed so that people do not starve or perish from disease. In addition to human rights, Rawls intends that people should be able to "take advantage of the rights, liberties, and opportunities of their society" (LP, 38n), which would require institu-

---

8. Principle number 8 of the Law of Peoples says: "Peoples have a duty to assist other peoples living under unfavorable conditions that prevent their having a just or decent political and social regime" (LP, 37). As a gloss upon this principle, Rawls says: "Certain provisions will be included for mutual assistance among peoples in times of famine and drought, and, insofar as it is possible, provisions for ensuring that in all reasonable liberal (and decent) societies people's basic needs are met. . . . By basic needs I mean roughly those that must be met if citizens are to be in a position to take advantage of the rights, liberties, and opportunities of their society. These needs include economic means as well as institutional rights and freedoms" (LP, 38).

9. Evidently, Rawls does not mean this list to be exclusive, for, he says, "Among the human rights are . . ."—after which follows the quotation in the text above.

tional rights and liberties, and economic means, that go beyond what is needed to exercise one's human rights.

Given the role of Rawls's idea of human rights in determining the extent of the duty of assistance, it is important to emphasize the basis for Rawls's account of human rights. Rawls is often criticized for not including certain liberal and democratic rights among the human rights: primarily, equal rights of political participation, freedom of speech and expression, and freedom of association, all of which are among the basic liberties that are part of Rawls's first principle of justice.[10] Many critics believe that Rawls's list of human rights, in addition to being truncated, is arbitrarily drawn, with no solid basis. Here one can add to this list of complaints that, in the case of the basic liberties, Rawls appealed to a conception of persons as free and equal democratic citizens with the two moral powers.[11] The basic liberties were regarded as fundamentally necessary to the exercise and development of the moral powers, and to enable democratic citizens to freely pursue a wide variety of permissible plans of life.[12] In the case of human rights, however, Rawls's list seems to be without any such foundation. Isn't Rawls's account of human rights then simply an appeal to unfounded intuitions?

Rawls apparently does not provide a conception of the person to ground his account of human rights, and, more generally, the Law of Peoples, because there is no shared conception of the person that will provide a basis for the public reason of the Society of Peoples. Decent societies, in particular, rely upon comprehensive religious and philosophical doctrines that will conflict with almost any conception of the person that might be acceptable to liberal peoples and other decent peoples. This does not mean, however, that Rawls's list of human rights is conjured out of thin air. It is a list of rights that, he says, is not distinctly liberal, and that all liberal and decent peoples can agree to on the basis of their liberal and decent comprehensive views. Moreover, the list does not depend upon a particular religious or philosophical doctrine, not even (Rawls contends) upon liberalism. Rather, it has a substantial foundation that is part of the Law of Peoples itself. What is the basis, then, for Rawls's account?[13] Oddly, critics of Rawls rarely, if ever, discuss the substantial basis Rawls provides for his account

10. See Charles Beitz, "Rawls's Law of Peoples," *Ethics* 110 (July 2000): at 683–86; and Allen Buchanan, "Rawls's Law of Peoples: Rules for a Vanished Westphalian World," *Ethics* 110 (July 2000): 718–19 (on Rawls's "rather lean set of individual rights").

11. The two moral powers are a capacity for a sense of justice (to understand, apply, and act from principles of justice) and a capacity for a rational conception of the good (to form, revise, and pursue a rational conception of the good). See *PL*, 19, 81,103–4. Rawls calls these powers, respectively, the capacities to be reasonable and to be rational. They are, in effect, the capacities for practical reasoning as applied to matters of justice, which, Rawls believes, are necessary for social cooperation.

12. See Rawls, "The Basic Liberties and Their Priority," lecture 8, *PL*, 289–371.

13. Thomas Pogge conjectures that Rawls's account of human rights is based in a concern to accommodate nonliberal peoples' rejection of liberal rights, in the hope that they can at least accept a smaller list of human rights. See Pogge, "An Egalitarian Law of Peoples," *Philosophy and Public Affairs* 23, no. 3 (Summer 1994): 195–224. This implies that the Law of Peoples is a modus vivendi between liberal and decent peoples, a claim that Rawls denies. Pogge's interpretation dis-

of human rights: "What have come to be called human rights are recognized as necessary conditions of any system of social cooperation. When they are regularly violated, we have command by force, a slave system, and no cooperation of any kind" (*LP*, 68).

Rawls has nothing more to say about social cooperation in *The Law of Peoples*, but in *Political Liberalism* he says: First, social cooperation is by its nature voluntary, and involves an absence of forced servitude and other conditions that would prevent us from holding people responsible for their conduct. Second, social cooperation is to be distinguished from efficiently coordinated behavior, when people are working in a group but their behavior is regulated simply for the sake of effectively achieving purposes that none of them may endorse. Prisoners in a work gang are not engaged in social cooperation, though they might work quite efficiently as a group (repairing roads, picking up trash, etc.). By contrast with efficiently coordinated behavior, the idea of social cooperation for Rawls assumes that each person has an idea of his or her good and is benefited in some way that he or she would acknowledge by engaging in cooperation with others. Presumably, if a person's good were not in any way furthered by interaction, then his or her actions would not be rational or even voluntary. Finally, for Rawls social cooperation also involves an idea of reciprocity and fair terms of cooperation, which provide a sense of what is "reasonable." These are norms that members of the cooperating group rely upon and use to guide their conduct and regulate the distribution of benefits and burdens among themselves. Moreover, the members mutually recognize these fair terms and refer to them not only to regulate but to criticize and assess one another's conduct. These terms are, in this regard, public standards, not just strategic norms (*PL*, 16).

For Rawls, then, social cooperation incorporates a distinctly moral component—a notion of fair terms of cooperation, understood as "reciprocity," which provide standards of reasonableness. Rawls distinguishes reciprocity from mutual advantage, which can be explicated entirely in terms of a person's good and what is rational for her to do (the third aspect of social cooperation mentioned above). People who are engaged in social cooperation normally are not focused exclusively on their own good, in the sense that they are ready to take advantage of others and free-ride whenever circumstances permit. This does not mean that people have to be altruistic to cooperate with others; but they do normally have a sense of fairness or justice—a settled disposition to comply with terms of cooperation, and do their part, even on occasions when it is not to their benefit (so long as others manifest a like disposition). For Rawls, one thing that distinguishes "decent peoples" from "states" (as traditionally understood) is that they have moral motives and a sense of justice as a people that enable them willingly

---

counts the centrality of social and political cooperation to Rawls's account of human rights, and also to his account of distributive justice. Pogge's interpretation also ignores the fact that human rights are agreed to among liberal peoples themselves, as being among the conditions whose violation is necessary to justify intervention in the affairs of other liberal peoples. If respect for human rights is adequate for the ideal case of a Society of Liberal Peoples, then how can it be a compromise designed to accommodate decent peoples?

to comply with their duties under the Law of Peoples and not take advantage of weaker peoples whenever it seems favorable to do so.[14]

It is this sense of social cooperation that Rawls seems to rely upon in drawing up his list of human rights. The right to life, freedom from involuntary servitude, the right to hold and use at least some personal property, and other human rights that Rawls mentions are minimal reasonable terms necessary to social cooperation. The right to vote and the right to run for office, however central to democratic societies, are not necessary for social cooperation as such; other methods of decision making are compatible with social cooperation. Historically, most people in most societies have not enjoyed democratic rights, and even in societies where they do, these rights often willingly go unexercised. This option is not true of human rights generally. To contend that democratic rights of political participation are on a par with, and just as important as, the right to life, freedom from involuntary servitude, the right to hold personal property, and other human rights that Rawls mentions, is implausible and unreasonable. And while it may not be as unreasonable to say that liberal freedom of association and freedom of speech are equally fundamental to social cooperation, it is still unconvincing. Some degree of freedom of speech and of association surely must be a human right and can be included under what Rawls calls the "right to liberty" (*LP*, 65). For example, fundamentalist Muslim societies that punish women for just talking with men who are not family members surely violate human rights. But Rawls denies that among the human rights must be included liberal freedoms of speech and association, with all that they include (for example, the right to defile or destroy national or sacred symbols, or enjoy pornography, or rights to same-sex marriage). To hold otherwise is not to take the idea of human rights seriously.

The idea of social cooperation also is central to Rawls's account of social justice. It underlies his distinction between "domestic justice" and the Law of Peoples. Moreover, the idea of social cooperation informs Rawls's account of the difference principle. What makes social cooperation possible for Rawls are the basic institutions that constitute "the basic structure of society."[15] Here it is crucial that, for Rawls, political cooperation under the terms of a political constitution, including the legal system that it regulates, is a central aspect of the basic structure of society. For Rawls, political cooperation is part of social cooperation; it makes social cooperation according to the terms of other institutions (particularly economic institutions) possible and is necessary to those institutions. (One important example: The institution of property is presupposed by economic

---

14. Cf. *LP*, 17, 28–29. "A difference between liberal peoples and states is that just liberal peoples limit their basic interests as required by the reasonable" (ibid., 29).

15. The primary basic institutions that constitute the basic structure of society are the following: the political constitution; the legal system of trials and other legal procedures it supports; the institution of property; markets and the myriad laws and conventions making economic production, exchange, and consumption possible; and the institution of the family, which enables a society to raise and educate children and reproduce itself as an ongoing system over time. See *TJ*, 7–8/6–7 rev. See also Rawls, *Justice as Fairness: A Restatement*, ed. Erin Kelly (Cambridge, MA: Harvard University Press, 2001), secs. 4, 15, and 16 (cited in text as *Restatement*).

cooperation; property is largely a legal institution and cannot exist—except perhaps in primitive form—in the absence of political cooperation according to the terms of a political constitution and a legal system.) When Rawls says that the political constitution is part of the basic structure, he does not just mean the procedures that specify how laws are enacted and that define offices and positions of political authority. He means more or less the entire legal system, including most public and private law, that is the product of the constitution in this procedural sense. Modern legal systems, such as the federal system in the United States, are made up of countless acts of legislation, administration, judicial precedent, and other legal rulings that are issued by the multiple legal bodies with lawmaking authority. An economic system that is regulated by the legal norms that are issued by the political constitution is also part of the basic structure. Here, of course, the legal norms of property, contract, commercial law, intangibles, and so on that are essential for economic production and exchange are to be included in the basic structure. What makes possible the incredibly complicated system of legal norms that underlie economic production, exchange, and consumption is a unified political system that specifies these norms and revises them to meet changing conditions.

Nothing comparable to the basic structure of society exists on the global level. Moreover, if Rawls is correct—if a stable "world state" that assumes the primary functions of governments is not feasible—then nothing comparable to the basic structure of society can ever stably endure on a global level (see LP, 36, 48). This means that social cooperation is and must remain distinct from the kinds of relations that hold between different societies individuated by their own separate political systems. This does not mean that different societies do not cooperate; of course they do. But they do not engage in social cooperation in Rawls's sense of cooperation framed within the basic structure of society. Cooperation among peoples (to use Rawls's terms) is a qualitatively different kind of cooperation from social cooperation, and it has its own distinctive fair terms of cooperation. These terms ideally are the Law of Peoples, the terms of cooperation for the Society of Peoples. Some of Rawls's critics confidently claim that "there is a global basic structure"[16] and argue that, for this reason, there must be principles of global distributive justice. This simply begs the question, however. Rawls does not need to deny a "global basic structure" in some sense, but clearly he would contend that it is very different from the basic structure of society. For Rawls, the global basic structure would just be the set of institutions that are needed to give effect to the Law of Peoples. Rather than "global basic structure," Rawls refers to "the basic structure of the Society of Peoples" (LP, 61). Whatever we call it, the important point is that these global institutions are very different—qualitatively different—from the basic structure of a society that makes social cooperation possible. It is only because there are societies, with their distinct basic structures of political, social, and economic institutions, that

---

16. Allen Buchanan asserts this and sees the existence of a global basic structure as sufficient grounds for a global distribution principle. See "Rawls's Law of Peoples," 705. As I argue in the text, this conclusion does not follow.

we can take seriously and regard as feasible any kind of "global basic structure." Global cooperation and global institutions are supervenient upon social cooperation and basic social institutions.

Why is the basic structure of society qualitatively different from the basic structure of the Society of Peoples, and from any other realistic and stable "global basic structure"? The Society of Peoples is not a political society, and thus has no original political jurisdiction or effective basic political power. (Here I use the terms "political society" and "political power" in John Locke's sense to include the idea of political authority, or having the right to rule.) The effective political power and jurisdiction that global institutions exercise are possessed by these institutions only to the degree that they have been granted such power and jurisdiction by independent peoples. Global political authority (such as it is) then exists only as a result of the legal acts of independent peoples—"legal" insofar as these acts are authorized by their own constitutions. So long as independent peoples can withdraw or revise the grant of political power transferred to global institutions (granted there may be significant costs in doing so), global political power remains supervenient upon the political power of independent peoples. This is what it means to say that global political authority and jurisdiction is not "basic" or "original." Basic political authority resides only within the basic structure of societies. This is not a necessary truth, but it is a significant empirical truth, assuming that a world government would not be capable of any enduring stability (LP, 36). Basic political authority resembles the idea of political sovereignty, but it does not carry the connotations of absolute political power that reside within the idea of sovereignty. Of course, no political power is absolute *de jure*, not even the power of peoples. The legitimacy of all political power (not to mention its justice) is subject to respect for human rights and the other conditions that Rawls imposes upon a decent (hierarchical) society.

Thus, social cooperation, in Rawls's sense, is not the only kind of cooperation. There is cooperation among peoples, and there are also different kinds of cooperation that exist within families, universities, churches, and other associations and groups. Naturally, all cooperation is social in a sense, but cooperation among members of a society—that is, among people who share the same basic structure—is a distinct kind that Rawls calls "social cooperation" (*Restatement*, 6). To avoid confusion, we might refer to cooperation within groups or associations in society as "associational cooperation." (Here we might provide each of these many different forms of associational cooperation with distinct names, to distinguish them all from social cooperation—familial cooperation, religious cooperation, etc.) For each of these different kinds of cooperation, there are rules that specify the fair terms of cooperation among members of that cooperative institution. These are the rules of "local justice" for lesser associations that exist within the basic structure of society (*Restatement*, 11). To be just or fair, however, these rules need not all be the same. (For example, children should not have equal say with their parents, or teammates equal authority with their coach, and employees need not have equal sway along with managers in order for the work rules internally regulating firms to be fair.)

Rawls says, "Justice as fairness starts with domestic justice—the justice of the basic structure. From there it works outward to the Law of Peoples, and inward to local justice" (ibid.). What is distinctive about the basic structure of society is not simply that it exercises profound effects on individuals' aims, characters, and future prospects. The same can be said, of course, about the institution of the family, or the religious institutions that provide moral structure for many people's lives. It is the purportedly profound effects that global institutions and economic relations exercise on people's lives that advocates of a global difference principle or other global distribution principle point to when they contend that there is nothing distinctive about the basic structure of a society. Rawls need not deny the significant (though not equally profound) effects of global cooperation to claim that domestic justice, the justice of the basic structure, concerns a different kind of institutional cooperation than does global justice, and that it therefore warrants its own principles of justice. Nor does Rawls even need to deny that there are global principles of justice that regulate global cooperation in order to claim that domestic justice, the justice of the basic structure, has a kind of priority over other forms of justice. But it is part of Rawls's "political constructivism" that terms of social cooperation must be worked out first, independently of the principles of justice of other institutions, whereas the principles of global and local associational justice presuppose the principles of justice for the basic structure. Principles of social (or domestic) justice constrain or limit, but do not entirely determine, principles of local justice. That is, we cannot fully specify the rights and obligations family members have to one another until we first work out the principles of social justice. (For, parents must respect the rights of their children, and have certain duties to educate and support them, in ways required by justice.) We can, however, specify the rights, duties, and obligations that citizens of a democratic society owe to one another without first working out the terms of the Law of Peoples. What we cannot do is decide the duties that different peoples owe to one another as peoples, and how they are to act toward one another as peoples in their political relations, before the principles of domestic justice are decided. This is how Rawls understands political constructivism: the principles that appropriately regulate social and political relations depend upon the kinds of institutions or practices to be regulated, and these principles are to be "constructed" on the basis of ideas that are central to the functioning of those institutions or practices and people's awareness of them.

Political constructivism is, I believe, integral to Rawls's rejection of cosmopolitanism and a global principle of distributive justice. Cosmopolitanism, as a view about distributive justice, claims that "the content of social justice cannot be arrived at by considering the individual society as a closed system in isolation from all others."[17] As such, cosmopolitanism is or at least involves an epistemological/methodological claim that denies the possibility of political constructivism. What ultimately underlies Rawls's political constructivism are his views regarding moral justification. The justification of principles of justice ultimately involves bringing into a "wide reflective equilibrium" the considered convictions of justice that we share regarding social institutions or practices. Practices and institutions each

---

17. See Samuel Scheffler, "Conceptions of Cosmopolitanism," in *Boundaries and Allegiances* (Oxford: Oxford University Press, 2001), 116.

have their own rules that are constitutive of the practice or institution. So long as we do not question the existence of the institution itself, it is the role of a conception of justice to provide principles for the regulation of these rules constituting practices or institutions. Of course, it may be that as a matter of justice itself (the justice of society, or global justice), certain practices or institutions should not exist or should be radically revised. (Many people have raised questions regarding the institutions of marriage and the family, for example, arguing that for reasons of social justice they should be radically revised, and in the case of civil marriage, even eliminated.) Anarchists, of course, argue that the state, and political society among people, is inherently unjust and should not exist. Some cosmopolitans contend that the state or political society as traditionally conceived (as an independent and autonomous entity, with exclusive control over a territory) should not exist, and that justice requires a world government of some kind.

In response, Rawls's account of the Law of Peoples is based upon certain empirical assumptions and theoretical commitments that, taken together, require the existence of separate societies, each regulated by its own basic structure. Rawls assumes that justice and social cooperation too (at least under modern conditions) are not possible without governments and complicated legal systems, and that what social justice involves, in large part, are principles for structuring and defining the powers of political institutions. He also assumes that a politically autonomous world-state is utopian (i.e., a state that is capable of serving the functions that different peoples with their governments controlling their own territories now perform). For Rawls, this means that attempts to provide principles of justice on the assumption of conditions that could obtain only within (or that optimally obtain only within) a world-state are misguided, since in an important sense these principles are not compatible with human nature, the human good, or the possibilities of stable human society.

What does this mean? On the face of it, the practical impossibility of a world government might not seem to pose any problem in formulating global principles of justice. For example, a utilitarian would say that a just global distribution is one that maximizes the sum of global happiness. The utilitarian then might contend: "The fact that a world government is not feasible is not relevant to the justification of the principle of utility as a standard for global distributive justice (and everything else). It is, rather, a pragmatic consideration relevant to the application of the principle of utility to decide how institutions should be feasibly designed to achieve global justice. But the fact that one or another institution is not feasible has no bearing on standards for distributive justice and whether they are to apply locally or are global in reach. Philosophical conceptions of justice should not be made hostage to contingencies, but are a priori, the product of (if you will) 'pure reason.'"

The role of empirical considerations and natural regularities in the justification of a conception of justice is a far more complicated question than can be addressed here.[18] This much should be said: For Rawls, our considered convic-

---

18. G. A. Cohen challenges Rawls's reliance on facts in justifying the principles of justice. See G. A. Cohen, "Facts and Principles," *Philosophy and Public Affairs* 31, no. 3 (Summer 2003): 211–45.

tions of justice arise within the practices and institutions we live with, and are attuned to the structure and demands of those institutions. Our considered judgments regarding individual liberties and just distributions originate within the framework provided by the basic structure of society. Moreover, they primarily apply to those institutions (for example, what constitutional rights should people have? how should the system of property and taxation be structured? and so on). Our considered judgments regarding global distributive justice are more tentative and much less secure, since there are few global institutions that give rise to them or anchor them. For many reasonable persons, it is hard to know where to even begin in considering these issues.

Among our more abstract considered convictions of justice that a conception of justice must accommodate is, Rawls assumes, that principles of justice that regulate social and political relations should be publicly knowable and reasonably acceptable to people whose lives and relations these principles regulate. This is part of what it is to be a free person for Rawls—to know, understand, and be able to reason about the bases of social and political relations, and not be under any illusions about them. For Rawls, this suggests that principles of justice should be capable of serving as principles of practical reasoning and justification among people who conceive of themselves as free and responsible agents. It is also a requirement of democracy for Rawls that citizens be in a position to know the bases of their political relations; hence, a publicity condition is incorporated into political liberalism. To serve this public role, however, principles of justice have to be generally acceptable to reasonable people as a public basis for deliberation and justification. This is necessary to citizens' and a democratic people's political autonomy. Moreover, the institutions that these principles presuppose and support, if they are to be publicly acceptable among free persons, must be feasible and capable of enduring over time; and to meet these requirements, they must gain citizens' willing support. As Rawls says, institutions should be "stable for the right reasons" (PL, xlii, 390), that is, acceptable to citizens on the basis of their sense of justice (LP, 15).

Now, assuming that what we are looking for is a conception of justice that (1) fits with our considered convictions of justice, as reasonable persons; (2) is publicly acceptable to free and equal persons who are also reasonable, and can serve them as a basis for public justification; and (3) is feasible and will endure over time and across generations while serving this public role; then it should follow that this public conception must be one that (4) takes into account and is responsive to the permanent facts about human beings and their living together in social groups, including how they conceive of their good. To put the point another way: Assuming that we are concerned with achieving the freedom and equality of real persons in the world, given their nature and limitations as human beings, a conception of justice must be responsive to facts about human nature if it is to be stable by engaging people's sense of justice.

Consider, now, the fact that human beings are sociable creatures who develop within and are profoundly affected by the basic institutions of their society. Consider, also, that a world government and basic structure that includes all the world within one society, and is capable of enduring and remaining stable on reasonable terms over time, is not empirically feasible. For a variety of reasons, the existence of a number of different societies, each with their own political institutions, is a permanent fact about social life. If this is true—if there is no escaping the fact of independent societies each with their own basic structure—and if what we seek is a publicly acceptable conception of justice, then there is no escaping the need for an independent conception of social justice that applies domestically to regulate the basic structure of society. This is required, not simply because of considerations of stability of social groups but because a conception of justice, for Rawls, has the role of providing a basis for public justification among people who regard themselves as free and as equals. (From the fact that a world-state is not feasible, it should also follow that there is no global conception of distributive justice that is acceptable as a basis for public justification among free and equal persons that is feasible and can remain stable across generations. But this separate issue will be addressed in the next section.)

Assuming all this is true (of course, many will contest it), the following problem arises: once the conception of justice for the basic structure of society is in place, there is a further need for an account of how different societies are to interrelate with one another. An account of international justice, or "the Law of Peoples," is in this regard an extension (not a precondition) of an account of social justice, and presupposes it. This claim was already implicit in *A Theory of Justice*, where Rawls remarked on the need "to extend the theory of justice to the law of nations" in order to guide the foreign policy of a nation regulated by the principles of justice (*TJ*, 377–80/331–33 rev.). This claim is only slightly modified in *The Law of Peoples*, where Rawls says:

> I emphasize that, in developing the Law of Peoples within a liberal conception
> of justice, we work out the ideals and principles of the *foreign policy* of a reason-
> ably just *liberal* people. This concern with the foreign policy of a liberal people
> is implicit throughout. (*LP*, 9–10, emphasis in original; cf., 83)

This is what Rawls means when he says the Law of Peoples arises "within political liberalism" (*LP*, 9). Since the Law of Peoples basically concerns the foreign policy of liberal peoples, questions of global justice are already confined to a narrow range of issues, relatively speaking, within the Law of Peoples. Many questions that occupy advocates of cosmopolitan justice do not even arise, having been preempted, in effect, by the problems that the Law of Peoples is designed to address. In the following section, I indicate in more detail how the question of global distributive justice is among these preempted issues.

III. Cosmopolitan Objections to the Law of Peoples

I turn now to more specific objections to Rawls's account in *The Law of Peoples*, especially those relevant to distributive justice. Rawlsian cosmopolitans (as I call them) criticize Rawls for failing to take into account a number of considerations in designing the Law of Peoples. Three of the main criticisms they make are the following.

1. With regard to Rawls's account of human rights: The parties to the original position among liberal peoples, where parties are representatives of (liberal) peoples, should carefully consider the list of human rights, and when they do, they will agree that the liberal rights that are a part of Rawls's first principle of justice, and are generally endorsed in all liberal societies, should be regarded as human rights enforceable over all the world by the Law of Peoples.[19] After all, what's good for the (liberal) goose should be good for the (nonliberal) gander. If so, then it is not at all clear that liberal societies will agree to tolerate decent (but nonliberal) societies in the way Rawls suggests.

2. Regarding natural resources: The representatives to the original position for liberal and decent peoples naturally should be concerned about the level of resources that their people respectively control. Not knowing this level, since they are behind the veil of ignorance, they should all insist that resource-poor nations be provided with resources from resource-rich nations. After all, as Rawls says in relation to domestic justice, no one deserves the resources he is born with, so no one deserves to be born rich or poor (e.g., *TJ*, 101–2/89 rev.). By the same token, resource-rich nations do not deserve the natural resources that happen to be deposited by nature on their territory. These resources should be redistributed to resource-poor nations (or at least subject to a resource tax upon extraction) until those nations receive their fair share, and the rational representatives of liberal and decent peoples will insist on as much in the interest of those they represent.[20]

3. Regarding distributive justice: Since representatives of peoples behind the veil of ignorance are ignorant not only of natural resources but also of the level of talent, knowledge, technology, capital, and culture their people enjoy, they should want to protect themselves not just against resource poverty but also against occupying globally less-advantaged positions. As a result, and for the same reasons as the parties in the domestic original position, they should choose a principle of global distributive justice. Here some critics argue that for the same reasons that parties agree to it in the domestic original position, the global principle of distributive justice should be the difference principle. (Charles Beitz, Thomas Pogge, Brian Barry, David Richards, K. C. Tan, and others have made this argument.) Others contend that Rawls's argument for the difference principle is mistaken and the global distribution principle should be another principle of justice. (Allen Buchanan makes this argument.) A third group contends that the difference principle should domestically apply within nations, subject to the requirements of a different global distribution principle which determines the share that each nation receives and to which they are to apply the domestic difference principle. (Pogge and Tan have suggested this position in conversation.)

19. See, for example, Pogge, "An Egalitarian Law of Peoples," 214–16; and K. C. Tan, *Toleration, Diversity, and Global Justice* (State College, PA: Penn State University Press, 2000), 28, 79–80.

20. See Pogge, "An Egalitarian Law of Peoples," 199ff.; and Charles Beitz, *Political Theory and International Relations* (Princeton, NJ: Princeton University Press, 1979; 2nd ed., 1999), 138, 141.

One feature that is common to all three of these main criticisms is that they seem to assume that Rawls has made a mistake in applying the terms of his own argument from the original position. I do not think this assumption is warranted. In this section, I address the first two criticisms. In section IV, I turn to the criticism regarding Rawls's rejection of a global difference principle or other global distribution principle.

A. Why Liberal Rights Are Not Incorporated into the Law of Peoples

1. Human Rights

In response to the first main criticism, the claim that liberal rights should be human rights, I have already discussed in section II the connection Rawls forges between human rights and the minimally necessary conditions for social cooperation. To defend his distinction between human rights and liberal rights against the cosmopolitan argument that it would not be accepted by liberal peoples within the original position, it is important, first, to see how Rawls sets up the original position in his discussion of the Law of Peoples. For simplicity's sake, I will call this the "original position among (liberal or decent) peoples," to be distinguished from the "global original position" among representatives of all world-inhabitants that is argued for by Rawlsian cosmopolitans. The first original position among peoples consists of representatives of liberal peoples (not representatives, one for each person in the world, like a global original position), with all peoples regarded as equals regardless of the size of their populations. These representatives of liberal peoples are subject to a veil of ignorance; they do not know specific contemporary or historical facts about their own and other societies (their population, resources, wealth, and so on). They do know, however, that they are regulated by a conception of liberal justice—if not specifically justice as fairness then some other liberal conception that guarantees the basic liberties and their priority, and an adequate social minimum. Importantly, and as in the case of Rawls's domestic original position, the representatives of liberal peoples are concerned solely with promoting the "fundamental interests" of the individual society that each one represents. Unlike the parties to the domestic original position, however, these representatives are not moved only by a purely rational motive, to procure a greater share of the primary goods. Rather, their main aim is to obtain terms of cooperation among peoples that best guarantee liberal justice within their own society and among their own people (*LP*, 33, 40). But while the parties are moved by a concern for justice for their own peoples, they are not moved by benevolence toward other peoples or even by a concern that liberal justice be done to them for its own sake. They are mutually indifferent in this regard. In this respect, the original position among liberal peoples does not differ from the domestic original position.[21]

---

21. Here there is an important point of interpretation. Earlier in section 2.3 of *The Law of Peoples*, Rawls sets forth four fundamental interests of liberal peoples: "They seek [1] to protect their

Given this concern for liberal justice among their own people, and assuming that other liberal peoples already recognize the basic liberties and their priority, there is no reason for a liberal people to agree to enforce liberal rights against other liberal peoples. To begin with, other liberal peoples already accept and domestically enforce requirements of liberal justice—this is what entitles them to take part in the agreement among liberal peoples. Moreover, even if an injustice is done by another liberal government against one of its own people (suppose, for example, that a liberal people falsely convicts a member of a minority group that a majority dislikes), this poses no danger of injustice to other liberal peoples. Given their interests in liberal justice in their own societies, there is insufficient reason for the representatives of liberal peoples to incorporate liberal basic liberties into the Law of Peoples that regulates their foreign relations with one another.

What about liberal peoples' relations with nonliberal peoples? Here Rawls invokes the original position a third time, and imagines an agreement, not among liberal peoples and decent peoples but only among decent hierarchical peoples themselves. They, too, Rawls contends, would agree to the same Law of Peoples as would liberal peoples, including respect for everyone's human rights. For this reason, Rawls concludes that liberal peoples should tolerate decent hierarchical peoples and accept them as equal members in the Society of Peoples (LP, 84). The apparent reason for this claim is that liberal peoples have nothing to fear from a people if the latter endorses the Law of Peoples. For, a people that endorses this Law respects other peoples' integrity and political autonomy; moreover, it also respects the human rights of its own members and of other individuals, and seeks to realize a common-good conception of justice among its own people. Decent peoples, then, do not present a threat to liberal peoples or to anyone else, so there is no reason for the representatives of liberal peoples to refuse to tolerate decent peoples and recognize them as equals.

Here enters the objection (posed by Beitz, Tan, and others) that if a liberal people is genuinely concerned about enforcing liberal rights among its own citizens, then it should also be concerned about enforcing the same rights among nonliberal peoples. As we have just seen, however, the representatives of lib-

---

territory, [2] to ensure the security and safety of their citizens, and [3] to preserve their free political institutions and the liberties and free culture of their civil society. Beyond those interests, a liberal people tries [4] to assure reasonable justice for all its citizens and for all people" (LP, 29). In section 3.3 Rawls adds a further interest, "a people's proper self-respect of themselves as a people" (LP, 34). It is important to my argument above (and, I believe, to Rawls's argument as well) that a distinction be drawn between the fundamental interests of liberal peoples and the motivations of their representatives in the original position. It is a fundamental interest of liberal peoples "to assure reasonable justice . . . for all people"; this is what it means for a people to "have a moral nature." But as for the representatives of peoples in the original position, they are not moved by this moral motive. Like the parties to the domestic original position, they are "modeled as rational" in Rawls's sense (LP, 32, 33), which means they are not morally motivated and are indifferent toward the interests of other parties and peoples they do not represent (except insofar as it promotes the fundamental interests of their own people). This motivational assumption of mutual indifference of the parties is necessary for the structure of the original position, in order for it to do the work Rawls assigns to it: namely, to regulate rational judgments (regarding the interests of those one represents) by reasonable constraints (the veil

eral peoples in the original position have no motivation to enforce liberal rights among nonliberal peoples. This is not their assigned role. This is not to say that as individuals, representatives of liberal peoples do not care about the extension of liberal rights—they may care quite a lot that all the world adopt liberalism. But in their capacity as the legal representatives of their peoples' own interests, they are not motivated to enforce liberal rights around the world. Instead, they seek a Law of Peoples that secures the conditions of liberal justice for their own people. It is not their responsibility, charge, or jurisdiction to agree on a cosmopolitan conception of justice providing liberal rights for all peoples (any more than it is any other trustee's or legal representative's charge or responsibility to concern himself with the rights and interests of third parties or the general population as a whole). So long as nonliberal peoples can accept and respect the Law of Peoples, and thus respect the integrity of other peoples and their human rights, there is no need for them also to accept liberal rights for their own people; such acceptance is not necessary to secure the conditions of liberal justice for a liberal people.

The general point is that there is no room in the original position for the argument that nonliberal people should not be tolerated because they do not accept liberal rights. That question simply does not arise. Of course, here it might be objected that this is arbitrary, due simply to the artifice of the original position and how the interests of the parties are defined by Rawls. But that is a different objection from the one we have been considering, namely, that Rawls's argument from the original position fails and is inconsistent since it does not address certain legitimate concerns the parties may have.

In response to this defense of Rawls, it may be said that if the representatives in the original position were only concerned about justice among their own peoples, why would they agree to tolerate only decent peoples? For, there are many "outlaw" and "burdened" states whose rulers do not respect the human rights of their own people, but nonetheless present no danger to liberal peoples (for example, the rulers of many African states). Why not tolerate these "harmless outlaws," too, so long as they present no threat to one's own security?[22] This suggests that Rawls, by his own arguments, puts himself into the position of having to accept a realist foreign policy, in spite of his efforts to do otherwise, and must

of ignorance and other constraints of right). Nevertheless, the fact that the parties' representatives are modeled as purely rational and indifferent to one another and other peoples does not by any means imply that liberal peoples themselves are purely rational and indifferent. Indeed, Rawls is careful to emphasize in section 9 that what primarily distinguishes peoples from states is that peoples have a moral nature; thus, they are not moved solely by their own interests and are not indifferent to one another, but do seek "to assure reasonable justice . . . for all peoples" (LP, 29). The reason this is an important point of interpretation is that, if the parties to the original position were motivated to do justice, not just for their own people but for all peoples, then this would open the way for the argument that the representatives of liberal peoples should also be concerned that nonliberal peoples accept liberal justice, including all the liberal basic liberties. If so, then liberal peoples would not have reason to tolerate nonliberal decent peoples, at least not for the reasons Rawls suggests. K. C. Tan, among others, has made this argument, and my remarks here are intended as a response to him. See Tan, *Toleration, Diversity, and Global Justice,* chap. 2.

22. Charles Beitz raises considerations along these lines in "Rawls's Law of Peoples," 685.

tolerate gross injustices and violations of human rights by some nations so long as they do not jeopardize other nations' security.

One reply to this argument is that liberal people do indeed have a good deal to fear from a state that has no respect for human rights or other principles of the Law of Peoples.[23] One only has to look at the dislocation of individuals and the disruption and war among neighboring nations that is caused by violations of human rights in Africa today. Behind the veil of ignorance, a representative does not know whether a neighboring country is liberal, decent, or an outlaw regime, nor does he know its relative size or strength in comparison with other peoples. Moreover, putting the original position and the motivations of its parties aside, the fact is that liberal peoples themselves do value human rights for their own sake, and seek "reasonable justice . . . for all peoples" (LP, 29). Peoples as peoples have a moral nature, and as such they have a sense of justice and are concerned with respect for human rights for their own sake. (They are also concerned with respect for liberal rights for their own sake, with the important qualification that people who enjoy them conceive of themselves as free and as equal citizens.) The objection stems from focusing on the motivations of the parties to the original position. Just because, from the point of view of the parties to the original position, respect for human rights by other peoples is important for instrumental reasons, this does not mean that the Law of Peoples regards human rights purely instrumentally or from a self-interested perspective. (The parallel here is with citizens in a well-ordered society of justice as fairness, who value justice for its own sake, and their representatives in the original position, who are not motivated by considerations of justice in the original position.) To say that Rawls's justification of human rights is purely "instrumental" is to fail to see that the parties in the original position are only part of a larger argument. They are not real people but merely embody rational considerations regarding the good of those they represent, whose interests are then subjected to the moral constraints of the original position, and the moral nature of free and equal people.

Here it bears emphasizing that the parties' toleration of nonliberal decent peoples, and their failure to include liberal rights in the list of human rights that the Law of Peoples protects, does not mean that liberal citizens or liberal societies do not regard liberal rights as universally applicable or as an ideal all societies ought to aspire to. Clearly, most liberal citizens do, as do most liberal government officials. Nevertheless, as a people (if not individually), they also respect well-ordered decent peoples as free and equal peoples and as politically autonomous, capable of self-determination and capable eventually of coming to an acceptance of liberal rights themselves. Recall that in a well-ordered decent hierarchical society, all reasonable and rational members of society accept its nonliberal terms of cooperation, and likely accept, too, the nonliberal comprehensive doctrine that is used to justify these terms of cooperation. To regard all

23. Rawls says: "Liberal and decent peoples have extremely good reasons for their attitude. Outlaw states are aggressive and dangerous; all peoples are safer and more secure if such states change, or are forced to change, their ways. Otherwise they deeply affect the international climate of power and violence" (LP, 81).

liberal rights as human rights and insist they should be enforced by the Law of Peoples is to impose upon nonliberal but decent peoples, for reasons they cannot accept, terms of cooperation that are universally at odds with the moral and political views of nearly everyone in that society. There is no justification within the public reason of the Society of Peoples for such measures. Moreover, such measures would fail to respect decent peoples as politically autonomous, both as individuals and as a people. Finally, there is the practical consideration that nonliberal decent peoples will not come to accept and endorse liberal rights under coercive terms or if they are made to feel that they and their own comprehensive views are disdained and not worthy of respect by liberal peoples.

2. The Duty of Assistance

Since liberal peoples have reason to care about reasonably just institutions and practices, including human rights, for their own sake, and not simply because they are themselves benefited, we can see why Rawls argues for a duty of assistance for burdened peoples. To begin with, for Rawls, the human right to life includes a "basic right" to the means of subsistence as well as security (*LP*, 65). Subsistence includes "minimum economic security" (*LP*, 65 n. 1). To justify a basic right to minimum economic security, Rawls says that "the sensible and rational exercise of all liberties, of whatever kind, as well as the intelligent use of property, always implies having general all-purpose economic means" (*LP*, 65). The question is, Who has the duty to see to it that this right is satisfied? Clearly, the government that is the agent responsible for a people has the primary duty to see to it that the means of subsistence for all its members are provided.[24] But when a government is incapable of providing or refuses to provide economic means sufficient to meet its members' subsistence needs (and basic needs as well), it falls to the Society of Peoples to fill this duty. The eighth Law of Peoples says: "Peoples have a duty to assist other peoples living under unfavorable conditions that prevent their having a just or decent political and social regime" (*LP*, 37). Here it appears that the duty of assistance requires more than simply providing for the subsistence needs of a burdened people, which is a human right they have. For, Rawls's gloss on the eighth Law of Peoples refers to "basic needs," which is clearly a broader category than subsistence needs since it includes "those [needs] that must be met if citizens are to be in a position to take advantage of the rights, liberties, and opportunities of their society. These needs include economic means as well as institutional rights and freedoms" (*LP*, 38 n. 47). The duty of assistance is keyed to this broader concept of basic needs, and this suggests that the duty of assistance extends beyond meeting a burdened peoples' subsistence needs.[25] The implica-

---

24. Rawls says that for a government to allow its people to starve when starvation is preventable reflects a "lack of concern for human rights" (*LP*, 109).

25. It is fairly clear that Rawls sees the duty of assistance as providing more than basic means of subsistence for people. He says that the aim of the duty of assistance "is to help a people manage their own affairs reasonably and rationally" (*LP*, 111) and to help them "to be able to determine the path of their own future for themselves" (*LP*, 118). "When the duty of assistance is fulfilled, and each people has its own liberal or decent government . . . each people adjusts the significance and importance of

tion is that while it may not be a human right to have all one's "basic needs" met, as defined, still, the Society of Peoples has a duty of assistance to meet basic needs until burdened peoples can provide for all their members themselves and become self-sustaining members of the Society of Peoples. Rawls says that the "target" of assistance is to enable "burdened societies to be able to manage their own affairs reasonably and rationally and eventually to become members of the Society of well-ordered Peoples" (*LP*, 111). The "final aim of assistance" is "freedom and equality for the formerly burdened societies." Particularly important, as we will see, is his claim that the purpose of the duty of assistance is to "assure the essentials of *political autonomy*" or the capacity of a people "to determine the path of their own future for themselves" (*LP*, 118; italics in original).

This duty of assistance can be quite extensive, then, especially if it is made contingent upon both a society's capacity for political autonomy and also the culture of particular societies and the resources needed to take advantage of the opportunities they offer. It would suggest, for example, a duty to provide in some way for the educational needs of a burdened people, so that they can find employment and be economically self-sufficient and can actively participate in the life of their culture. Rawls has too little to say here. He does say that what the representatives of peoples discuss in the original position, instead of competing conceptions of the Law of Peoples, are different formulations and interpretations of the eight principles of the Law of Peoples (*LP*, 40). This seems to leave it open for further determination that the duty of assistance might impose rather exacting demands upon members of the Society of Peoples to assist burdened peoples. This is an important point in responding to the argument against Rawls for his failure to provide for a principle of global distributive justice (a subject I will return to in section IV).

B. A Resource Redistribution Principle?

Still, the duty of assistance has both a "target" and a "cutoff," and does not amount to an open-ended principle of distributive justice (as Rawls uses that term [*LP*, 119]). Once peoples' basic needs are met and they are self-sustaining members

---

the wealth of its own society for itself. If it is not satisfied, it can continue to increase savings, or, if that is not feasible, borrow from other members of the Society of Peoples" (*LP*, 114). Either alternative assumes that a people is in a position to create wealth well above what is needed to provide means of subsistence for all its members. Here again, the argument cannot be made that Rawls's reliance on a duty of assistance and his rejection of a global distributive principle allows corrupt governments to borrow money and saddle their people with poverty for generations. This criticism, based on contemporary practices by corrupt regimes and their relations with affluent nations, refuses to acknowledge that the Law of Peoples is formulated for the ideal feasible case of well-ordered decent societies governed by a common-good conception of justice. Nothing in the Law of Peoples implies that peoples now should tolerate the exploitation of less-developed peoples either by their own governments or by multinational corporations. Quite the contrary: since the aim of the Law of Peoples is that all peoples should be members of a well-ordered Society of Peoples, the implication is that historical practices of exploitation of one people by another or by private interests should be prohibited, since such practices impede the development and independence of burdened peoples.

of the Society of Peoples, the duty of assistance to other peoples is fully satisfied by other members of the Society of Peoples. There is no further duty arising from a principle of distributive justice to continually provide once-burdened societies with additional resources. The implication of this lack of a distribution principle is that no real limit is imposed on the degree of inequality that can exist among peoples (other than the limit implied by the duty of assistance).

Here it is objected (by Beitz, Pogge, Martha Nussbaum, and others) that Rawls is guilty of (yet another) inconsistency in his argument. In his argument for principles of domestic justice, Rawls makes much of the fact that people do not deserve either the greater natural talents or the social position with which they are born.[26] But if no person deserves his starting position in life, or to be born with greater (or lesser) natural and social advantages than anyone else, then surely it must also be true that no nation or people deserves to be "born" with greater or lesser natural resources than other peoples either. Charles Beitz says, "Like talents, resource endowments are arbitrary in the sense that they are not morally deserved."[27] But the natural resources a people controls contribute decisively to the level of income and wealth its members enjoy and their comparative (dis)advantages.

In his earlier work, Beitz argues that the parties to an international original position would insist on a resource redistribution principle; they would do this, not simply because it is fair, but to protect their own interests. "Not knowing the resource endowments of their own societies, the parties would agree on a resource redistribution principle that would give each society a fair chance to develop just political institutions and an economy capable of satisfying its members' basic needs."[28] Is Beitz's claim true when applied to the original position among peoples that Rawls sets forth in his discussion of the Law of Peoples, which involves separate agreements among liberal peoples and among decent peoples? Why wouldn't liberal peoples (and, then, decent peoples) agree at least among themselves to redistribute resources, in order to protect themselves from the eventuality that they may represent resource-poor peoples? Here, surely, we have a different case from the preceding one, where liberal peoples had insufficient reason to agree to enforce liberal rights globally.

If we focus just on the artifice of the original position, I think it must be said once again (though here the argument is not as conclusive) that the original position is structured so that the question of redistributing resources does not arise. The

---

26. Here again, as discussed in chapter 4, it is important to emphasize that Rawls does not say that people do not deserve their natural talents. This is a common misreading, and it leads to much criticism of Rawls. What Rawls in fact says is that we do not deserve to be "better endowed" than others (*TJ*, 14/13 rev.), and that "it seems to be one of the fixed points of our considered judgments that no one deserves his place in the distribution of natural endowments, any more than one deserves his initial starting place in society" (*TJ*, 104/89 rev., see also 312/274 rev., where Rawls repeats this claim). He means, here, simply that people do not deserve the inequalities in natural talent or social position they are born with. No one deserves to be born smarter or richer than anyone else. This seems obvious to Rawls, a "fixed point in our considered judgments" (*TJ*, 311/274 rev.).

27. Beitz, *Political Theory and International Relations*, 139.

28. Beitz, *Political Theory and International Relations*, 141.

purpose of the agreement within the original position is to establish principles of
foreign policy among liberal peoples; its purpose is not to arrive at principles of
compensation or at a conception of cosmopolitan justice. Of course, the parties
might be concerned with the level of natural resources that they have. But would
their concern lead them to insist upon redistributing natural resources among
peoples as a condition of cooperating as peoples? (Or, we might ask, would it
lead them to insist upon a global resource tax, as Pogge argues?) Here they would
need to take into account the burdens and the degree of interference with their
independence that may be involved in redistributing natural resources discovered
in their territory: Is it to be done in kind? If so, who is responsible for extracting
resources? If instead of going to the enormous trouble of redistributing resources in
kind, poor peoples are to be compensated monetarily, then where is this money to
come from and what is the periodic rate of payment? Are the peoples of resource-
rich countries to be taxed, and can they afford this? Or is a resource-rich country
to flood the world market with its resources—thus driving down the price—to
raise money to pay compensation to resource-poor nations? Many questions like
this arise, which might give representatives of peoples pause in considering the
wisdom of a resource redistribution principle.[29] Just as the representatives to Rawls's domestic original position do not agree to a resource redistribution principle
per se, or to a principle that compensates people proportionately for the degree of
their disadvantage, but instead agree to a principle of distributive justice that structures the economy so as to maximally benefit the worst off, so it would seem to be
more rational for the parties to the extended original position to simply agree to a
principle of distributive justice to deal with issues of resource inequality.

Nevertheless, even dealing with the problem that way might be questionable, for reasons Rawls himself suggests. Rawls gives short shrift to the resource
redistribution argument. Basically, he denies its claim that the natural resources
a people controls determine its members' income and wealth. Pointing to the
people of Japan and other resource-poor but still well-to-do peoples (and also to
the people of Argentina and other resource-rich but still-poor peoples), he says
that how a nation fares has much more to do with its political culture than with
the natural resources it controls within its boundaries:

> There is no society anywhere in the world—except for marginal cases—with
> resources so scarce that it could not, were it reasonably and rationally organized
> and governed, become well-ordered. . . . The crucial element in how a country
> fares is its political culture—its members' political and civic virtues—and not
> the level of its resources. (LP, 108, 117)

Given the centrality of political culture to a society's well-being, Rawls says,
"The arbitrariness of natural resources causes no difficulty" (LP, 117). I think an

---

29. Here it might be said that these are simply questions of the application of a global resource
principle. However, if we accept the publicity condition on principles, then I think that more is
involved here than simply the application of a vague principle. Why should representatives of peoples
want to accept a principle that inevitably will give rise to interminable disputes among peoples?

important assumption underlying Rawls's argument here is that, on Rawls's view, the duty of assistance should be set at a level that assures political autonomy, the capacity of a people "to be able to determine the path of their own future for themselves" (*LP*, 118). It is only once that the political autonomy of a people is procured that the level of wealth a country enjoys can become largely a matter of its political culture (as opposed to being a matter of the natural resources it has on hand [see *LP*, 117–18]). Here again, it is important to emphasize that Rawls's argument applies to well-ordered societies in a well-ordered Society of Peoples. It is under those circumstances, where there is an absence of internal political corruption and external exploitation by other peoples and by multinational business interests that a people's level of well-being will largely be decided by its political culture, and the natural resources it controls will not be such a significant factor.

We can assume that the parties to Rawls's original position have this general knowledge. Thus, if Rawls's argument is convincing, then it is questionable whether it is rational for the representatives of peoples to be worried about instituting a resource redistribution principle or about compensating the resource-poor at all, especially given all the potential problems that arise with administering such a principle.

One response to Rawls's argument is this: Why should the inhabitants of poor countries have to take responsibility for the miserable political and social culture they are born into any more than they should have to take responsibility for the level of resources they are born with? From the perspective of individuals, it is just as arbitrary for one to be born into a culturally impoverished country as it is for one to be born into a resource-poor country. This raises the question of the need for a global distribution principle (as opposed to a global resource redistribution principle), a subject that will be considered in the next section. For his part, Beitz, in his response to Rawls, says that the question of the degree to which political culture, natural resource endowments and the lack thereof, technology and human capital, and other factors contribute to economic backwardness is in dispute; moreover, it may not even be an intelligible question, given developing societies' enmeshment in a world economy.[30] I would argue, however, that to refute Rawls's position, one would have to make a more convincing empirical case that political culture cannot be relatively independent and self-determining even under ideal conditions. In any case, Beitz, in later works, seems to drop his earlier insistence on a resource redistribution principle, and resolves problems of differences in natural resource endowment with a global principle of distributive justice. Here again, it has to be kept in mind that Rawls is focused on the possibility of political autonomy and a people's control over its political and social culture under conditions of well-ordered societies, all of which are members of the Society of Peoples. The importance of this point will be emphasized again in the next section in my discussion of a global principle of distributive justice. But the main point I want to make here is that these criticisms of Rawls's position—for failure to include a resource redistribution principle and, perhaps, a principle of

30. Beitz, "Rawls's Law of Peoples," 690.

distributive justice, also—indicate the degree to which the cosmopolitan position depends (frequently, if not always) upon what is often called "luck egalitarianism," or the idea that it is the role of a conception of justice to correct for and equalize the effects of natural and social chances and accidents. The degree to which many of Rawls's cosmopolitan critics are luck egalitarians is evident when they suggest that Rawls is inconsistent in this argument.[31] They claim that if Rawls is bothered by the luck of the draw in the natural and social lottery in the domestic case, he should also be bothered by the luck of the draw among peoples in the "resource lottery." This contention underlies many arguments for the resource redistribution principle and for a global distribution principle. For Beitz and others who advocate a resource redistribution principle, being engaged in a cooperative endeavor is not a condition for the application of this principle. Indeed, a cooperation requirement would be contrary to the purpose of the principle, since the opportunity for cooperation is itself nearly as dependent upon arbitrary factual contingencies as other facts that influence distributions of benefits. Why should the natural resources a country has at its disposal depend upon whether it cooperates (economically, politically, etc.) with other nations? After all, the lack of natural resources has a direct bearing upon an impoverished people's inability to cooperate.

Luck egalitarians, who include the Rawlsian cosmopolitans, often refer to Rawls's claim that no one deserves greater natural talents or his starting position in society, and that the outcome of the natural lottery "is arbitrary from a moral perspective" (see *TJ*, sec. 12), and contend that there is an inconsistency in Rawls's argument. They use the same idea to support their position that the consequences of chance should be equalized or at least neutralized in the distribution of natural resources among peoples. Here it is relevant that, when Rawls says in *A Theory of Justice* that no one deserves his place in the distribution of native endowments (*TJ*, 104/89 rev.) and that this natural distribution is morally arbitrary (*TJ*, 75/64 rev.), he is making this point within the context of an argument for principles of justice that apply to societies' basic structures, as ongoing socially cooperative endeavors. As argued earlier in chapter 4 of this volume, the inference he draws is not that a society should seek to equalize distributions that are the consequences of chance, or neutralize the effects of chance. It is, rather, that the natural (or social) endowments one is born with should not be allowed to "improperly influence" one's place in the distribution of income and wealth; instead, some other principle should determine the proper degree of influence of natural and social contingencies upon distributions. This principle is the difference principle. The difference principle is not a luck egalitarian principle, or, as Rawls says, it "is not the principle of redress" (*TJ*, 100–101/86–87 rev.). That is not its point. It does not try to equalize the results of birth, social class, and other contingencies, or compensate the disadvantaged for their unfortunate circumstances. Rather, it is a principle that "distributes" the benefits and burdens that result from natural and social differences, regardless of whether or not they are the product of chance, so as to maximally benefit the least advantaged. As I

---

31. Cf. Beitz, *Political Theory and International Relations*, 137–38.

discussed earlier, the difference principle presupposes, and is designed to apply to, the basic institutions constituting the basic structure of society. Rawls's point is not that luck or natural facts should never determine or affect distributions of income and wealth of any kind. (How would that be possible? No matter what we do, morally arbitrary natural facts are going to affect distributions of assets in some way.) It is, rather, that, within socially cooperative frameworks, the distribution of natural assets should be allowed to determine the distribution of income and wealth only if and to the degree that it maximally benefits the least-advantaged members of society. It does not follow that one may generalize this point and apply it globally, where there is an absence of socially cooperative frameworks and a shared basic structure. Such a move rejects Rawls's position that social cooperation and the special political and social relationships of a shared basic structure matter to distributive justice. I conclude that Rawls is not guilty of the inconsistency he is accused of on this point.[32]

IV. Problems with a Global Distribution Principle

The argument is frequently made that Rawls's difference principle, or some other principle, should globally apply to determine the distribution of income and wealth.[33] In this section, I discuss some potential problems with the idea of a global difference principle and, more generally, some reasons why Rawls rejects the idea of global distributive justice.

It is sometimes suggested that, in rejecting a global distribution principle, Rawls wrongly assumes that laissez-faire among peoples is the default position for global economic distribution. Thomas Pogge, for example, says that Rawls, in effect, gives a Nozickian reply to arguments for a global difference principle. For Rawls, "it is somehow natural or neutral to arrange the world economy so that each society has absolute control over, and unlimited ownership of, all natural resources within its territory."[34] However, Pogge claims, Rawls gives no reason for this assumption, nor does he show why the opposite assumption should not be

32. On problems with luck egalitarianism, see Samuel Scheffler, "What Is Egalitarianism?" *Philosophy and Public Affairs* 31, no. 1 (Winter 2003): 5–39. For a more general discussion, see Susan Hurley, *Justice, Luck, and Knowledge* (Cambridge, MA: Harvard University Press, 2003); my comments on Hurley's book can be found in chapter 4 of this volume.

33. For example, Thomas Pogge says: "Taken seriously, Rawls's conception of justice will make the life prospects of the globally least advantaged the primary standard for assessing our social institutions." Pogge, "Rawls and Global Justice," *Canadian Journal of Philosophy* 18, no. 2 (1988): 227–56, at 233. And Charles Beitz has said: "It seems obvious that an international difference principle applies to persons in the sense that it is the globally least advantaged representative person (or group of persons) whose position is to be maximized." Beitz, *Political Theory and International Relations*, 152. T. M. Scanlon also once suggested that the difference principle should apply globally. See T. M. Scanlon, "Rawls's Theory of Justice," in *Reading Rawls*, ed. Norman Daniels (Palo Alto, CA: Stanford University Press, 1989), 202.

34. Pogge, "An Egalitarian Law of Peoples," 212–13. See also Pogge, "Rawls and Global Justice," where he says that Rawls leaves international economic interactions up to "libertarian rule-making" (250) and that "the economic order of Rawls's utopia . . . is shaped by free bargaining" (252).

made, namely, that the difference principle or some other distributive principle should be the default position and should apply globally.

I would argue, however, that Rawls does not assume that the difference principle globally applies for the simple reason that he believes that claims of distributive justice are already settled at the domestic level. For reasons I will discuss momentarily, it would make no sense to argue that the difference principle should apply a second time, before or after it is domestically applied. Moreover, the disanalogies with Nozick's libertarianism are too numerous for Pogge's comparison to be of critical value. Rawls does not assume absolute property rights or laissez-faire economic relations among peoples. For Rawls, the duty of assistance to burdened societies is a condition upon a society's use of its resources; by contrast, in Nozick's libertarianism, there is no political duty to assist anyone in need. Moreover, on Rawls's view, the Society of Peoples has requisite authority to restrict or regulate nations' and corporations' detrimental uses of resources in ways that would not be recognized by libertarians. Finally, the analogy between a people's independent control of a territory and an individual's rights over property (however extensive) is unfitting. By exercising political jurisdiction over a territory, a people establishes a system of property, which is a complicated system of rules and interdependent expectations. By contrast, individuals do not establish systems of property; rather, they hold and use possessions within property systems, subject to the systems' legal rules and expectations. A people's control over a territory is not a kind of property; it is the condition for the existence of the social institution of property. More generally, it is a condition for social and political cooperation and the very existence of a political people.

Why does Rawls reject the global application of the difference principle? There are several reasons.

1. First, Rawls regards the difference principle as a principle of reciprocity, designed to apply under conditions of social cooperation to the basic structure of society, where the members of society are regarded as engaging in a complex web of political and social institutions that make up the basic structure. People engaged in social cooperation in a common basic structure of institutions are confronted with a crucial question: How are the terms of cooperation to be structured among themselves as they each pursue their individual purposes and conceptions of the good? The difference principle is designed to express the idea of reciprocity from a benchmark of equality that (for Rawls) defines the terms of social cooperation among free and equal democratic citizens. Assuming that the members of a democratic society are engaged in a common social and political endeavor, advances in the position of those better off should not at any point come at the expense of the worse off; rather, the worse off should consistently benefit from changes in the terms of cooperation that benefit the more advantaged members of society.[35] To say that the difference principle should apply globally, and regardless of the kind of cooperation that exists among people, implies that there is nothing special about social and political cooperation within the

---

35. I refer here to Rawls's graphical depiction of the difference principle in A *Theory of Justice*, sec. 13, figure 6, and in *Restatement*, sec. 18, figure 1, 62.

basic institutions of society; moreover, it implies that democratic social and political cooperation is of no consequence to questions of distributive justice. This is
explicit in the objection of those luck egalitarians who argue that the difference
principle should apply globally since people cannot control which society they
are born into or whom they are destined to cooperate with. The luck egalitarian
will say: "If cooperation and whom you cooperate with are just as arbitrary as are
the talents and social position you are born with, then the fact of cooperation
should not act as a limit upon the application of the difference principle."[36] But
if society is to be possible at all among individuals, there must be special terms of
cooperation that apply to members of the group that do not apply to those who
are not members. Among these, Rawls contends, are principles of distributive
justice based on the idea of reciprocity.

2. Luck egalitarianism is one basis for a global distribution principle. Another
potential basis is more Rawlsian: it is the claim that global cooperation and a
global basic structure exist, particularly in economic relations, and that by Rawls's own criteria a global distribution principle is appropriate in order to reward
all those poorer peoples who do their part in global economic production. Allen
Buchanan, among others, argues that "it is unjustifiable to ignore the global basic
structure in a theory of international law,"[37] and that if Rawls had recognized the
influence of the global basic structure on individuals' and peoples' prospects, he
would have accepted a global distribution principle. Constituting the global basic
structure for Buchanan are the following institutions: regional and international
economic agreements (including the General Agreement on Tariffs and Trade,
North American Free Trade Agreement, and various European Union treaties),
international financial regimes (including the International Monetary Fund, the
World Bank, and various treaties governing currency exchange mechanisms), an
increasingly global system of private property rights, including intellectual property rights that are of growing importance as technology spreads across the globe,
and a set of international and regional legal institutions and agencies that play an
important role in determining the character of all the preceding elements of the
global basic structure.[38]

If this is what Buchanan means by "global basic structure," it is incorrect
to suggest that Rawls ignores it. For Rawls, institutions like these are an integral
part of the Society of Peoples, but he refuses to regard them as a global basic
structure of the kind that warrants principles of distributive justice. Buchanan
and others put greater emphasis on these international institutions since they

36. As K. C. Tan argues, on Rawls's account of distributive justice, "Citizens of disadvantaged
countries are collectively held accountable for their country's unsound domestic policies, even when
a majority of them had no part in the making of these policies. And this is clearly inconsistent with
Rawls's own moral individualism. On Rawls's own reasoning, a person born into a society with poor
population control and economic policies cannot be said to deserve her fate any more than another
born into more favorable circumstances deserves her[s]. These are mere accidents of birth, and are
as morally arbitrary as is being born into wealth or poverty in the domestic context." Tan, "Critical
Notice of John Rawls, *The Law of Peoples,*" *Canadian Journal of Philosophy* 31 (March 2001): 122.

37. Buchanan, "Rawls's Law of Peoples," 706.

38. Buchanan, "Rawls's Law of Peoples," 706.

believe they affect people's future prospects just as a domestic basic structure does.[39] But there is really no comparison between the basic structure of society and the effect of global institutions. The difference is not simply a matter of the (far) greater degree to which domestic institutions affect people's lives. Nor is it simply that international institutions are supervenient upon national ones: they presuppose the complicated basic institutions (the many systems of property and contract, for example) of the basic structures of the many societies whose practices they regulate. Rather, it is also that these international institutions are the product of independent peoples' exercise of their original political jurisdiction as members of the Society of Peoples, which they agree to in order to maintain their own basic structure of society, over which they exercise political autonomy. Simply put, there is no global basic structure mainly because there is no world-state, with all it would entail. (For example, as I discuss below, since there is no world-state, there is no independent global property system to apply a principle of distributive justice to, such as the difference principle; international property conventions presuppose and are confined by the terms of the rules of property systems of politically independent peoples). There is, then, a fundamental difference between Rawls's and his cosmopolitan critics' assumptions regarding the conditions of social cooperation and distributive justice.

3. A third reason for rejecting a global difference principle is that Rawls regards the difference principle as a political principle in the sense that it is to guide legislators in defining and regulating the uses of property, setting commercial policies, specifying schemes of taxation, specifying the terms of and regulating securities and negotiable instruments, defining conditions for copyrights, patents, royalties, and other forms of intellectual property, and establishing the other indefinitely many laws and regulations that structure an economy. (Compare Rawls's remarks regarding application of the difference principle at the legislative rather than the constitutional stage [PL, 229–30].) Strictly applied, the difference principle would require legislators and other officials to consider the effect of laws and regulations upon the prospects of the worst off members of society. While they may not need to scrutinize each decision to determine if it maximizes the prospects of the worst off, governing officials should at least determine that the least advantaged are not disadvantaged indirectly by decisions made, and that any benefits created by political and economic policies also redound to an appropriate degree to the benefit of the worst off. There are an enormous number of laws, regulations, legal precedents, and conventions that structure property and economic systems (literally millions in the U.S. federal system). In the absence of political authority and political cooperation, it is hard to see how the difference principle could be applied to influence, much less determine, these innumerable laws, rules, and social practices. The primary practical problem with the cosmopolitan suggestion that the difference principle should be globally applied is that, in the absence of a world-state, there is no political agent with authority to apply it on a global level. Here it might be suggested that each government representing the world's many peoples should apply the difference principle, if

39. Buchanan, "Rawls's Law of Peoples," 706.

not jointly then at least severally. This would require that each nation calculate the effects of its many decisions upon the worst-off members of the world. This is not feasible, nor would it have the desired (or even desirable) effects. The coordination problems of many nations separately trying to tailor their many decisions to affect peoples in distant lands over whom they have no political authority seem insurmountable in the absence of a world-state. This does not mean that, in making their laws regulating economic institutions, societies should not take into account the adverse effects of their economic policies and property norms upon other peoples, particularly less-advantaged peoples. But this would not be equivalent to instituting the difference principle on a global scale, since it would not require governments to choose only those policies that maximally benefit the (world's) least advantaged. Moreover, there is no need for a global difference principle, or a global distribution principle of any other sort, to induce governments to take into account and restrict the adverse effects of their policies on the world's least-advantaged nations. The duty of assistance already implies a duty to consider and rectify adverse effects of economic policies upon burdened peoples. Furthermore, in reference to the "guidelines for setting up cooperative organizations," "standards of fairness for trade," and "provisions for mutual assistance," Rawls states: "Should these cooperative organizations have unjustified distributive effects, these would have to be corrected in the basic structure of the Society of Peoples" (LP, 115). Presumably, he means here the "Confederation of Peoples" and international economic institutions with regulatory oversight may impose duties over economic agents as they engage in trade, international investment, and other economic transactions.[40] Nothing Rawls says implies that standards for fairness of trade and "distributive effects" are to be decided (as Pogge and other critics suggest) at the global level by a doctrine of unmitigated laissez-faire or libertarian entitlement principles. On the contrary, the implication is that economic relations among peoples are to be regulated with the aim of rendering them all independent and self-sustaining members of the Society of Peoples, each of whose individual members' basic needs are met so that all persons are able to actively participate in their particular society and take advantage of the rights, liberties, and opportunities it offers them (cf. LP, 38 n. 47).

4. It has been suggested (by Pogge, K. C. Tan, et al.) that since there is global economic cooperation, the difference principle should doubly apply, both at the global and at the national level. The thought here seems to be that just as the members of a family can distribute their resources according to principles of local justice once they obtain their fair share under the difference principle in their (liberal) society, so too a society can apply the difference principle to distribute its fair share of the global product once the global difference principle has been satisfied. But the difference principle is not like a principle that applies to a fixed allocation of goods—it's not as if the total global product is like a big cake that we can keep slicing into shares at the global, domestic, and then familial levels. The difference principle can apply only once to structure economic and property institutions, either globally or domestically. It cannot apply to both. (Among

40. See LP, sec.4.5, 42–43, on cooperative organizations.

other reasons, we can seek to maximize the position of the globally least advantaged, or the domestically least advantaged, but not both, for we can maximize only one thing.) In this way, the analogy between the dual application of the difference principle at the global and domestic levels differs from the dual application of the difference principle first domestically and then within the family. The economy and the family are two different kinds of institutions, whereas domestic and global economic relations are not. It is not clear what sense could be given to the idea of first structuring economic institutions so that they maximize the position of the worst off in the world, then structuring domestic economic and legal institutions so that they maximize the prospects of the domestically worst off within each society.

5. Not only is there the problem (mentioned in item 3 above) of who is to apply a global difference principle to achieve its intended effects but there is also a problem regarding just what a global difference principle is supposed to apply to. In the absence of a world-state, there is no global legal system regulating relations among individuals. To take one important example, one role of the difference principle is to specify rights and permissible uses of property interests and to regulate transactions involving property. However, there is no global property system to apply a global difference principle to. There are economic relations among peoples and members of different peoples. But even here, in the case of international trade, it is (in the absence of treaties setting out specific rules) the property and contract laws of one or another country that apply to regulate economic transactions and to decide disputes about rights when they break down. There is very little international property law that applies to international trade, and the international law that does exist is largely the result of treaties among peoples and is dependent in many ways upon existing laws in various countries.

6. Let us suppose, however, that we can make sense of the idea of a global difference principle, independent of a basic structure of society and a world-state (and leaving aside questions of how it is to be implemented among nations and whether it can practicably serve as a public conception of justice that guides the actions of independent peoples or individuals). Rawls's explicit reason for rejecting a global difference principle, or any other global principle of distributive justice, is that since a global distribution principle would continuously apply to all wealth without a cut-off point, it would be unfair to politically independent peoples. He gives two examples, both of which assume the ideal case of well-ordered societies that are members of the Society of well-ordered Peoples. The first example involves two societies beginning with the same level of wealth, one of which saves and invests its resources in industrialization and over time becomes wealthier, the other of which prefers to remain "a more pastoral and leisurely society" of modest means. It would be "unacceptable," Rawls says, to tax the incremental wealth of the richer society and redistribute it to the poorer nation. The second example runs parallel to the first, but assumes a rather high rate of population growth. One society undertakes population control measures to restrain the high rate of growth and achieves zero-growth, while the other society, for religious and cultural reasons "freely held by its women" does not. (Rawls's example here presupposes "the elements of equal justice for women" as required by a well-ordered

society [*LP*, 118n].) Over time, the per-capita income of the society practicing population control is higher. Again, it "seems unacceptable" to tax the wealth of the richer nation and redistribute it to the poorer nation that has freely chosen to maintain its population at higher levels for religious reasons (*LP*, 117–18).

Importantly, Rawls's rejection of a global distribution principle rests upon the assumption that it is possible for a well-ordered people to exercise political autonomy, that its members are economically self-sufficient (relatively speaking) and not subject to manipulation by external forces beyond their control, and that they can control their level of wealth through savings, investment, population control, and other measures.[41] Rawls's critics seem to question this crucial assumption of the independence of peoples under ideal conditions of a well-ordered Society of Peoples. It has been said, for example, that the inequalities of resources for which Rawls's account allows will inevitably lead to political corruption and the exploitation of less-developed peoples by richer peoples. As Thomas Pogge says, "In a world with large international inequalities, the domestic institutions of the poorer societies are vulnerable to being corrupted by powerful political and economic interests abroad."[42] Again, it is important to recall that the Law of Peoples is drawn up for the ideal case of well-ordered societies joined into a well-ordered Society of Peoples. The Law of Peoples includes a duty of peoples to provide for material and other conditions that enable all peoples to be politically autonomous and independent. These and other requirements should protect less-advantaged peoples from "being corrupted by powerful political and economic interests abroad" (as Pogge says, ibid.). If critics claim that such corruption is nonetheless inevitable so long as inequality exists, then clearly Rawls is more sanguine here than his critics are regarding human nature and the possibilities for a "realistic utopia" of politically autonomous and independent well-ordered peoples.

Let us put this dispute aside, since it involves largely empirical conjectures about the capacity for political autonomy and the workings of an economy, both domestically and worldwide, under conditions of a well-ordered Society of Peoples. What I want to focus on instead is Rawls's claim that the argument for a global distribution principle made by cosmopolitans is grounded in concern for "the well-being of individuals and not the justice of societies" (*LP*, 119). What are the origins of this claim? I believe we can understand its origins by examining the two examples I discussed earlier, involving rich and poor societies. A global distribution principle would require that wealth be transferred from richer peoples to poorer peoples in these two examples, even though the relative levels of wealth were (we are assuming) the result of each well-ordered people's free decisions. The insistence that such redistribution should nonethe-

41. See *LP*, 117–18, where Rawls indicates that well-ordered liberal and decent peoples are "free and responsible and able to make their own decisions," and "able to determine the path of their own future for themselves."

42. See Pogge, "An Egalitarian Law of Peoples," 213. Pogge further argues against the inequality of wealth allowed by Rawls's account, saying that "relative poverty breeds corruptibility and corruption," and that "it is entirely unrealistic to expect that such foreign-sponsored corruption can be eradicated without reducing the enormous differentials in per capita GNP" (ibid., 213, 214).

less be effected can only be based in an ultimate concern for the well-being of individuals, independent of the choices made by their own political culture and even by themselves, assuming they agree with the decisions of their political culture. This goes beyond my earlier suggestion that cosmopolitan accounts of distributive justice are ultimately guided by a kind of luck egalitarianism, or the idea that distributions of income and wealth should not in any way reflect outcomes due to chance. It says that transfers of wealth should occur from richer to poorer without regard to either chance or choice, and should be decided purely on the basis of comparative welfare. Rawls's rejection of welfarism is integral to his rejection of a global distribution principle. In the domestic case, the end of social justice is not individual welfare but the freedom and equality of citizens. Similarly, in the international case, the end of the Law of Peoples is not the total welfare of a people (*LP*, 119–120). (It is not even the welfare of its least-advantaged individuals, though all individuals' basic needs are to be met so that they can participate in the social and political life of their culture.) The end of the Law of Peoples is rather the justice and political autonomy of peoples, which includes the freedom and equality of a people as members of the Society of well-ordered Peoples (*LP*, 118, 119). Essential to this is that a society should be in a position to meet the basic needs of all its members so that they can participate in the social and political life of their culture. Recall that this is the basis for the duty of assistance, as opposed to a principle of distributive justice. Here again, however, cosmopolitans may object that, if not welfare then at least the freedom and equality of individuals, and not of peoples, should be the aim of an account of international justice. But Rawls focuses on peoples rather than individuals in the global case, we have seen, because of the priority he assigns to the basic structure of society and the central role that political cooperation, political culture, and political autonomy play in his account of social justice.[43] This focus is precisely the result of his concern for the freedom and equality of individuals, which is in the background throughout in *The Law of Peoples*. (Recall that the book's purpose is to "work out the ideals and principles of *foreign policy* of a just *liberal* people" [*LP*, 10, emphasis in original].) A condition of the freedom and equality of individuals, as Rawls conceives these basic democratic values, is politically autonomous citizenship within the basic structure of a democratic society that itself exercises political autonomy (that is, its citizens are "able to make their own decisions" and "able to determine the path of their own future for themselves" [*LP*, 118]). In the end, Rawls's rejection of a global distribution principle does not rest simply upon the assumption that a people can exercise political autonomy, that its members can be economically self-sufficient (relatively speaking) and not subject to manipulation by external forces beyond their control, and that they can control their level of wealth through savings, investment, population control, and other measures. It also rests upon his ideal conception of the freedom and equality of democratic

---

43. Cf. Rawls's claim: "It is surely a good for individuals and associations to be attached to their particular culture and to take part in its common public and civic life. . . . This is no small thing. It argues for preserving significant room for the idea of a people's self-determination" (*LP*, 111).

citizens, and the social and political conditions that must hold if that ideal of the person is to be realized.

7. Finally, there is an issue that requires more discussion than I can give it here, but which I take up in more detail in the next chapter. Rawls envisions the difference principle when conjoined with fair equality of opportunity to encourage widespread ownership and control of capital and the means of production, either in a "property-owning democracy" or in a liberal socialist economy.

> The background institutions of property-owning democracy work to disperse the ownership of wealth and capital, and thus to prevent a small part of society from controlling the economy, and indirectly, political life as well. By contrast, welfare-state capitalism permits a small class to have a near monopoly of the means of production.
>
> Property-owning democracy avoids this, not by the redistribution of income to those with less at the end of each period, so to speak, but rather by ensuring the widespread ownership of productive assets and human capital (that is, education and trained skills) at the beginning of each period, all this against a background of fair equality of opportunity. (*Restatement*, 139)

Rawls was attracted to such ideas as a "share economy" (where workers own stock in firms they work in), workers' cooperatives, public provision of capital to encourage workers to become independent economic agents or to start up small businesses, and other measures for the widespread distribution of control over the means of production.[44] He continues the passage above:

> The intent is not simply to assist those who lose out through accident or misfortune (although that must be done), but rather to put all citizens in a position to manage their own affairs on a footing of a suitable degree of social and political cooperation. . . . The least advantaged are not, if all goes well, the unfortunate and unlucky—objects of our charity and compassion, much less our pity—but those to whom reciprocity is owed as a matter of political justice among those who are free and equal citizens along with everyone else. (*Restatement*, 139)

Now, because there is no global basic structure, advocates of a global difference principle are required to envision the difference principle as a reallocation principle, where the income and wealth of more-advantaged societies are reallocated to less-advantaged peoples "at the end of each period, so to speak" (see quote above). But since this principle does not apply to any substantial basic structure to shape property, control over capital, and other economic relations, and is not conjoined with a principle of fair equality of opportunity, the allocative model of the global difference principle can do little to further Rawls's primary aims of enabling citizens to take control of their lives and achieve economic independence and political autonomy.

---

44. See, for example, *Restatement*, 176, 178, where Rawls endorses Mill's idea of worker-owned cooperatives as part of a property-owning democracy. On Mill, see also *LP*, 107n.

This is not to say that the difference principle, when applied domestically, has no role in allocating income to the less advantaged (primarily in the form of income supplements for workers who earn too little to achieve economic independence [*TJ*, 285/252 rev.]). As Rawls makes clear, however, the difference principle specifically, and distributive justice more generally, should not be confused with measures for alleviating poverty or misfortune; nor is its purpose to assist those with special needs or handicaps, or to compensate the unfortunate for bad luck, natural inequalities, and other accidents of fortune. Any number of principles, domestic and global, can provide a decent social or global minimum and serve the role of poverty alleviation and meeting special needs. There is no need to appeal to a dysfunctional "global difference principle" for these purposes. (Rawls's duty of assistance to meet basic needs already serves to address problems of global poverty.)

The general point, then, is that Rawls does not regard distributive justice in terms of the alleviation of poverty or misfortunes; rather, he transforms the issue from a narrow question of the allocation of a fixed product of wealth in order to address a larger set of issues. Distributive justice is made part of the larger question about how to fairly structure economic and property relations among socially cooperative citizens who regard themselves as free and equal, and each of whom does his or her fair share in producing the social product. Rawls joins the question of distributive justice with the larger question of how a democratic society is to structure economic relations and control of wealth among free and equal citizens, in a way that affirms their independence, self-respect, freedom, and equality. The robust conception of reciprocity implicit in the difference principle is a response to this general issue. It is not the proper response to the problem of global poverty, or to meeting handicaps and special needs, redressing misfortune, and so on. These are specific problems to address by reference to moral duties of assistance, mutual aid, and so on, and are to be determined by citizens' democratic deliberations, on the basis of their knowledge of available resources once the demands of distributive justice are in place and satisfied. These alleviatory problems of nonideal theory raise issues that are separate from the question of determining appropriate standards for just distributions among socially productive democratic citizens who are cooperative members of a well-ordered society.

V. Conclusion

A central theme running through this chapter is the centrality of political cooperation and political autonomy to Rawls's account of distributive justice, human rights, and the Law of Peoples. Political autonomy is essential to his idea of social cooperation and the basic structure of society. It accounts for his position regarding distributive justice as a requirement of domestic rather than global justice. Finally, political autonomy provides the basis for his account of the Law of Peoples. We would, perhaps, be making too strong a claim if we said that, for Rawls, political autonomy of individuals and well-ordered societies would not be possible if there were a global principle of distributive justice. But given the centrality of the difference principle to his account of domestic justice and the task of democratic legislation, the claim is not too far off the mark. For this reason, I conclude that the dilution of political autonomy of a (democratic) people that is required by a global distribution principle entails the dilution of the ideal of free and equal democratic citizens around which Rawls's account of justice and political liberalism is constructed.

I am grateful to K. C. Tan for many helpful discussions and criticisms of this chapter. I am also grateful to the other contributors to volume 23, issue 1, of *Social Philosophy and Policy* for their comments, and to Ellen Paul for her many helpful suggestions in preparing the final version of this chapter.

9

Distributive Justice and the Law of Peoples

I. Introduction: Justice and the Division of Institutional Labor

In *A Theory of Justice*, Rawls says that the distribution of income and wealth within a society is just when laws and economic institutions are designed so as to maximally benefit the least advantaged members of that same society.[1] This standard for domestic distributive justice is to apply worldwide, to determine just distributions in every society in the world. In this regard, Rawls has an account of global distributive justice. But he does not have, and he does not endorse, a global distribution principle. The difference principle applies globally, within each society, but it is not global in reach.

Neither *Political Liberalism* nor *The Law of Peoples* retracts or alters this position. The primary focus of political liberalism is not ideal justice but liberal legitimacy. It implies that laws regulating distributions in a democratic society can be legitimate, hence, worthy of respect, even if they are not wholly just.[2] Unlike the basic liberties and their priority, the difference principle is not required by liberal legitimacy; for legitimacy, it suffices that a liberal society provide an adequate social minimum (adequate to enable free and equal persons to realize the moral powers and effectively exercise equal basic liberties). The difference principle is one among several standards that satisfy the legitimacy test, all of which meet the criterion of reciprocity and the requirements of public reason. A society that protects the basic liberties and their priority, and affords equal opportunities and an

---

1. John Rawls, *A Theory of Justice* (Cambridge, MA: Harvard University Press, 1971; rev. ed., 1999) (cited in text as *TJ*; sometimes referred to as *Theory*).

2. Rawls, *Political Liberalism* (New York: Columbia University Press, 1993; paperback edition, 1996, 2004) (cited in text as *PL*; references are to paperback edition); and *The Law of Peoples* (Cambridge MA: Harvard University Press, 1999) (cited in text as *LP*). For Rawls's distinction between the aims of *A Theory of Justice* and *Political Liberalism*, see "The Idea of Public Reason Revisited," sec. 7, in *The Law of Peoples*, 179–80.

adequate social minimum, is "reasonably just." It is not "fully just," since liberal justice for Rawls still requires guaranteeing the fair value of the political liberties, fair equal opportunities, and an economy designed to satisfy the difference principle. But the argument for this "most reasonable" political conception of justice is a matter of reasonable disagreement among free and equal persons; consequently, (Rawls finally came to believe) justice as fairness would not likely be acceptable to all reasonable citizens in a well-ordered liberal society because of differences in their reasonable comprehensive views (LP, 180). What could be generally accepted and agreed to among reasonable citizens are the basic liberties and their priority, and the duty of society to guarantee a social minimum adequate to exercising the basic liberties.

In The Law of Peoples, Rawls does not retract his earlier position that the principles of justice are required in every society in the world. It is not the purpose of the Law of Peoples to say what social justice is. Instead, the Law of Peoples is an extension of political liberalism. It, too, has a limited aim: Given the justification of a liberal conception of social justice, such as justice as fairness, what principles are to govern the relations among different societies in the world? "The Law of Peoples proceeds from the international political world as we see it, and concerns what the foreign policy of a reasonably just liberal people should be" (LP, 83).

The foreign policy of a liberal people includes a duty of assistance, to meet the basic needs of "burdened peoples" (LP, 38, 105–13). But it does not include a duty of distributive justice that applies to the world at large (LP, 113–20). Distributive justice for Rawls is socially, hence, domestically, established. Distributive justice exists globally when every society designs its institutions so as to maximally benefit the least advantaged members of its own society.

Here cosmopolitans criticize Rawls's starting position, his beginning with principles of social justice, among members of the same society, instead of justice among all individuals in the world. For, principles of social justice seem to preempt much of the territory that would be covered by a theory of global justice, including a global distribution principle. Cosmopolitans say: "But how can we decide distributive shares within a society until we first decide such global distribution questions as whether societies have exclusive rights to control the resources within their territory?" This question (purportedly) requires principles of global distributive justice.

Rawls thought that a world government is unrealistic and even undesirable; many of his critics now appear to agree (Pogge, Beitz, Buchanan, Tan, et al.). (I will argue later that the impracticality of a world state implies the unfeasibility of a global difference principle.) But while Rawls regarded a world state and a global difference principle as unfeasible, he did not seem to regard as unfeasible a Society of Peoples, all of whom were liberal (however unlikely this may be). For, there is nothing in Rawls's account about human nature or the fixed realities of social cooperation that would forestall a world of liberal societies. This would be the most ideal feasible world, according to A Theory of Justice. Even so, Rawls distinguishes between liberal basic liberties and human rights. Liberal basic liberties are required of a society for it to be "reasonably just." Human rights are different: they are a "special class of urgent rights" (PL, 79); urgent because they are "necessary to any system of social cooperation" (*LP*, 68). Human rights, unlike liberal rights, are among the conditions of social cooperation. There is an idea of minimal justice built into the idea of social cooperation. This suggests why human rights might have a distinctive role in Rawls's account. For, it is social cooperation, conceived in terms of basic social institutions and their basic structure, that provides Rawls with the starting point for considerations of justice (and in the case of distributive justice, the reference point).[3] By no means does this imply that justice is exclusively a social duty, owed only to members of one's own society. We have all kinds of duties of justice according to the Law of Peoples to other societies and their members, as well as duties of "local justice" to others with whom we share membership in some social group (e.g., the family and voluntary associations). But within Rawls's political constructivism, principles and duties of social justice are worked out first and provide the basis for determining principles and duties of justice among peoples. Now assume the most-ideal case, a world of liberal societies: so long as all liberal societies respect the human rights of their members, liberal peoples are not to interfere with one another's domestic institutions. This is just the Law of Peoples liberal societies would agree to, and it remains true even if members of a liberal society act non-liberally to infringe some citizens' liberal rights (e.g., a denial of freedom of certain kinds of speech or a denial of voting rights to a minority). Instead, other liberal peoples would have a duty to allow a liberal people to politically (re)establish liberal justice on their own.

It is, in part, because decent hierarchical societies also respect the human rights of their members, are non-aggressive, and pursue a common good conception of justice that advances in some way the good of all its members, that Rawls extends this standard of toleration among liberal societies to decent societies as well. For, from a decent people that respects human rights and the remaining Law of Peoples, a liberal people has nothing to fear. The same Law of Peoples that would apply in the fully ideal case of a world of well-ordered liberal peoples ought also to apply in the less-than-ideal case of a world with liberal and non-liberal but well-ordered decent peoples. This suggests that it is not because Rawls seeks initially to accommodate decent peoples, as a kind of modus vivendi, that he defines standards for toleration and noninterference in terms of respect for human (rather than liberal) rights. Nor is it because Rawls finds decent hierarchical societies "morally on an equal footing" with liberal societies, for he does not—he says they are guilty of injustice.[4] For, the Law of Peoples is defined with regard to the ideal case of relations among well-ordered liberal peoples, without reference to decent peoples. This means that the Law

---

3. Why choose social cooperation as a starting point for justice and not simply the basic needs of humanity as such (or the needs of free and equal persons)? It is largely due to the role of society and social cooperation in defining not just a person's basic needs and future prospects, but also the centrality for Rawls of political cooperation in making social cooperation possible. (More on this later.)

4. See *LP* 62, 83. Thomas Pogge makes this accusation of Rawls, even though he recognizes that "Rawls himself deems them [decent hierarchical societies] morally flawed." See Pogge, "Rawls on International Justice," *The Philosophical Quarterly* 51 (2003): 247–48.

of Peoples cannot be (as Thomas Pogge contends) a "stopgap model to be super-ceded, in a hoped for future era when nearly all societies will have become lib-eral,"[5] for in effect it is already designed to apply to this very case of a fully ideal world of liberal peoples.

Liberal cosmopolitans believe, however, that it is the duty of liberal peoples to enforce liberal rights over all the world. But Rawls does not regard it as the role of one people to establish standards of liberal justice for another people when it is decent (in his sense). So long as a well-ordered society, liberal or decent, respects human rights—the moral conditions necessary for social cooperation—and evi-dences concern for all its members by pursuing a common good conception of justice, and also respects the Law of Peoples, its people should be permitted by other peoples to establish justice on their own in the hopes that they will eventually make liberal institutions part of their political culture. Rawls endorses this position, not simply for the pragmatic reason he cites, namely, that liberal institutions cannot take hold and stably endure without a peoples' widespread support. He endorses it also because of the priority assigned to social and politi-cal cooperation, and to public justification, in his account of justice. It is, he suggests, *unreasonable* for liberal societies to enforce liberal liberties as a condi-tion of cooperation with decent hierarchical societies—unreasonable for a liberal people to insist that decent societies be fully reasonable, if you will. I return to this seeming paradox momentarily.

This institutional division of labor in establishing justice is a fundamental point in understanding Rawls's account of toleration of decent peoples:[6] social justice for Rawls requires liberal justice, and it is the role and duty of all govern-ments to establish liberal social justice among the people they represent. But it is not any government's role to establish liberal justice for individuals over all the world. The kind of justice that governments are to establish over the world is the Law of Peoples. The principle of toleration of decent peoples has what some see as a peculiar result in that it requires liberal people to enforce justice among their own people but tolerate injustice in decent peoples so long as they respect human rights (narrowly defined) and advance a common good. Some see this as an "asymmetry" or "incoherence."[7] After all, on Rawls's own account we all have a natural duty of justice to establish just liberal and democratic institutions (*TJ*, secs. 19, 51), and surely this duty must apply over all the world. And so we do; but the natural duty of justice to promote liberal justice is a duty for individuals and not a duty for all institutions. As individual democratic citizens you and I have a duty to not discourage and perhaps even encourage unjust peoples to afford lib-eral rights to all their members—through discussion or by contribution to liberal

---

5. Pogge, "Rawls on International Justice," 249.

6. On the idea of the division of labor in Rawls, see Samuel Scheffler, "The Division of Moral Labour: Egalitarianism Liberalism as Moral Pluralism," *Proceedings of the Aristotelian Society*, supp. vol. 79 (2005).

7. See Pogge, "The Incoherence between Rawls's Theories of Justice," *Fordham Law Review* 77 (April 2004): 1739–60; and K. C. Tan, *Toleration, Diversity, and Global Justice* (University Park: Pennsylvania State University Press, 2000), chaps. 2–3.

advocacy organizations, for example. But it is not the role of our political representatives to do so; the duty of justice that applies to them is different. The duty of justice they have is not a natural but an institutional duty, namely, to respect the Law of Peoples. This position may seem odd if one believes all persons and institutions have a duty to directly promote maximally good consequences (in this case, liberal rights and democratic institutions). But I see no "asymmetry" or "incoherence" about it—not any more than the rule that requires each family to attend to the nurturing, well-being, and education of its own members, and does not impose a duty on everyone to equally secure the same for children all over the world. It is part of Rawls's view of the importance of the division of labor among persons and institutions.

To understand liberal toleration of and "due respect" for decent peoples and other perplexities in Rawls's Law of Peoples, it is essential to keep in mind that Rawls's Law of Peoples is (like his principles of social justice) specified to apply in the first instance for the ideal case, among "well-ordered societies." How the Law of Peoples is to be applied in our world, "with its great injustices," is a separate issue (LP, 89). It is the nature of a well-ordered society that its members have a "moral nature": they generally accept and have a sense of justice that motivates them to comply with the conception of justice that regulates society, and this is common knowledge (LP, 23). In well-ordered liberal societies, all reasonable citizens conceive of themselves as free and equal and they publicly endorse one or another liberal conception of justice (all of which guarantee the basic liberties and their priority, equal opportunities, and a social minimum). In decent hierarchical societies, all members endorse the non-liberal, common good conception of justice that regulates their society. Common good conceptions, by definition, promote a conception of the good of each member of society. This does not mean that the common good promoted is the same that we accept (a liberal and democratic conception, for most of us); nor does it mean that everybody in a well-ordered decent society accepts all its laws designed to promote their common good. (For example, some will object to restrictions on their freedom of speech.) But still, all do accept the common good conception invoked to publicly justify those laws even if they do not agree with all its interpretations and applications.

This stipulation is important in understanding Rawls since it stymies the point of a great many objections that contend that the Law of Peoples allows for all sorts of gross injustices (racial discrimination, ethnic cleansing, etc.).[8] These accusations are simply not true. This objection misconstrues the role of the Law of Peoples. It resembles a claim that Rawlsian distributive justice allows for lying and violations of freedom of speech, for, after all, these wrongs are not specifi-

---

8. See, for example, Simon Caney, "Cosmopolitanism and the Law of Peoples," *The Journal of Political Philosophy* 10, no.1 (March 2002): 102, where he says: "Rawls's schema, thus, allows racial discrimination, the political exclusion of ethnic minorities, the forcible removal of members of some ethnic communities (that is, ethnic cleansing), the reduction of some to just above subsistence whilst other members of that society luxuriate in opulent splendor, and the perpetuation of grossly unequal opportunities and political power." None of these accusations is correct.

cally prohibited by the difference principle. But like the difference principle, the Law of Peoples is but one part of a liberal conception of justice, and it has a specific function that covers but one domain of justice: relations among liberal peoples and among liberal and decent peoples. Nothing about the Law of Peoples implies that violation of liberal rights, or an absence of a democratic franchise, denial of equal opportunities, or economic exploitation are not unjust. On the contrary, these practices are unjust wherever they occur. "A decent hierarchical society . . . does not treat its own members reasonably or justly as free and equal citizens" (LP, 83). The Law of Peoples does not provide separate standards of justice for non-liberal societies that sanction these wrongs, even if societies are decent. Instead, it sets forth minimal standards of domestic justice that all peoples must meet if they are to avoid intervention and remain in good standing with other peoples. A society does not have to be fully or even reasonably just to avoid intervention and sanction, and to be tolerated by other peoples. So long as it is decent—respects human rights, meets basic needs, and enforces a widely accepted common good conception of justice—its domestic politics will not be interfered with by other peoples, and it will be allowed to establish liberal justice according to its own timetable. This is what Rawls's critics cannot abide. For them, injustice *by* anyone is intolerable *for* anyone; so *all* persons, institutions and governments must have a duty to promote *all* requirements of justice and combat *all* injustices wherever they appear. The division of labor implicit in Rawls's institutional approach rejects this position.

The formulation of the Law of Peoples for the ideal case of well-ordered (liberal and decent) societies—where all reasonable persons endorse their societies' public conception of justice—also clarifies why Rawls thinks it would be unreasonable to enforce liberal rights against decent hierarchical societies: unreasonable, that is, for liberal peoples to enforce the "fully reasonable" among peoples who are domestically unreasonable in denying liberal rights (LP, 61). Rawls's reasons for the position and the importance he attaches to a people's self-determination are several: (1) The most discussed but probably least significant is Rawls's purportedly "communitarian" avowal of the good for individuals of belonging to a culture and taking part in its public and civic life (cf. LP, 61). More important is (2) the centrality Rawls assigns to social cooperation itself, through basic social institutions, and the self-determination of society's basic structure through *political* means. (I emphasize this centrality of political cooperation to Rawls's account of social justice in the previous chapter.) Also, (3) Rawls's account of liberal toleration of decent peoples is connected with the idea of public reason and the centrality of public justification in Rawls's account. If a well-ordered decent people generally endorses, and its members individually aspire to realize, a non-liberal common good conception of justice, then there is no basis in their public reason upon which to argue that they should accept a liberal political conception. For, since "it lacks the liberal idea of citizenship" (LP, 83), a decent society and its members do not conceive of themselves or their common good in terms of the freedom and equality of democratic citizens—which is the basis for public reasoning in the liberal case. There is, then, no shared basis for justification between decent and liberal societies that extends beyond the Law of Peoples itself and its seminal ideas. If not, then there is no basis for reasoning on liberal grounds with decent peoples, and persuading them that they should abandon their non-liberal common good conception in favor of a liberal political view. Sanctions and coercive measures are then the only way to enforce liberalism among them. Rawls finds this unreasonable, for it is a failure to show "due respect" for a people, their culture and their history, and their sincere affirmation of a common good. It undermines their self-respect as a people, "frustrate[s] their vitality" (LP, 62), and "may lead to great bitterness and resentment" (LP, 61). The problem is not simply that there is no substantial likelihood that sanctions and coercive means will meet with success and instill a sense of liberal justice in nonliberal people—indeed, it may have the opposite effect. More problematic is the failure to provide a justification to decent peoples (who have a "moral nature") in reasonable terms they can understand and accept; this imposes an unreasonable expectation, for it is a failure of mutual and, hence, "due" respect. For Rawls, where sanctions or coercive means are employed against reasonable persons—persons with a moral nature and a desire to do what is right and just—respect for them as persons requires that the sanctioning agent provide a justification to them as reasonable persons with a moral nature—not simply a justification that is acceptable to reasonable persons who conceive of themselves as free and equal.[9]

To conclude this discussion, Rawls's cosmopolitan critics have long contended that there is an inconsistency in his position regarding the scope of liberal justice. Though he proceeds from a commitment to equal respect for persons as individuals in his account of domestic justice, his Law of Peoples is constructed upon a "morality of states." This is problematic if not inconsistent: if respect for persons as free and equal requires that they enjoy liberal rights, then people should have liberal rights without regard to national boundaries. Therefore, liberal justice should be established and enforced all over the world.[10]

I have suggested that Rawls can concede that people should enjoy liberal rights over all of the world, but that the question still remains, Who should establish and enforce requirements of liberal justice among a people? Rawls contends, not unreasonably, that only a people themselves should enforce liberal rights among themselves, upon their development of a liberal sense of justice and acceptance of liberal principles as part of their political culture. In no regard does this imply that Rawls wavers in his commitment to liberal justice. The idea of toleration does not imply that one embraces all that another stands for; indeed,

9. The requirement of public justification and justification to others as reasonable persons explains, I believe, why Rawls sees toleration of decent peoples as an important virtue. Charles Beitz contends that this kind of toleration is simply a pre-theoretical intuition of Rawls's, but I believe Rawls's "intuition" has ample support in other considerations. Charles Beitz, "Rawls's Law of Peoples," Ethics 110, no. 4 (July 2000): 681. Some may respond that to be reasonable is just to be a liberal, but Rawls denies this. Decent people can be reasonable too, though not fully reasonable. Abraham Lincoln was reasonable, but rejected a universal franchise (women and blacks), and endorsed segregation of races, and much else that we would regard as protected by freedom of speech and other basic liberties.

10. The term "morality of states" is used by Charles Beitz in his important work Political Liberalism and International Relations (Princeton, NJ: Princeton University Press, 1979, 1999), pp. 8, 127. For the claim that Rawls is inconsistent, see K. C. Tan, Toleration, Diversity, and Global Justice (University Park: Pennsylvania State University Press, 2000), 30.

it is a misnomer to say that we "tolerate" people whose values we share. Toleration implies that one believes that the persons or practices tolerated are wrong in
some important respect.[11] A decent hierarchical society is wrong about justice,
for it "does not treat its own members reasonably or justly as free and equal citizens" (LP, 83). But this does not mean that it is the role of liberal peoples to make
decent peoples free and equal, or even to insist that they must be as a condition
of cooperation and respect as an equal people.

II. A Global Distribution Principle?

(A) Even if liberal peoples' toleration of decent peoples seems reasonable, leaving them to establish liberal basic liberties on their own, Rawls's division of institutional labor may seem less reasonable when used to defend the domestic scope
of the difference principle. For, whereas ideally the same liberal rights should be
domestically established throughout all the world, the most-ideal feasible case
of domestic enforcement of the difference principle (or any domestic distribution principle) by every society implies that citizens similarly situated in different societies will have markedly different economic prospects. Critics ask: "Why
should the least advantaged people born into poorer societies have different life
prospects than the least advantaged people born into wealthier societies? For, if
differences in the social class and natural talents one is born with are arbitrary
from a moral point of view (TJ, sec.12), so, too, must be the country into which
a person happens to be born and live.[12] Why, then, shouldn't a people have the
duty to structure their economic relations to maximize the position of the least
advantaged people, not in their own society but in the world at large?"
    Some of Rawls's most sympathetic critics have argued that the difference
principle should apply globally rather than domestically (among others, Beitz,
Pogge, Tan, Barry, even Scanlon in his early review of TJ[13]), and that it would be
chosen in a global original position. I argue that, in the absence of a world state,
a global legal system, and global property, the suggestion makes little sense. Critics' immediate response here may be that, if not the difference principle, then
some other global distribution principle should apply to fairly distribute natural
resources and the products of industry. I address this more general objection first,
before turning to the difference principle in section III.
    Begin with an internal objection, raised by many (Pogge, Beitz, Tan, etc.),
namely, Why don't the representatives of peoples in the original position agree to
the difference principle, or at least some global distribution principle from their
original position? If they reasoned according to the maximin criterion of choice

11. On this point, see T. M. Scanlon, "The Difficulty of Toleration," in The Difficulty of Toleration (Cambridge, MA: Cambridge University Press, 2004), 187.
    12. See K. C. Tan, Justice without Borders (Cambridge, UK: Cambridge University Press,
2004), 101, 159–160, for the claim that a person's national membership is as morally arbitrary as the
talents a person happens to be born with.
    13. T. M. Scanlon, "Rawls' Theory of Justice," in Reading Rawls, ed. Norman Daniels (New
York: Basic Books, 1974).

that Rawls uses in the domestic original position, it would seem that they should. And even if they did not employ maximin, but (because of the veil of ignorance) "were equally concerned with rich and poor peoples' interests alike," they should agree to some global (re)distribution principle (such as a global resource tax, as suggested by Beitz and Pogge).[14]

Rawls emphasized in later works that the maximin rule of choice is not sufficient to argue for the difference principle, and, by implication, any other principle of distributive justice.[15] The reason is that reasoning from maximin is rational for parties in the original position only if among the alternatives for choice there is but one alternative that is acceptable if the worst transpires. This condition mainly applies when the only alternatives are justice as fairness and utilitarianism or other conceptions that do not guarantee a social minimum. But where the alternative to justice as fairness is a "mixed conception" in which basic liberties and a social minimum are assured, maximin cannot be used, for then the least advantaged position becomes tolerable whatever the outcome. The argument Rawls instead provides for the difference principle rests on a strong conception of reciprocity and "stability for the right reasons."[16] Later, I will contend that this argument will not succeed in the case of the original position among peoples, since peoples are not engaged in social cooperation, which for Rawls is needed for the robust conception of reciprocity used to argue for the difference principle.

But this does not respond to critics' larger question; namely, "If not the difference principle, why don't the representatives of peoples agree to at least some global principle of distributive justice?" To many, it appears that Rawls simply asserts that they do not, and stipulates instead that they argue over different interpretations of the Law of Peoples he sets forth (*LP*, 41–42, 86).

There is more here than meets the eye. Rawls assumes that while we have duties of humanitarian assistance to burdened peoples, distributive justice is different and presupposes social cooperation. Social cooperation involves not only a multiplicity of shared social norms and institutions but also presupposes political cooperation and the capacity of a people to politically determine their social and economic fates. The basic ideas behind Rawls's views regarding distributive justice as a problem of social cooperation are as follows:

1. For Rawls, distributive justice is not an allocation problem, to divide up and redistribute for consumption a product that is produced by some unrelated external process. Distribution of product, though important, is a secondary issue, dependent upon how the social process of production is structured. Distributive justice in the first instance poses the general problem of fairly designing the sys-

14. See Pogge, "Rawls on International Justice," 252, on the parties' reasoning from maximin, or at least having "equal concern" for rich and poor peoples. On Pogge's argument that Rawls's own argument commits him to a global resource tax, see "An Egalitarian Law of Peoples," *Philosophy and Public Affairs* 23, no. 3 (Summer 1994): 195–224.

15. See Rawls, *Justice as Fairness: A Restatement*, ed. Erin Kelly (Cambridge, MA: Harvard University Press, 2001), 43n3, 94–95, 96 (cited in text as *Restatement*).

16. See Rawls, *Restatement*, 36–37.

tem of basic legal institutions and social norms that make production, exchange, distribution, and consumption possible among free and equal persons.[17]

2. The system of property and economic norms are social and legal institutions and can be designed in many ways. How property and the economy should be designed is the first subject of distributive justice. Distributive justice is, then, in the first instance, a feature of *basic social institutions*, including the legal system of property, contract, and other legal conditions for economic production, transfers and exchanges, and use and consumption.

3. Basic social institutions and legal norms that make production, exchange, and use and consumption possible are *political products*, one of the primary subjects of political governance. It is not just fiscal policies, taxation, public goods, and welfare policies that are involved here; more basically, it is political decisions about the multiplicity of property rules and economic norms and institutions that make possible these policies, and economic and social cooperation as well. The primary role for a principle of distributive justice is to provide standards for designing, assessing, and publicly justifying the many legal and economic institutions that structure daily life.

4. Since these basic institutions are social and political it should follow that distributive justice is social and political. If so, then in the absence of a world state, there can be no global basic structure on a par with the basic structure of society. Indeed, there is nothing in global relations anywhere near to being comparable to a society's basic structure of political, legal, property, and other economic institutions. Of course, there is global cooperation and there are some global institutions, but these are not *basic* institutions. Rather, global political, legal, and economic arrangements are *secondary* institutions and practices: they are largely the product of agreements among peoples and are supervenient upon the multiplicity of basic social institutions constituting the basic structures of many different societies.

5. Consequently, the only feasible global basic structure that can exist is also secondary and supervenient: It is nothing more than "the basic structure of the Society of Peoples," and its governing principles are the Law of Peoples (*LP*, 61).

The crucial point perhaps is that Rawls transforms the problem of distributive justice from an allocation question into a question of the political design of basic social (economic and legal) institutions. Modern property systems, and contractual and commercial norms consist of innumerable laws (in the United States, literally millions of legislative acts, judicial rulings, administrative regulations, etc.) that provide basic structure and content to property and economic activity, including norms regarding the productive control, the use and consumption, and transfer and disposal of economic goods and other possessions. It is not just that global norms pale by comparison but that they are secondary and

---

17. The focus on basic institutions is needed to make distribution a matter of pure procedural justice. Why this is important ultimately goes to Rawls's reasons for focusing on the basic structure in the first place. This is a complicated topic; the short answer is that it is needed to guarantee conditions for moral pluralism and citizens' free pursuit of a plurality of goods.

supervenient on these and other basic social institutions. An example of what I mean by the "secondary" nature of global norms and institutions is when firms contract for goods and labor on the international market their contracts, property rights, powers, duties, and liabilities are specified and enforced according to the laws of one or another society. It is a society's legislative specification of property systems, contract law, commercial instruments, corporate and securities law, and others—of the myriad rights, powers, duties, liabilities, and so on that make them up—that is crucial here, not their coercive legal enforcement (see "H" of this section). Also, even in cases where international norms do exist independent of any nation's particular laws (much has been made here of a meager international property law), these norms do not issue from any global political body with non-derivative original political and legal jurisdiction, for there are none. Whatever jurisdiction global regulators and courts have is not original, but they have been granted and continue to enjoy it only by virtue of the political acts of different peoples.

For Rawls, then, distributive justice presupposes social and political cooperation since distributive principles apply to structure basic institutions and these are socially and politically specified, sustained, and enforced. Social and political cooperation, not global cooperation, provide the multiplicity of laws and norms that define people's expectations and structure and govern their everyday life. This is not to deny that production and consumption in one country affects people's lives and prospects in another, or that countries are economically dependent upon each others' trade or consumption patterns. Rawls's argument for social rather than global distributive justice does not rely upon a false assumption of autarky. But trade alone or causal influences of consumption patterns on other peoples do not amount to social cooperation.

(B) Rawls's critics confidently refer to "global economic institutions" and a "global basic structure," as if Rawls had simply ignored the fact, clear to all, that basic global institutions and all-pervasive global norms exist.[18] I contend that the economic and political relations they mention (few and far between) are secondary, not basic institutions. They are secondary in that they are based upon the property, contract, and commercial laws of one or another people's political society, and arise as a result of treaties and agreements between nations. There is no global basic structure because there are not *basic* global institutions—no world state, no independent global legal order, no global property system, no independent global contract law, negotiable instruments law, securities law, and so on. The rules and institutions that make global economic cooperation possible are national, and they apply internationally only due to agreements among peoples.

The one significant practice or norm Rawls's critics allude to which might at first appearance be regarded as a basic global institution is peoples' recognition that nations have "ownership" or control of the land and natural resources in the territories they occupy. Pogge, K. C. Tan, and others see this example as

---

18. See, for example, Allen Buchanan, "Rawls's Law of Peoples: Rules for a Vanished Westphalian World," *Ethics* 110, no. 4 (July 2000): 697–721, at 705–706.

justifying a need for a global distribution principle to regulate this practice, and decide how global resources are to be distributed. But it is a mistake to regard this norm as a basic institution, on a par with the institution of property. For, control and jurisdiction over a territory by a people is sui generis: it is the condition of the possibility of the existence of a people and their exercising political jurisdiction. As such, it is not a kind of property; for, among other reasons, it does not have the incidents of property. It is not legally specified and enforced, nor is it alienable or exchangeable, but it is held in trust in perpetuity for the benefit of a people. But more importantly, rather than being a kind of property, a people's control of a territory provides the necessary framework for the legal institution of property and other basic social institutions. Finally, peoples can control and have controlled territories without norms of cooperation or even recognition by other peoples at all. Indeed, this has been true of many countries for most of history; they have existed in a Hobbesian state of war. The point is not that there is anything just about this situation—on the contrary, it has been sustained by aggression and injustice for most of history—but that, unlike property and other basic social institutions, a people's control of a territory is not necessarily cooperative or in any way institutional. It is, then, misleading to call a people's control of a territory and recognition of others' boundaries "property," a "basic institution" or part of a "global basic structure," simply in hopes of showing an inconsistency in Rawls and smuggling in a global principle of distributive justice. There are surely global norms of respect for another people's territory—indeed this is part of the Law of Peoples. But there are no global basic institutions, because there is no global polity. And insofar as there is a "global basic structure," it can be nothing more than the basic structure of the Society of Peoples, which is to be regulated by the Law of Peoples.

(C) Rawls's critics often rely upon the fact of gross inequality and world poverty to argue for a global distribution principle.[19] World poverty is certainly a problem of justice, for it is largely due to the great injustice that currently exists in many peoples' governments and in world economic relations. But on Rawls's account, it is an injustice that is to be addressed by the duty of assistance, by preventing the unfair exploitation of a people's resources by other nations and international business, and by requiring corrupt governments to respect human rights and satisfy the basic needs and promote the good of their members. A global distribution principle is not needed to address the problem of severe global poverty, and, indeed, is an inappropriate remedy. For, distributive justice applies among peoples whether or not they are poor. If some day all the peoples of the world had adequate income and wealth to enable their members to pursue their chosen way of life, global principles of distributive justice would still apply. This suggests that there must be some other foundation than poverty for global principles of distributive justice.

Contrary to some critics, Rawls's duty of assistance is not a charitable duty. Rather, it is a duty of justice that well-ordered peoples owe to burdened peoples

---

19. See, for example, Thomas Pogge, "An Egalitarian Law of Peoples" and "Rawls on International Justice."

existing under unfavorable circumstances. The duty of assistance is as much a duty of justice as is the domestic duty to save for future generations. Rawls discusses "the similarity" between these two duties; "[they] express the same underlying idea" (LP, 106–7). The duty of assistance also resembles another natural duty of justice, of mutual aid.[20] Apparently for Rawls, the duty of assistance to burdened peoples, to meet their basic needs, is to be satisfied, like the just savings principle, before determining the distributive shares of the least advantaged in one's own society under the difference principle.[21] Rawls then seems to afford a kind of importance to meeting basic human needs worldwide that moderates claims of distributive justice within a society.

(D) Many assertions of a global distribution principle appear to be based in a kind of egalitarianism that Rawls simply rejects. This is the kind of egalitarianism which says that equality (of resources, or of welfare, or perhaps of capabilities) is good for its own sake. Taken strictly, the idea that equality of resources is good for its own sake implies that, even if people equally endowed voluntarily decide to use their resources in ways that create great inequalities—suppose you save your earnings and I spend mine drinking expensive wines—there are considerations that speak in favor of restoring equal distribution, hence, transferring part of your savings to me so I can buy still more expensive wine. Most egalitarians, understandably, do not endorse this position. They claim not that equal distributions per se are intrinsically good but that what is desirable are equal distributions in so far as they are not the product of people's free and informed choices (under appropriate conditions). The egalitarian position here is, then, one that seeks to equalize the products of fortune—"luck egalitarianism" so-called. So long as the relevant products of fortune have been equalized or neutralized (e.g., people have been compensated for misfortune), then inequalities in resources, welfare, capabilities—whatever the relevant good—are warranted, assuming they are based in people's free and informed choices.

I suspect that luck egalitarianism drives many cosmopolitan calls for a global distribution principle; the idea that people cannot help being born into one society rather than another. Whether or not this is so, luck egalitarianism is not Rawls's position. Justice does not require that we equalize or even neutralize the products of brute fortune (whether the products of social or natural endowments or just brute bad luck). Instead, social justice requires that society use these inevitable inequalities of chance so as to maximally benefit the least advantaged members of society. (On Rawls and luck egalitarianism, see chap. 4 of this volume.)

Rawls also rejects the position that equal income and wealth are good for their own sake (cf. LP, 114–15). Equal respect for persons, equal basic liberties, equality of fair opportunities, equal worth of political rights and liberties—these equalities are good for their own sake, but not the equal distribution of income and wealth, or of welfare or opportunities for welfare, or of capabilities for func-

20. "One aim of the law of nations is to assure the recognition of these [natural] duties in the conduct of states" (TJ, 115/99 rev.).
21. "Thus the complete statement of the difference principle includes the savings principle as a constraint" (TJ, 292/258 rev.).

tioning. For, equality of these things for their own sake would require, other things being equal, making some worse off in these regards without improving anyone else's situation. There seems no point in that, unless needed to protect fundamental interests.

(E) Thomas Pogge contends that Rawls's Law of Peoples is subject to "libertarian rule-making" and "free bargaining" among peoples, where economic distributions among peoples are determined by negotiated treaties and trade agreements.[22] The references to "libertarian rule-making" and so on can be misleading. Trade agreements between peoples are not "free bargains" between self-interested economic agents, but political agreements among peoples' representatives, each of whom has "due respect" for one another as an equal people, and a duty not to undermine their political autonomy and independence. One has to be careful not to confuse agreements between well-ordered peoples or societies with bargains between individual economic agents, and draw the conclusion that, because economic relations between individuals in separate societies is regulated by trade agreements between their governments, final distributions to these and other individuals are also (therefore) determined by "free bargaining" and "libertarian rule making." In "Rawls' utopia"[23] final distributions to individuals are not determined by libertarian free bargaining, but should in all cases be determined by the difference principle. This is not altered by the fact that trade relations between peoples is decided by trade agreements among their governments. For, whatever individuals gain via international commerce is always subject to regulation/redistribution according to the difference principle applied within their own society.

If so, then what must be bothersome to Pogge is that the collective wealth controlled by some peoples enables them to impose on less wealthy peoples terms of trade that unfairly take advantage of their bargaining power. Of course this happens all the time in the world as we know it, where corporations exercise undue influence over governments. But why should we expect the same political corruption to be the rule in Rawls's well-ordered Society of Peoples? Pogge and others just assume that, because Rawls does not have a global distribution principle, then it must be the case that relations between more- and less-advantaged peoples will be exploitive of the less affluent.[24] This assumption is simply unwarranted in Rawls's ideal case of well-ordered societies that are members of the Society of Peoples, who have a moral nature and "due respect" for one another as an independent people. Indeed, Rawls takes for granted that non-exploitive principles of fair trade would be agreed to among such peoples, determined behind a veil of ignorance regarding wealth and the size of one's economy (LP, 42–43). He also assumes that peoples will observe their duty to respect and not undermine the political autonomy and independence of other peoples, so that they "may be able to determine the path of their future for themselves" (LP, 118).

---

22. Pogge, "Rawls on International Justice," 25–52. See also Pogge, "An Egalitarian Law of Peoples," 212; and Pogge, "Priorities of Global Justice," *Metaphilosophy*, 32, nos. 1–2 (January 2001): 16.
23. Ibid.
24. See, for example, Pogge, "Rawls on International Justice," 251.

(F) Again, Pogge says: "Like the existing global economic order, that of Rawls's Society of Peoples is then shaped by free bargaining." Consequently, "Rawls's account of international justice renders all but invisible the question of whether the global economic order we currently impose is harming the poor by creating a headwind against economic development in the poorest areas and is therefore unjust." Underlying this is the idea that nothing in Rawls's Law of Peoples prevents the current practice by "affluent and powerful societies" in imposing "a skewed global economic order that hampers the economic growth of poor societies and further weakens their bargaining power."[25] Among the unjust exploitive practices, Pogge says, which cause global poverty are (1) corporations' bribery payments to corrupt officials in undeveloped nations, which are tolerated by those corporations' home governments; (2) the "international resource privilege" allowing corrupt officials to sell off a poor nation's resources to corporations in rich nations, thereby ransacking poor countries' wealth; and (3) international borrowing by corrupt governments to support their regimes, which saddle poor nations with debts that endure long after corrupt governments have been replaced.[26]

Pogge's account of the extent of severe world poverty, the huge discrepancies in wealth between nations, and the very modest sacrifices that richer nations would need, but refuse, to make to help alleviate the worst global poverty, are sobering. But his arguments against Rawls are misguided. To begin with, as Pogge recognizes, Rawls's duty of assistance, requiring that richer peoples contribute to meet impoverished people's basic needs, imposes stringent duties upon nations to alleviate the miseries of the status quo. But more to the point, Rawls recognizes the many injustices of the current global situation that Pogge points to, and he clearly rejects them. Rawls says: "If a global principle of distributive justice for the Law of Peoples is meant to apply to our world as it is with its extreme injustices, crippling poverty, and inequalities, its appeal is understandable" (LP, 117). This can be understood to imply that, as a transitional principle to establishing a well-ordered Society of Peoples, Rawls would support some sort of global distribution principle—if not the difference principle, then some other redistributive principle. (More on this momentarily.) But with respect to Pogge's arguments, the corrupt governments Pogge cites are outlaw regimes; for even if they do respect human rights of their members (which is doubtful since they do not provide means of subsistence [LP, 65]), still they exploit their people and do not pursue anything resembling a common good conception of justice. As outlaws, they have no claim to be tolerated under the Law of Peoples, much less bargained with, and it would be wrong for well-ordered peoples to do anything to perpetuate them. On Rawls's account, developed countries are not simply authorized but would have a duty to prohibit their corporations from participation in exploitation of a burdened people. For, surely if a government can sanction outlaw governments for abuse of their people and even intervene, it can also prevent its own domestic corporations from aiding and abetting outlaw governments' exploitation of their people.

25. Pogge, "Priorities of Global Justice," 16–17.
26. Pogge, "Priorities of Global Justice," 17–22.

The problem with Pogge's contention that the Law of Peoples does nothing to alleviate current global injustice is that, like so many criticisms of Rawls, it ignores the fact that the Law of Peoples is drawn up for the ideal case of well-ordered societies and peoples. As Rawls maintains in the case of social justice, the transition principles that apply to the non-ideal case to bring about a well-ordered society often must go beyond the principles of justice, and by implication beyond the Law of Peoples, to establish remedial conditions that would not be appropriate in a well-ordered society. So just as Rawls might have supported as a provisional measure preferential treatment of minorities, though it infringes fair equality of opportunity, in order to remedy generations of pernicious discrimination, so, too, he could have supported as a temporary measure a global distribution principle, to rectify the history of exploitation, expropriation, and gross violation of human rights endured by burdened peoples around the world. But the important point is that such a global principle would be remedial, not permanent, for the reasons Rawls suggests. What are these reasons?

(G) Namely, that in well-ordered Society of Peoples, among peoples, each of whom are themselves internally well-ordered and pursue a common good conception that all their members accept, there would be no cut-off point for transfers from more advantaged to less advantaged nations, even when the least advantaged are well-to-do. Rawls gives two examples (*LP*, 117–18): one is where a people in Society B freely chooses to remain "pastoral and leisurely" rather than industrialize; the other where Society B "because of its prevailing religious and social values, freely held by its women, does not reduce the rate of population growth and it remains rather high." In both cases, he says it would be "inappropriate" to redistribute wealth to B from a wealthier Society A that had deliberately undertaken industrial development or controlled its population in order to increase its wealth.

If it is held that, even though each person in Society B freely endorses the population policies leading to a lesser standard of living, nonetheless, there still should be a redistribution of wealth from Society A to B, then we then go well beyond luck egalitarianism to a position that says that, in matters of distributive justice, not only are people not to be held responsible for the luck affecting their future prospects but they are not even to be held responsible for the consequences of their preferences when in line with their society's decisions. For, in Rawls's example, all members of Society B prefer living in their Society with its increasing population and the cultural advantages this provides for them, to living in Society A with its restrained population policies and the greater wealth it enjoys. It is under these conditions, Rawls says, that it would be "inappropriate" to transfer wealth from A to B. To insist on the contrary that it is nonetheless fair seems to be a difficult if not untenable position.

It might be countered here that, in the absence of liberal institutions, people's choices in support of Society B's common good conception and its resulting population policies cannot be truly voluntary. But that, too, is a difficult position to argue. (It implies, for example, that for most of history, individuals have not made voluntary decisions, and that most of the world does not even now.) If the bar for voluntary responsible choice is raised that high, why stop there? After all, most people even in liberal societies do not engage in the critical reflection that liberal liberties allow, but follow convention or their peers, just as do people in non-liberal societies. Why are their choices any more voluntary than the decisions of people in non-liberal decent societies who accept the commonly held view? The direction of the objection inclines toward the position that full autonomy is a condition of voluntariness and responsibility—another difficult position to maintain.

Finally, nothing about Rawls's examples strictly implies that Society B is not fairly wealthy or even a liberal society to begin with. It's highly unlikely, of course, that in a liberal society all will endorse traditional population policies and the comprehensive doctrines behind them. But the force of Rawls's example does not depend on the assumption that Society B is non-liberal. The question, rather, is, Regardless of whether the poorer Society B is liberal or not, and moderately wealthy or not, should there be a redistribution from Society A to B when all reasonable and rational inhabitants of B endorse the pastoral and population policies in place, or the social conception of justice and the conception of the good that led to their adoption? A negative response is sufficient, it seems, to show that a global principle of distribution is not appropriate for the ideal case. What that ideal case implies for our current situation, "with its great injustices," is a separate issue, but it does speak against the cosmopolitan position favoring a global distributive principle in all cases (LP, 89).

Cosmopolitans often contend that such Kantian ideas as "equal respect and concern for persons" (Tan), "respect for human dignity," and "respect to humanity as such" (Nussbaum) require a global distribution principle.[27] Offhand, it is hard to see why this must be so. Kant himself, though reputed by some to be a cosmopolitan (e.g., Onora O'Neill), regarded national boundaries as morally significant and did not endorse a global distribution principle. Why is it not sufficient to show respect for persons as such, that we respect and enforce others' human rights and take measures to make them effective? Why is Rawls's duty of assistance requiring that peoples meet one another's basic needs not adequate to this task? It begs the question to simply assert that those who do not endorse an egalitarian global distribution principle do not take equality between persons as such to be of concern.[28] Given that so many current liberal conceptions of domestic distributive justice are already based in or elucidate a conception of respect for persons (e.g., Rawls, Dworkin, Nagel, Ackerman, etc.), it is hard to know what to make of bald assertions that respect for persons implies a global distribution principle. At least we should be provided, for purposes of comparison, with an alternative systematic conception supporting a global distribution principle; and this we do not have yet. Cosmopolitan theory is as yet extremely under-theorized. It needs to get beyond the stage at which it seeks to show (futilely, I believe) that Rawls's own ideas commit him to a global distribution principle.

---

27. Tan, *Justice without Borders*, 151–156; Martha Nussbaum, *For Love of Country* (Boston: Beacon Press, 1996), 13, 15.

28. Such claims stem I believe from luck egalitarian assumptions that national membership is arbitrary and should not affect distributive justice. Cf. Tan, p. 101.

Finally, it is also said that views which reject a global distribution principle take the state, not the individual, as the basic moral unit.[29] But if, as I've claimed on Rawls's account, each state has a duty to domestically establish the difference principle, and each state has a duty to provide assistance to burdened peoples so that they can meet the basic needs of all their members, how is it that Rawls's refusal to establish a global distribution principle implies that states, rather than individuals, are taken as the basic units for moral consideration? It cannot be because Rawls simply refuses to give liberal states the authority to require other peoples (liberal or decent) to domestically enforce the difference principle, or any other distribution principle.[30] For that is simply a matter of the institutional division of labor for Rawls, not a Hegelian endorsement of the state as a basic unit of moral consideration.

(H) Thomas Nagel also has recently grounded distributive justice socially but on different grounds, namely in the need to associate socially under the auspices of a coercive state. Nagel contends that, unlike global cooperation, adherence to political institutions is not voluntary, and it is in that coercive context that special obligations of justice arise towards members of our own societies. My position here (which is also Rawls's, I believe) differs from Nagel's in that it does not hinge on coercive legal enforcement, but rather on the need for cooperative social and political institutions that legislate and sustain (whether coercively or not) the cooperative institutions of distributive justice.[31] Also, my position (I believe Rawls's, too) differs from Nagel's to the degree that he grounds justice more generally—as opposed to duties of humanitarian assistance—in the legal enforcement of social norms. Nagel appears to say that, while we have humanitarian duties to people generally, justice is a different kind of duty, and depends upon being members of the same society. But for Rawls, peoples have certain duties of justice to other peoples in their economic and other cooperative relations, which do not depend upon being members of the same society or any coercive legal framework. The Law of Peoples itself imposes requirements of justice for Rawls. Moreover, the fact that peoples participate in certain cooperative institutions is sufficient to give rise to other duties of justice, such as procedural fairness, taking everyone's legitimate interests and concerns into account, and so on. It is only duties of social and distributive justice that peoples lack towards one another in Rawls's account, not all duties of justice.

---

29. Cf. Tan, *Justice without Borders*, 35–39.

30. Tan does recognize that accounts of social justice like Rawls's do not have to be "state-centric." "Methodological statism," he says, holds that states are the units for distributive justice since this is the best way to insure equality between individuals globally. Yet he dismisses this approach since existing states have not gone in a more egalitarian direction, but rather inequalities have only increased. The problem here is that Tan's appeal to the status quo, like Pogge's, is not an effective argument against Rawls's approach, which is ideal theory. See Tan, *Justice without Borders*, 36–38.

31. See Thomas Nagel, "The Problem of Global Justice," *Philosophy and Public Affairs* 33, no.2 (Spring 2005): 113–147 at 132–33.

III. Problems with Globalizing the Difference Principle

(A) I cannot in the confines of this paper fully vindicate Rawls's position against a global distribution principle, or reply to the many criticisms by Rawls's cosmopolitan critics. For example, it is not easy to respond in short order to Thomas Pogge's argument that the parties to Rawls's original position representing peoples would choose a global resources tax to benefit less advantaged peoples. For me to respond that Rawls sets up the original positions among liberal peoples and among decent peoples respectively so that this question does not arise seems an unsatisfactory answer—though I believe this is true and is the beginning of the right answer. I think the main reason Pogge's global resource tax seems intuitively attractive is due to both the severe poverty that so many people suffer and to the many injustices that developed nations have and continue to impose upon poorer peoples. Rawls's Law of Peoples responds to these problems, with, among other things, the humanitarian duty of assistance. Perhaps a better test of Pogge's proposal is to ask whether a global resource tax would be appropriate under ideal conditions, in a well-ordered Society of Peoples, where all reparations have been paid, and all peoples domestically enforced the difference principle and were at least moderately prosperous. Would a resource-poor yet wealthy country (such as Japan), or even moderately wealthy country, be due compensation in that case? I believe not, but no doubt some will think otherwise. If the response is that Japan is not poor, and thus should not receive anything under a global resource tax, then this confirms my conjecture that the intuitive force of Pogge's proposal depends upon past injustices or the severe impoverishment of a people, and peoples' humanitarian duty to relieve poverty; it does not depend upon the distributive injustice of failing to compensate for the relative lack of natural resources of resource-poor peoples. Other than the humanitarian duty to relieve poverty and to make reparations for past injustices, the only other idea that seems to underlie Pogge's suggestion is a luck egalitarian intuition—that undeserved adverse inequalities should be compensated; but this, we have seen, Rawls simply rejects as a basis for distributive justice (see chap. 4).

(B) Even if a fuller case against a global distribution principle or resource tax cannot be made here, I do think suggestions of a global difference principle can be dispatched. Once we consider the kind of principle the difference principle is and what would be needed to globalize it, the proposal is not feasible, if it makes sense at all.

What is usually envisioned by proponents of a global difference principle is a reallocation of wealth from wealthier to poorer societies, periodically and in lump sum payments. The problem with this reallocation model is that it is not Rawls's difference principle. We've seen that the difference principle does not apply simply to allocate existing sums of wealth without regard to how or by whom they are produced and their expectations (cf. *TJ*, 88/77 rev.). This is not its proper role. Rather, it applies in the first instance to structure basic legal and economic institutions that enable individuals to exercise control over economic resources. The crucial point is that the difference principle is a *political* principle: it requires legislative, judicial, and executive agency and judgment for its application, interpretation, and enforcement. There is no invisible hand that gives rise to the myriad complexities of the basic institutions of property, contract law, commercial instruments, and so on. If *political* design of these and other basic economic and legal institutions is primarily what the difference principle is about, and if distributions to particular individuals are to be left up to pure procedural justice once this design of the basic economic structure is in place, then there must exist political authority with legal jurisdiction, and political agents to fill these functions and positions, and to monitor and "fine tune" the system. So in addition to complex economic practices and a legal system of property, contract, commercial instruments, securities law, and so on, the difference principle requires for its application political authority with the normal powers of governments.

There is no global political authority to apply the difference principle; nor is there a global legal system or global system of property to apply it to. So a global difference principle would be without both agency and object—*no legal person* to implement it, and *no legal system* to which it is applicable. In this regard, one can see why advocates of a global difference principle might want to regard it as an allocation principle. But their global allocation principle is not a political principle that political agents can apply to any basic institutions or basic structure. Such a principle is not the difference principle, but is something quite different.

(C) There may be other ways to apply the difference principle globally and still preserve its role as a political principle that applies to a basic structure. Consider "global difference principle 2," the proposal that the governments of many different peoples severally should apply the difference principle to their own basic institutions, with an eye towards advancing the position of the least advantaged, not in their own society but in the world at large. This is a peculiar proposal, given the inevitable lack of coordination among the world's governments in severally applying the difference principle in this way, and given also each society's inability to directly influence the practices and laws of peoples where the world's least advantaged reside. To apply the difference principle in this way is less likely to make the world's poorest better off than if governments were to follow some other policy.

The cosmopolitan proponent of the global difference principle may say: "What is important is not what principle governments directly apply but the end result of making the least advantaged as well off as they can be. So governments should not directly appeal to a global difference principle, since obviously its direct application severally by many peoples will not have the intended effect. They should observe a method of indirection, applying whatever policies make their own economy prosperous. Whatever principles or combination of principles they severally follow that maximally benefit the world's least advantaged is the best." Call this indirect position "global difference principle 3." It is compatible with a global economy where each nation applies Rawls's domestic difference principle, just as he advocates, to maximally benefit the least advantaged in their own society. (Then, too, it is potentially compatible with any number and combination of economic principles and policies observed by nations.)

It may well be that the domestic application of the difference principle in every society would maximally benefit both the least advantaged in each society and also simultaneously the least advantaged in the world. The best way to maximally benefit the world's poorest would then be for each people to focus on its own members and maximize the position of the poorest among them. This would be an interesting coincidence, ironical perhaps from both cosmopolitans' and Rawls's perspectives. But why would we call this eventuality the "application" of a *global* difference principle" when no such global principle is directly applied by anyone? What we have instead is the application of Rawls's domestic difference principle in every society worldwide, with the coincidental effect of maximally benefiting the world's least advantaged. But since this effect is coincidental, and global difference principle 3 is not publicly known or applied in any legislative or other public deliberations, it is not a *public political principle* of justice. Since it does not effectively guide anyone's reasoning or deliberations, it is not clear why we should call it a "principle" at all. What if (contrary to evidence) the best way to maximally benefit the world's poorest now just happened to be that each nation observe the classical liberal laissez-faire policies advocated by the IMF (International Monetary Fund) and current U.S. policy. Would we then say that each nation was applying the global difference principle? Whatever the case, not being a public political principle, global difference principle 3 has little to do with Rawls's difference principle.

Finally, "global difference principle 4": It has been suggested (by Pogge in conversation) that the difference principle should apply, not to all economic institutions worldwide, or to the total product of all world economies, but to global institutions (lending policies, trade agreements, etc.) and the marginal product that results from economic cooperation among peoples. (One example, assuming that annually 15–17% of the U.S. wealth stems from global trade, this percentage of our gross national product should be applied to maximally benefit the world's least advantaged.) But this is not the difference principle either, for it does not apply broadly to structure all economic institutions and property relations, but either applies simply to allocate the marginal product of global economic cooperation (following the rule, "to each so as to maximize the welfare or share of the least advantaged"); or it applies the difference principle narrowly to structure certain specific procedures (e.g., loan policies should be arranged to maximally benefit the poorest nations). It is questionable whether or how much this piecemeal application of the difference principle will actually improve the situation of the worst off in the world, all things considered, not to mention make them as well off as they can be. (Granted, this would be an empirical issue. But, for example, it would impose an enormous deterrent on global trade for goods and labor if resulting wealth had to be subjected to a global then a domestic difference principle.) In any case, this piecemeal difference principle, since it applies to but a marginal portion of the world's wealth, seems little more than an afterthought to Rawls's position. It abandons the basic cosmopolitan position that distributive justice should be globally, not domestically, determined.

(D) I have argued that, in the absence of basic global institutions—a world state, a world legal system with comprehensive jurisdiction, a unified global property system, and so on—a "global difference principle" is not even a shadow of its domestic self. But there are even more formidable dissimilarities between Rawls's domestic difference principle and a global difference principle. To begin with, Rawls's arguments for the difference principle rely upon a robust idea of social cooperation and of reciprocity among the members of a *democratic* society. "Democratic Equality" and a "property-owning democracy"[32] are the terms he uses for the economic system structured by the difference principle and fair equality of opportunity. Democratic social and political cooperation does not exist at the global level, and most likely never will. The natural question, then, is: Even if we agree that there is some kind of global distribution principle, why should it be the difference principle? Outside the confines of a democratic society, Rawls's arguments for the difference principle do not travel well when considered from the perspective of a global original position. But if the argument from democratic reciprocity cannot be relied on, what, then, could be the argument for a global difference principle?

More to the point, Rawls envisions the difference principle to structure property institutions so as to encourage (when conjoined with fair equality of opportunities) widespread ownership and control of the means of production, either in a "property-owning democracy" or a liberal socialist economy. He says: "The intent is not simply to assist those who lose out through accident or misfortune (although that must be done), but rather to put all citizens in a position to manage their own affairs on a footing of a suitable degree of social and political cooperation. . . . The least advantaged are not, if all goes well, the unfortunate and unlucky—objects of our charity and compassion, much less our pity—but those to whom reciprocity is owed as a matter of political justice among those who are free and equal citizens along with everyone else" (*Restatement*, 139).

Like J. S. Mill, Rawls believed that for workers to have as their only real option a wage relationship with capitalist employers undermines individuals' freedom and independence, blunts their characters and imaginations, diminishes mutual respect among income classes, and leads to the eventual loss of self-respect among working people. For this and other reasons, Rawls was attracted to such ideas as a "share economy" (where workers have part ownership of private capital), workers' cooperatives, public provision of capital to encourage workers in becoming independent economic agents or to start up their own businesses, and other measures for the widespread distribution of control of means of production.[33]

Since it does not apply to any substantial basic structure to shape property and other economic relations, and is not conjoined with a principle of fair equal opportunities, cosmopolitans' allocation model of the global difference principle can do little to further these aims. This is not to deny that the difference principle, when applied domestically, does have an allocative role (primarily in the form of supplementary income payments for workers who earn too little for eco-

---

32. See *TJ*, secs. 13 and 42; *Restatement*, sec. 41.

33. See, for example, *Restatement*, 176, 178, where Rawls endorses Mill's idea of worker-owned cooperatives as part of a property-owning democracy. See also *LP*, 107–8n, on Mill on the "stationary state" and the "labouring class."

nomic independence [*TJ*, 285–86/252 rev.]). But the difference principle (1) is not an instrument for alleviating poverty or misfortune (though it incidentally does that); (2) is not meant to assist those with special needs or handicaps; and (3) cannot compensate the unfortunate for bad luck, natural inequalities and other accidents of fortune. Regarding 1 — poverty — any number of principles, domestic and global, can provide a decent social or global minimum and serve the role of poverty alleviation. There is no need to appeal to a dysfunctional "global difference principle" for that purpose. Rawls's duty of assistance to meet basic needs is already sufficient to serve that role.

As for 2 — assisting those with handicaps or special needs — in the domestic case, Rawls envisions other principles to be decided at the legislative stage to serve this role, based in considerations of assistance and mutual aid similar to those behind the global duty of assistance (cf. the natural duties of mutual aid and of mutual respect, *TJ*, secs.17, 51). Here objections by Sen, Nussbaum, and many others — that Rawls misdefines the least advantaged and does not take into account the needs of the handicapped in his account of distributive justice — misconceive the role of the difference principle in structuring production relations and property systems among free and equal democratic citizens. To oversimplify, perhaps, the difference principle focuses initially on the side of production, not consumption. It is because of Rawls's focus on social cooperation in the production of wealth among members of a democratic society that he is able to insist upon reciprocity in its final distribution, as specified by the difference principle. As a principle of reciprocity the difference principle is not suited to deal with problems of meeting people's special needs. We could always spend more upon those who are especially handicapped, and to apply the difference principle to their circumstances would severely limit if not eliminate the share that goes to the economically least advantaged (unskilled workers at the minimum income) and who make a contribution to production.

Finally, regarding 3, Rawls says, "The difference principle is not of course the principle of redress. It does not require society to try to even out handicaps as if all were expected to compete on a fair basis in the same race" (*TJ*, 101/86 rev.). Rawls suggests that "luck egalitarianism" by itself, taken as a conception of distributive justice, is implausible, for it does not take into account production relations, measures needed to advance the common good, or to improve standards of living. "It is plausible as most such principles are as a prima facie principle" (ibid.).

The general point, then, is that Rawls does not regard distributive justice in an alleviatory manner; rather, he transforms the issue from a narrow question of allocation of a fixed product of wealth for alleviatory or other purposes, in order to address a larger set of issues. "We reject the idea of allocative justice as incompatible with the fundamental idea by which justice as fairness is organized: the idea of society as a fair system of social cooperation over time. *Citizens are seen as cooperating to produce the social resources on which their claims are made*" (*Restatement*, 50; emphases added). Distributive justice is, then, made part of the larger question about how to fairly structure economic and property relations among socially cooperative productive agents, who regard themselves as free and equal and each of whom does his or her fair share in creating the social product.

Rawls therewith incorporates the question of distributive justice into the tradition of Mill and Marx, where the primary focus is on how to fairly structure production relations in a way that affirms the freedom, equality, dignity, and self-respect of socially productive agents. "What men want is meaningful work in free association with others, these associations regulating their relations to one another within a framework of just basic institutions" (*TJ*, 290/257 rev.). The robust conception of reciprocity implicit in the difference principle responds to this more general issue. The difference principle is not a proper response to the problem of global poverty or to other alleviatory issues mentioned (meeting handicaps and special needs, redressing misfortune, etc.). These are specific problems to address in non-ideal theory, by reference to moral duties of assistance, mutual aid, and so on, and are to be determined by citizens' democratic deliberations, on the basis of their knowledge of available resources. These alleviatory problems of non-ideal theory raise issues separate from the question of ideal theory of determining appropriate standards for just distributions among socially productive democratic citizens who are cooperative members of a well-ordered society.

IV. Conclusion

There may be other reasons why Rawls provides distributive justice with a social rather than a global reference point. I have not sought to connect the social bases of distributive justice with Rawls's all-too-brief remarks regarding the good of participation in the civic and public life of one's culture (*PL*, 61). My view is that this argument from the good of community, however significant such values might otherwise be, is not of much importance to Rawls's social grounding of distributive justice. Instead, I have argued that the main reasons for Rawls's social grounding of distributive justice are political and institutional—they concern the social conditions needed for the creation, distribution, and enjoyment of income and wealth under conditions of democratic society and compatible with its fundamental values.

It is a serious failing of cosmopolitan accounts of distributive justice that they discount the significance of social cooperation and regard distributive justice as asocial and apolitical.[34] Like Nozick's libertarianism, cosmopolitans regard distributive justice as determined pre-cooperatively, and see social and political cooperation themselves as simply arbitrary facts, irrelevant to the central questions of distributive justice. But social cooperation is not just one way; rather, it is the only possible way that production of goods and services takes place and economic value is created. In this and other regards, global cooperation is secondary; it may be conducive to but it is not necessary for production, use, and enjoyment of income and wealth. These facts should be of fundamental significance to distributive justice.

What bothers many cosmopolitans is that global capitalism has created ways to elude political control by the world's governments. For example, Wal-Mart

---

34. I am indebted to Samuel Scheffler for the ideas in this and the next paragraph, and to Joshua Cohen for the conjectures in the final paragraph.

might employ entire villages in developing countries, whose members make only one product. There is a problem of justice here, and part of the problem is that there is no global basic structure to deal with it. Perhaps some additions need to be made to Rawls's Law of Peoples to deal with this and other problems, for example, making room for international institutions that regulate global business practices to insure fair business and labor practices and guard against exploitation. Rawls clearly leaves room for this in his Law of Peoples. For example, such measures might be justified by a people's duty to enable burdened peoples to become politically autonomous and maintain their status as an independent peoples. But cosmopolitans seek the wrong solution to this problem. It is not a problem that can be addressed, much less resolved, by a global distribution principle that simply reallocates wealth from richer nations to poorer people in developing nations.

Finally, though Rawls doubted the feasibility of a world state, he did not deny that global economic cooperation could evolve gradually its own institutions, and that these might eventually multiply into an intricate and complex network of independent institutions, with widespread effects upon peoples' future prospects. I do not think that anything Rawls says rules out the appropriateness of standards of justice applying to these cooperative institutions, constraining economic relations in various ways to the benefit of less advantaged peoples, or perhaps even imposing a principle of distributive justice were these institutions extensive and pervasive enough. It would not be the difference principle because of the absence of democratic reciprocity among peoples but rather some other principle or condition that would have to exist together with and qualify the domestic difference principle (like the just savings principle qualifies the difference principle). In the absence of an outline of what this global institutional framework would be like and the degree of cooperation it envisions, it is perhaps fruitless to conjecture what principles might be appropriate to it. The point is that Rawls does not seem to rule out the possibility of a global distribution principle supplementing the difference principle in the event of the eventual evolution of complex global economic institutions. It is not a situation he addressed, but conforms to his view of the institutional basis for distributive justice.

For helpful comments, I am grateful to Samuel Scheffler, Eric Rakowski, Chris Kutz, and other members of the Kadish Center workshop at the School of Law, UC–Berkeley; to Pavlos Eleftheriadis, Neil MacCormick, Jon Tasioulas, and other participants at the 2005 Legal Philosophy Conference, Baillol College, Oxford; and to Joshua Cohen. I am especially grateful to K. C. Tan for his helpful criticisms. Thanks, also, to David Reidy and Rex Martin for their helpful suggestions.

Appendix A

Remarks on John Rawls (Memorial Service, Sanders Theater, Harvard University, February 27, 2003)

For those of us who knew John Rawls's modesty and gentleness, it is sometimes hard to grasp the profound impact he has had on the contemporary intellectual landscape. The fact that *A Theory of Justice* has been translated into 27 languages after only thirty years in print is extraordinary for a philosophy book. Just last month, I received mail from a Chinese philosopher in Beijing who asked for help in making some of Rawls's *Collected Papers* available in Chinese. The broad international reach of Rawls's work attests to his world-historical significance.

I want to say something about what I take to be the lifelong motivations behind John Rawls's work. For his entire career, he was primarily occupied by two related questions. First, what does justice require of us? Second, given what justice requires, are humans capable of it? Each of Rawls's three main books (*A Theory of Justice*, *Political Liberalism*, and *The Law of Peoples*) and most of his papers address these two questions. Rawls's lifelong interest in these questions developed out of his early concern with the religious question of why evil exists among humankind. This was the subject of his honors thesis at Princeton. As a student, he planned to go into the Episcopal priesthood eventually, but World War II intervened. Upon graduation, in January 1943 he enlisted in the army and served three years, mainly in the Pacific theater—in New Guinea, the Philippines, and later in occupied Japan. He suffered a grazing head wound from a sniper's bullet which left a scar on his head, and he witnessed the nuclear ruins of Hiroshima after the Japanese surrender. By the end of the war, Rawls had given up his plans to become a minister, and apparently he gave up religion too. But, largely because of the brutality and devastation of the war, which he experienced firsthand, Rawls was led to reflect anew on the problem of evil, now in the form of the question whether human nature is capable of justice, or whether our nature is so selfish, scarred, and corrupt as to put justice beyond human capabilities. In all his works, Rawls rejects this desolate view of humankind, which is, in effect, the orthodox Christian doctrine of original sin. Instead, he holds that a just society which affirms the freedom, equality, and self-respect of all its citizens is within human reach.

When I first read *A Theory of Justice* in the late 1970s, what impressed me about it most was its affirmation of the potential for human goodness. Rawls is often criticized for being utopian. But to say Rawls affirmed our potential for human goodness does not mean that he was optimistic about our achieving a just society of equals. How could he be in the present political climate, of which he complained of politicians "selling the public trust" to corporations who (for example) are allowed into congressional committee meetings to draft legislation favorable to themselves? He was appalled by the practice, saying of the congressional leaders who permitted it, "They are destroying our democracy." If it is utopian to hold out the hope of something better, and not give in to cynicism about the possibilities for a democratic society, then Rawls may be called utopian. But he thought a society of equals committed to advancing the good of all persons a "*realistic* utopia" (as he sometimes called it).

One of the last sentences John Rawls wrote and published has a kind of somberness about it that contrasts with the end of *A Theory of Justice*. He says in the concluding sentence of *The Law of Peoples* (128):

> If a reasonably just Society of Peoples is not possible . . . and human beings are largely amoral, if not incurably cynical and self-centered, one might ask, with Kant, whether it is worthwhile for human beings to live on the earth.

It was to avoid this sense of hopelessness about humanity that drove John Rawls's philosophy his entire career. He offers an inspiring yet intellectually compelling vision of the possibility of a just society grounded in the better side of human nature.

For all the seriousness of his work, there was a lighter side to Jack which came through in his relationships with colleagues and friends. He was stubbornly modest. For example, when I told him a picture of him was needed for the front cover of *The Cambridge Companion to Rawls*, he objected, saying that he did not see why anyone cared what he looked like. Only after he was convinced that each of the more than 30 volumes in that series carried portraits of the philosopher concerned did he relent and allow one of his wife Mardy's handsome watercolor portraits to be used on the front cover of the book.

Jack also had a self-effacing sense of humor. For example, Paul Freund once told him that there were not one but two local judges on the federal courts in Chicago named "Julius Hoffman." To keep them straight, Chicago lawyers called one judge, who was highly respected by them, "Julius the Just." The other Judge Julius Hoffman had notoriously presided over the Chicago Seven trial in the 1970s. They called him "Just Julius." So Jack took to signing letters and inscribing books for his friends as "Just Jack." However much he thought of himself, and wanted others to think of him, as Just Jack, he was indeed Jack the Just, the preeminent theorist of justice in the twentieth century.

John Rawls: Friend and Teacher (*Chronicle Review: The Chronicle of Higher Education,* December 13, 2002)

The Philosopher John Rawls has died at 81. He had an enormous influence on academic discussions of social, political and economic justice. His 1971 book *A Theory of Justice* is widely recognized as the most significant work in political philosophy since J. S. Mill. In the time since John Rawls died, there have been a number of tributes that focus on his formidable intellectual contributions. Here, I offer more personal reflections based on my experience of him.

Rawls's lifelong interest in justice developed out of his early concern with the basically religious question of why there is evil in the world and whether human existence is nonetheless redeemable. This concern, originating during World War II while an undergraduate and later a soldier in the Pacific, led him to inquire whether a just society is realistically possible. His life's work was aimed at discovering what justice requires of us, and then showing that it is within human capacities to realize a just society and a just international order.

John Rawls was born in Baltimore into a well-to-do family. His father was a prominent lawyer and his mother was active in local politics. I was one of Rawls's PhD students in the early 1980s, but was inspired by him even before we met. Upon reading *A Theory of Justice,* I decided to leave a career in law and begin graduate work in philosophy. I never dreamed then that I would have the great good fortune to work with Rawls, much less become his friend. Although I cannot be sure, I think Jack warmed to me because his father, like me, was from North Carolina; Jack felt at ease with a relaxed Southern manner. He appreciated my friendly teasing of him and his position. For example, at the turn of the millennium, the editors of the Modern Library ranked the top 100 nonfiction works in English in the twentieth century. *A Theory of Justice* placed 28th, high for a philosophy book, but it was still bested by Russell's and Whitehead's seminal work in logic, *Principia Mathematica,* ranked 23rd. When I told Jack of this, he said little, although he seemed pleased to be in such august company. But when I said, "Jack, you should have worked harder, and then *you* could have been 23rd," he laughed heartily.

Jack was a quiet, modest, and gentle man. He did not seek fame, and he did not enjoy the spotlight. A private person, he devoted himself either to research and teaching, or to relaxing with his family and friends. He declined almost all requests for interviews and chose not to take an active role in public life. In part, this is because he felt uncomfortable speaking before strangers and large groups and often stuttered in those settings. But he also believed that philosophers are almost always misunderstood when they address the public, and that, while political philosophy has considerable influence on people's lives, its effects are indirect, taking many years to become part of society's moral awareness.

In 1999, Jack agreed to accept a National Humanities Medal by President Clinton, and also the Rolf Schock Prize in Logic and Philosophy. Prior to that, he had regularly declined honors and invitations. Big prizes and awards made him uncomfortable. Mardy, his wife of 53 years, reports that Jack always said that if he ever won a Nobel Prize he would decline it. Knowing this, in the late 1990s, when offered the Japanese Kyoto Prize, which carries a $500,000 award, she declined on his behalf without even consulting him. When she told Jack, he said he might like to accept it, depending on the conditions. Upon learning, however, that acceptance of the prize required not only that he give three public lectures but also that he have lunch and dinner with the Emperor, Jack reaffirmed his initial disclaimer. His daughter Liz said Jack was willing to do a lot of things, but not have lunch with the Emperor. Indeed, Jack denounced the practice of royalty and the corrupting effects of privilege. He often praised his Oxford friend and teacher, H. L. A. Hart, for refusing to accept a knighthood.

Jack's rejection of privilege explains his fondness for Abraham Lincoln. He admired Lincoln because he saw him as the president who most appreciated the moral equality of human beings, and because he was the rare statesman who did not compromise with evil. Jack frequently quoted Lincoln's assertion—"If anything is wrong, slavery is wrong"—as the best example of a fixed moral conviction that anyone with a sense of justice must believe.

The rightward drift of American politics distressed Jack. He said of Congress under Newt Gingrich's management, "They are destroying our democracy." He was appalled by the practice of allowing business lobbyists into committee meetings to draft legislation favorable to themselves. This, together with our system of corporate financing of political campaigns, he condemned as "selling the public trust." He judged the current administration and Congress by the same high standards.

Jack was a conscientious teacher. His lectures were carefully prepared and written out, and he continually revised them after reading the most recent scholarship and rethinking his positions. He made his lecture notes available to students, saying that he sometimes stuttered and was not sure he could be understood. A better reason, surely, is that his lectures were very intense and hard to digest upon one hearing (or even two or three). His lectures were nearly ready for publication in the form he left them. He resisted publication initially but was encouraged by former students, especially Barbara Herman, who appealed to his sense of fairness by saying that while his own students continued to benefit professionally from his teachings, others could not. He also resisted publishing his collected papers; he said that he saw his papers as opportunities to experiment with ideas, which would later be revised or rejected in a book. When told that students and scholars were spending hours hunting down his many papers in libraries, he agreed to issue them in one volume.

Unlike the work of most analytic philosophers, Rawls's work was systematic and driven by a comprehensive vision. He did not directly address problems discussed by contemporary analytic philosophers. For the most part, his work was a dialogue with the great figures in modern moral and political philosophy—the contractarians Hobbes, Locke, and Rousseau; the utilitarians Hume, Mill, and Sidgwick; and the German Idealists Kant, Hegel, and Marx. Not only in its structure but also in its prose, *Theory of Justice* reads like the work of a nineteenth-century philosopher. (As his colleague and close friend Burton Dreben said, it reads as if translated from the original German.) In all his works, Jack was very generous in citing others, even when what they said had little to do with the points he made. Only very rarely did he respond to his critics (most notably to H. L. A. Hart on liberty), and only then when he felt their criticisms were serious and constructive. Most often, he thought that his critics (who are legion) misunderstood him. While self-effacing in person and in print, Jack was also sparing in his praise. I think he probably believed (though not in this particular instance) what Hume said in criticizing Locke's social contract: namely, there is little ever new in philosophy, and that which is new is almost always wrong. It was not easy handing over one's work to Jack to read.

Jack was a tall, lanky man, with piercing blue eyes. He participated in sports at Princeton and was an excellent sailor. He exercised until well into his 70s, biking, jogging, and hiking, and he took daily walks until a few days before his death. Popular legend (and some obituaries) to the contrary, he never played professional baseball. This rumor was fabricated by a Leveritt House Master at Harvard after Jack had hit a number of home runs in an intramural softball game. Losing students were distressed at being humiliated by an aging professor, and the house master assuaged them by saying Jack was a "ringer" for the Yankees.

Jack also had a taste for oatmeal cookies served with tea. Recently, I spent part of an afternoon with him as his wife went out to play tennis. She left a large cookie for him. As I got up to leave, he asked me to go look through the kitchen cabinets for a bag of oatmeal cookies, which he asked me to leave with him as I left. I guiltily complied. The next afternoon, he asked me if I wanted more than the two cookies I had eaten. I told him that, as good as they were, I had better not eat any more. He then announced definitively to his wife, "Mardy, Sam wants another cookie, and I think I'll have another one, too." Jack had a mischievous streak.

In mid-October, I drove out to his rambling house in Lexington, Massachusetts, carrying the newly published *Cambridge Companion to Rawls*, only the second volume in that wide-ranging series devoted to a living philosopher (Habermas is the other). Many of Jack's students and friends contributed articles. The portrait of him on the cover was painted by his wife Mardy. Earlier, he had objected vigorously to any picture, saying that he did not see why people cared what he looked like. When I told him every single volume in the series had portraits, he ceased protesting. He appreciated the tribute, saying, "It looks great, Sam."

It was to be the last time I would see Jack. His wife called on Sunday, November 24, saying that Jack died at 9:30 in the morning, peacefully, of heart failure at home. He had his wits until the very end. He will be cremated; his ashes will be put to rest with other Harvard luminaries at the Mt. Auburn Cemetery in Cambridge. He will be greatly missed.

Index